vSphere Virtual Machine Management

Create vSphere virtual machines, manage performance, and explore advanced capabilities

Rebecca Fitzhugh

BIRMINGHAM - MUMBAI

vSphere Virtual Machine Management

Copyright © 2014 Packt Publishing

All rights reserved. No part of this book may be reproduced, stored in a retrieval system, or transmitted in any form or by any means, without the prior written permission of the publisher, except in the case of brief quotations embedded in critical articles or reviews.

Every effort has been made in the preparation of this book to ensure the accuracy of the information presented. However, the information contained in this book is sold without warranty, either express or implied. Neither the author, nor Packt Publishing, and its dealers and distributors will be held liable for any damages caused or alleged to be caused directly or indirectly by this book.

Packt Publishing has endeavored to provide trademark information about all of the companies and products mentioned in this book by the appropriate use of capitals. However, Packt Publishing cannot guarantee the accuracy of this information.

First published: March 2014

Production Reference: 1140314

Published by Packt Publishing Ltd.
Livery Place
35 Livery Street
Birmingham B3 2PB, UK.

ISBN 978-1-78217-218-5

www.packtpub.com

Cover Image by Tony Shi (shihe99@hotmail.com)

Credits

Author
Rebecca Fitzhugh

Reviewers
James Bowling
Andy Grant
Christopher Kusek
Brian Wuchner

Acquisition Editor
Joanne Fitzpatrick

Content Development Editor
Ankita Shashi

Technical Editors
Kunal Anil Gaikwad
Monica John
Pramod Kumavat
Mukul Pawar
Adrian Raposo
Siddhi Rane

Copy Editors
Alisha Aranha
Sayanee Mukherjee
Adithi Shetty

Project Coordinator
Wendell Palmer

Proofreaders
Lawrence A. Herman
Amy Johnson

Indexer
Mariammal Chettiyar

Graphics
Ronak Dhruv
Yuvraj Mannari
Abhinash Sahu

Production Coordinator
Conidon Miranda

Cover Work
Conidon Miranda

About the Author

Rebecca Fitzhugh is an independent VMware Consultant and VMware Certified Instructor (VCI). Her focus is on designing and delivering solutions as an infrastructure architect as well as delivering various authorized VMware courses. Prior to becoming a consultant and instructor, she served for five years in the United States Marine Corps, where she assisted in the buildout and administration of multiple enterprise networks residing on virtual infrastructure.

Rebecca currently holds multiple IT industry certifications, including VMware Certified Advanced Professional (VCAP) in Data Center Design (DCD), Data Center Administration (DCA), and Cloud Infrastructure Administration (CIA). You can follow her on Twitter (`@RebeccaFitzhugh`) or contact her using LinkedIn (`www.linkedin.com/in/rmfitzhugh/`).

First and foremost, I would like to thank my sister, Robyn, and my brother, Joe. There are not enough words in this world to express how deeply grateful I am for you. I also want to thank my hilarious and brilliant niece and nephew, Katalyna and Kellan, for inspiring me each and every day. To all my friends around the world who have supported me and encouraged me: I'm so glad that there are people like you in my life with whom I can share my adventures.

A big thanks to the editors, technical editors, and reviewers who went through my writing. This book was written across three continents, much of it while sitting in the planes and airports. Jet lag is not conducive to writing coherent sentences; so, I truly appreciate your patience as I worked on trying to get my thoughts written down.

About the Reviewers

James Bowling is a VCAP5-DCD, VCAP5-DCA, VCP5-DCV/IaaS, VCP-Cloud, VMware vExpert (x3), Cisco Champion for Data Center, Houston VMUG Leader, and virtualization enthusiast living in Houston, TX with over 13 years of experience. He has received the 2009 COMMON/IBM Power Systems Innovation Award for Energy Efficiency for his design and implementation of the United States Bowling Congress (USBC) Datacenter in Arlington, TX. James has held presentations on automation and orchestration at VMworld US and EMEA. His experience spans designing, deploying, and maintaining large-scale cloud infrastructures. He is currently a Cloud Architect for General Datatech, LP in Dallas, Texas. He can be reached on Twitter (`@vSential`) or through his virtualization blog (`vsential.com`).

Andy Grant is a Technical Consultant for HP Enterprise Services. Andy's primary focus is datacenter infrastructure and virtualization projects across a number of industries, including government, healthcare, forestry, financial, gas and oil, and international contracting. He currently holds a number of technical certifications such as VCAP4/5-DCA/DCD, VCP4/5, MCITP:EA, MCSE, CCNA, Security+, A+, and HP ASE BladeSystem. Outside of work, Andy enjoys hiking, action pistol sports, and spending time adventuring with his son.

Christopher Kusek is a technology visionary and Internet personality known as @cxi on Twitter. A VMware vExpert, he has worked for enterprise vendors such as EMC and NetApp, leading global teams of Virtualization and Cloud Professionals. He is currently leading the charge for virtualization for the war effort in Operation Enduring Freedom in Afghanistan.

Brian Wuchner is a Senior Systems Administrator for a government agency. He has over 10 years of industrial experience with specialties in infrastructure automation, directory services, and data center virtualization. Brian holds the VCA-Cloud, VCA-WM, and VCP5-DCV certifications and was awarded the vExpert title from VMware for 2011-2013. He can be contacted on LinkedIn (http://www.linkedin.com/in/bwuch), on Twitter (@bwuch), or through his blog at http://enterpriseadmins.org.

www.PacktPub.com

Support files, eBooks, discount offers, and more

You might want to visit www.PacktPub.com for support files and downloads related to your book.

Did you know that Packt offers eBook versions of every book published, with PDF and ePub files available? You can upgrade to the eBook version at www.PacktPub.com and as a print book customer, you are entitled to a discount on the eBook copy. Get in touch with us at service@packtpub.com for more details.

At www.PacktPub.com, you can also read a collection of free technical articles, sign up for a range of free newsletters and receive exclusive discounts and offers on Packt books and eBooks.

http://PacktLib.PacktPub.com

Do you need instant solutions to your IT questions? PacktLib is Packt's online digital book library. Here, you can access, read, and search across Packt's entire library of books.

Why Subscribe?

- Fully searchable across every book published by Packt
- Copy and paste, print, and bookmark content
- On demand and accessible via web browser

Free Access for Packt account holders

If you have an account with Packt at www.PacktPub.com, you can use this to access PacktLib today and view nine entirely free books. Simply use your login credentials for immediate access.

Instant Updates on New Packt Books

Get notified! Find out when new books are published by following @PacktEnterprise on Twitter, or the *Packt Enterprise* Facebook page.

Table of Contents

Preface	**1**
Chapter 1: Virtual Machine Concepts	**7**
vSphere virtual machines	**8**
Virtual machine components	**9**
Uses of virtual machines	**12**
The primary virtual machine resources	**13**
CPU	14
Memory	15
Network	16
Disk	17
Virtual machine files	**18**
Configuration files	19
Swap files	22
Virtual disks	22
Snapshot files	24
Other files	24
Viewing virtual machine files	25
Using the vSphere Client	25
Using the vSphere Web Client	27
Using command line	28
VMware Tools	**28**
Summary	**31**
Chapter 2: Creating a Virtual Machine Using the Wizard	**33**
vSphere Client versus vSphere Web Client	**33**
Creating a VM using the typical configuration wizard	**34**
Name and Location	36
Storage	37
Guest Operating System	38

Network	39
Create a Disk	40
Ready to Complete	42
Editing the settings	43
Creating a VM using the custom configuration wizard	**46**
Name and Location	47
Storage	48
Virtual Machine Version	49
Guest Operating System	50
CPUs	52
Memory	53
Network	54
SCSI controller	55
Creating a new virtual disk	57
Using an existing virtual disk	59
Raw Device Mappings	62
Do not create disk	67
Ready to Complete	68
Creating a VM using vSphere Web Client	**69**
Select a name and folder	70
Select a compute resource	71
Select storage	72
Select compatibility	73
Select a guest OS	74
Customize hardware	75
Ready to complete	76
Summary	**77**
Chapter 3: Other Ways to Provision a Virtual Machine	**79**
Configuring virtual machine customizations	**79**
Copying Sysprep files to vCenter directory	80
Creating a customization	82
New VM Guest Customization Spec	83
Set Registration Information	84
Set Computer Name	84
Enter Windows License	86
Set Administrator Password	86
Run Once	88
Configure Network	88
Set Workgroup or Domain	90
Set Operating System Options	91
Ready to complete	92
Creating a virtual machine from a template	**92**
Creating a template	93

Deploying VMs from the template	94
Select a name and folder	94
Select a compute resource	95
Select storage	96
Select clone options	97
Creating a virtual machine by cloning	**99**
Creating a virtual machine from an OVF file	**100**
Select source	101
Review details	101
Accept EULAs	102
Select name and location	102
Select storage	103
Setup networks	104
Customize template	104
Ready to complete	105
Creating a virtual machine using VMware vCenter Converter	**106**
Source System	108
Source Machine	108
Destination System	109
Destination Virtual Machine	110
Destination Location	111
Options	112
Summary (pane)	114
Summary	**114**
Chapter 4: Advanced Virtual Machine Settings	**115**
Introducing the virtual machine monitor	**116**
Understanding monitor modes	116
Enabling CPU hot plug / memory hot add	**120**
The CPUID mask	**122**
The CPU affinity setting	**123**
Setting the .vswp location	**124**
Viewing other advanced options	**126**
The General Options section	127
The VMware Remote Console Options section	128
The VMware Tools section	128
The Boot Options section	130
Installing VMware Tools	**131**
Installing VMware Tools in a Windows virtual machine	131
Installing VMware Tools in a Linux virtual machine	135
Summary	**137**

Chapter 5: Managing Multitiered Applications with vApps — 139
- What is a vApp? — 140
- Creating a vApp — 141
- vApp options — 145
  - IP addressing policies — 146
  - Virtual machine startup/shutdown order — 149
- Exporting a vApp — 150
- Cloning a vApp — 152
- Summary — 157

Chapter 6: Virtual Machine Performance and Resource Allocation — 159
- Resource performance concepts — 159
  - CPU virtualization — 160
  - Memory reclamation — 161
    - Transparent page sharing (TPS) — 162
    - Ballooning — 163
    - Compression — 163
    - Swapping to host cache — 165
    - Hypervisor swapping — 168
  - Network constraint — 170
  - Storage constraint — 170
- Understanding resource controls — 170
  - Shares — 171
  - Limits — 173
  - Reservations — 175
- Resource pools — 177
  - Creating a resource pool — 178
  - Expandable reservations — 181
- Network I/O Control — 182
- Storage I/O Control — 187
  - vSphere Storage APIs — 191
- Disk alignment — 192
- Performance tuning — 192
  - Traditional performance practices — 193
  - Performance problems — 193
  - Troubleshooting performance — 194
- Summary — 195

Chapter 7: Monitoring Virtual Machines — 197
- Performance charts — 197
  - Overview performance charts — 198
  - Advanced performance charts — 199

Using esxtop	**203**
Monitoring CPU	205
Monitoring memory	205
Monitoring network	207
Monitoring storage	208
The esxtop options	209
Using alarms	**210**
Creating condition-based alarms	210
Creating event-based alarms	214
Other places to find information	**215**
Summary	**219**
Chapter 8: Migrating Virtual Machines	**221**
vMotion	**221**
Configuring for vMotion	222
Migration using vMotion	228
Migration using Storage vMotion	**231**
Cross-host Storage vMotion	**237**
Summary	**243**
Chapter 9: Balancing Resource Utilization and Availability	**245**
Clusters	**245**
Creating a cluster	246
Distributed Resource Scheduler (DRS)	**247**
Overview of DRS	248
Enabling and configuring DRS	248
DRS recommendations and monitoring DRS	251
Affinity/Anti-affinity rules	255
High Availability	**256**
Overview of HA	257
Configuring HA	259
Storage Distributed Resource Scheduler (SDRS)	**265**
Overview of SDRS	266
Configuring SDRS	267
Applying SDRS recommendations	272
Anti-affinity rules	273
Summary	**274**
Chapter 10: Virtual Machine Design	**275**
Comparing provisioning methods	**275**
Provisioning using templates	276
Using clones for provisioning	277

Using virtual appliances	277
OVF templates	277
Virtual hardware and resource configuration	**278**
Virtual machine maximums	278
Memory	279
CPU	280
Storage	282
The Disk Provisioning types	282
Disk Mode	284
The SCSI controller	284
Raw Device Mapping (RDM)	285
The virtual network adapters	286
Other considerations	**287**
Renaming virtual machines	287
Upgrading virtual hardware version	287
Using tags	290
NTP configuration	291
Disabling unused virtual hardware	293
VMware Tools	296
Summary	**297**
Index	**299**

Preface

Ever since VMware was founded in 1998, it has been creating stable x86 virtualization platforms that allow multiple guest operating systems and applications to run on a single physical server. VMware has truly revolutionized how a datacenter is managed. By consolidating and running more workloads on fewer servers, the datacenter requirements are reduced including space, power, cooling, and cabling. Using virtualization also transforms the way servers are provisioned; virtual machines are deployed within a few minutes rather than the much longer process of deploying physical servers. There's hardly any need to mention that there are many advanced features that improve the availability and continuity of virtual machines.

This book aims at assisting vSphere administrators, new and experienced, to improve their knowledge of virtual machine configuration and administration. This is not meant to replace any vSphere administration or installation guides but merely to supplement them.

What this book covers

Chapter 1, *Virtual Machine Concepts*, covers the fundamental ideas of virtual machines as well as understanding the components that VMs are comprised of.

Chapter 2, *Creating a Virtual Machine Using the Wizard*, explains the step-by-step process of how to create a virtual machine using the wizard in the vSphere Client and vSphere Web Client.

Chapter 3, *Other Ways to Provision a Virtual Machine*, covers how to build a template and provision VMs from template, by cloning, or from physical machines using VMware vCenter Converter. Also, guest OS customizations are covered so that potential IP conflicts, hostname conflicts, and duplicate SIDs are avoided.

Chapter 4, *Advanced Virtual Machine Settings*, discusses a few advanced settings, how to make the configurations, and how these configurations will affect the virtual machine's functionality and performance.

Chapter 5, *Managing Multitiered Applications with vApps*, discovers why a vApp is the perfect container for a multitiered application. Also, included herein are instructions on how to create, configure, and manage VMware vSphere vApps.

Chapter 6, *Virtual Machine Performance and Resource Allocation*, explores different settings that may improve a virtual machine's performance, if needed. Also, discussed in the chapter are resource allocation settings that affect the amount of resources given to a virtual machine and how virtual machines compete in contention.

Chapter 7, *Monitoring Virtual Machines*, discusses how an administrator can monitor a virtual machine using esxtop and performance graphs.

Chapter 8, *Migrating Virtual Machines*, explains how to migrate a virtual machine using vMotion and Storage vMotion, if the need arises, as well as how to configure these features.

Chapter 9, *Balancing Resource Utilization and Availability*, gives a general understanding of how to configure and use vSphere Distributed Resource Scheduler (DRS), Storage DRS, and High Availability.

Chapter 10, *Virtual Machine Design*, focuses on how the administrator should move forward in the creation and deployment of virtual machines taking everything discussed into consideration.

What you need for this book

This book is technical in nature, so the reader should have a basic understanding of the following:

- VMware vSphere
    - Hypervisor basics
- vCenter basics
- Active Directory
    - Domain authentication
    - Replication

- Windows Server
    - Basic administration skills
- Linux
    - Basic administration skills
- Experiencing managing DHCP and DNS
- Understanding of basic networking

Who this book is for

Typical readers of this book would be those who have a general understanding of VMware vSphere fundamentals and who want to build up knowledge of virtual machine administration, configuration, and monitoring. This book was written not only to appeal to beginners but also to supply a generous amount of information for advanced users.

Conventions

In this book, you will find a number of styles of text that distinguish between different kinds of information. Here are some examples of these styles, and an explanation of their meaning.

Code words in text, database table names, folder names, filenames, file extensions, pathnames, dummy URLs, user input, and Twitter handles are shown as follows: "Once authenticated, type `esxtop` to begin running this utility."

A block of code is set as follows:

```
displayName = "SampleVM"
extendedConfigFile = "SampleVM.vmxf"
virtualHW.productCompatibility = "hosted"
memSize = "384"
```

New terms and **important words** are shown in bold. Words that you see on the screen, in menus or dialog boxes for example, appear in the text like this: "Click on **OK** after configuring this feature."

> Warnings or important notes appear in a box like this.

> Tips and tricks appear like this.

Reader feedback

Feedback from our readers is always welcome. Let us know what you think about this book—what you liked or may have disliked. Reader feedback is important for us to develop titles that you really get the most out of.

To send us general feedback, simply send an e-mail to `feedback@packtpub.com`, and mention the book title via the subject of your message. If there is a topic that you have expertise in and you are interested in either writing or contributing to a book, see our author guide on `www.packtpub.com/authors`.

Customer support

Now that you are the proud owner of a Packt book, we have a number of things to help you to get the most from your purchase.

Errata

Although we have taken every care to ensure the accuracy of our content, mistakes do happen. If you find a mistake in one of our books—maybe a mistake in the text or the code—we would be grateful if you would report this to us. By doing so, you can save other readers from frustration and help us improve subsequent versions of this book. If you find any errata, please report them by visiting `http://www.packtpub.com/submit-errata`, selecting your book, clicking on the **errata submission form** link, and entering the details of your errata. Once your errata are verified, your submission will be accepted and the errata will be uploaded on our website, or added to any list of existing errata, under the Errata section of that title. Any existing errata can be viewed by selecting your title from `http://www.packtpub.com/support`.

Piracy

Piracy of copyright material on the Internet is an ongoing problem across all media. At Packt, we take the protection of our copyright and licenses very seriously. If you come across any illegal copies of our works, in any form, on the Internet, please provide us with the location address or website name immediately so that we can pursue a remedy.

Please contact us at copyright@packtpub.com with a link to the suspected pirated material.

We appreciate your help in protecting our authors, and our ability to bring you valuable content.

Questions

You can contact us at questions@packtpub.com if you are having a problem with any aspect of the book, and we will do our best to address it.

1
Virtual Machine Concepts

Ever since VMware was founded in 1998, it has been creating stable x86 virtualization platforms that allow multiple guest operating systems and applications to run on a single physical server. Before an administrator can begin creating and configuring vSphere virtual machines, it is important to understand what a virtual machine is and the concepts behind virtualizing hardware.

In this chapter, you will learn:

- What a virtual machine is
- Components of a virtual machine
- Why to use virtual machines
- Files that make up a virtual machine
- The four primary resources
- VMware Tools

The multiple instances of Windows or Linux systems that are running on an ESXi host are commonly referred to as a **virtual machine** (**VM**). Any reference to a guest **operating system** (**OS**) is an instance of Linux, Windows, or any other supported operating system that is installed on the VM.

vSphere virtual machines

At the heart of virtualization lies the virtual machine. A virtual machine is a set of virtual hardware whose characteristics are determined by a set of files; it is this virtual hardware that a guest operating system is installed on. A virtual machine runs an operating system and a set of applications just like a physical server. A virtual machine comprises a set of configuration files and is backed by the physical resources of an ESXi host. An **ESXi host** is the physical server that has the VMware hypervisor, known as ESXi, installed. Each virtual machine is equipped with virtual hardware and devices that provide the same functionality as having physical hardware.

Virtual machines are created within a virtualization layer, such as ESXi running on a physical server. This virtualization layer manages requests from the virtual machine for resources such as CPU or memory. It is the virtualization layer that is responsible for translating these requests to the underlying physical hardware.

Each virtual machine is granted a portion of the physical hardware. All VMs have their own virtual hardware (there are important ones to note, called the **primary 4**: CPU, memory, disk, and network). Each of these VMs is isolated from the other and each interacts with the underlying hardware through a thin software layer known as the **hypervisor**. This is different from a physical architecture in which the installed operating system interacts with installed hardware directly.

With virtualization, there are many benefits, in relation to portability, security, and manageability that aren't available in an environment that uses a traditional physical infrastructure. However, once provisioned, virtual machines use many of the same principles that are applied to physical servers.

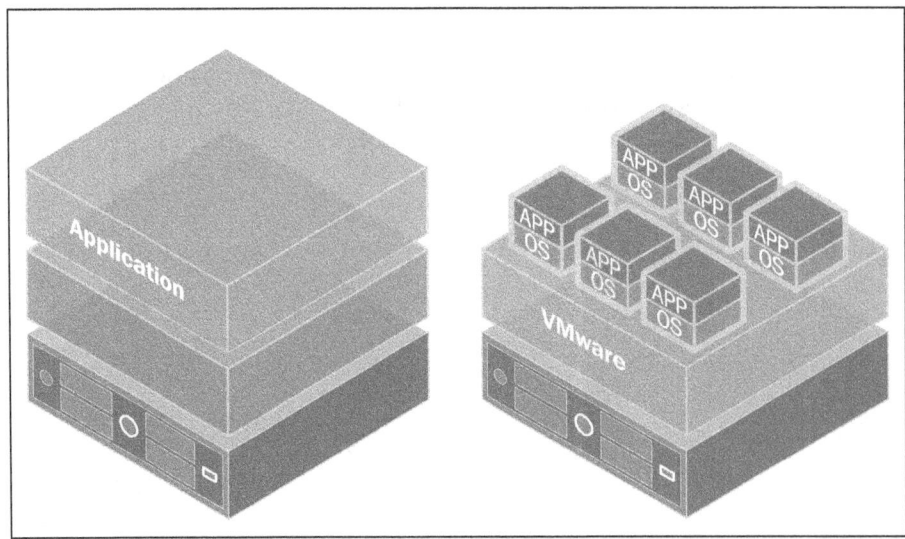

The preceding diagram demonstrates the differences between the traditional physical architecture (left) and a virtual architecture (right). Notice that the physical architecture typically has a single application and a single operating system using the physical resources. The virtual architecture has multiple virtual machines running on a single physical server, accessing the hardware through the thin hypervisor layer.

Virtual machine components

When a virtual machine is created, a default set of virtual hardware is assigned to it. VMware provides devices and resources that can be added and configured to the virtual machine. Not all virtual hardware devices will be available to every single virtual machine; both the physical hardware of the ESXi host and the VM's guest OS must support these configurations. For example, a virtual machine will not be capable of being configured with more vCPUs than the ESXi host has logical CPU cores.

The options and configurations for these devices will be explained further in *Chapter 2, Creating a Virtual Machine Using the Wizard*. For example, we'll explore the effects of assigning virtual sockets versus that of assigning virtual cores on the virtual machine's vCPU.

The virtual hardware available includes:

- **BIOS**: Phoenix Technologies 6.00 that functions like a physical server BIOS. Virtual machine administrators are able to enable/disable I/O devices, configure boot order, and so on.
- **DVD/CD-ROM**: NEC VMware IDE CDR10 that is installed by default in new virtual machines created in vSphere. The DVD/CD-ROM can be configured to connect to the client workstation DVD/CD-ROM, an ESXi host DVD/CD-ROM, or even an .iso file located on a datastore. DVD/CD-ROM devices can be added to or removed from a virtual machine.
- **Floppy drive**: This is installed by default with new virtual machines created in vSphere. The floppy drive can be configured to connect to the client device's floppy drive, a floppy device located on the ESXi host, or even a floppy image (.flp) located on a datastore. Floppy devices can be added to or removed from a virtual machine.
- **Hard disk**: This stores the guest operating system, program files, and any other data associated with a virtual machine. The virtual disk is a large file, or potentially a set of files, that can be easily copied, moved, and backed up.

- **IDE controller**: Intel 82371 AB/EB PCI Bus Master IDE Controller that presents two **Integrated Drive Electronics** (**IDE**) interfaces to the virtual machine by default. This IDE controller is a standard way for storage devices, such as floppy drives and CD-ROM drives, to connect to the virtual machine.
- **Keyboard**: This mirrors the keyboard that is first connected to the virtual machine console upon initial console connection.
- **Memory**: This is the virtual memory size configured for the virtual machine that determines the guest operating system's memory size.
- **Motherboard/Chipset**: The motherboard uses VMware proprietary devices that are based on the following chips:
    - Intel 440BX AGPset 82443BX Host Bridge/Controller
    - Intel 82093 AA I/O Advanced Programmable Interrupt Controller
    - Intel 82371 AB (PIIX4) PCI ISA IDE Xcelerator
    - National Semiconductor PC87338 ACPI 1.0 and PC98/99 Compliant Super I/O
- **Network adapter**: ESXi networking features provide communication between virtual machines residing on the same ESXi host, between VMs residing on different ESXi hosts, and between VMs and physical machines. When configuring a VM, network adapters (NICs) can be added and the adapter type can be specified.
- **Parallel port**: This is an interface for connecting peripherals to the virtual machine. Virtual parallel ports can be added to or removed from the virtual machine.
- **PCI controller**: This is a bus located on the virtual machine motherboard, communicating with components such as a hard disk. A single PCI controller is presented to the virtual machine. This cannot be configured or removed.
- **PCI device**: DirectPath devices can be added to a virtual machine. The devices must be reserved for PCI pass-through on the ESXi host that the virtual machine runs on. Keep in mind that snapshots are not supported with DirectPath I/O pass-through device configuration. For more information on virtual machine snapshots, see `http://vmware.com/kb/1015180`.
- **Pointing device**: This mirrors the pointing device that is first connected to the virtual machine console upon initial console connection.

- **Processor**: This specifies the number of sockets and core for the virtual processor. This will appear as AMD or Intel to the virtual machine guest operating system depending upon the physical hardware.
- **Serial port**: This is an interface for connecting peripherals to the virtual machine. The virtual machine can be configured to connect to a physical serial port, a file on the host, or over the network. The serial port can also be used to establish a direct connection between two VMs. Virtual serial ports can be added to or removed from the virtual machine.
- **SCSI controller**: This provides access to virtual disks. The virtual SCSI controller may appear as one of several different types of controllers to a virtual machine, depending on the guest operating system of the VM. Editing the VM configuration can modify the SCSI controller type, a SCSI controller can be added, and a virtual controller can be configured to allocate bus sharing.
- **SCSI device**: A SCSI device interface is available to the virtual machine by default. This interface is a typical way to connect storage devices (hard drives, floppy drives, CD-ROMs, and so on) to a VM. SCSI device that can be added to or removed from a virtual machine.
- **SIO controller**: The **Super I/O** controller provides serial and parallel ports, and floppy devices, and performs system management activities. A single SIO controller is presented to the virtual machine. This cannot be configured or removed.
- **USB controller**: This provides USB functionality to the USB ports managed. The virtual USB controller is a software virtualization of the USB host controller function in a VM.
- **USB device**: Multiple USB devices may be added to a virtual machine. These can be mass storage devices or security dongles. The USB devices can be connected to a client workstation or to an ESXi host.
- **Video controller**: This is a VMware Standard VGA II Graphics Adapter with 128 MB video memory.
- **VMCI**: The **Virtual Machine Communication Interface** provides high-speed communication between the hypervisor and a virtual machine. VMCI can also be enabled for communication between VMs. VMCI devices cannot be added or removed.

Uses of virtual machines

In any infrastructure, there are many business processes that have applications supporting them. These applications typically have certain requirements, such as security or performance requirements, which may limit the application to being the only thing installed on a given machine. Without virtualization, there is typically a 1:1:1 ratio for server hardware to an operating system to a single application. This type of architecture is not flexible and is inefficient due to many applications using only a small percentage of the physical resources dedicated to it, effectively leaving the physical servers vastly underutilized. As hardware continues to get better and better, the gap between the abundant resources and the often small application requirements widens. Also, consider the overhead needed to support the entire infrastructure, such as power, cooling, cabling, manpower, and provisioning time. A large server sprawl will cost more money for space and power to keep these systems housed and cooled.

Virtual infrastructures are able to do more with less—fewer physical servers are needed due to higher consolidation ratios. Virtualization provides a safe way of putting more than one operating system (or virtual machine) on a single piece of server hardware by isolating each VM running on the ESXi host from any other. Migrating physical servers to virtual machines and consolidating onto far fewer physical servers means lowering monthly power and cooling costs in the datacenter. Fewer physical servers can help reduce the datacenter footprint; fewer servers means less networking equipment, fewer server racks, and eventually less datacenter floor space required. Virtualization changes the way a server is provisioned. Initially it took hours to build a cable and install the OS; now it takes only seconds to deploy a new virtual machine using templates and cloning.

VMware offers a number of advanced features that aren't found in a strictly physical infrastructure. These features, such as High Availability, Fault Tolerance, and Distributed Resource Scheduler, help with increased uptime and overall availability. These technologies keep the VMs running or give the ability to quickly recover from unplanned outages. The ability to quickly and easily relocate a VM from one ESXi host to another is one of the greatest benefits of using vSphere virtual machines.

In the end, virtualizing the infrastructure and using virtual machines will help save time, space, and money. However, keep in mind that there are some upfront costs to be aware of. Server hardware may need to be upgraded or new hardware purchased to ensure compliance with the **VMware Hardware Compatibility List** (HCL). Another cost that should be taken into account is the licensing costs for VMware and the guest operating system; each tier of licensing allows for more features but drives up the price to license all of the server hardware.

The primary virtual machine resources

Virtualization decouples physical hardware from an operating system. Each virtual machine contains a set of its own virtual hardware and there are four primary resources that a virtual machine needs in order to correctly function. These are CPU, memory, network, and hard disk. These four resources look like physical hardware to the guest operating systems and applications. The virtual machine is granted access to a portion of the resources at creation and can be reconfigured at any time thereafter. If a virtual machine experiences constraint, one of the four primary resources is generally where a bottleneck will occur.

In a traditional architecture, the operating system interacts directly with the server's physical hardware without virtualization. It is the operating system that allocates memory to applications, schedules processes to run, reads from and writes to attached storage, and sends and receives data on the network. This is not the case with a virtualized architecture. The virtual machine guest operating system still does the aforementioned tasks, but also interacts with virtual hardware presented by the hypervisor.

In a virtualized environment, a virtual machine interacts with the physical hardware through a thin layer of software known as the virtualization layer or the hypervisor; in this case the hypervisor is ESXi. This hypervisor allows the VM to function with a degree of independence from underlying physical hardware. This independence is what allows vMotion and Storage vMotion functionality. The following diagram demonstrates a virtual machine and its four primary resources:

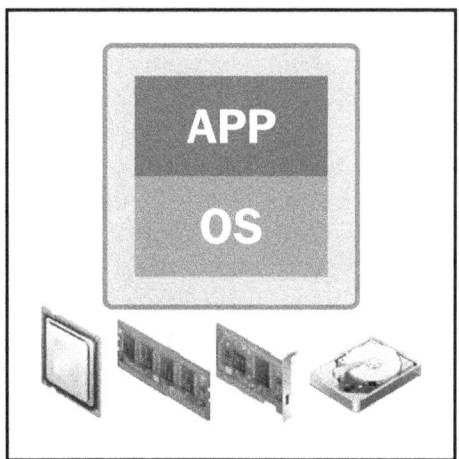

This section will provide an overview of each of the "primary four" resources. Configurations for these resources will be discussed in *Chapter 2, Creating a Virtual Machine Using the Wizard* and *Chapter 4, Advanced Virtual Machine Settings*.

CPU

The virtualization layer runs CPU instructions to make sure that the virtual machines run as though accessing the physical processor on the ESXi host. Performance is paramount for CPU virtualization, and therefore will use the ESXi host physical resources whenever possible. The following image displays a representation of a virtual machine's CPU:

A virtual machine can be configured with up to 64 virtual CPUs (vCPUs) as of vSphere 5.5. The maximum vCPUs able to be allocated depends on the underlying logical cores that the physical hardware has. Another factor in the maximum vCPUs is the tier of vSphere licensing; only Enterprise Plus licensing allows for 64 vCPUs. The VMkernel includes a CPU scheduler that dynamically schedules vCPUs on the ESXi host's physical processors.

The VMkernel scheduler, when making scheduling decisions, considers socket-core-thread topology. A **socket** is a single, integrated circuit package that has one or more physical processor cores. Each core has one or more logical processors, also known as threads. If hyperthreading is enabled on the host, then ESXi is capable of executing two threads, or sets of instruction, simultaneously. Effectively, hyperthreading provides more logical CPUs to ESXi on which vCPUs can be scheduled, providing more scheduler throughput. However, keep in mind that hyperthreading does not double the core's power. During times of CPU contention, when VMs are competing for resources, the VMkernel timeslices the physical processor across all virtual machines to ensure that the VMs run as if having a specified number of vCPUs.

VMware vSphere Virtual Symmetric Multiprocessing (SMP) is what allows the virtual machines to be configured with up to 64 virtual CPUs, which allows a larger CPU workload to run on an ESXi host. Though most supported guest operating systems are multiprocessor aware, many guest OSes and applications do not need and are not enhanced by having multiple vCPUs. Check vendor documentation for operating system and application requirements before configuring SMP virtual machines.

Memory

In a physical architecture, an operating system assumes that it owns all physical memory in the server, which is a correct assumption. A guest operating system in a virtual architecture also makes this assumption but it does not, in fact, own all of the physical memory. A guest operating system in a virtual machine uses a contiguous virtual address space that is created by ESXi as its configured memory. The following image displays a representation of a virtual machine's memory:

Virtual memory is a well-known technique that creates this contiguous virtual address space, allowing the hardware and operating system to handle the address translation between the physical and virtual address spaces. Since each virtual machine has its own contiguous virtual address space, this allows ESXi to run more than one virtual machine at the same time. The virtual machine's memory is protected against access from other virtual machines.

This effectively results in three layers of virtual memory in ESXi: physical memory, guest operating system physical memory, and guest operating system virtual memory. The VMkernel presents a portion of physical host memory to the virtual machine as its guest operating system physical memory. The guest operating system presents the virtual memory to the applications.

The virtual machine is configured with a set of memory; this is the sum that the guest OS is told it has available to it. A virtual machine will not necessarily use the entire memory size; it only uses what is needed at the time by the guest OS and applications. However, a VM cannot access more memory than the configured memory size. A default memory size is provided by vSphere when creating the virtual machine. It is important to know the memory needs of the application and guest operating system being virtualized so that the virtual machine's memory can be sized accordingly.

Network

There are two key components with virtual networking: the virtual switch and virtual Ethernet adapters. A virtual machine can be configured with up to ten virtual Ethernet adapters, called **vNICs**. The following image displays a representation of a virtual machine's vNIC:

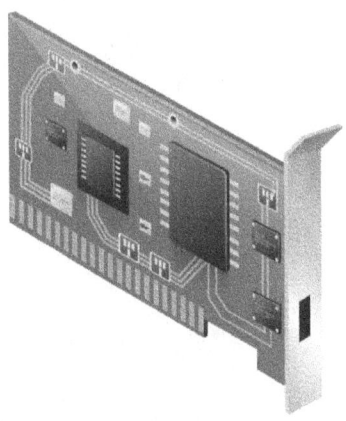

Virtual network switching is software interfacing between virtual machines at the vSwitch level until the frames hit an uplink or a physical adapter, exiting the ESXi host and entering the physical network. Virtual networks exist for virtual devices; all communication between the virtual machines and the external world (physical network) goes through vNetwork standard switches or vNetwork distributed switches.

Virtual networks operate on layer 2, **data link**, of the OSI model. A virtual switch is similar to a physical Ethernet switch in many ways. For example, virtual switches support the standard VLAN (802.1Q) implementation and have a forwarding table, like a physical switch. An ESXi host may contain more than one virtual switch. Each virtual switch is capable of binding multiple vmnics together in a **network interface card** (**NIC**) team, which offers greater availability to the virtual machines using the virtual switch.

There are two connection types available on a virtual switch: a port group and a VMkernel port. Virtual machines are connected to port groups on a virtual switch, allowing access to network resources. VMkernel ports provide a network service to the ESXi host to include IP storage, management, vMotion, and so on. Each VMkernel port must be configured with its own IP address and network mask. The port groups and VMkernel ports reside on a virtual switch and connect to the physical network through the physical Ethernet adapters known as **vmnics**. If uplinks (vmnics) are associated with a virtual switch, then the virtual machines connected to a port group on this virtual switch will be able to access the physical network.

Disk

In a non-virtualized environment, physical servers connect directly to storage, either to an external storage array or to their internal hard disk arrays to the server chassis. The issue with this configuration is that a single server expects total ownership of the physical device, tying an entire disk drive to one server. Sharing storage resources in non-virtualized environments can require complex filesystems and migration to file-based **Network Attached Storage** (**NAS**) or **Storage Area Networks** (**SAN**). The following image displays a representation of a virtual disk:

Shared storage is a foundational technology that allows many things to happen in a virtual environment (High Availability, Distributed Resource Scheduler, and so on). Virtual machines are encapsulated in a set of discrete files stored on a datastore. This encapsulation makes the VMs portable and easy to be cloned or backed up. For each virtual machine, there is a directory on the datastore that contains all of the VM's files. A datastore is a generic term for a container that holds files as well as .iso images and floppy images. It can be formatted with VMware's **Virtual Machine File System** (**VMFS**) or can use NFS. Both datastore types can be accessed across multiple ESXi hosts.

VMFS is a high-performance, clustered filesystem devised for virtual machines that allows a virtualization-based architecture of multiple physical servers to read and write to the same storage simultaneously. VMFS is designed, constructed, and optimized for virtualization. The newest version, VMFS-5, exclusively uses 1 MB block size, which is good for large files, while also having an 8 KB subblock allocation for writing small files such as logs. VMFS-5 can have datastores as large as 64 TB. The ESXi hosts use a locking mechanism to prevent the other ESXi hosts accessing the same storage from writing to the VMs' files. This helps prevent corruption.

Several storage protocols can be used to access and interface with VMFS datastores; these include Fibre Channel, Fibre Channel over Ethernet, iSCSI, and direct attached storage. NFS can also be used to create a datastore. VMFS datastore can be dynamically expanded, allowing the growth of the shared storage pool with no downtime.

Virtual Machine Concepts

vSphere significantly simplifies accessing storage from the guest OS of the VM. The virtual hardware presented to the guest operating system includes a set of familiar SCSI and IDE controllers; this way the guest OS sees a simple physical disk attached via a common controller. Presenting a virtualized storage view to the virtual machine's guest OS has advantages such as expanded support and access, improved efficiency, and easier storage management.

Virtual machine files

vSphere administrators should know the components of virtual machines. There are multiple VMware file types that are associated with and make up a virtual machine. These files are located in the VM's directory on a datastore. The following table will summarize and provide a quick reference and short description of the files that make up a virtual machine:

File	Example filename	Description
.vmx	\<vmname\>.vmx	Configuration file
.vmfx	\<vmname\>.vmfx	Additional configuration file
.vmtx	\<vmname\>.vmtx	Template file
.nvram	\<vmname\>.nvram	BIOS/EFI configuration
.vswp	\<vmname\>.vswp	Swap files
	vmx-\<vmname\>.vswp	
.log	vmware.log	Current log file
	vmware-##.log	Old log file entries
.vmdk	\<vmname\>.vmdk	Virtual disk descriptor
-flat.vmdk	\<vmname\>-flat.vmdk	Data disk
-rdm.vmdk	\<vmname\>-rdm.vmdk	Raw device map file
-delta.vmdk	\<vmname\>-delta.vmdk	Snapshot disk
.vmsd	\<vmname\>.vmsd	Snapshot description data
.vmsn	\<vmname\>.vmsn	Snapshot state
.vmss	\<vmname\>.vmss	Suspend file

Depending on the state and configuration of the virtual machine, not all files may be present in the virtual machine directory.

Let's explore these virtual machine files in more detail.

Configuration files

The `.vmx` file describes the current configuration information and hardware settings for the VM. This can contain a large variety of information regarding the virtual machine, to include its specific virtual hardware configuration (amount of RAM, NIC settings, CD-ROM information, parallel/serial port information, and so on), as well as its advanced resource and power settings, VMware tools options, and so forth. It is possible to make changes and directly edit this file; however, do this at your own risk. Generally, it is recommended to have a backup of this file first and to not edit until recommended by VMware support.

The `.vmx` file is a plain-text file that functions as the structural definition of the VM. The `.vmx` file can be copied from the datastore and opened using a program that supports creation and saving of files using UTF-8 encoding, such as WordPad. The following excerpt shows an example of a `.vmx` file for a virtual machine named ExampleVM:

```
.encoding = "UTF-8"
config.version = "8"
virtualHW.version = "10"
nvram = "ExampleVM.nvram"
pciBridge0.present = "TRUE"
svga.present = "TRUE"
pciBridge4.present = "TRUE"
pciBridge4.virtualDev = "pcieRootPort"
pciBridge4.functions = "8"
pciBridge5.present = "TRUE"
pciBridge5.virtualDev = "pcieRootPort"
pciBridge5.functions = "8"
pciBridge6.present = "TRUE"
pciBridge6.virtualDev = "pcieRootPort"
pciBridge6.functions = "8"
pciBridge7.present = "TRUE"
pciBridge7.virtualDev = "pcieRootPort"
pciBridge7.functions = "8"
vmci0.present = "TRUE"
hpet0.present = "TRUE"
displayName = "SampleVM"
extendedConfigFile = "ExampleVM.vmxf"
virtualHW.productCompatibility = "hosted"
memSize = "384"
sched.cpu.units = "mhz"
powerType.powerOff = "soft"
```

```
powerType.suspend = "hard"
powerType.reset = "soft"
scsi0.virtualDev = "lsilogic"
scsi0.present = "TRUE"
ide1:0.deviceType = "cdrom-image"
ide1:0.fileName = "/vmfs/volumes/5099c3c8-d8fe7ee8-2961-005056903273/
win2k3srvsp2.iso"
ide1:0.present = "TRUE"
floppy0.startConnected = "FALSE"
floppy0.clientDevice = "TRUE"
floppy0.fileName = "vmware-null-remote-floppy"
ethernet0.virtualDev = "e1000"
ethernet0.networkName = "Production"
ethernet0.addressType = "vpx"
ethernet0.generatedAddress = "00:50:56:bc:c0:47"
ethernet0.present = "TRUE"
scsi0:0.deviceType = "scsi-hardDisk"
scsi0:0.fileName = "ExampleVM.vmdk"
scsi0:0.present = "TRUE"
guestOS = "winnetenterprise"
toolScripts.afterPowerOn = "TRUE"
toolScripts.afterResume = "TRUE"
toolScripts.beforeSuspend = "TRUE"
toolScripts.beforePowerOff = "TRUE"
uuid.bios = "42 3c 4c d6 12 1e 5e c2-a4 a3 b6 89 95 9f 7a 75"
vc.uuid = "50 3c 6f a7 75 fb 68 7c-d1 42 df f7 f8 9b f5 f2"
chipset.onlineStandby = "FALSE"
sched.cpu.min = "0"
sched.cpu.shares = "normal"
sched.mem.min = "0"
sched.mem.minSize = "0"
sched.mem.shares = "normal"
sched.swap.derivedName = "/vmfs/volumes/5099c3c8-
d8fe7ee8-2961-005056903273/ExampleVM/ExampleVM-7f1e3e76.vswp"
uuid.location = "56 4d 9b 08 ee d9 6c e2-ab 67 3a dc 63 16 cb fe"
replay.supported = "FALSE"
replay.filename = ""
scsi0:0.redo = ""
pciBridge0.pciSlotNumber = "17"
pciBridge4.pciSlotNumber = "21"
```

```
pciBridge5.pciSlotNumber = "22"
pciBridge6.pciSlotNumber = "23"
pciBridge7.pciSlotNumber = "24"
scsi0.pciSlotNumber = "16"
ethernet0.pciSlotNumber = "32"
vmci0.pciSlotNumber = "33"
vmci0.id = "-1784710539"
hostCPUID.0 = "0000000b756e65476c65746e49656e69"
hostCPUID.1 = "000106a50002080080b822291fabfbff"
hostCPUID.80000001 = "00000000000000000000000128100800"
guestCPUID.0 = "0000000b756e65476c65746e49656e69"
guestCPUID.1 = "000106a500010800809822010fabbbff"
guestCPUID.80000001 = "00000000000000000000000128100800"
userCPUID.0 = "0000000b756e65476c65746e49656e69"
userCPUID.1 = "000106a500020800809822010fabbbff"
userCPUID.80000001 = "00000000000000000000000128100800"
evcCompatibilityMode = "FALSE"
vmotion.checkpointFBSize = "4194304"
cleanShutdown = "TRUE"
softPowerOff = "FALSE"
ide1:0.startConnected = "TRUE"
toolsInstallManager.lastInstallError = "0"
tools.syncTime = "FALSE"
tools.remindInstall = "FALSE"
toolsInstallManager.updateCounter = "1"
unity.wasCapable = "FALSE"
```

Reading through this file gives us important information regarding the configuration of the virtual machine. Here are a few examples:

- The VM's configured guest operating system can be derived from the `guestOS` line.
- Based upon the `memsize` line, it is known that the VM was configured for 384 MB of memory.
- The virtual machine only has one network adapter configured for the VM network port group based on the `ethernet0` lines.
- The virtual machine's vNIC has a MAC address of `00:50:56:bc:c0:47`, specified by the `ethernet0.generatedAddress` line.

A virtual machine's `.vmx` file is most commonly edited to modify the MAC address so that it matches the effective MAC address set within the guest operating system.

The `.vmx` file is extremely important to the virtual machine. However, keep in mind that it only structurally defines the VM's virtual hardware composition. It does not hold any actual data from the guest OS running within the VM. The virtual machine's data is stored in its virtual disk file. Here is an overview of the configuration and BIOS files:

- `.vmtx`: When a virtual machine is converted to a template, the virtual machine configuration file (`.vmx`) is replaced by the template configuration file (`.vmtx`).
- `.nvram`: This is generally a fairly small file that contains the BIOS settings that the VM uses upon boot. This is similar to how a physical server that has a BIOS chip allows hardware configuration options. The virtual BIOS settings, contained in the `.nvram` file, can be accessed by pressing *F2* when the virtual machine is powered on.

Swap files

The `.vswp` file is created when the virtual machine is powered on. The size of the `.vswp` file is equal to that of a configured memory, unless there is a reservation. When a memory reservation is configured for a VM, then the `.vswp` file size would equal the configured memory size minus the memory reservation. This file is used as a last resort when the hypervisor is reclaiming physical memory from its virtual machines, due to contention. Memory reclamation techniques are discussed in *Chapter 6, Virtual Machine Performance and Resource Allocation*.

Looking at the previous table, you may have noticed the `vmx-<vmname>.vswp` file. This file is for the overhead memory created for a VM, a new feature in vSphere 5.x. Historically, this memory overhead was not swappable. Though there was a memory reservation to back this, the entire address space did not actually have to reside in memory. This file helps to reduce the reservation requirements for virtual machines.

Virtual disks

The following are some of the virtual disk files:

- `.vmdk`: **Virtual disk descriptor**, which holds information such as the size and disk geometry of the virtual disk, information that makes the VM believe it has a real hard disk and not files on a datastore. Such information includes the virtual disk's adapter type, drive sectors, heads, and cylinders. This descriptor file also contains a pointer to the larger data file for the virtual disk or the `-flat.vmdk` file. An example of this information is demonstrated in the following screenshot:

```
# Disk DescriptorFile
version=1
encoding="UTF-8"
CID=fffffffe
parentCID=ffffffff
isNativeSnapshot="no"
createType="vmfs"

# Extent description
RW 6291456 VMFS "CustomVM-flat.vmdk"

# The Disk Data Base
#DDB

ddb.deletable = "true"
ddb.virtualHWVersion = "8"
ddb.longContentID = "33ab0a4a64bf2e315b197c09fffffffe"
ddb.uuid = "60 00 C2 99 75 82 d9 36-df b7 af f8 d1 c6 5a 3b"
ddb.geometry.cylinders = "391"
ddb.geometry.heads = "255"
ddb.geometry.sectors = "63"
ddb.thinProvisioned = "1"
ddb.adapterType = "lsilogic"
```

- -flat.vmdk: This file actually contains the virtual disk's data. This is created by default when a virtual hard drive is added to a virtual machine that is not using the **Raw Device Mapping** (**RDM**) option. When created as a thick provisioned disk, it will be sized approximately to what was specified in the creation wizard. The different disk provisioning types will be discussed in *Chapter 2, Creating a Virtual Machine Using the Wizard*.

- -rdm.vmdk: This is the mapping file for the **Raw Device Mapping** (**RDM**) option, managing the RDM device's mapping data. The virtual machine isn't aware of this since the mapping file is presented to the ESXi host as a traditional disk file and available for normal filesystem operations. The storage virtualization layer presents the mapped device as a virtual SCSI device to the VM. An -rdm.vmdk file exists for each RDM configured for the virtual machine. RDMs will be discussed in more detail in *Chapter 2, Creating a Virtual Machine Using the Wizard* and *Chapter 10, Virtual Machine Design*.

Snapshot files

The following are the snapshot files:

- `-delta.vmdk`: These files are only used when creating snapshots. When a snapshot is created, the original `-flat.vmdk` file is no longer written to; it becomes read only. All changes that are written to the virtual disk are now being written to the `-delta.vmdk` files instead. Due to the fact that these `-delta.vmdk` files are bitmaps of changes made to a virtual disk, the `-delta.vmdk` file cannot exceed the size of the original `-flat.vmdk` file. A `-delta.vmdk` file is created for each snapshot that is generated. These `-delta.vmdk` files are updated in 16 MB increments as changes are written to the virtual disk.
- `.vmsd`: This file is a snapshot descriptor that contains information regarding which files are used by each snapshot, description, display name, and any associated UIDs. There is only one `.vmsd` file per virtual machine, regardless of how many snapshots the virtual machine has. This file is updated each time a new snapshot is created or a snapshot is deleted.
- `.vmsn`: This file stores the virtual machine's state at the time the snapshot was taken. The size of this file varies depending on whether the option to include the VM's memory state was selected during snapshot creation. A separate `.vmsn` file will be created for each snapshot and will automatically be removed when the snapshot is deleted.

Other files

Let's take a look at some other files:

- `.vmss`: This file is used when a virtual machine is suspended so as to preserve the VM's memory contents; it is only present when the VM is suspended. When the virtual machine is resumed from the suspended state, it can start again right from where it left off. The contents of this file are written back to the ESXi host's physical memory when the virtual machine is brought out of a suspended state; however, the file will not be automatically deleted until the VM is powered off. This file will be approximately the same size as the configured memory for the virtual machine, unless memory contention is present.

- `.log`: Log files are created in order to log information regarding the virtual machine, typically used during troubleshooting efforts. The current log file is always named `vmware.log`, and by default up to six older log files will be retained. These older log files will have a number appended at the end of their names, which will be updated with each file (`vmware-2.log`).

Viewing virtual machine files

A virtual machine's files can either reside on a VMFS or a NFS datastore. The vSphere Client or the vSphere Web Client can be used to browse the datastore and display a virtual machine's files.

Using the vSphere Client

In order to figure out which datastore the VM resides on and browse the datastore by performing the following steps:

1. First select the virtual machine in the inventory.
2. On the VM's **Summary** tab, there is a **Resources** pane that lists all the datastores being used by the selected VM.
3. Right-click on a datastore and select **Browse Datastore...** from the available options.

   This is demonstrated in the following screenshot:

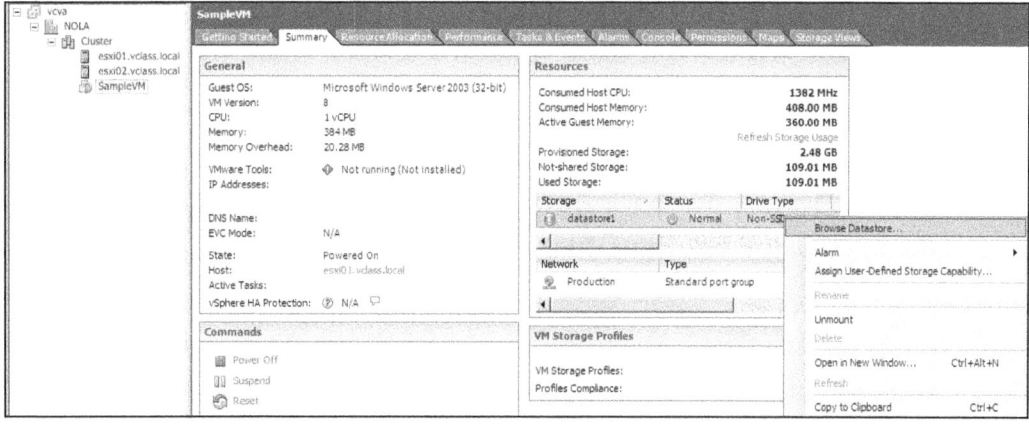

This process opens the Datastore Browser, which is a handy tool to quickly display the contents of any datastore. The virtual machine's files can be displayed by selecting the VM's directory, as shown in the following screenshot:

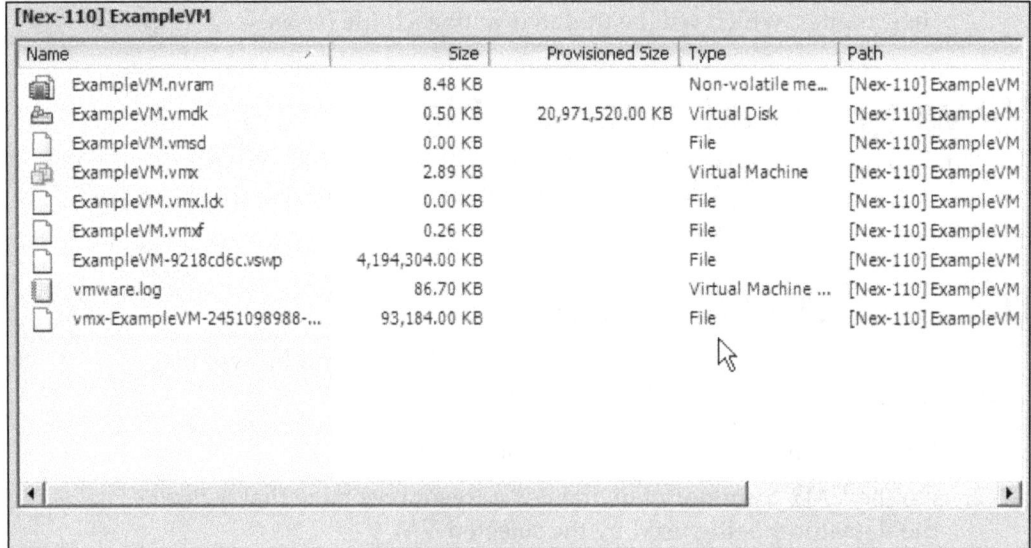

 The Datastore Brower shows that the virtual disk consists of only a single file, the .vmdk file. This is not indicative of reality; there are actually at least two files that make up the virtual disk, the .vmdk and -flat.vmdk files.

Another option in the vSphere Client is **Storage Views**; to access this option, perform the following steps:

1. Select the VM in the inventory and then the **Storage Views** tab.
2. There is a drop-down menu towards the left-hand side, click on it and select **Show All Virtual Machine Files**.

This is shown in the following screenshot:

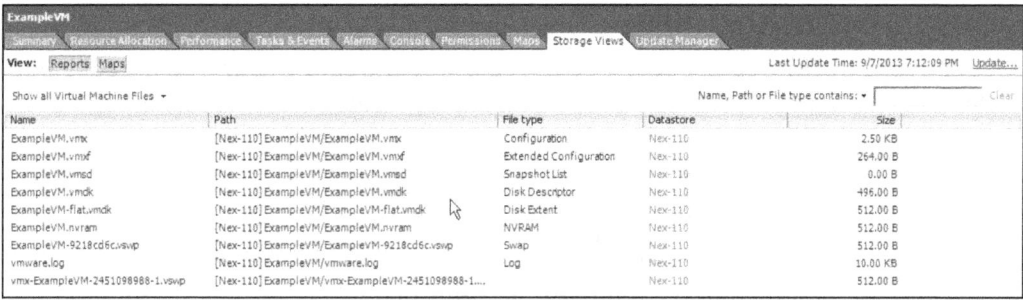

Notice that the -flat.vmdk file is displayed in this view. This is the only view in the vSphere Client where the -flat.vmdk file is shown. All other views show only the .vmdk file.

Using the vSphere Web Client

If the vSphere Web Client is installed, then the virtual machine files may also be viewed using it. This view is the vSphere Web Client equivalent to the vSphere Client's Datastore Browser. Once the vSphere Web Client is launched:

1. Browse to the **Datastore and Datastore Cluster** view.
2. Once in this view, select the datastore that the virtual machine resides on in the inventory pane.
3. From there, go to the **Manage** tab and select the **Files** button.
4. The datastore directories will be listed on the left-hand side. Select the virtual machine; the results will look similar to what is displayed in the following screenshot. Note that the -flat.vmdk file is not shown:

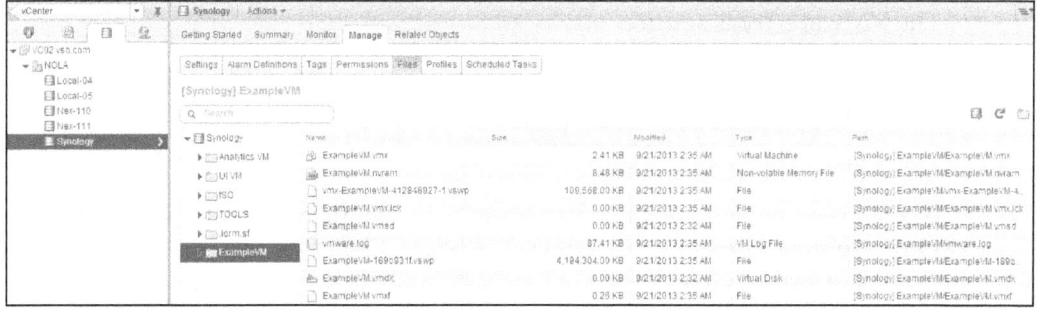

Using command line

Alternatively, the files can be displayed via a command line. Ensure SSH is enabled on the ESXi host that the virtual machine is located on and use an SSH client, such as PuTTy, to establish a connection. For steps on how to enable SSH, check http://vmware.com/kb/1017910. Navigate to the virtual machine's directory and use the `ls -l` command to view the files.

An example of the output from using the `ls -l` command, after navigating to the VM's directory, is shown in the following screenshot:

```
/vmfs/volumes/65b1b1cd-04d63456/ExampleVM # ls -l
-rw-------   1 42949672 42949672 4294967296 Sep  8 00:11 ExampleVM-9218cd6c.vswp
-rw-------   1 42949672 42949672 21474836480 Sep  8 00:08 ExampleVM-flat.vmdk
-rw-------   1 42949672 42949672       8684 Sep  8 00:11 ExampleVM.nvram
-rw-------   1 42949672 42949672        496 Sep  8 00:08 ExampleVM.vmdk
-rw-r--r--   1 42949672 42949672          0 Sep  8 00:08 ExampleVM.vmsd
-rwxr-xr-x   1 42949672 42949672       2961 Sep  8 00:11 ExampleVM.vmx
-rw-------   1 42949672 42949672          0 Sep  8 00:11 ExampleVM.vmx.lck
-rw-r--r--   1 42949672 42949672        264 Sep  8 00:08 ExampleVM.vmxf
-rw-r--r--   1 42949672 42949672      89527 Sep  8 00:14 vmware.log
-rw-------   1 42949672 42949672   95420416 Sep  8 00:11 vmx-ExampleVM-2451098988-1.vswp
/vmfs/volumes/65b1b1cd-04d63456/ExampleVM #
```

VMware Tools

VMware Tools is a utility suite that enhances the performance of a virtual machine's guest OS. If VMware Tools is not installed in the guest operating system, the guest will be lacking in some important functionality. The VMware Tools utility improves virtual machine management by replacing the generic OS drivers with VMware drivers optimized for virtual hardware. The following components are included after the installation of VMware Tools:

- The VMware Tools service
- VMware Tools device drivers
- The VMware user process
- VIX

The **VMware Tools service** passes information between guest operating systems and the ESXi host; service starts when the guest OS boots. This runs as a `vmtoolsd.exe` program in Windows, `vmware-tools-daemon` in Mac OS X, and `vmtoolsd` in Solaris, FreeBSD, and Linux guest operating systems.

This service can run scripts that help automate repetitive guest operating system operations. Synchronization of the guest operating system time with the time on the ESXi host (with the exception of Mac OS X) can be configured with VMware Tools, though this is not necessarily recommended. Another benefit is the ability to move the mouse cursor freely between a Windows guest operating system in the VM and the vSphere Client (otherwise, *Ctrl + Alt* must be pressed in order to release the cursor from the VM console). Windows operating systems have the ability to quiesce snapshots used by certain backup operations provided by the service. VMware Tools also provides the process that sends heartbeats to VMware products to indicate that the guest operating system is running.

VMware Tools device drivers refine mouse operations and improve performance of networking, sound, and graphics. The guest OS will determine which drivers are installed with VMware Tools. The following device drivers can be included with VMware Tools:

Driver	Description
SVGA driver	Replaces the default VGA driver (640 x 480 resolution and 16-color graphics), enabling 32-bit displays, high display resolution, and faster graphics performance. Windows OSes that are Vista or later will use the VMware SVGA 3D driver.
SCSI driver	The VMware Paravirtual SCSI driver is included with VMware Tools for use. Other storage adapter drivers are bundled with the OS or are available via third-party vendors.
Paravirtual SCSI driver	High performance storage adapter that can produce greater throughput and lower processor utilization. This is best suited for a VM with an application that produces a very high amount of I/O throughput.
VMXNET NIC drivers	When installed, the VMXNET family of adapters can replace the default emulated networking drivers. These paravirtualized VMXNET adapters improve network performance and increase features.
Mouse driver	Improves mouse performance.
Audio driver	Required for many Windows OSes.
vShield Endpoint	When using vShield, a custom VMware Tools installation can install the vShield Endpoint Thin Agent component. vShield Endpoint offloads antivirus scans to the hypervisor without a large agent.

Virtual Machine Concepts

Driver	Description
ThinPrint driver	Enables virtual printing for Windows VMs; printers will be listed in the guest OS that are added to the OS on the client or host.
Memory control driver	Used for efficient memory allocation between virtual machines, commonly called the **balloon driver**.
Modules and drivers for support of automatic virtual machine backups	Allows for third-party, vSphere integrated backup software to create application consistent snapshots. The virtual machine's disks are quiesced and certain processes are paused during the snapshot process. The **Volume Shadow Copy Services** (**VSS**) for Windows Server 2003 or newer, and the Filesystem Sync driver for older Windows OSes are installed.
VMCI and VMCI Sockets drivers	The Virtual Machine Communication Interface driver allows for efficient and fast communication between VMs on the same ESXi host.

The **VMware user process** starts when a user logs in to a Windows guest OS or starts a desktop environment session in Linux. The process' program file is called `vmtoolsd.exe` on Windows guest OSes and `vmusr` for FreeBSD, Solaris, and Linux operating systems. This allows for copy-and-paste interaction between the guest operating system and the vSphere Client, matching the screen display resolution of the guest with that of the vSphere Client.

VIX support is provided for using the VMware VIX API for guest operating system-bound API calls. The VIX API allows for the automation of virtual machine operations on the ESXi platform.

Summary

A vSphere administrator needs to understand virtual machine concepts before creating virtual machines. A virtual machine is a set of virtual hardware presented to a guest operating system whose characteristics are determined by a set of files. There are multiple VMware file types that are associated with and make up a virtual machine and are located in the VM's directory on a datastore. These files include the `.vmx`, `.nvram`, `.vswp`, `.vmdk`, `-flat.vmdk`, and `.log` files. Each virtual machine is equipped with virtual hardware and devices, such as one or more virtual CPUs, memory, video cards, IDE devices, SCSI devices, DVD/CD-ROM, parallel and serial ports, and network adapters, that provide the same functionality as physical hardware. Once the administrator understands that the virtual hardware is available, the next step is to learn how it can be configured. VMware Tools is a utility suite that enhances the performance of a virtual machine's guest OS. VMware Tools should be installed in every virtual machine to ensure the virtual machines aren't lacking in any functionality.

The next chapter will discuss how to create a virtual machine using the wizard and other associated configuration options.

2
Creating a Virtual Machine Using the Wizard

In *Chapter 1*, *Virtual Machine Concepts*, we discussed the conceptual idea and structural makeup of a virtual machine. Now it's time to discuss how to create a virtual machine from scratch using the creation wizard. Step-by-step instructions will be given on creating a virtual machine using vSphere Client and vSphere Web Client.

In this chapter, you will learn:

- How to create a virtual machine using the typical configuration wizard
- How to create a virtual machine using the custom configuration wizard
- How to create a virtual machine using vSphere Web Client
- Different virtual machine configuration options presented in the wizards

vSphere Client versus vSphere Web Client

There are now two possible graphical user interface client choices for managing your vCenter Server inventory. But you may not know which client should be utilized for daily use. Upon release of the full-featured vSphere Web Client in vSphere 5.1, VMware made it known that no new features would be added to vSphere Client. Since vSphere Web Client provides the new features of vSphere 5.1 and vSphere 5.5, it is the one that you want to use. Not only that, but vSphere Client can only be installed on a Windows operating system, whereas vSphere Web Client is a platform independent browser-based implementation. As of vSphere 5.5, Microsoft Internet Explorer 8, 9 (64-bit), and 10, Mozilla Firefox, and Google Chrome are supported on Windows operating systems. Mozilla Firefox and Google Chrome are also supported on Mac OS X.

Creating a Virtual Machine Using the Wizard

There are cases where you may be attempting to use a plugin that has not yet been updated to work with vSphere Web Client. You may not have a choice but to use vSphere Client for plugin access. However, keep in mind that this transition period where both clients are used will eventually end and vSphere Web Client will be the only option available. Vendors are working to update all plugins and features to work with vSphere Web Client, so it's best to begin the adjustment now.

In *Chapter 1, Virtual Machine Concepts*, as well as the current chapter, instructions are given for both vSphere Web Client and vSphere Client. For all future chapters, only vSphere Web Client will be discussed.

Creating a VM using the typical configuration wizard

In order to launch the virtual machine creation wizard, right-click on a container that a virtual machine can reside in (Cluster, ESXi host, and resource pool, among others). Select **New Virtual Machine...**.

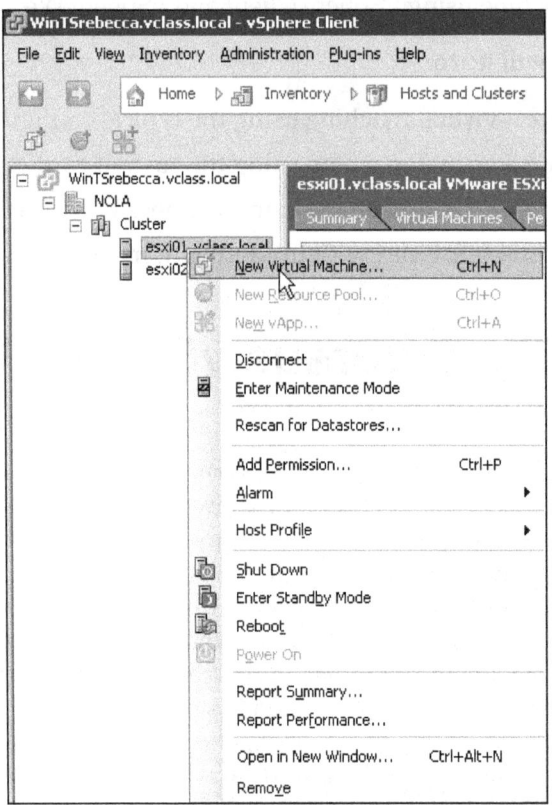

Once the **Create New Virtual Machine** wizard is launched, there are two options, **Typical** and **Custom**, as shown in the next screenshot. A typical configuration uses common virtual hardware and configurations based on the selection of the guest operating system. A custom configuration, which will be explored in the next section *Creating a VM using the custom configuration wizard*, allows you to modify the specifications of the virtual hardware.

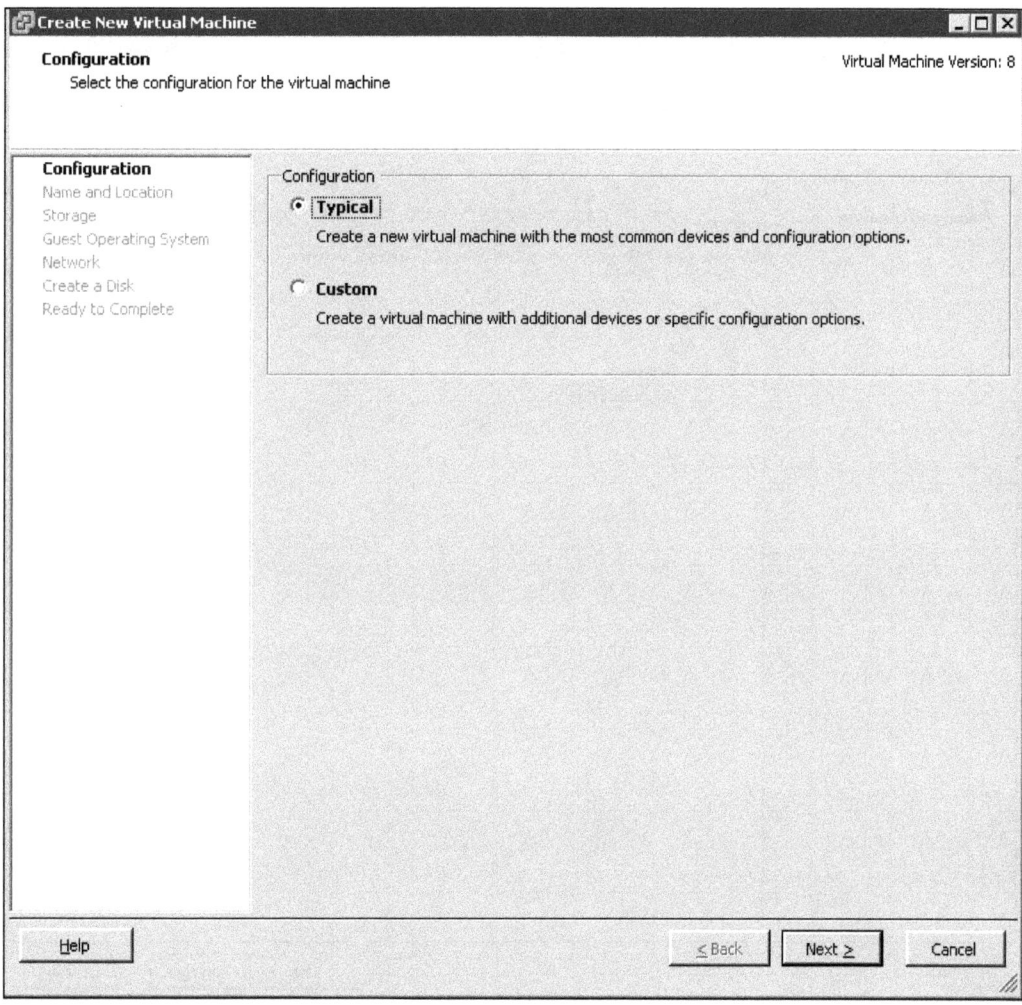

After selecting **Typical**, click on the **Next** button.

Name and Location

On the **Name and Location** pane, the virtual machine's name should be specified. Whatever name is specified for the virtual machine will result in all virtual machine files being named the same. The **Inventory Location** needs to be specified; this designates where the VM is placed in the VM and Template view in vCenter. This is demonstrated in the following screenshot:

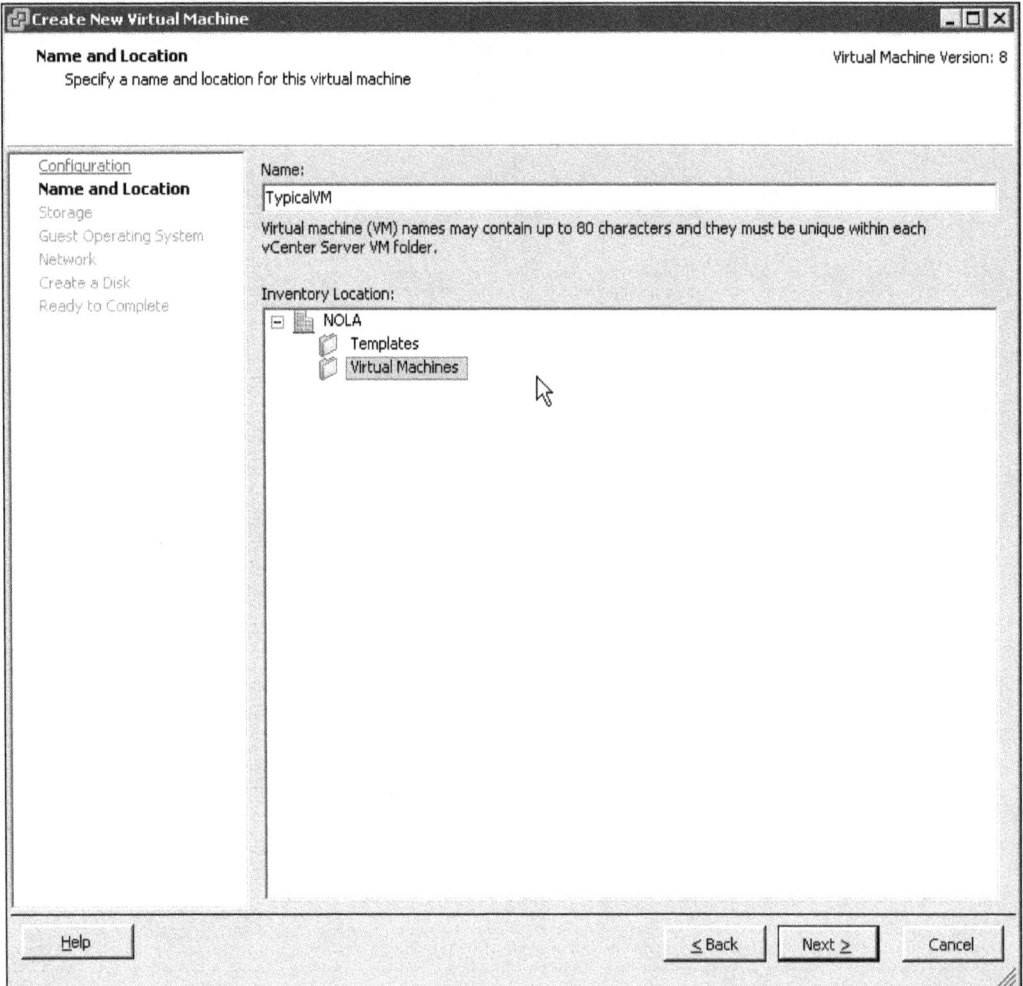

Upon selecting the folder in the VM and Template view, click on **Next**.

Storage

The next screenshot demonstrates the **Storage** pane, which prompts you to select on which datastore the virtual machine's directory and files should be created. This is not a permanent selection; the VM's files can be migrated to another datastore any time using **Storage vMotion**. If VM storage profiles or datastore clusters are set up in vCenter, select which **VM Storage Profile** or datastore cluster should be associated with the VM being created.

> Please note that profile-driven storage allows you to use storage capabilities and virtual machine storage profiles to help determine whether VMs are using a storage that guarantees a specific level of performance, availability, capacity, redundancy, and so on.

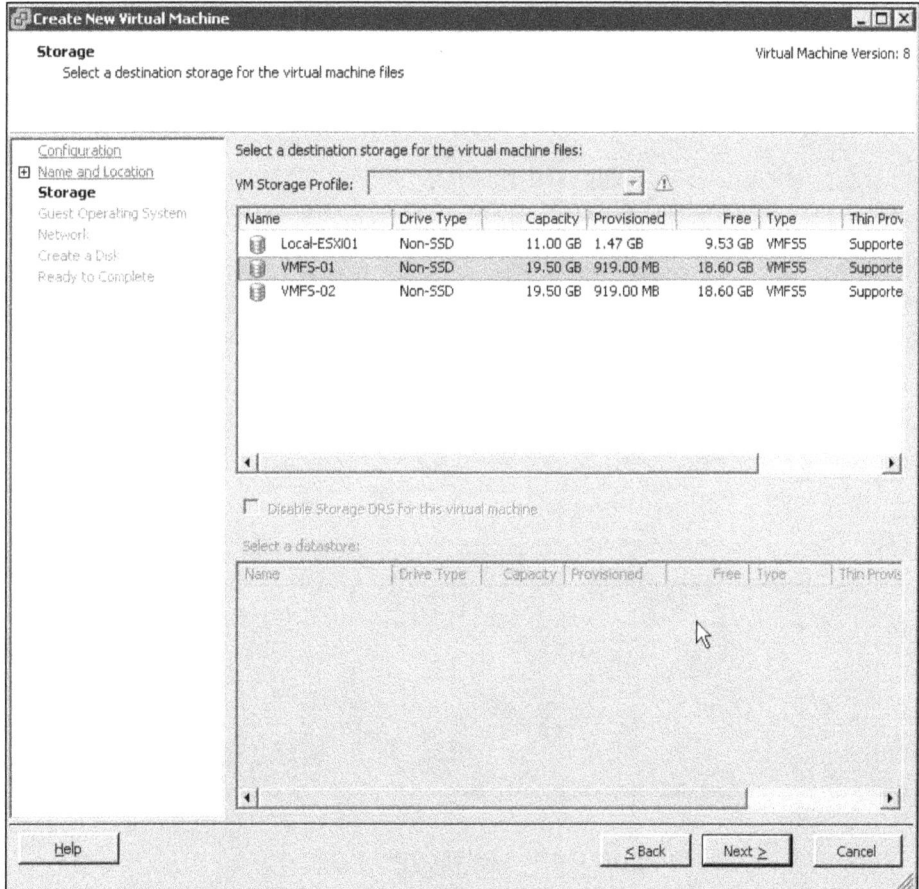

Once the datastore is selected, click on **Next**.

Creating a Virtual Machine Using the Wizard

Guest Operating System

Select the guest operating system that you plan to install from the list of choices, shown in the next screenshot. This is an important selection as it dictates which virtual hardware will be presented to the VM based on its compatibility with the guest OS.

The following screenshot shows the options of the various guest operating systems:

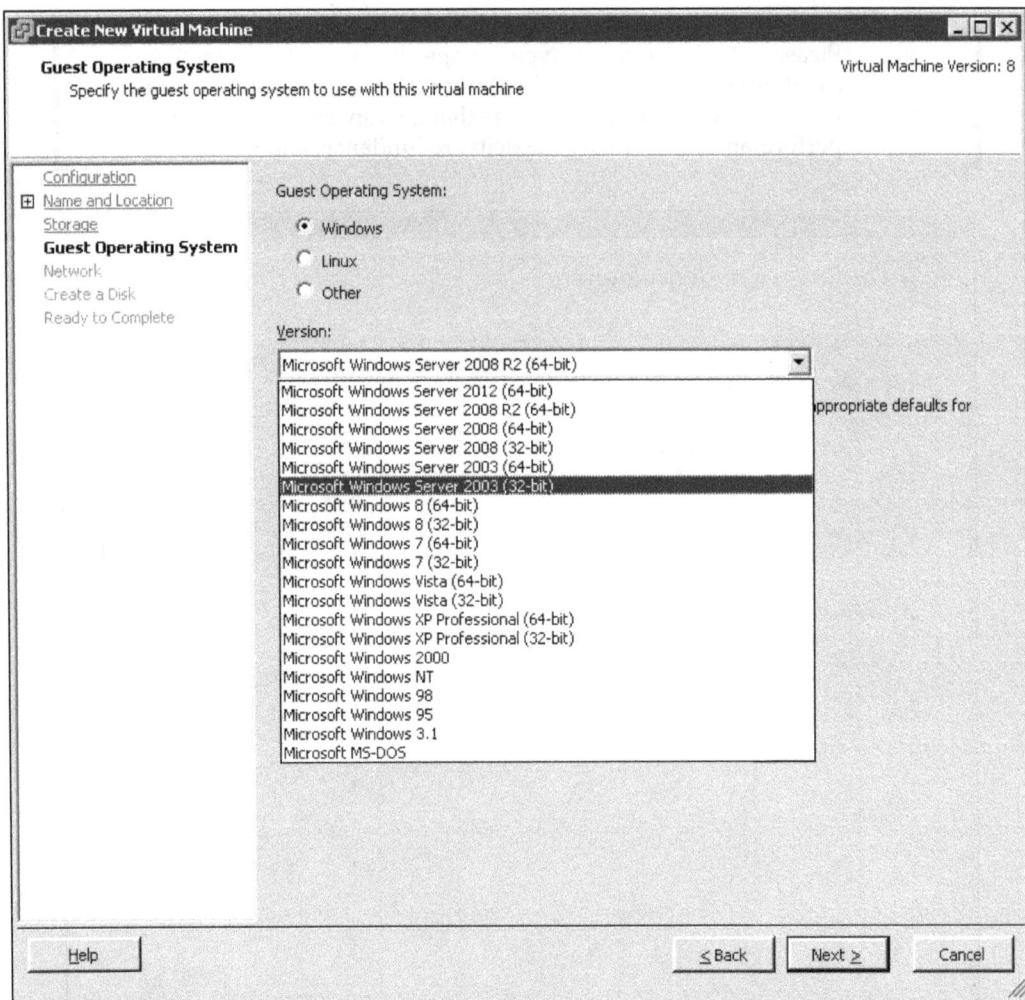

Click on **Next** after selecting the correct guest operating system.

[38]

Network

The following screenshot displays the **Network** pane. First, specify the number of NICs that the virtual machine will be configured with. The maximum is 10 vNICs for a single VM. For each NIC, select which **Network** (virtual machine port group) it will be connected to and which **Adapter Type** will be used. By default, the vNICs are connected at power on, but this can be deselected.

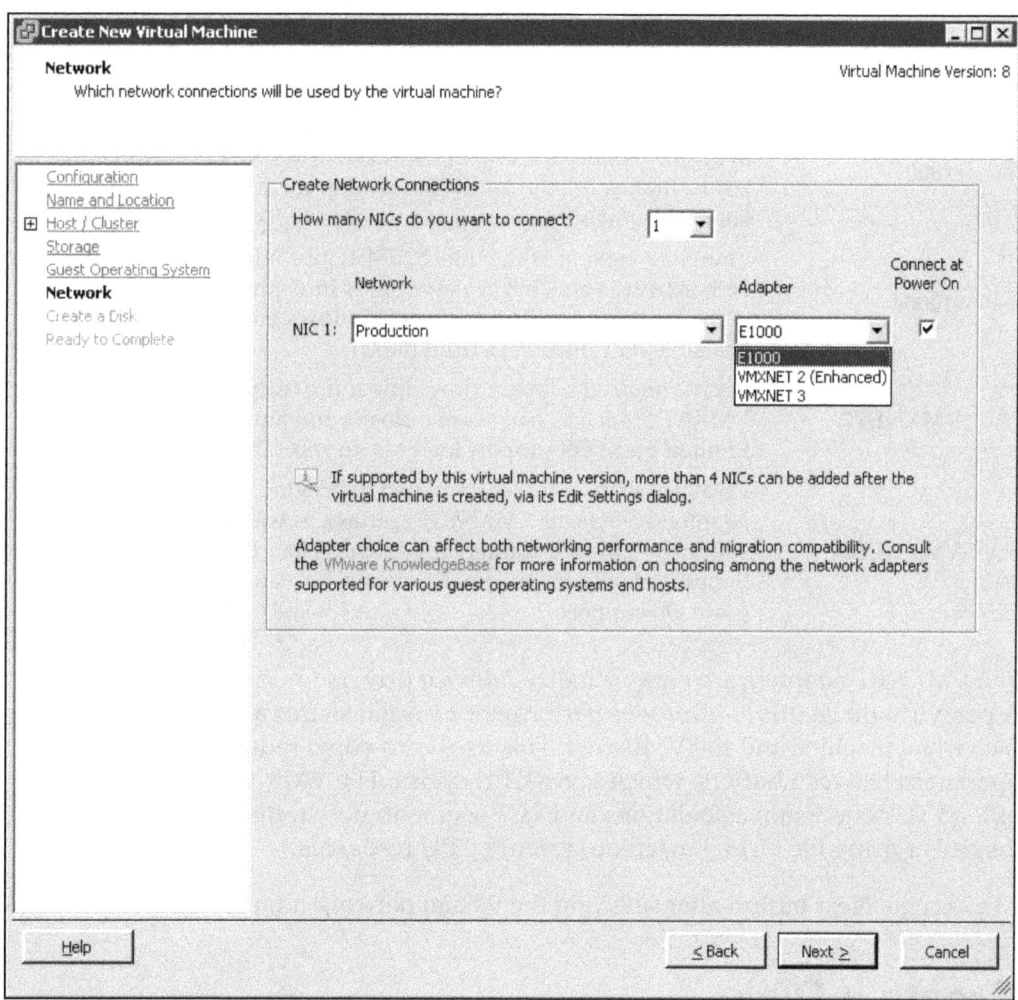

Creating a Virtual Machine Using the Wizard

The following table compares the different virtual network adapters that are available for a virtual machine.

Network Adapter	Description
vlance	Emulated version of the AMD 79C970 PCnet32. It's an older generation 10 Mbps NIC with drivers available in most 32-bit guest OSes, except Windows Vista and newer.
VMXNET	Paravirtualized adapter, optimized for performance in virtual machines. VMware Tools is required for VMXNET driver.
e1000	Emulated version of the Intel 82545EM 1Gbps NIC. Available in Linux versions 2.4.19 and later, Windows XP Professional x64 Edition and later, and Windows Server 2003 (32-bit) and later. No jumbo frames support prior to ESX/ESXi 4.1.
e1000e	Emulated version of the Intel 82574 1Gbps NIC. Only available on hardware version 8 or newer VMs in vSphere 5.x. Default vNIC for Windows 8 and newer Windows guest OSes. Not available for Linux OSes from the UI.
VMXNET2	Paravirtualized adapter, providing more features than VMXNET, such as hardware offloads and jumbo frames. Limited guest OS support for VMs on ESX/ESXi 3.5 and later.
VMXNET3	Paravirtualized adapter unrelated to previous VMXNET adapters. Offers all VMXNET2 features as well as NetQueue support, MSI/MSI-X interrupt delivery, and IPv6 offloads. Supported only for hardware version 7 or later with limited guest OS support.

The VMXNET adapters are paravirtualized device drivers for virtual networking. A paravirtualized driver improves performance since it shares a ring buffer between the virtual machine and the VMkernel. This uses zero-copy, reducing internal copy operations between buffers, which saves CPU cycles. The VMXNET adapters can offload TCP checksum calculations and TCP segmentation to the network hardware instead of using the virtual machine system's CPU resources.

Click on the **Next** button after selecting the virtual network adapter type.

Create a Disk

The next pane is **Create a Disk**. This should reflect the datastore chosen, as shown in the next screenshot, and display the space available on that datastore. In this pane, select the **Virtual disk size** and its provisioning type. The virtual disk can be up to 62 TB as of vSphere 5.5.

ESXi supports the following virtual disk types:

- **Thin Provision**: In this case, the disk is allocated and zeroed out on demand as needed rather than giving a full provisioning at creation, such as thick provisioning. This results in a thin provisioned disk having a shorter creation time. Subsequent writes to the blocks result in the same performance as eager-zeroed thick disks. There can be a more effective usage of the datastore space, but it can result in an over-provisioned datastore.
- **Thick Provision Eager Zeroed**: In this case, the disk space is allocated and zeroed out at disk creation. This increases the time taken to create the disk, but using this type of a disk results in the best performance, even upon first write to each block. This is required for using the Fault Tolerance feature with VMs.
- **Thick Provision Lazy Zeroed**: In this case, the disk space is allocated at disk creation, but each block is not zeroed out until the first write. Comparatively, this results in a shorter creation time than eager-zeroed. This is the default option in vSphere Client and is good for most cases.

The **Create a Disk** pane is shown in the following screenshot:

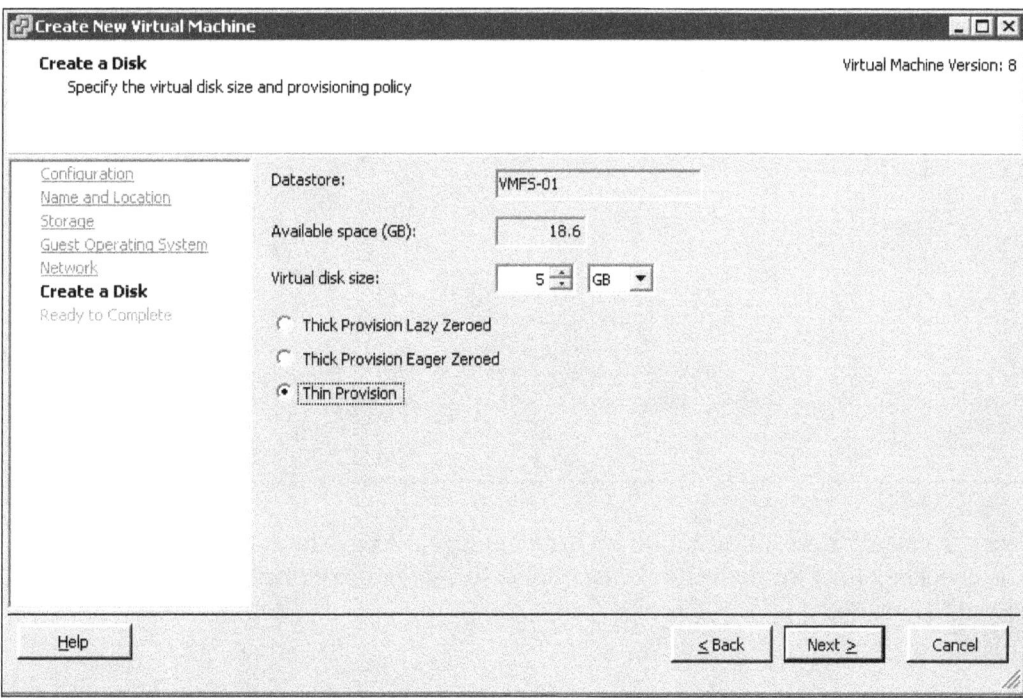

Click on the **Next** button once the virtual disk is configured.

Ready to Complete

The last section of the **Create New Virtual Machine** wizard is the review section, as shown in the following screenshot:

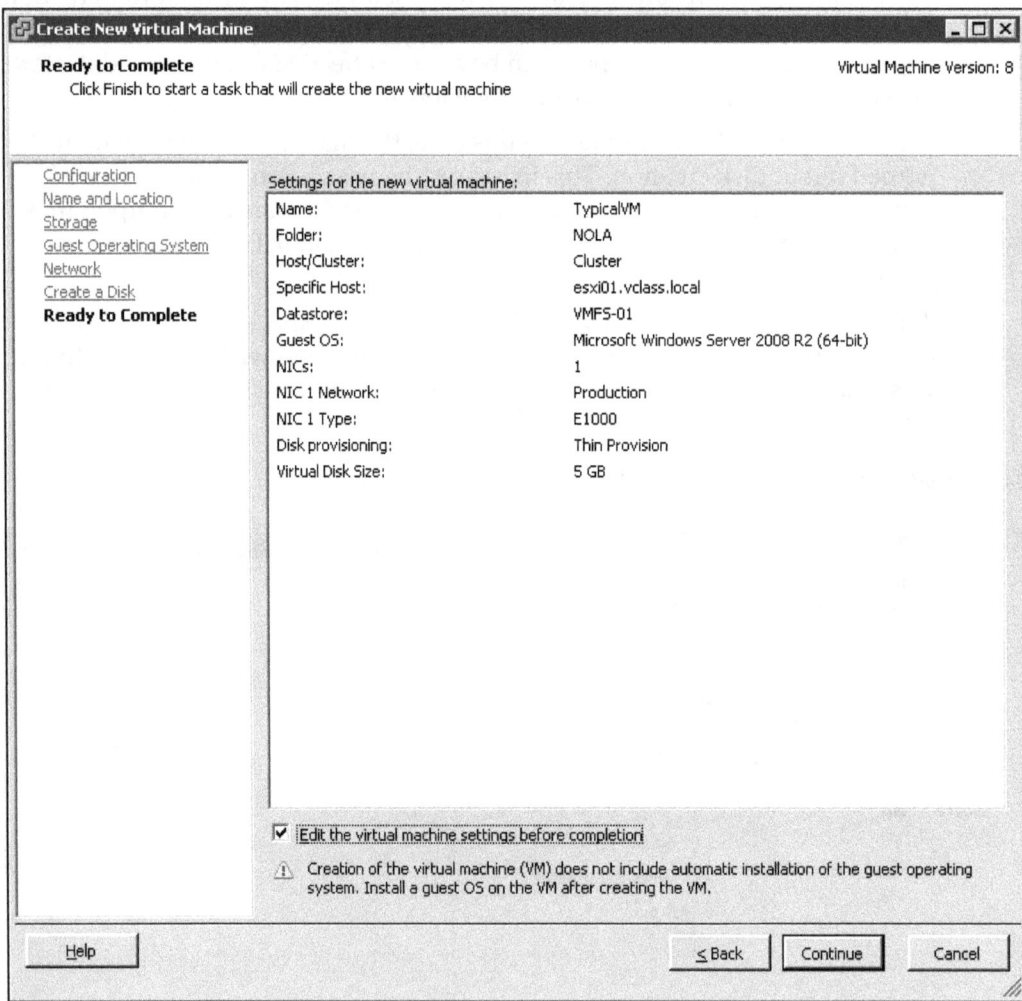

Ensure that all of the information is correct and select **Finish**, or click on the checkbox for **Edit the virtual machine settings before completion** and select **Continue**.

Editing the settings

If the aforementioned checkbox is selected, then the settings dialog will appear as shown in the following screenshot:

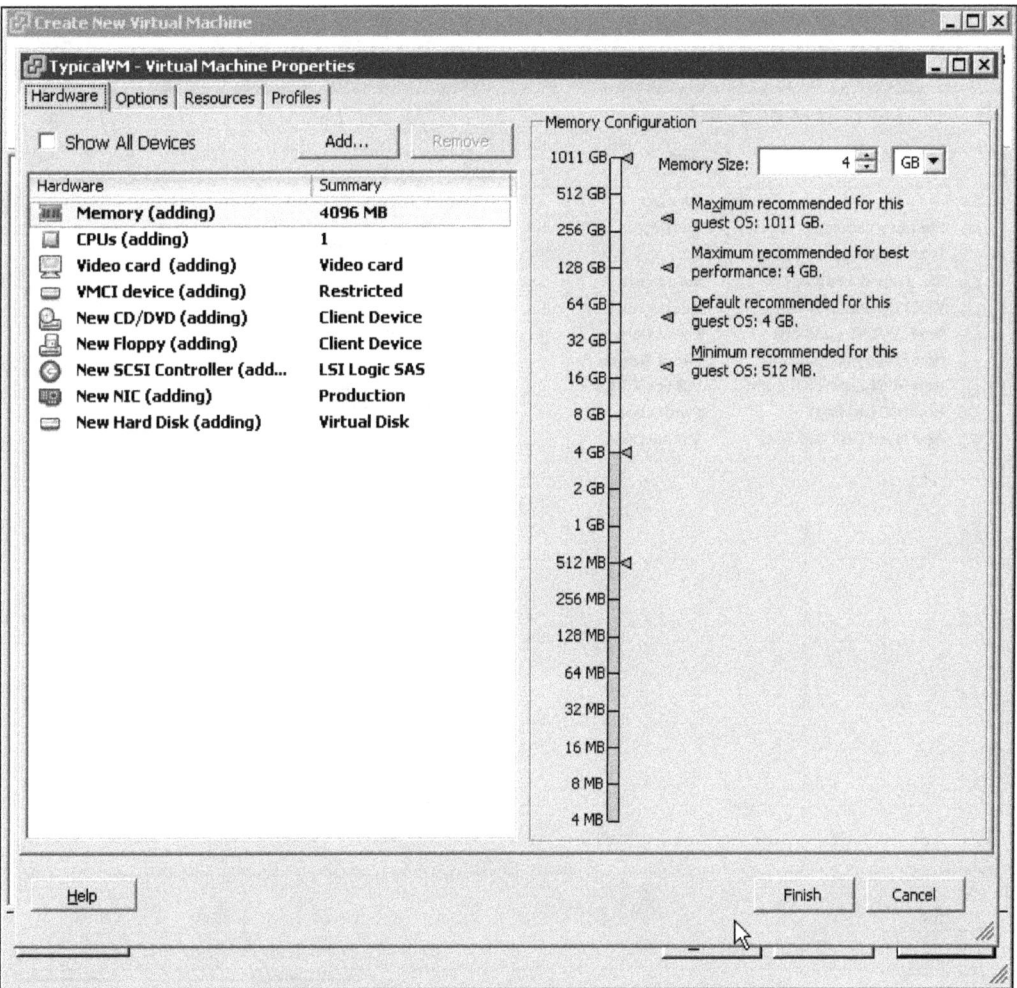

Creating a Virtual Machine Using the Wizard

From the settings of the virtual machine, you can review the default configuration. The preceding screenshot demonstrates the default memory size for the virtual machine's selected guest operating system. This can be adjusted as desired. The CPU configuration for the virtual machine is shown in the following screenshot:

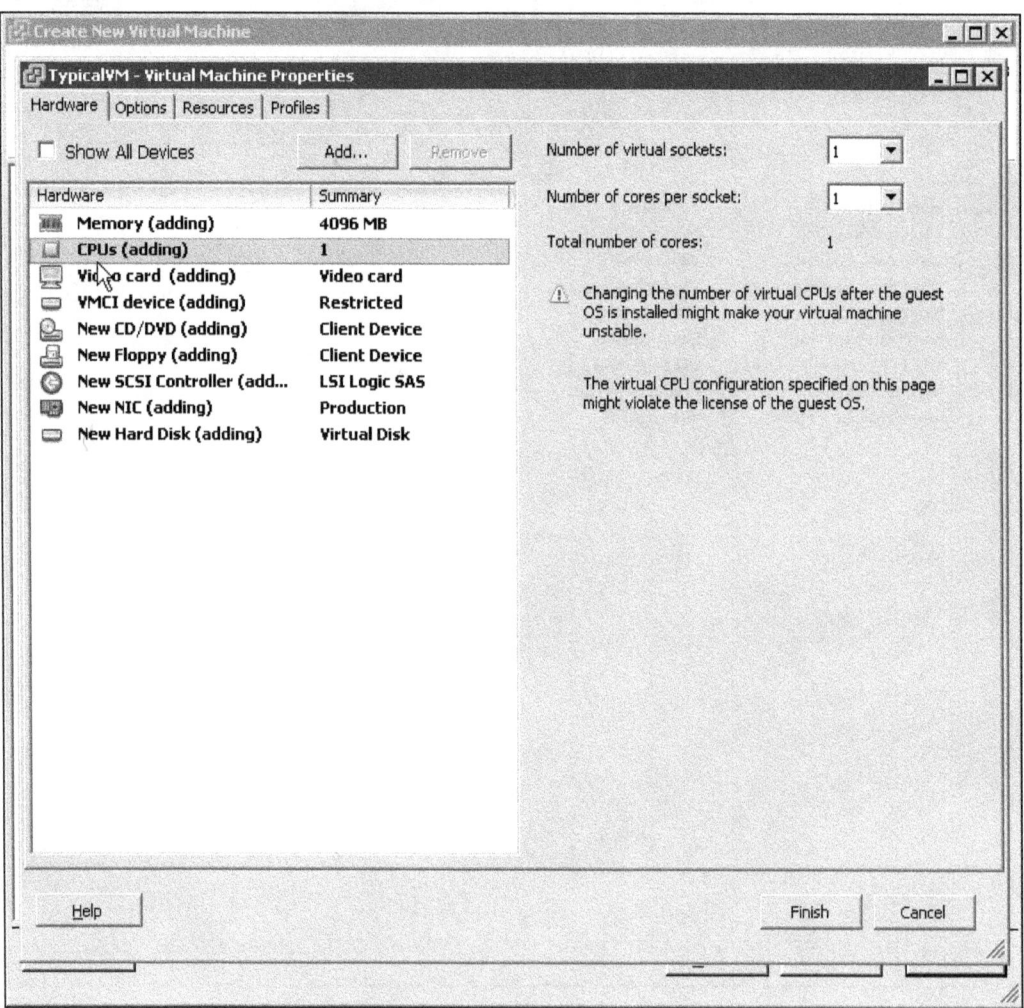

Notice that the default virtual machine CPU value is set to **1**. If how many vCPUs the virtual machine's application requires is not known, then it is recommended to start at 1 vCPU and adjust as needed.

Once the virtual machine's configuration is reviewed, then you can mount an ISO image for a guest operating system. Take a look at the following screenshot:

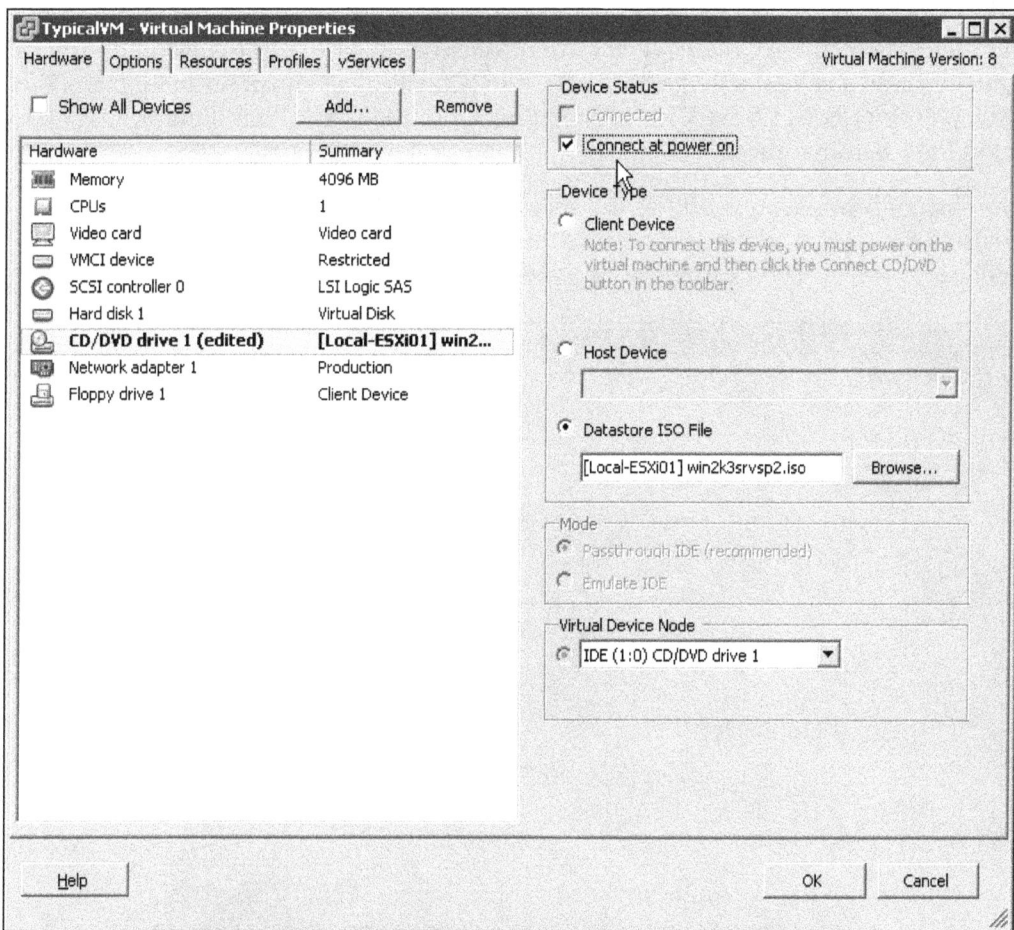

To mount an image, select **CD/DVD drive**, choose **Datastore ISO File**, and click on the **Browse...** button. Pick the correct ISO image for the selected guest operating system and ensure that the checkbox next to **Connect at power on** is selected. Click on **OK** and proceed to power on the VM.

Creating a VM using the custom configuration wizard

In order to launch the **Create New Virtual Machine** wizard, right-click on a container that a virtual machine can reside in (Cluster, ESXi host, resource pool, among others). Select **New Virtual Machine**. Once the wizard has launched, select the **Custom** option.

The custom configuration allows the specification of specific virtual hardware, whereas the typical configuration uses the default hardware based upon the guest operating system. The **Configuration** pane is shown in the following screenshot:

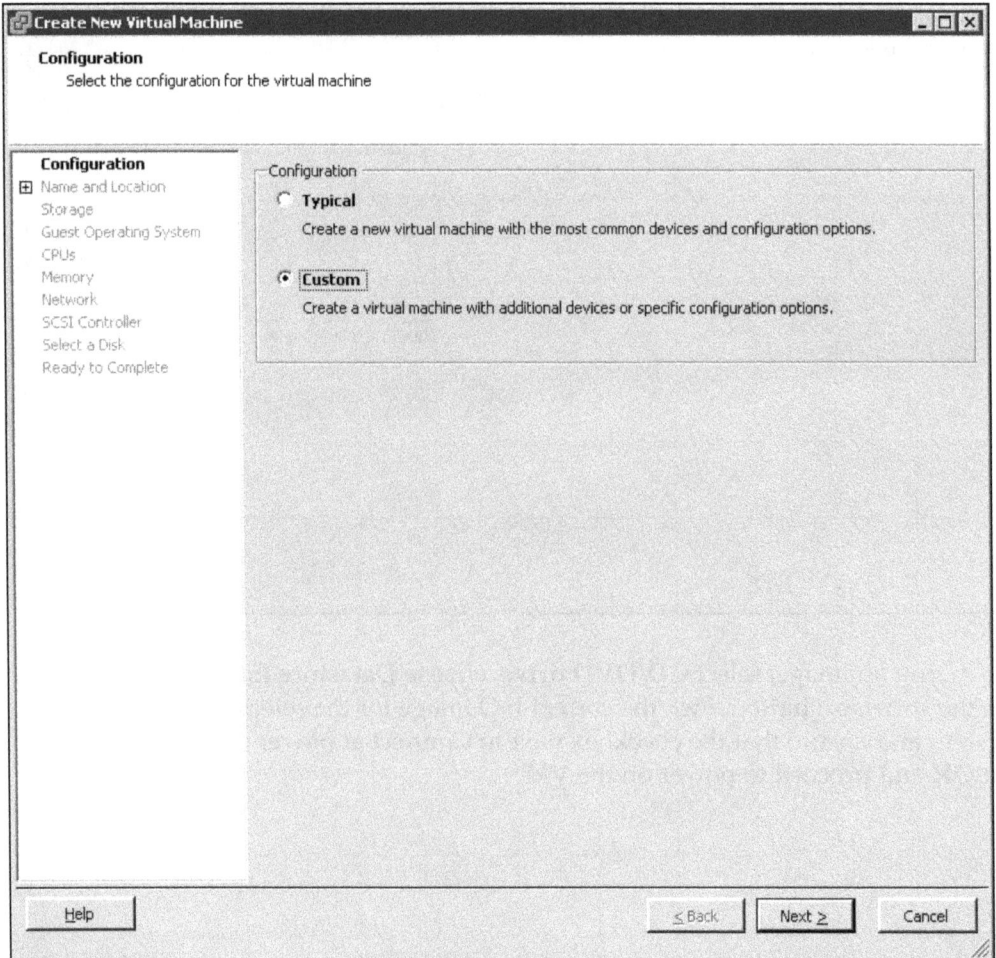

After selecting **Custom**, click on the **Next** button.

Name and Location

On the **Name and Location** pane, the virtual machine's **Name** should be specified. Remember that whatever name is specified here will also be used for the virtual machine directory and filenames. An **Inventory Location** that designates where the VM is placed in the inventory for the VM and Template view in vCenter needs to be specified.

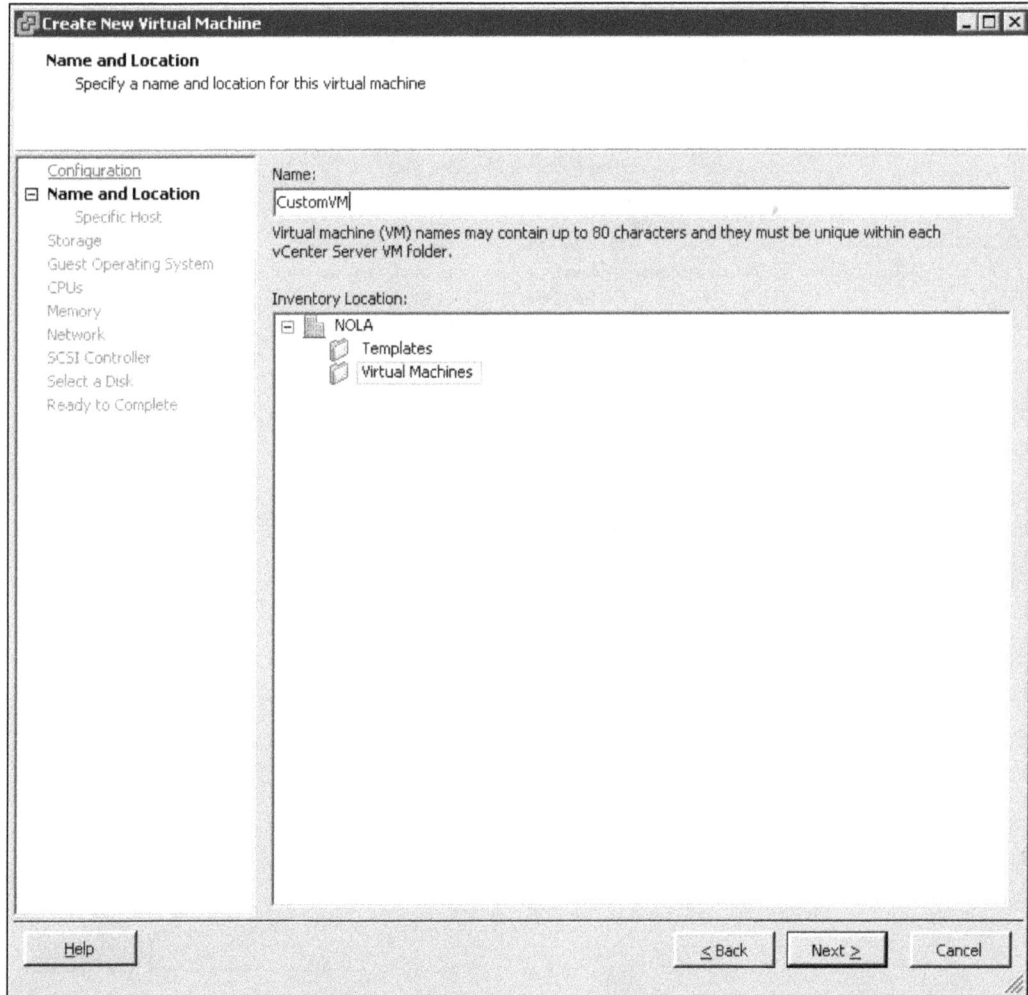

Once a folder is selected for the virtual machine's placement in the VM and Template view in vCenter, select **Next**.

Storage

The **Storage** pane prompts you to select the datastore on which the virtual machine's directory and files will be created. This is not a permanently binding selection; the VM's files can be migrated to another datastore at any time using Storage vMotion. If VM storage profiles are set up in vCenter, select which **VM Storage Profile** should be associated with the VM being created, so as to guarantee a level of service.

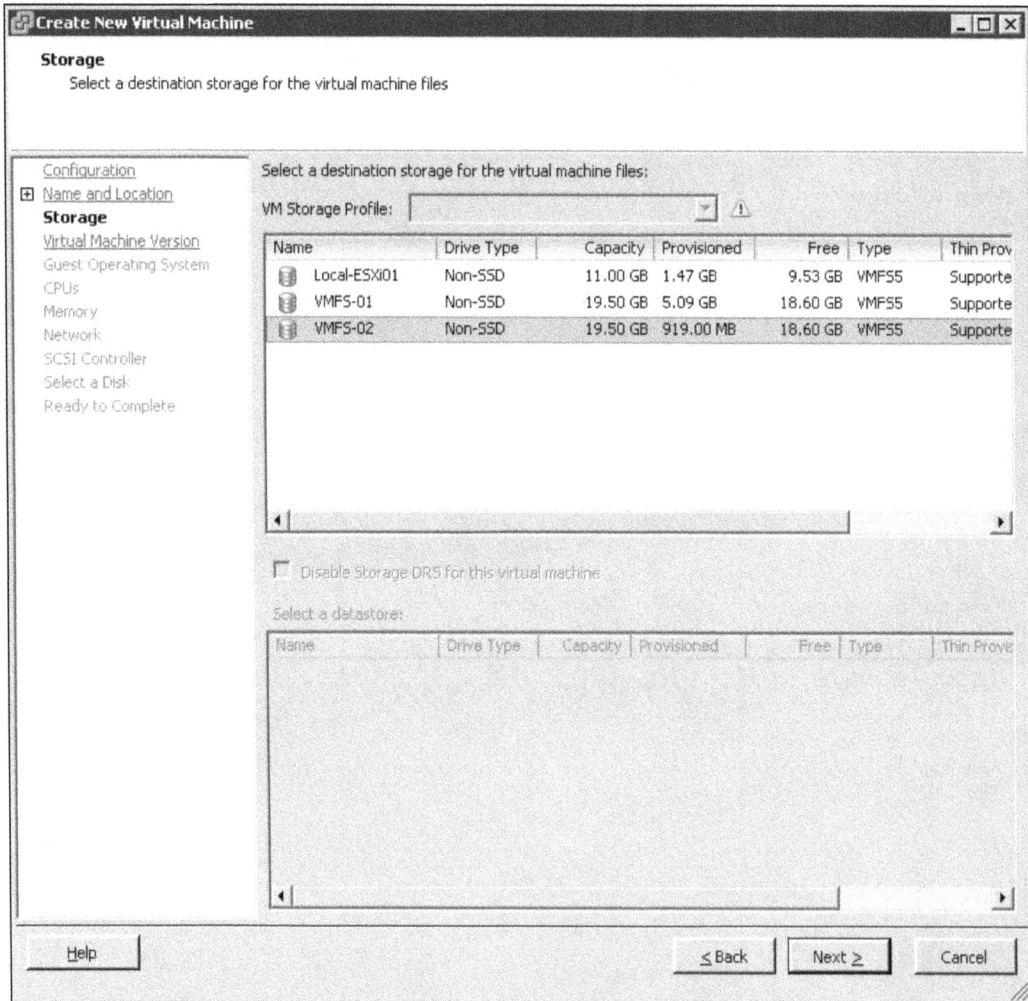

Notice that the option to select **Disable Storage DRS for this virtual machine** is unavailable to be selected. This is grayed out because these datastores are not currently in the datastore cluster managed by Storage DRS.

Click on **Next** after selecting the datastore.

Virtual Machine Version

The **Virtual Machine Version** pane, as seen in the next screenshot, is the selection of a virtual hardware version. Generally, you want to choose the newest hardware version so that the newest features and higher hardware maximums are available. However, for backward compatibility purposes, older versions may be chosen. Consult the following table for a compatibility chart. An ESXi host cannot power on a virtual machine with a virtual hardware version that is greater than what it supports.

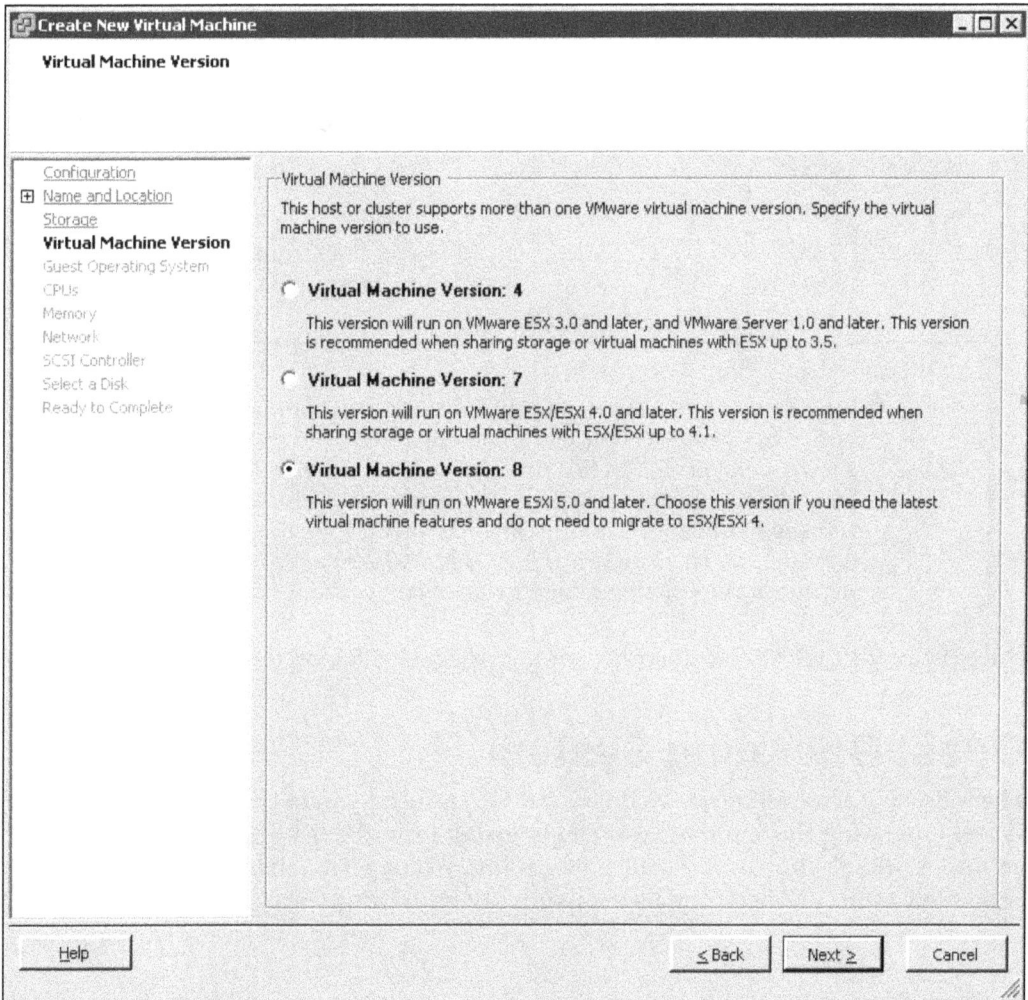

Notice that the highest level of virtual hardware available in vSphere Client is Version 8. Versions 9 and 10 are available to select when creating a virtual machine in vSphere Web Client. Once a virtual machine is upgraded to hardware version 10, the settings can no longer be edited in vSphere Client, they can only be edited in vSphere Web Client.

Version	Product Version	Max Memory Size	Max vCPUs	Additional Features
10	ESXi 5.5	1 TB	64	Extended vGPU support, SATA controller enhancements (up to 4 controllers and 30 devices per controller)
9	ESXi 5.1	1 TB	64	Improved 3D graphics
8	ESXi 5.0	1 TB	32	USB 3.0 device support
7	ESX/ESXi 4.x	255 GB	8	Hot Plug support for CPU and memory, VMXNET3
4	ESX 3.x	64 GB	4	

> Note that if a VM is created on an ESXi host that supports a given virtual hardware version and is then migrated to an ESXi host running a lower version of ESXi that does not support the virtual hardware level, the VM will not power on. For example, a virtual machine running hardware version 10 can only run on a vSphere 5.5 ESXi host, it cannot run on vSphere 4.1. See *Chapter 10, Virtual Machine Design,* for instructions on upgrading the hardware version.

Once the correct virtual hardware version is selected, click on the **Next** button.

Guest Operating System

The following screenshot shows the **Guest Operating System** pane. Select the **Guest Operating System** that you plan to install from the list of choices. This is an important selection as it dictates, by default, which virtual hardware will be presented to the VM based on its compatibility with the guest OS.

Chapter 2

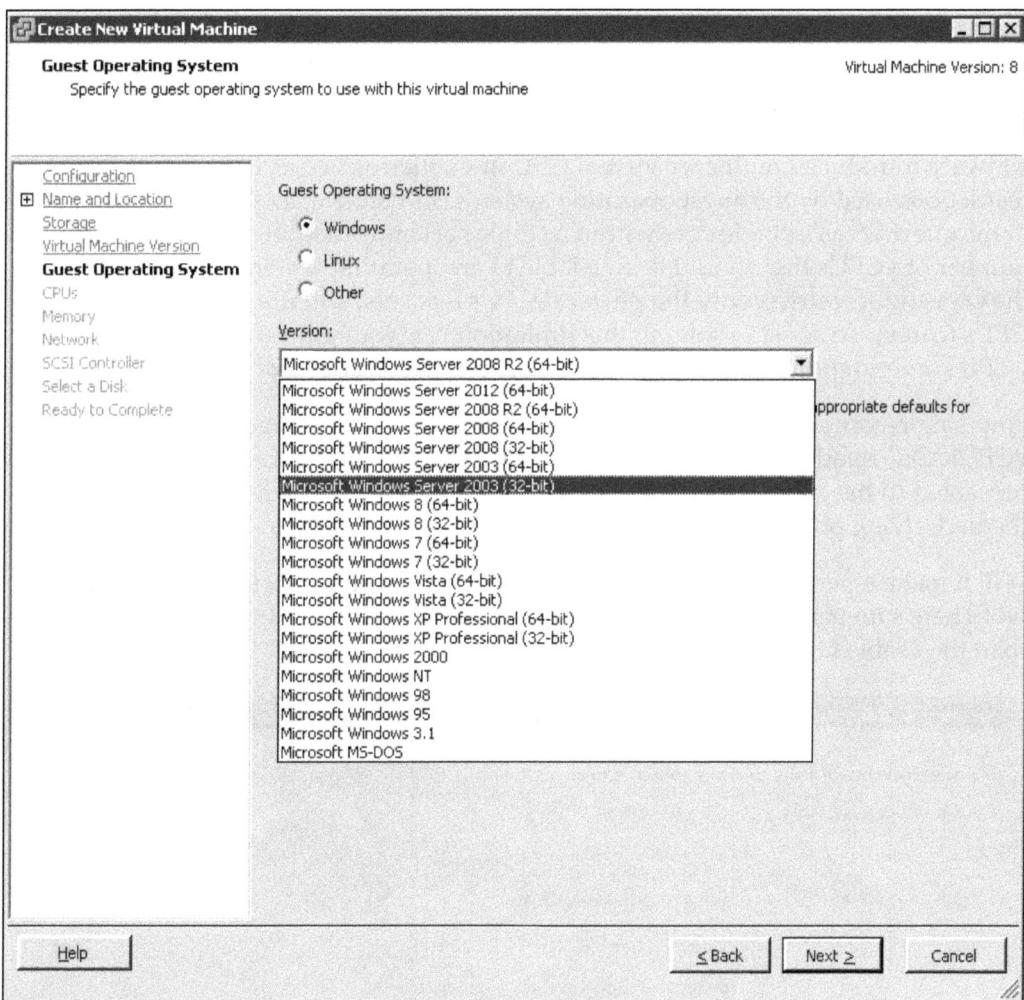

Upon selection of the guest OS, click on the **Next** button.

Creating a Virtual Machine Using the Wizard

CPUs

On the **CPUs** pane, demonstrated in the next screenshot, choose how many virtual sockets and virtual cores will be available to the guest operating system.

VMware introduced multicore virtual CPU in vSphere 4.1 so as to avoid socket restrictions used by the guest operating systems. In vSphere, a vCPU is presented to the guest OS as a single core within a single socket by default, which limits the number of vCPUs that should be available to an operating system. Generally, the OS vendor restricts only the physical CPUs (sockets) and not the logical CPUs (cores). To assist in solving this limitation, VMware introduced the vCPU configuration options of *virtual sockets* and *cores per virtual socket*.

Four single-core sockets equal four vCPUs. Two dual-core sockets also equal four vCPUs. One quad-core socket equals four vCPUs. The difference is how the CPU is presented to the guest operating system, not how the vCPUs will be scheduled on the underlying physical processors.

Will it make a performance impact whether we use multiple sockets or one socket? No! There's no performance impact between using virtual sockets or cores other than the usable number of vCPUs.

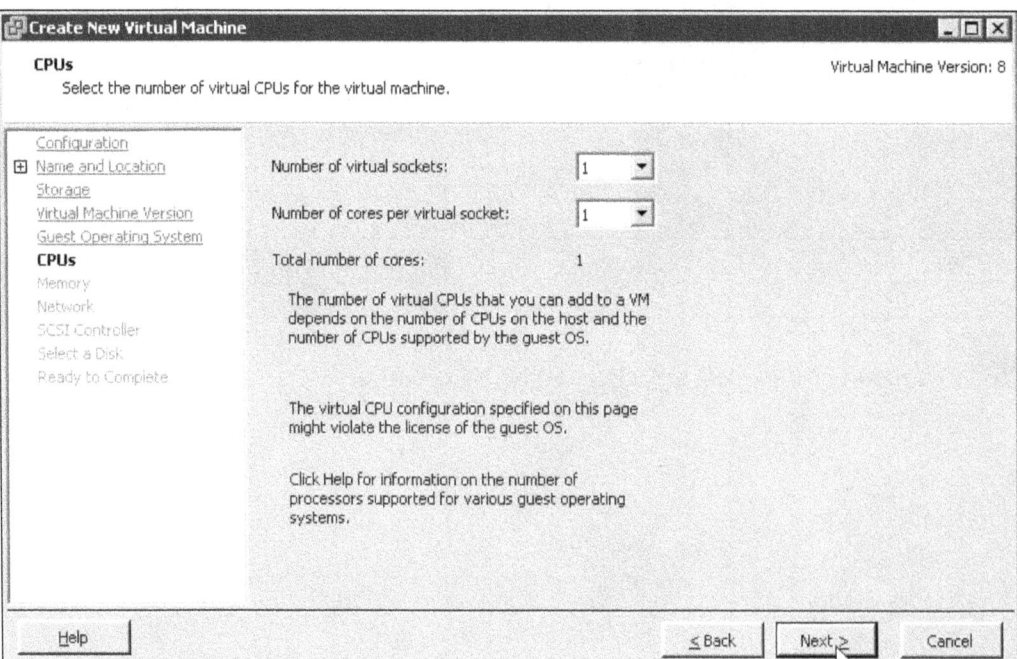

Click on **Next** once the CPUs have been configured.

Chapter 2

Memory

On the **Memory** pane, select the virtual machine's **Memory Size** in MB or GB. The recommended size for the selected guest OS is populated by default. This can be adjusted, as needed, depending on what application will be installed.

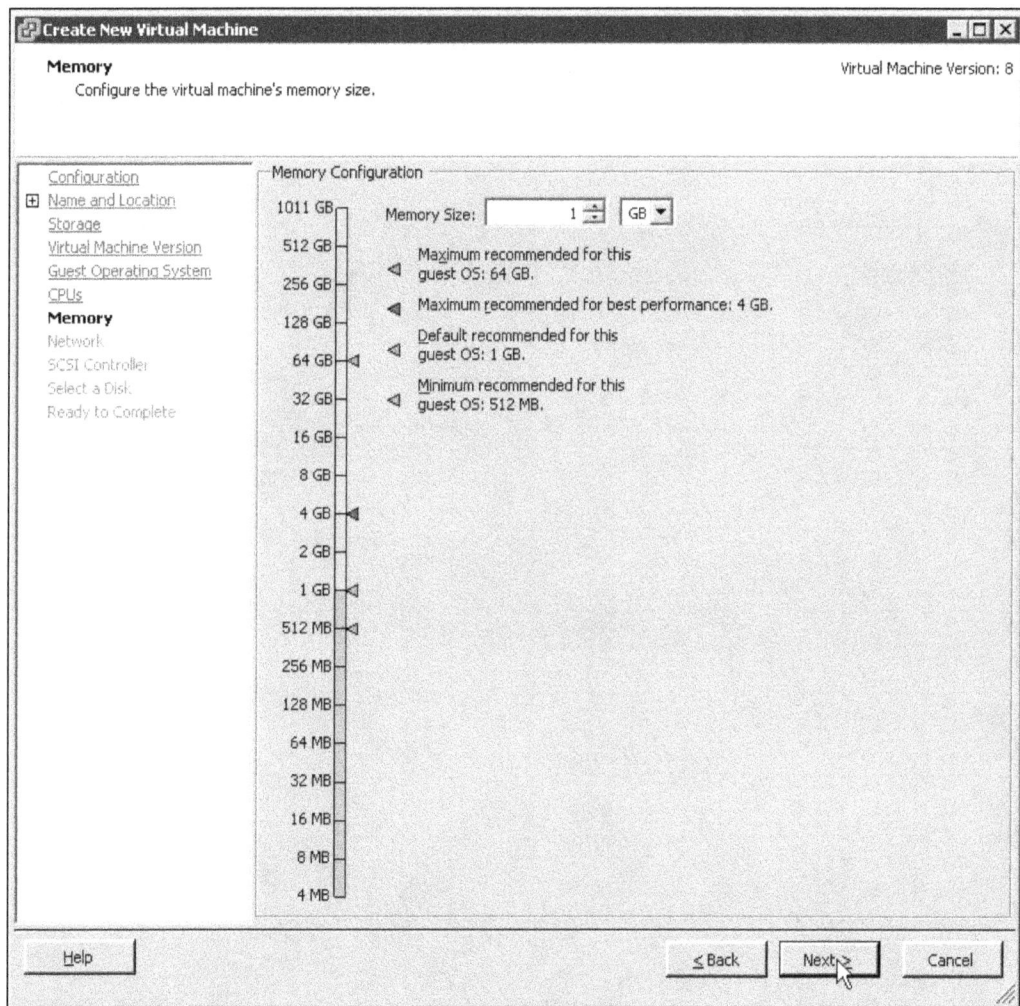

Once configured, click on **Next** to configure the networks.

Network

Select the number of NICs to configure for the virtual machine as well as which virtual machine port group to select. Consult the table in the *Network* subsection of the *Creating a VM using the typical configuration wizard* section to compare virtual adapter types and select the desired one. Ensure that **Connect at Power On** is selected for all adapters.

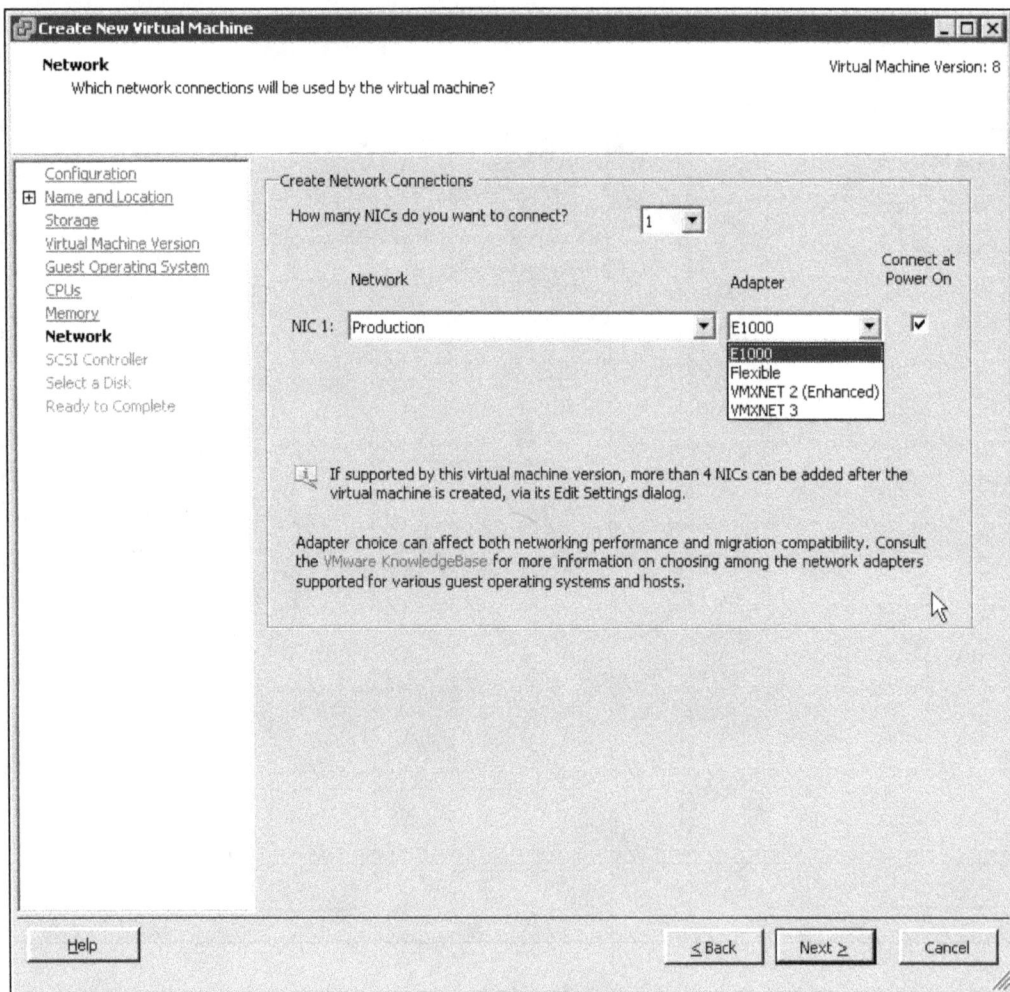

Click on **Next** upon selection of the network adapters.

SCSI controller

A virtual machine uses virtual SCSI controllers to access virtual disks. Whether or not the virtual disk is an IDE or SCSI disk, it is unaffected by the choice of SCSI controller. The wizard, based on the guest operating system that is selected on the **Guest Operating System** pane, preselects the correct default controller. The VMware Paravirtualized SCSI and LSI Logic SAS controllers are available only for virtual machines with hardware version 7 or later.

Paravirtualized SCSI adapters are high performance storage adapters that can result in lower CPU utilization and greater throughput. PVSCSI adapters are befitting virtual machines whose applications create a very high amount of I/O throughput. Check http://vmware.com/kb/1010398 for more information.

Disks with snapshots might not experience performance gains when used on LSI Logic SAS and LSI Logic Parallel controllers.

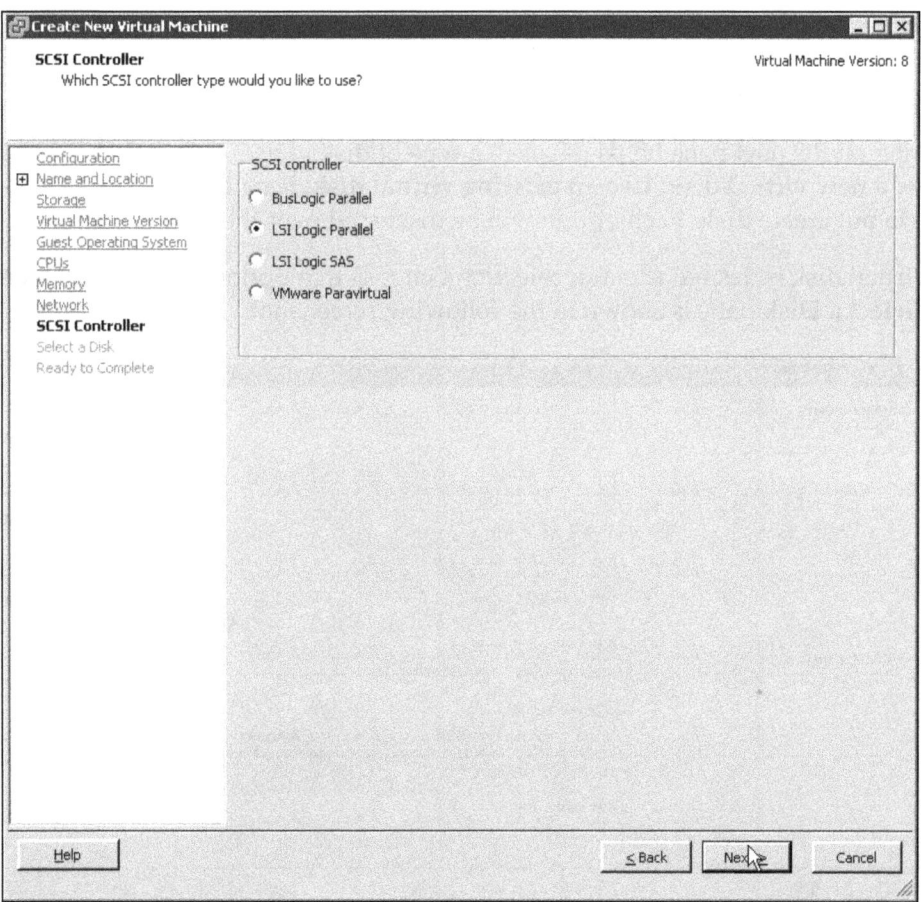

Creating a Virtual Machine Using the Wizard

The following table compares the different SCSI controllers available to assist in the selection process:

Adapter Type	Use Cases
BusLogic Parallel	• Default for Windows 2000 • Considered a legacy adapter, no current updates or enhancements
LSI Logic Parallel	• Default for Windows 2003, Vista, and Linux OSes • Most commonly used adapter and widely compatible
LSI Logic SAS	• Default for Windows 2008 and Windows 7 • Newer LSI driver and used for MSCS support
VMware Paravirtualized	• Used for high I/O VMs (over 2000 IOPS) • Lower CPU utilization but check for OS support

After selecting the SCSI adapter type, click on **Next**.

Clicking on the next pane helps us select a type of disk to use. The options include: **Create a new virtual disk**, **Use an existing virtual disk**, **Raw Device Mappings**, and **Do not create disk**. Each option will be discussed over the next few pages.

If a virtual disk is desired (default selection), choose that option and click on **Next**. The **Select a Disk** pane is shown in the following screenshot:

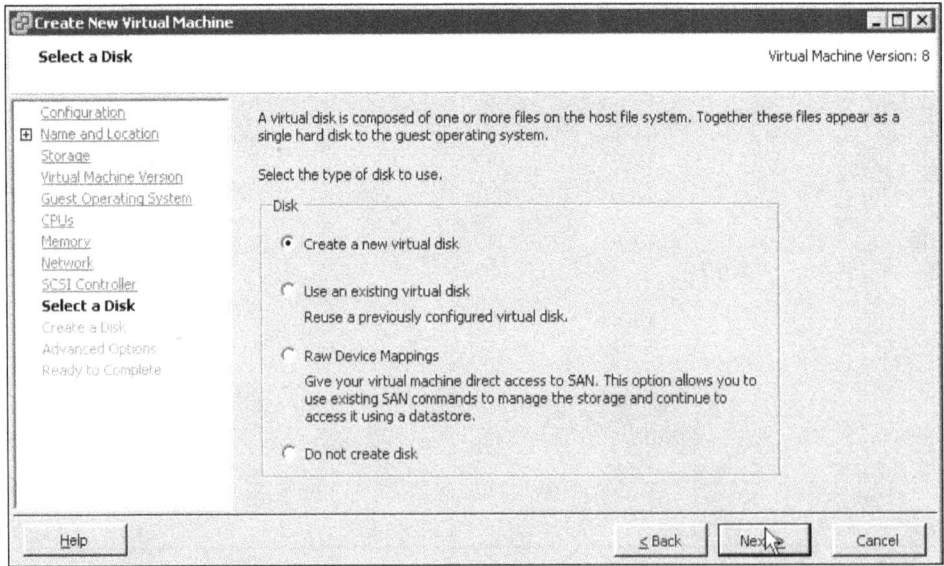

Creating a new virtual disk

Once the virtual disk creation option is selected, choose the **Disk Size** and **Disk Provisioning** type (refer to the *Creating a disk* subsection of the *Creating a VM using the typical configuration wizard* section for assistance).

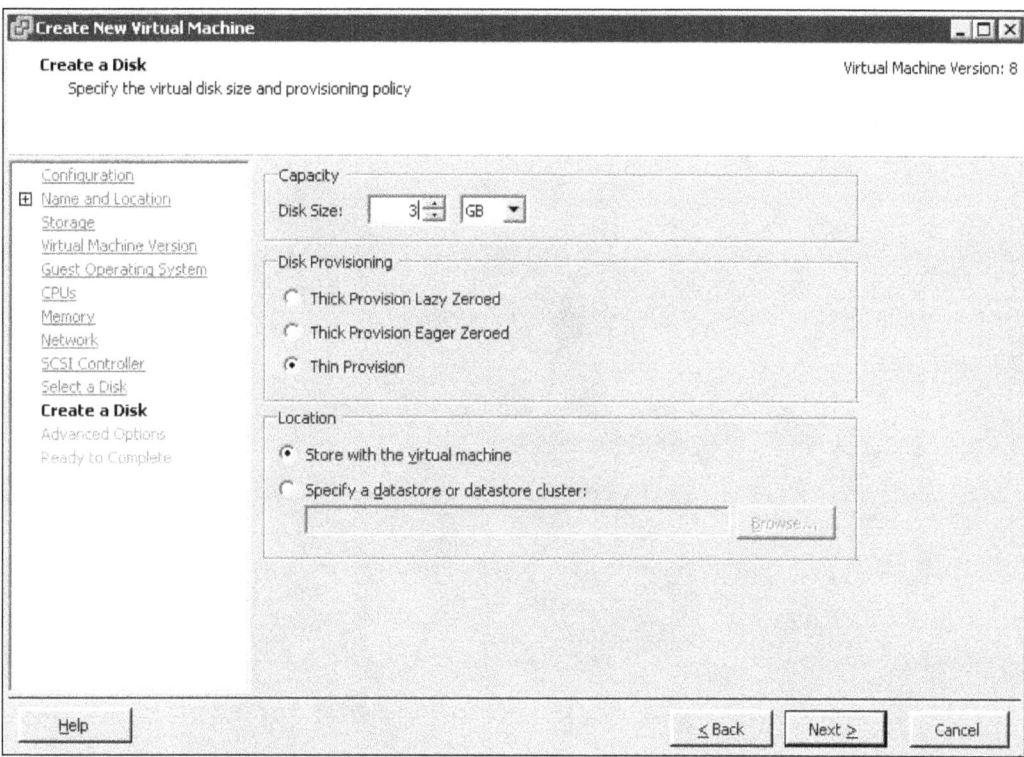

Location for the virtual disk can also be specified. By default, the virtual disk is stored with the rest of the virtual machine's files; however, it can be specified to save the new virtual disk on a different datastore. Click on **Next** after selections.

On the **Advanced Options** pane, select the **Virtual Disk Node** for creating a virtual disk. Specify whether to use **SCSI** or **IDE** and which controller and device number should be used. By default, the first available device on the first available controller is selected. If the virtual machine has multiple disks, some administrators will use different controllers for **Raw Device Mapping (RDM)**, when compared to virtual disks.

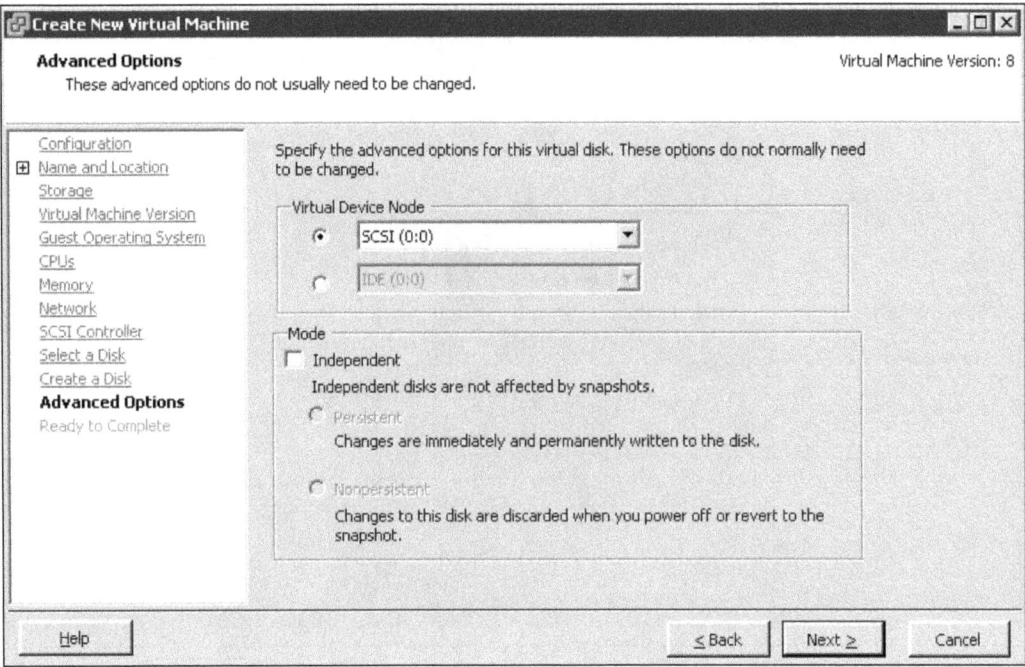

Under the **Mode** section, select whether the disk should be independent or not. This option tackles the question of what independent disks actually do, whether they are persistent or nonpersistent. If a disk is independent, then it can be omitted from a backup operation due to the fact that independent disks do not support snapshot operations. Think of independent disks as being *independent of snapshots*. The independent option under the **Mode** section includes two choices:

- **Persistent**: This option commits changes immediately and permanently to the disk. You will not see a delta file associated with this disk during a snapshot operation. This virtual disk file continues to behave as if there is no snapshot being taken of the virtual machine and all writes go directly to the disk. All changes to the disk are preserved upon snapshot deletion.

- **Nonpersistent**: When this configuration is chosen, a redo log is created to capture all subsequent writes to the disk. If the snapshot is deleted or if the virtual machine is powered off, the changes captured in that redo log are discarded.

In the case of cloning the virtual machine, an independent disk is not included in the resultant newly cloned virtual machine.

Once configured, click on **Next** to review all virtual machine settings before selecting **Finish**.

Using an existing virtual disk

Alternately, the **Use an existing virtual disk** option can be selected. This will allow you to browse and select a previously configured virtual disk. For example, if an application like Symantec Ghost has been used to create a preconfigured image, the application may be exported as a .vmdk file. This file can be mounted on a virtual machine using this process.

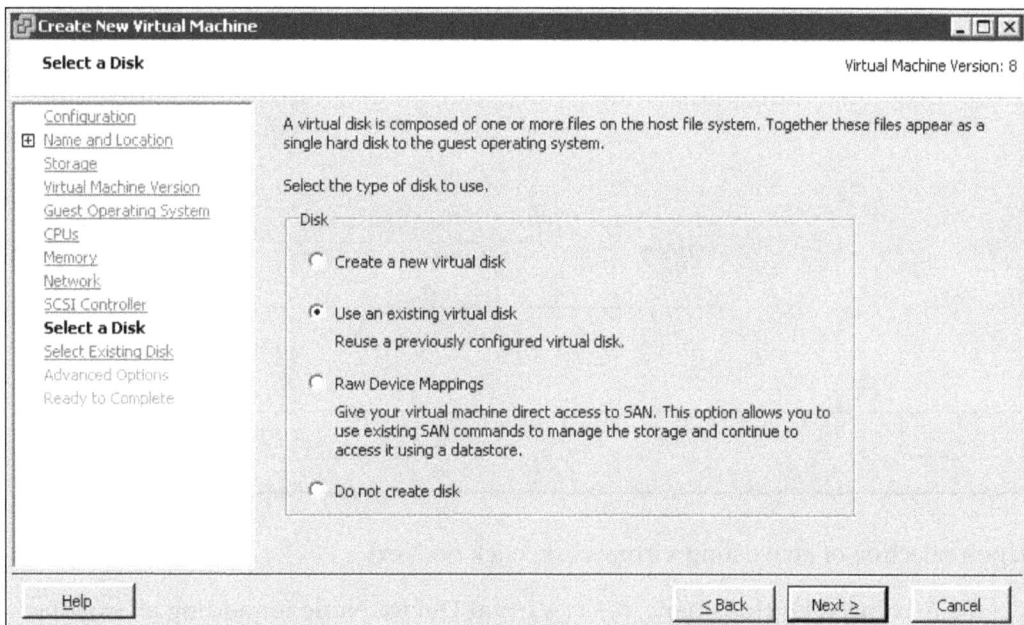

If this option is desired, select it and click on the **Next** button.

Creating a Virtual Machine Using the Wizard

To select an existing virtual disk, click on the **Browse...** button. This will bring up a list of datastores; navigate to the correct datastore until a .vmdk file is selected.

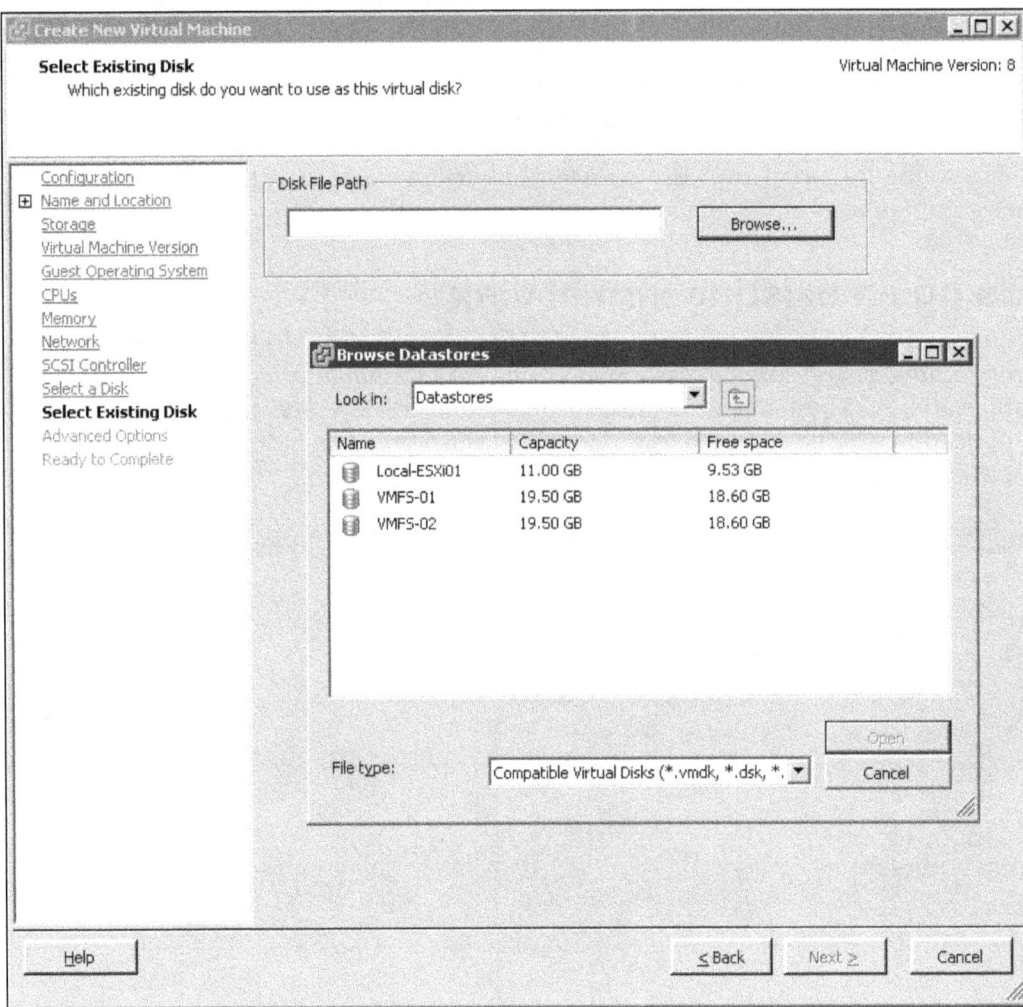

Upon selection of an existing virtual disk, click on **Next**.

On the **Advanced Options** pane, select **Virtual Device Node** for adding an existing virtual disk. Also specify the **Mode** option, which will determine whether or not the disk should be independent.

Chapter 2

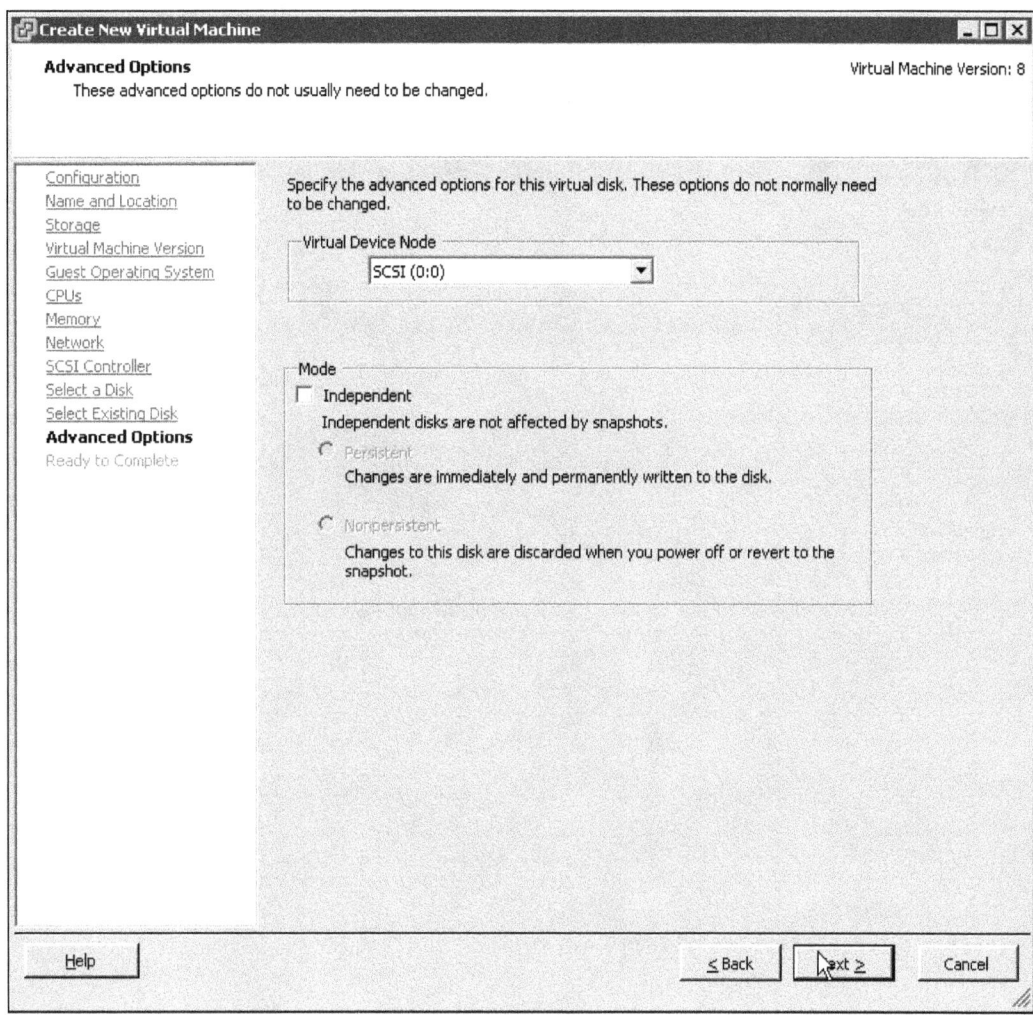

Click on **Next** to review all virtual machine settings upon configuration of the advanced options.

Creating a Virtual Machine Using the Wizard

Raw Device Mappings

Another option, when selecting what type of disk to use, is an RDM. An RDM configuration gives a virtual machine direct access to a raw LUN.

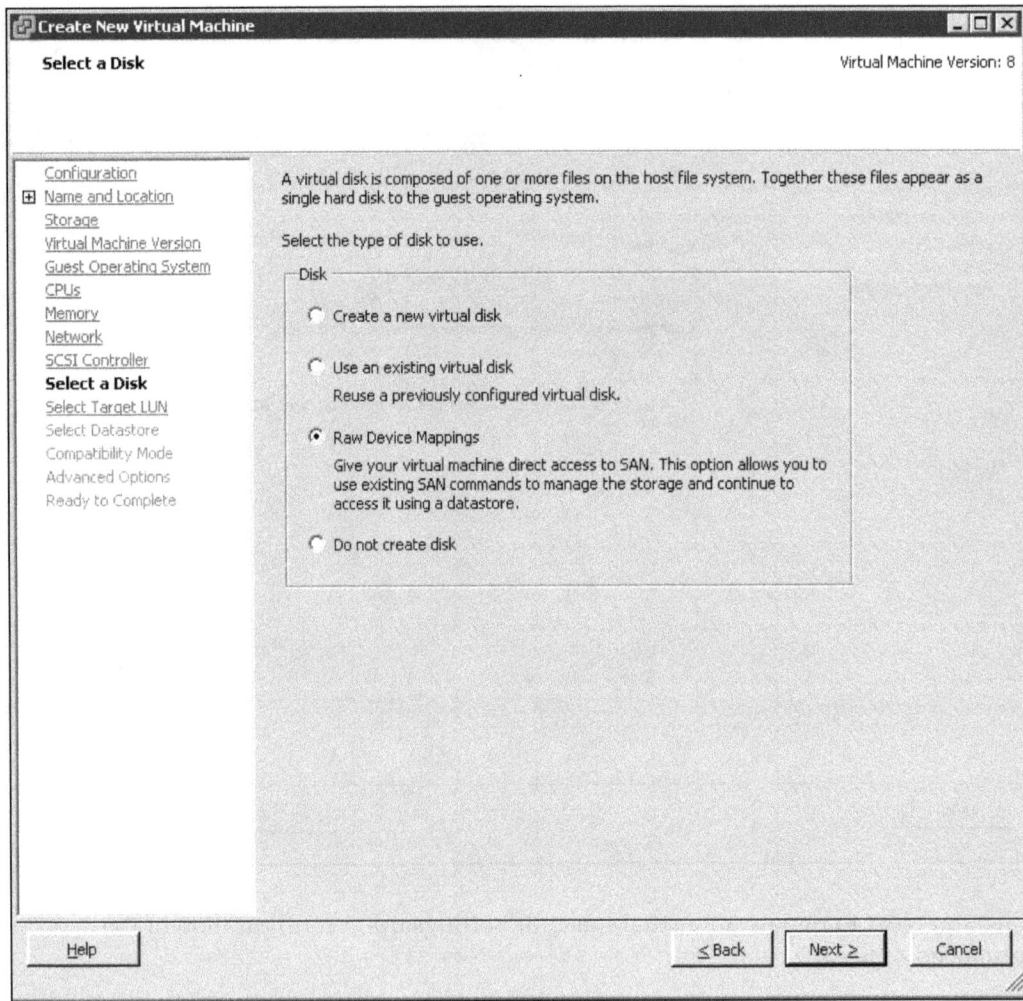

Select the **Raw Device Mappings** option and click on **Next**.

Chapter 2

The next pane displays what LUNs are available for use by Raw Device Mapping. The following screenshot only lists a single available LUN, but in many cases multiple LUNs will be listed. Make sure to expand the **Name** and **Path ID** columns to verify that you are selecting the correct LUN based on the canonical name and path ID.

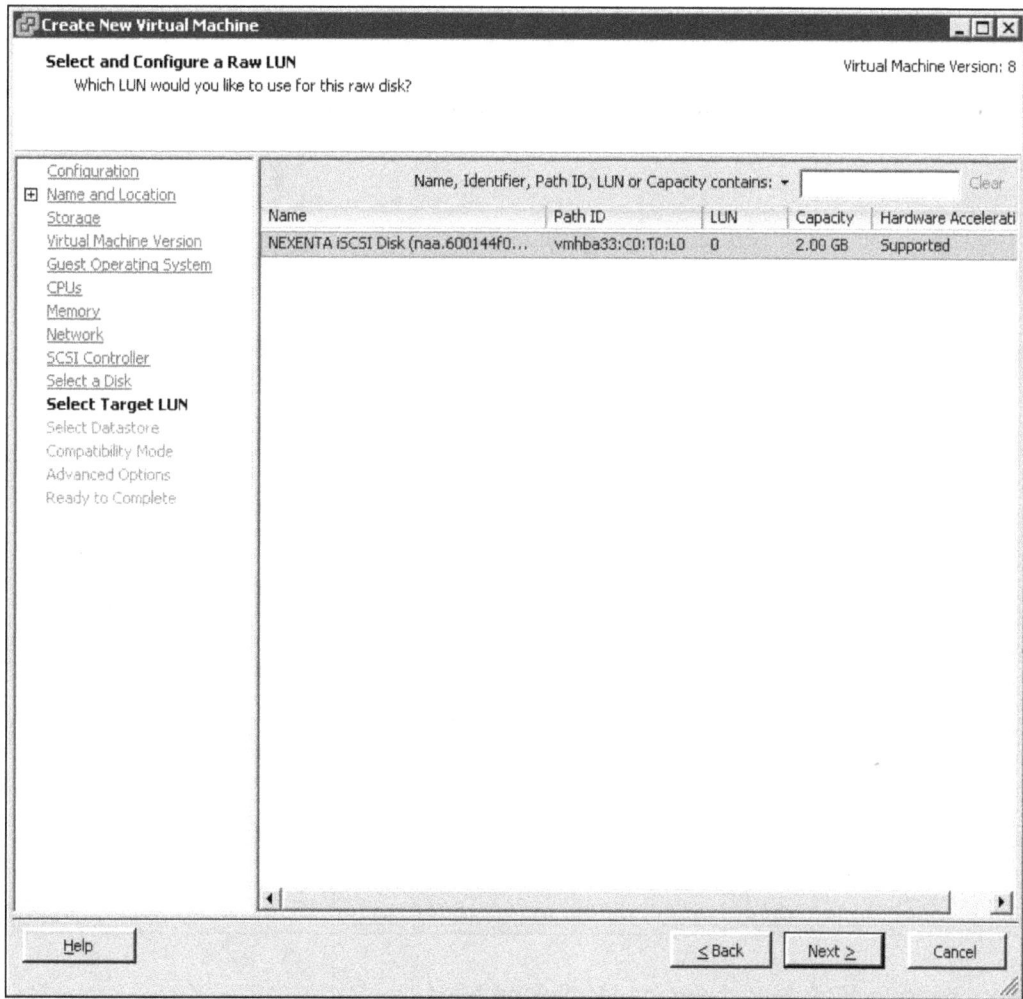

Upon selection of the LUN to be used, click on the **Next** button.

Creating a Virtual Machine Using the Wizard

The next pane displays the option for specifying where the -rdm.vmdk mapping file will be stored. By default, this file will be stored on the same datastore as the rest of the virtual machine's files. However, you can specify a different datastore if desired.

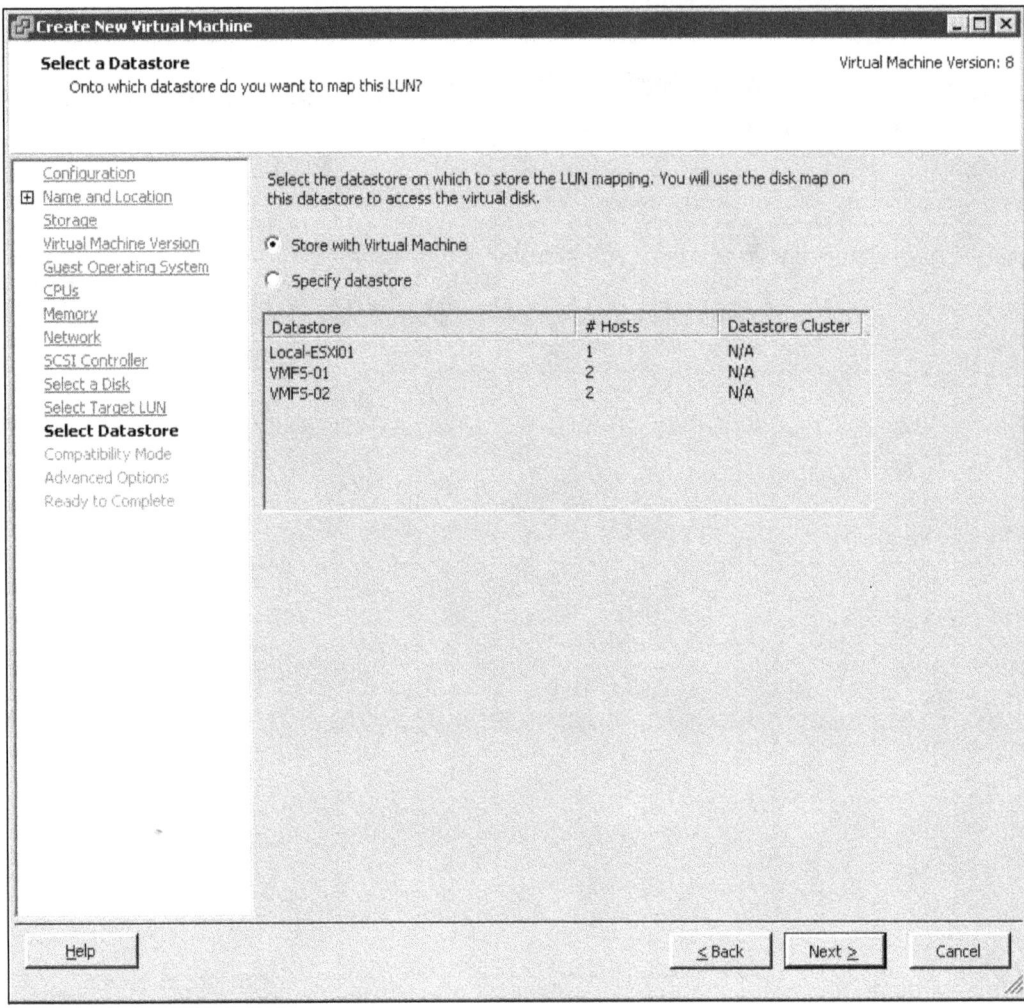

Once the selections have been made, click on **Next**.

[64]

The **Select Compatibility Mode** pane, as seen in the next screenshot, requires the selection of the RDM compatibility mode. There are two compatibility modes for an RDM:

- **Physical**: This mode specifies minimal SCSI virtualization of the mapped device and allows for greater flexibility of SAN management type software. The VMkernel passes all SCSI commands, with the exception of the REPORT LUNs command, to the device. The REPORT LUNs command is virtualized so that the VMkernel can isolate the LUN to the owning virtual machine. Other than that, all characteristics of the underlying hardware are exposed. The maximum size is 64 TB.

- **Virtual**: This mode specifies full virtualization of the mapped device, sending only READ and WRITE commands. The real hardware characteristics are hidden; the mapped device appears the same as a virtual disk file in a VMFS volume to the guest operating system. Due to this, the virtual mode is more portable across storage hardware because it presents the same behavior as the virtual disk file. The maximum size, as of vSphere 5.5, is 62 TB.

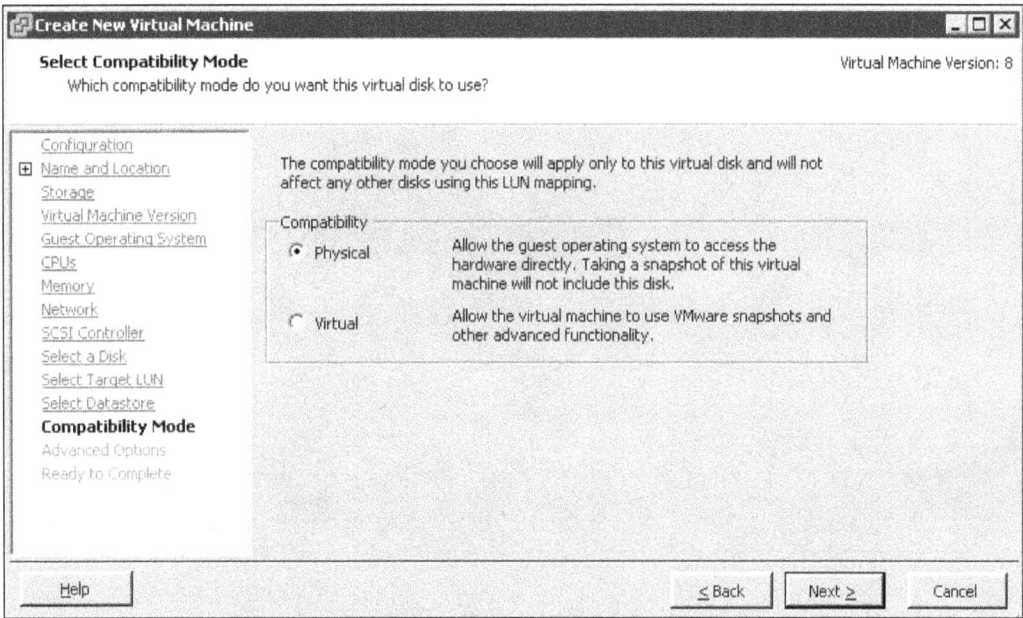

Click on **Next** upon selection of the RDM compatibility mode.

On the **Advanced Options** pane, select **Virtual Device Node** for creating the RDM (shown in the next screenshot). Specify which SCSI controller and device number should be used. By default, the first available device on the first available controller is selected.

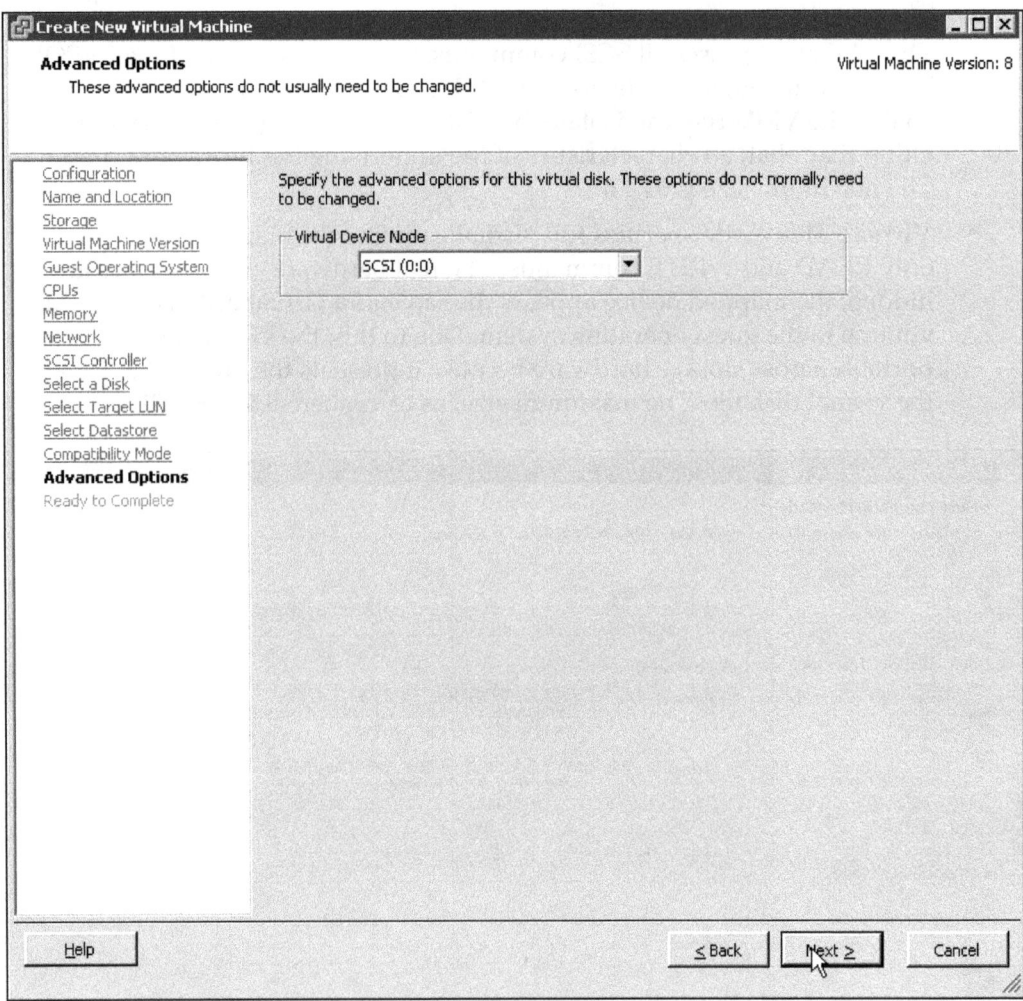

Click on **Next** upon selection of **Virtual Device Node**.

Do not create disk

The final option for the virtual disk pane is **Do not create disk**. If this option is selected, the virtual machine files will be created without a disk. This option is generally selected if it is planned that a virtual disk may be migrated later, and then subsequently mounted to the virtual machine.

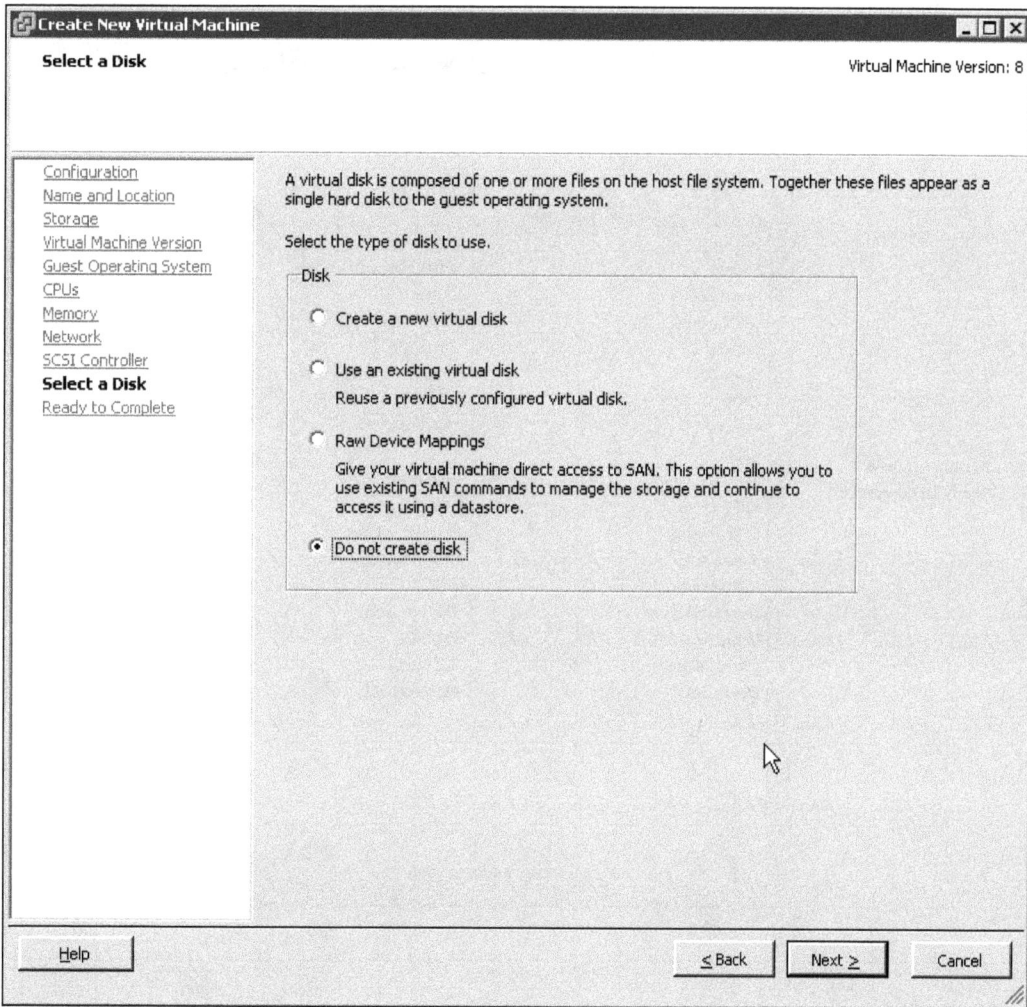

After selecting the virtual disk option, click on **Next**.

Ready to Complete

The final pane of the custom virtual machine creation wizard simply summarizes all the selections made. If any of the virtual hardware configurations are incorrect, select the corresponding hyperlink of the left column of the wizard to go back and make the correct selection. The **Ready to Complete** pane is shown in the following screenshot:

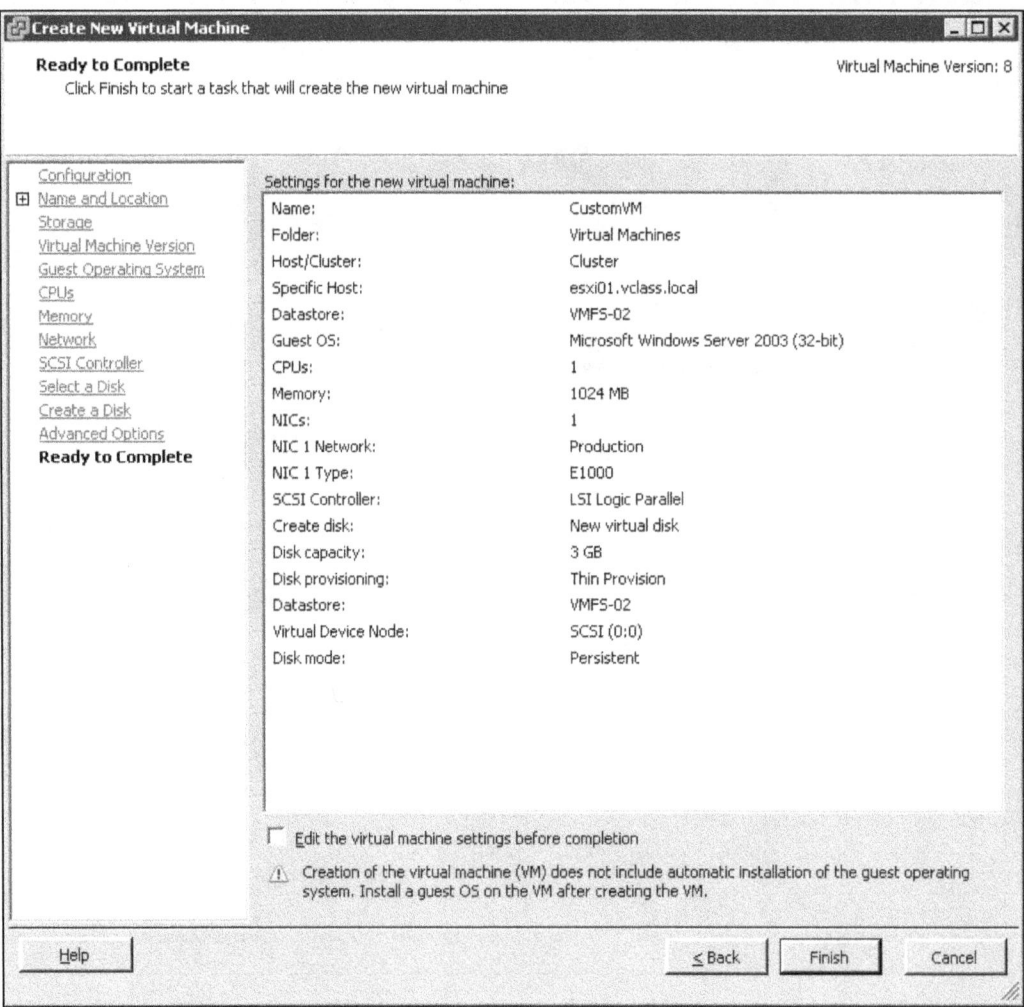

If further configurations are desired, mounting a guest operating system's .iso image, for instance, select the checkbox next to **Edit the virtual machine settings before completion**. Just click on **Finish** otherwise.

Chapter 2

Creating a VM using vSphere Web Client

The vSphere Web Client was released in vSphere 5.0, but it had only a subset of the features of vSphere Client until a fully featured vSphere Web Client was released in vSphere 5.1. VMware has made numerous improvements to vSphere Web Client in vSphere 5.5 (including drag-and-drop and Mac OS X support), further asserting it as the future of management interfaces. All the new vSphere 5.1 and 5.5 features have been made available solely in vSphere Web Client; due to this, it is important to familiarize ourselves with the Web Client.

In order to launch the virtual machine creation wizard, open **vSphere Web Client** and navigate to one of the vCenter views. From there, right-click on a container that a virtual machine can reside in (Cluster, ESXi host, resource pool, among others) and select **New Virtual Machine....**

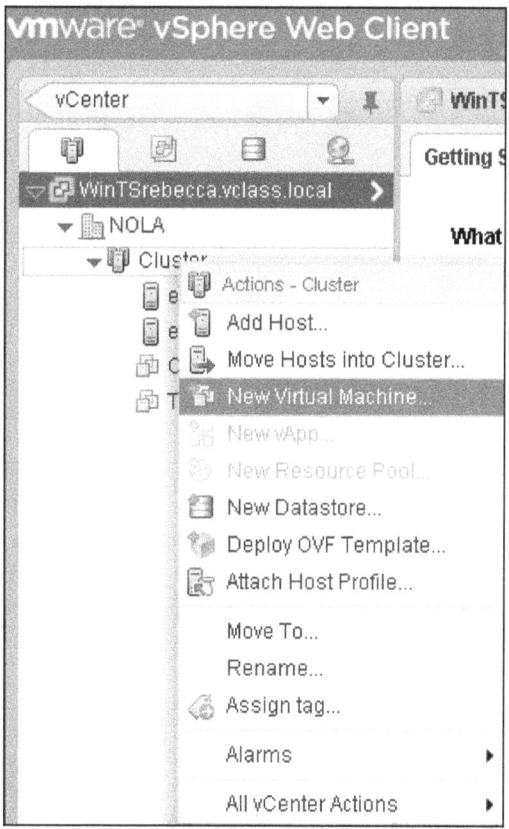

Creating a Virtual Machine Using the Wizard

The next screenshot shows all of vSphere Web Client's available options in the New Virtual Machine wizard. The other options will be discussed in *Chapter 3, Other Ways to Provision a Virtual Machine*.

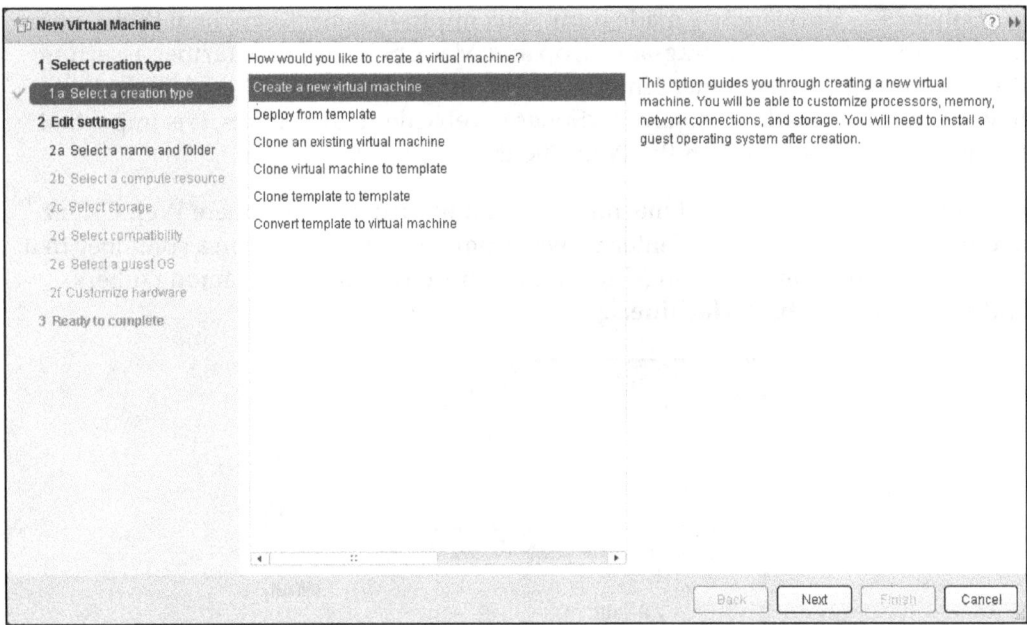

Select **Create a new virtual machine option** and click on **Next**.

Select a name and folder

First specify a name for the virtual machine being created in the **Select a name and folder** pane. Don't forget that whatever name is specified here will result in all the virtual machine's files as well as the virtual machine's directory being named the same. Towards the center of the following screenshot, a folder or datacenter should be selected for the virtual machine's placement in the VM and Template view within vCenter.

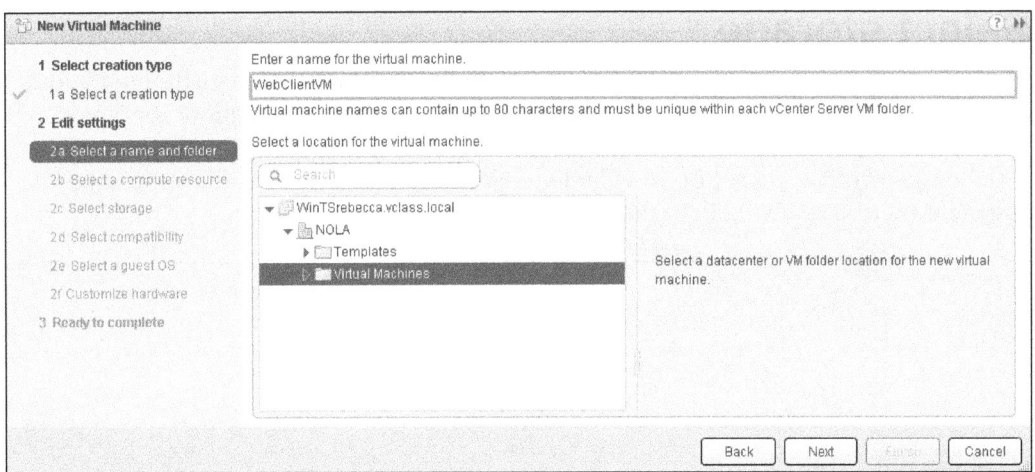

Once the virtual machine's name is specified and its location in the VMs and Template view is selected, click on **Next**.

Select a compute resource

The following screenshot shows the **Select a compute resource** pane; a cluster (if DRS enabled), ESXi host, resource pool, or vApp should be selected for placement of the virtual machine in the Hosts and Clusters view in vCenter.

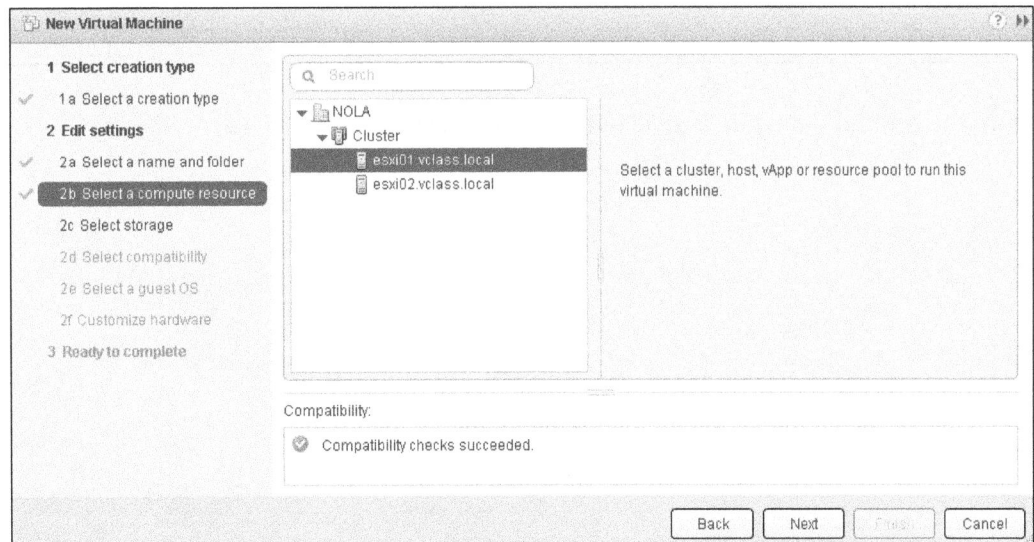

Once the desired compute resource is selected, click on **Next**.

Select storage

The **Select storage** pane prompts you to select which datastore the virtual machine's directory and files will be created on. This is not a permanent selection; the VM's files can be migrated to another datastore at any time using Storage vMotion. If VM storage profiles are set up in vCenter, select which storage profile should be associated with the VM being created.

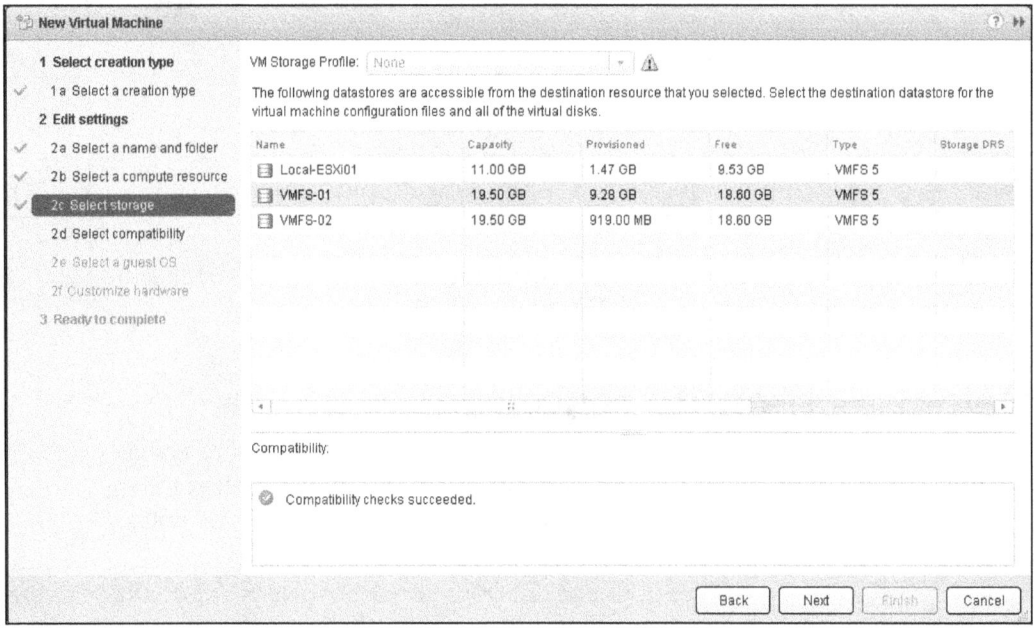

Once the desired datastore is selected, click on **Next**.

Select compatibility

The next screenshot presents the **Select compatibility** pane. By selecting a compatible version of ESXi, you are effectively setting the virtual hardware version of the virtual machine being created. Reference the table in the *Virtual Machine Version* subsection of the *Creating a VM using the custom configuration wizard* section for the virtual hardware version that is to be selected.

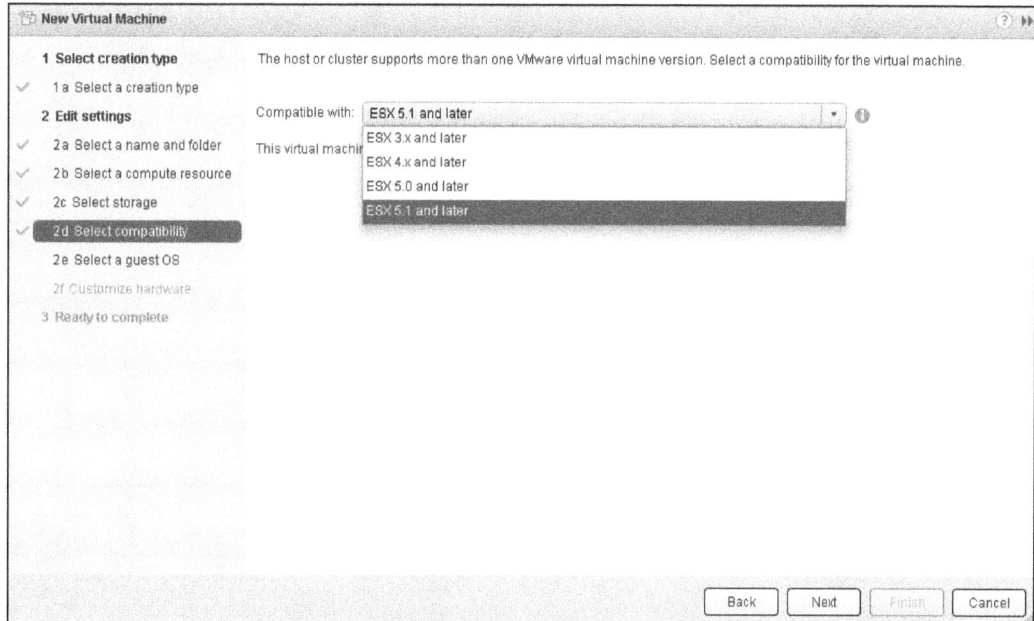

Once the compatible ESXi version is selected, click on **Next**.

Select a guest OS

Select **Guest OS Family** and **Guest OS Version** that you plan to install from the list of choices. This is an important selection as it dictates which virtual hardware will be presented to the VM based on its compatibility with the guest OS.

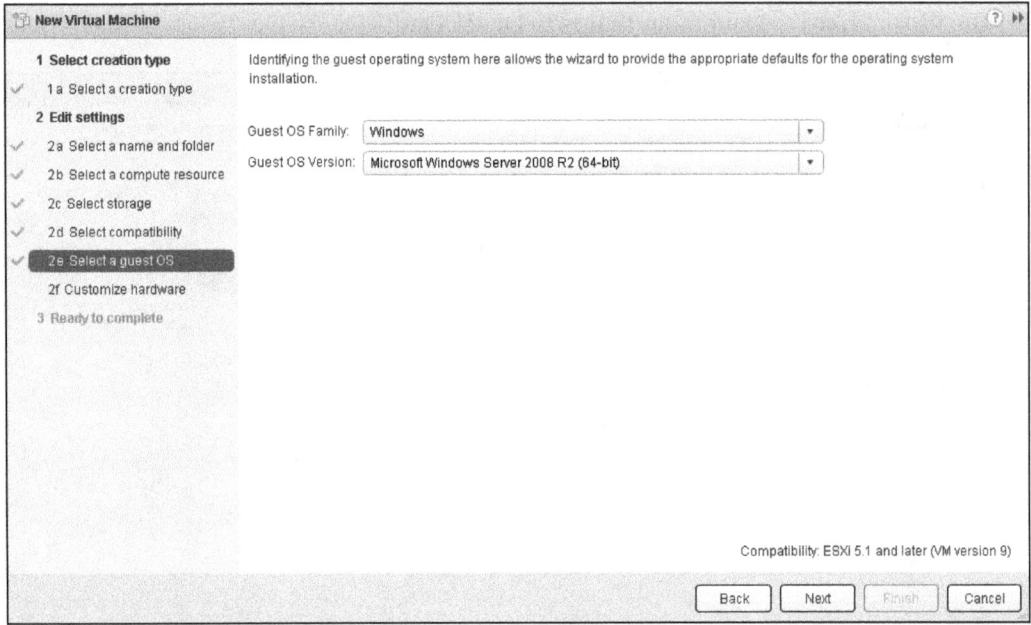

Once the guest operating system has been selected, click on **Next**.

Customize hardware

The **Customize hardware** pane, as seen in the following screenshot, allows for the selection of vCPUs, memory size, virtual disk size, and network selection, among others. You can expand the selection of virtual hardware to see all options by clicking on the black arrow to the left of the name. Notice that, from here, an .iso file can be mounted from this pane by dropping down the menu next to **New CD/DVD Drive** and selecting **Datastore ISO**.

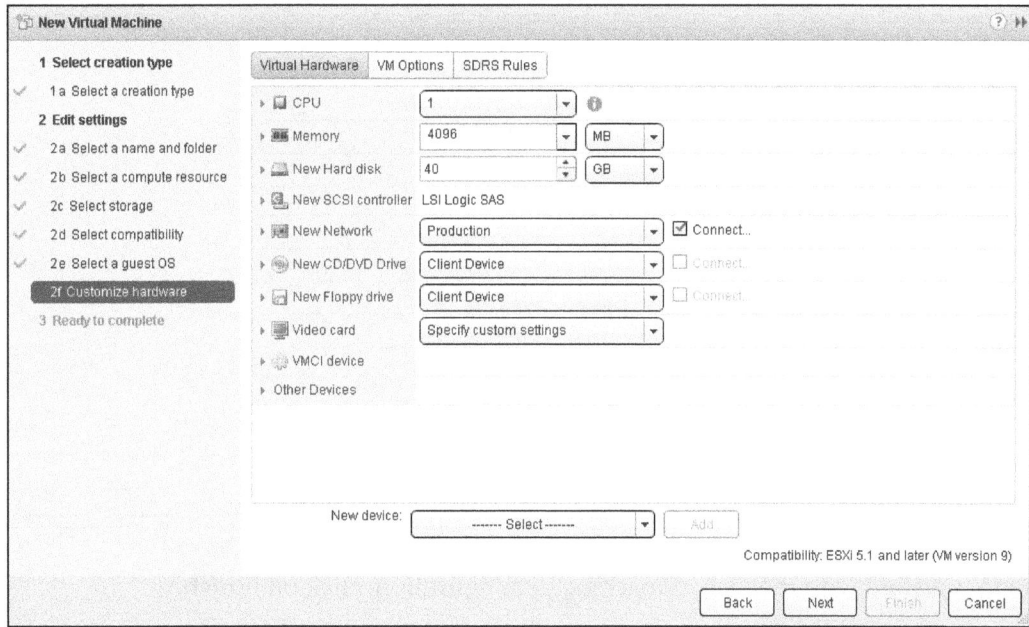

Once the virtual hardware has been configured as desired, click on the **Next** button.

Ready to complete

The last pane of the New Virtual Machine wizard summarizes the virtual machine's configuration for one last review prior to creation of the files. The **Ready to complete** pane is shown in the following screenshot:

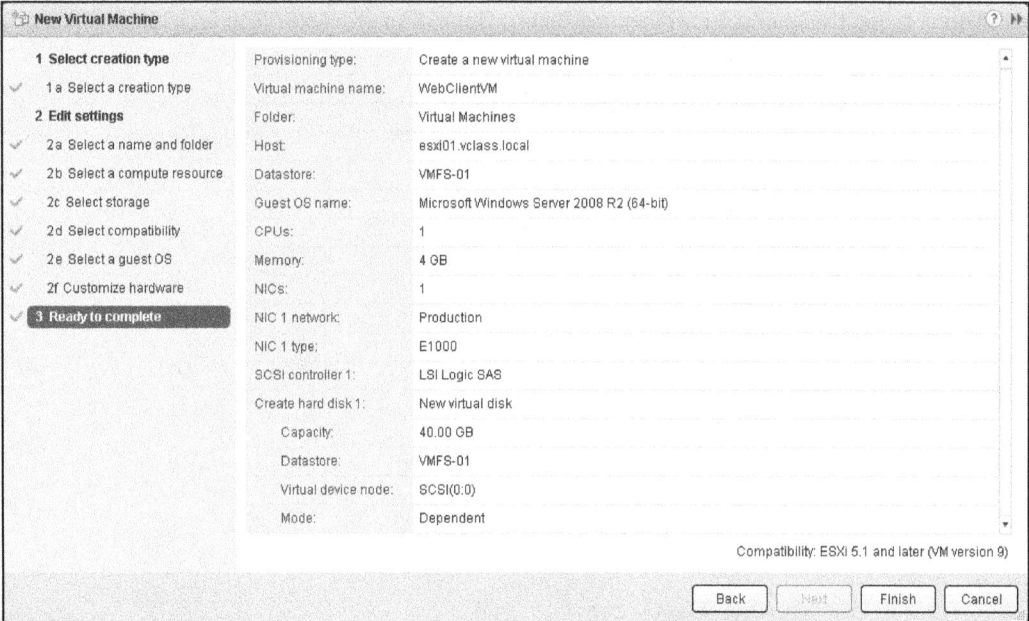

Once satisfied with the virtual machine's configuration, click on **Finish**.

Summary

A virtual machine can be created using both vSphere Client and vSphere Web Client. However, vSphere Client is less featured than vSphere Web Client in vSphere 5.5. The added functionality makes vSphere Web Client the preferred client for accessing and administering vCenter server. A typical creation of a virtual machine will result in the default selection for the virtual hardware, whereas a custom creation will allow for the specification of virtual hardware by the administrator. Each virtual machine is equipped with virtual hardware and devices that allow the same functionality as physical hardware. These include one or more virtual CPUs, memory, video card, IDE devices, SCSI devices, DVD/CD-ROM, parallel and serial ports, and network adapters. The selected virtual hardware version dictates compatibility with an ESXi host. Virtual hardware versions 9 and 10 are only available for selection using vSphere Web Client. Once a virtual machine is upgraded to hardware version 10, the settings can no longer be edited in vSphere Client, it can only be edited in vSphere Web Client.

There's more than one way to create a virtual machine; other provisioning methods will be discussed in the next chapter.

3
Other Ways to Provision a Virtual Machine

The previous chapter discussed how to create a virtual machine using the Wizard, but no administrator wants to create a virtual machine from scratch every single time. This chapter will cover how to build a template and provision virtual machines from the templates or from physical machines using VMware vCenter Convertor. Guest OS customizations will also be covered so that potential IP conflicts, hostname conflicts, and duplicate SIDs are avoided.

In this chapter, you will learn:

- How to configure and use virtual machine customizations
- How to create a virtual machine from a template
- How to create a virtual machine by cloning
- How to deploy a virtual machine from an **Open Virtualization Format** (**OVF**) file
- How to create a virtual machine using VMware vCenter Converter

Configuring virtual machine customizations

Customization specifications can be created and are XML files containing guest operating system settings for virtual machines. This can include changing certain properties such as the computer name, license settings, or even network settings. These customizations are created using the **Guest Customization** wizard provided and managed using the **Customization Specification Manager** option. The customization parameters are stored in the vCenter Server database. Anytime a password is entered into the customization, whether for a local administrator or a domain administrator, the passwords are stored in an encrypted format in the database.

Copying Sysprep files to vCenter directory

In order to use custom specifications for Windows virtual machines, the correct version of Sysprep for each operating system must be downloaded and placed in the correct vCenter Server directory. On a Windows 2008 or Windows 2012 server on which vCenter is installed, the file location is `C:\ProgramData\VMware\VMware VirtualCenter\sysprep\`. The Windows 2003 location is demonstrated in the next screenshot.

When using the vCenter Server Appliance, copy the Sysprep file to location `/etc/vmware-vpx/sysprep`, and then select the directory for the desired operating system.

The following screenshot demonstrates the `\sysprep` directory on a Windows 2003 vCenter Server. From here, select the operating system for which you intend to copy the correct Sysprep files:

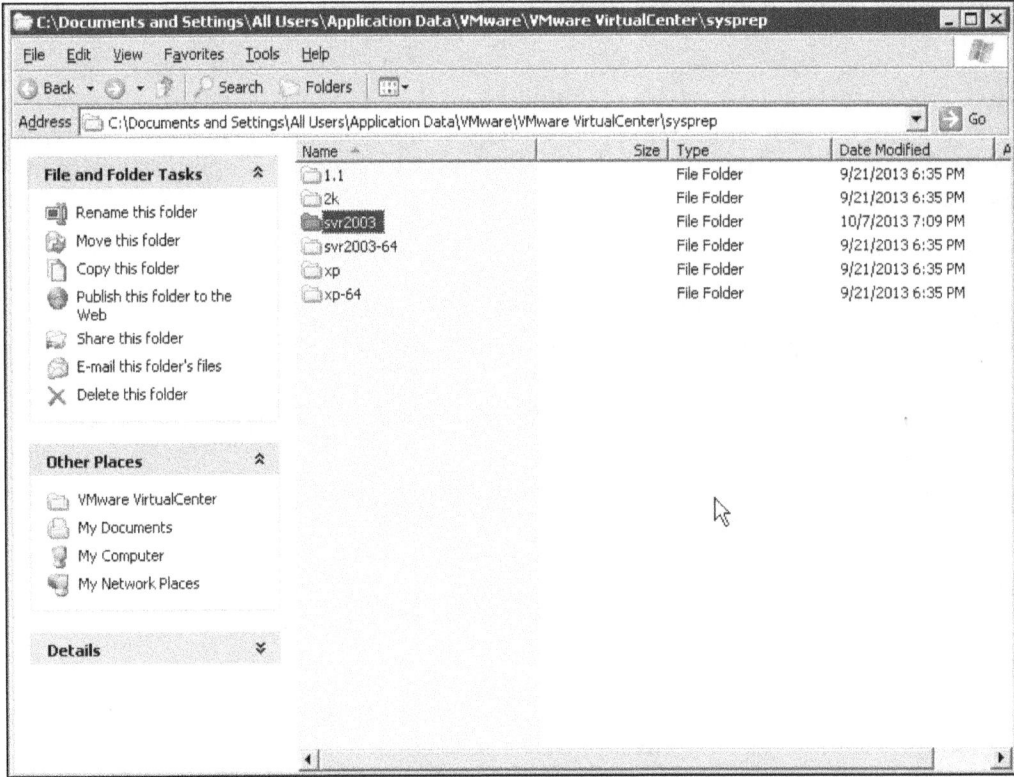

Chapter 3

The following screenshot shows Sysprep files copied to the coordinating directory. It demonstrates copying the correct Sysprep files for Windows 2003 into the `\svr2003` directory:

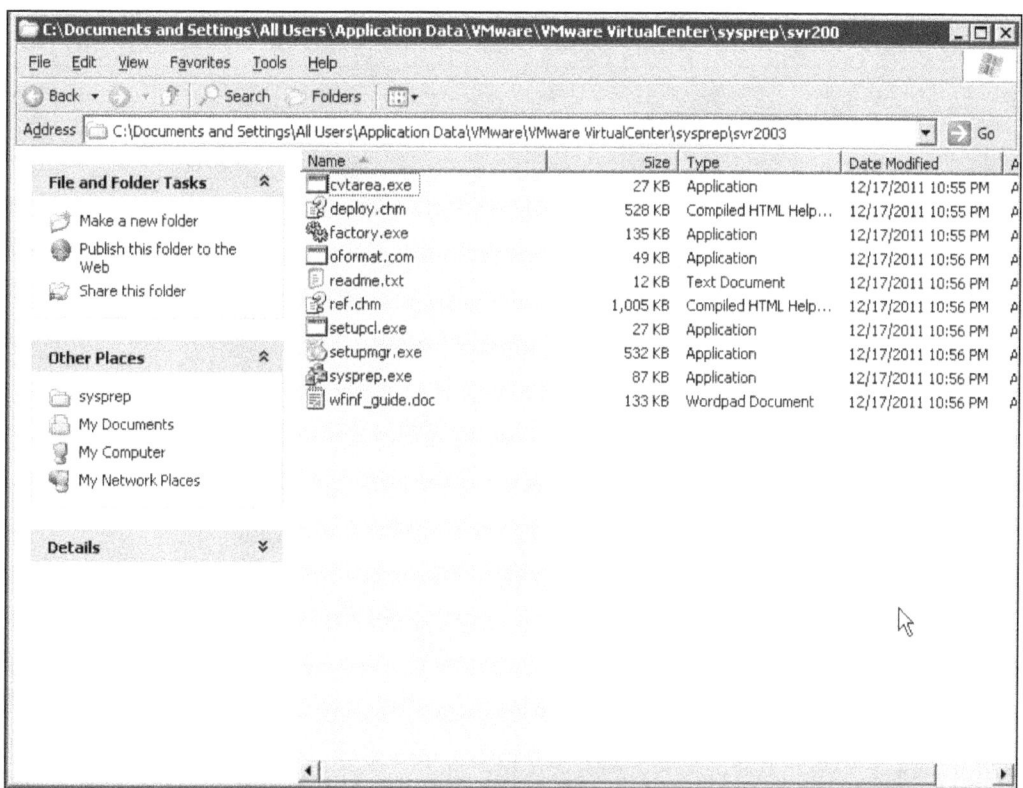

The Sysprep files need to be copied to each guest operating system's directory.

> Sysprep tools are built into Windows Server 2008, Windows Server 2012, Windows 7, and Windows 8 operating systems and do not have to be downloaded.

Once Sysprep files are copied to the correct location, a customization specification can be created.

Other Ways to Provision a Virtual Machine

Creating a customization

To create a customization, go to the **Home** page of vCenter Server using the vSphere Web Client. Select **Customization Specifications Manager** under the **Monitoring** section. This is shown in the following screenshot:

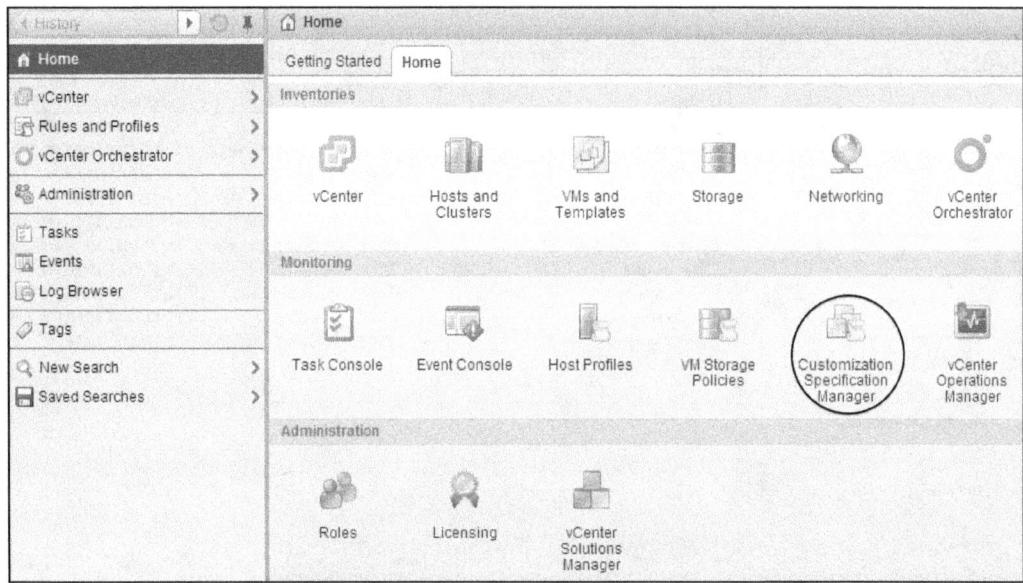

To create a new customization specification, select the New button (which displays the **Create a new specification** message when hovering the mouse on the New button), as shown in the following screenshot:

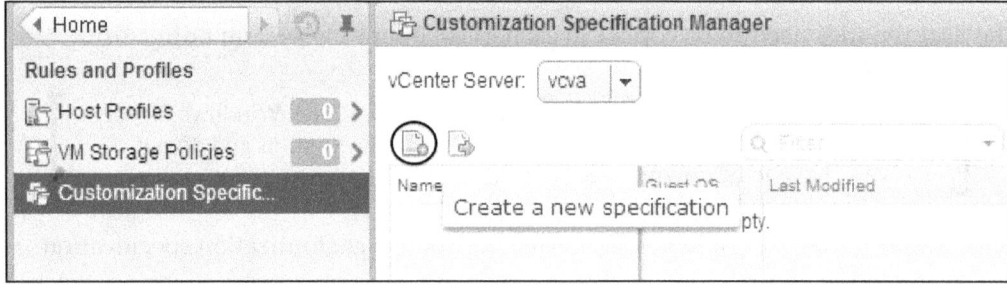

New VM Guest Customization Spec

On the **Specify Properties** pane of the customization wizard, select whether this customization will be used for a Windows or Linux operating system. Depending on the **Target VM Operating System** selection, the wizard will be modified to reflect the choice. This section will outline the process for creating a Windows customization. There is also an option to specify the use of a custom Sysprep answer file. Type a name and short description (if desired) to differentiate this customization from any other to be created, as shown in the following screenshot:

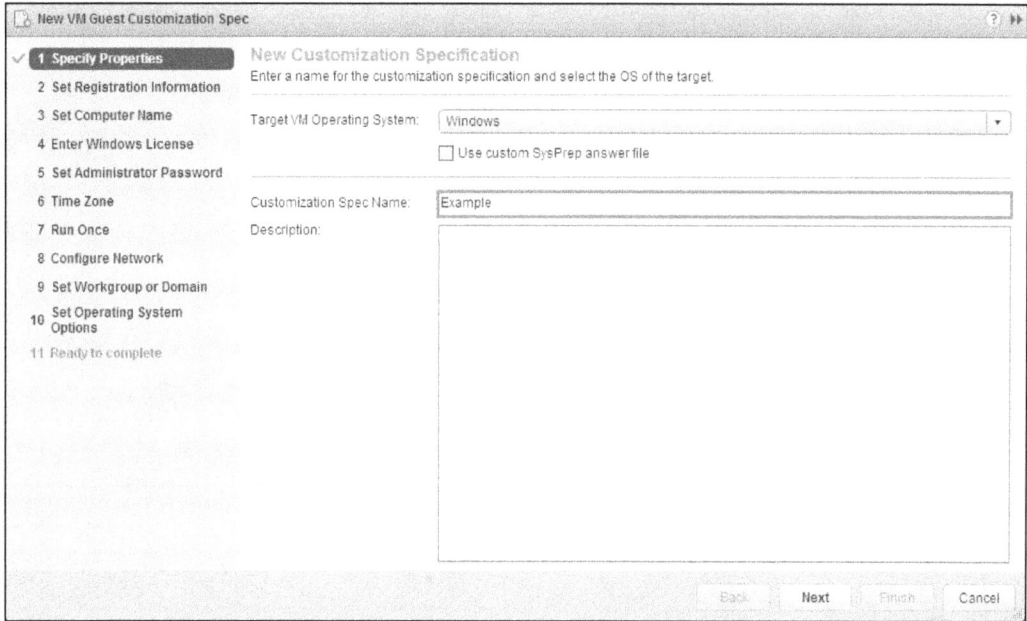

Click on **Next** after entering all the required information.

Set Registration Information

On the **Set Registration Information** pane, enter values against the **Name** and **Organization** fields for registration information for this copy of the guest operating system:

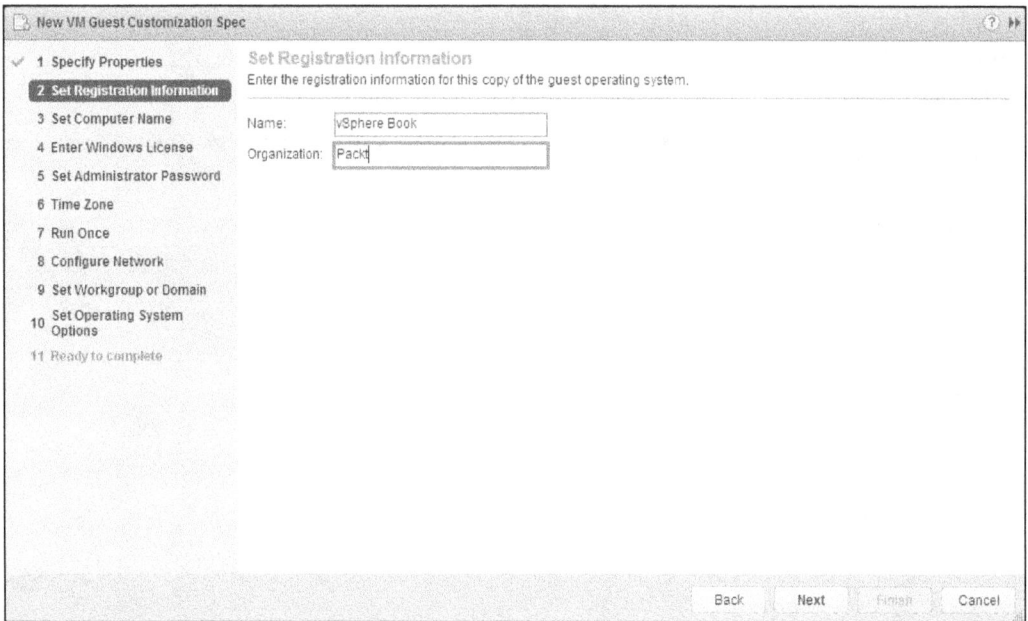

Select **Next** after filling out the information.

Set Computer Name

For the **Set Computer Name** pane, there are multiple options to choose from:

- The first option is **Enter a name** (as long as it is under 15 characters), but any virtual machine deployed using this customization will have the same computer name.

Chapter 3

- The second option is **Use the virtual machine name**, which will use whatever is specified as the virtual machine's inventory name as the computer name within the guest operating system.
- A third option is **Enter a name in the Clone/Deploy wizard**, which allows the specification of a computer name during a virtual machine's deployment from a template or cloning.
- Lastly, a name can be generated using a custom application configured within the vCenter Server, as shown in the following screenshot:

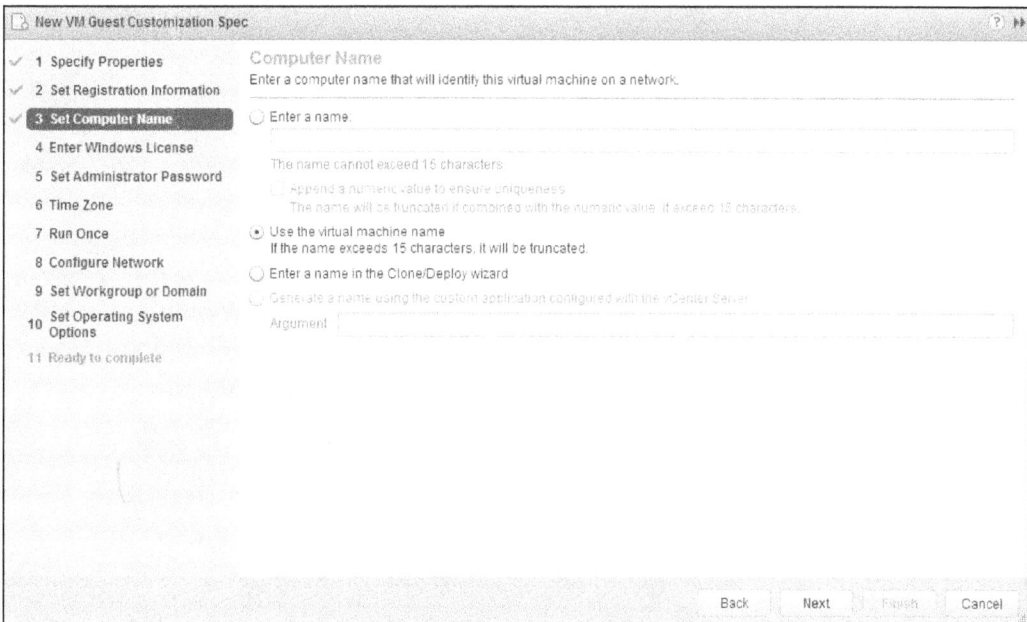

After selection, click on the **Next** button.

Enter Windows License

Since the Windows operating system was chosen in a previous screenshot, the pane for **Enter Windows License** is made available. Specify any licensing information needed, including the actual **Product Key** and which **Server License Mode** should be used. Leave this blank if the virtual machine doesn't require any licensing information due to something like volume licensing. The **Enter Windows License** pane is shown in the following screenshot:

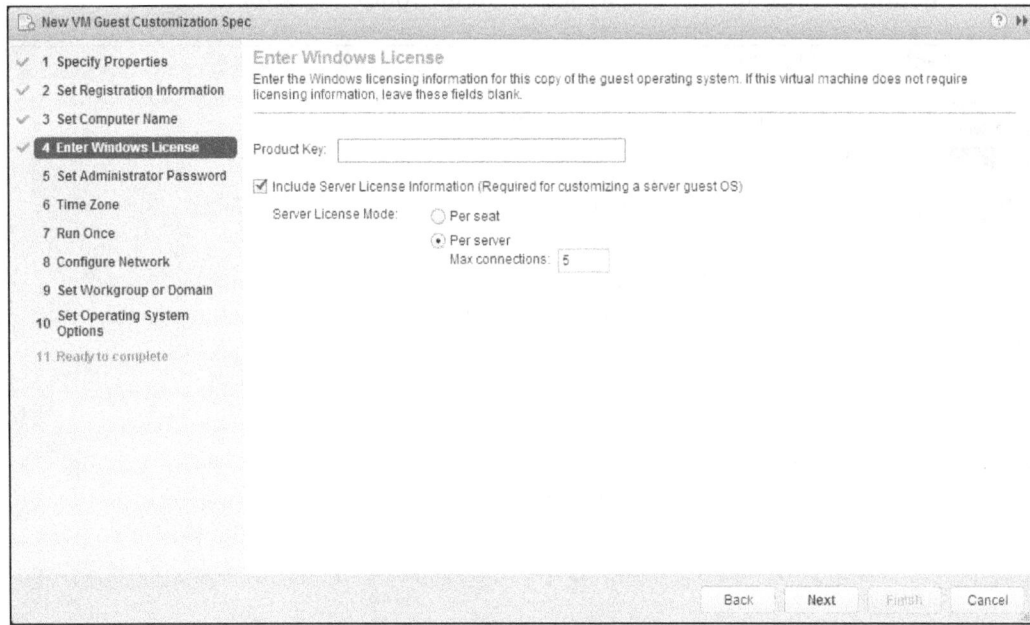

Click on **Next** upon completion of this pane.

Set Administrator Password

The next screenshot demonstrates the **Set Administrator Password** pane; this allows the customization creator to specify what password should be used for the local administrator account of the guest operating system. There is also an option that allows automatic login of the administrator, which is shown in the following screenshot:

Chapter 3

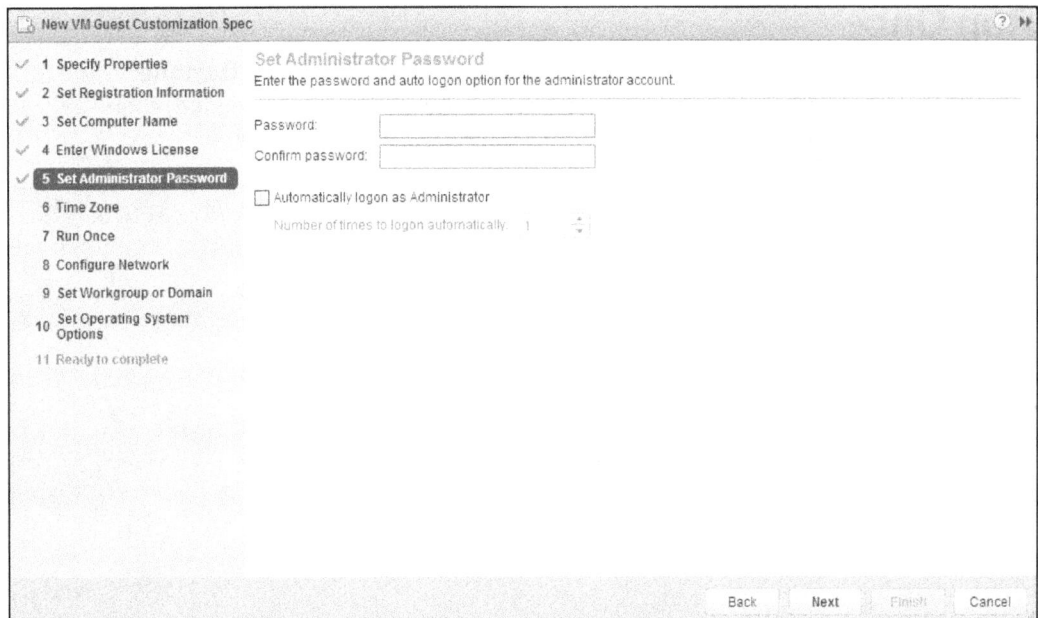

 The administrator passwords specified in the customization specifications are stored in the vCenter database and encrypted using the vCenter SSL certificate. Updating or changing the certificate will result in the passwords becoming invalid. Be sure to update the customization specifications and reenter the password.

After specifying the administrator password, click on **Next**.

The next pane will prompt for time zone selection. Click on **Next** again.

Run Once

If it is desired that a command be run the first time a user logs on, then this information should be input in the **Run Once** pane. If this is not needed, then leave the pane blank, as shown in the following screenshot:

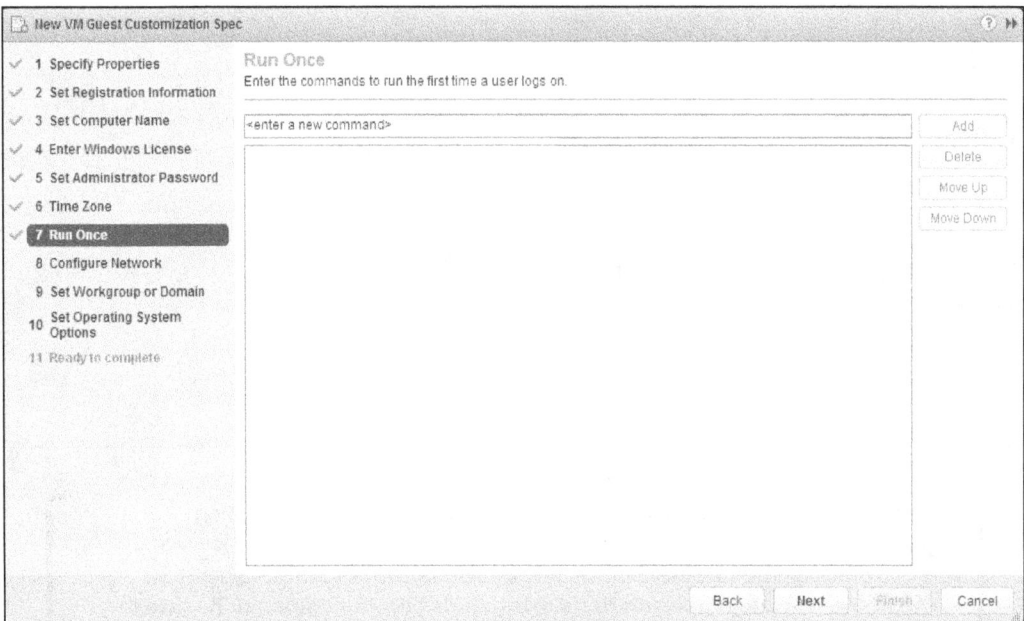

After configuring a command to be run, click on **Next**.

Configure Network

There are two options available on the **Configure Network** pane, **Use standard network settings for the guest operating system, including enabling DHCP on all network interfaces** and **Manually select custom settings**. Selecting the former results in vCenter Server configuring all network interfaces from a DHCP server by using default settings. The latter option allows for manual input of all network information, as shown in the following screenshot:

Chapter 3

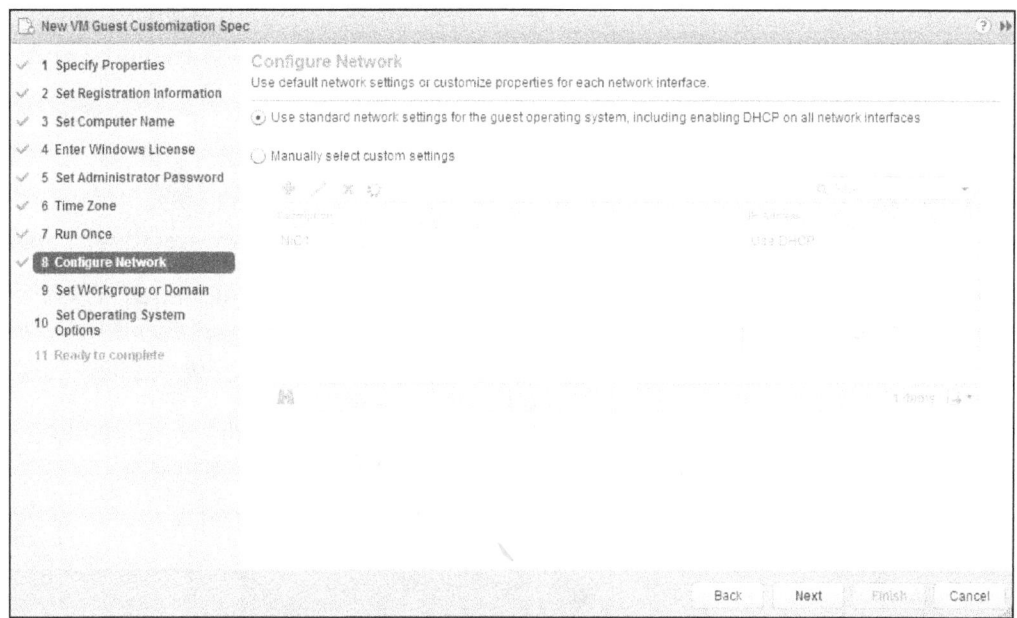

After selecting the **Configure Network** option, click on **Next**.

A list of configurable NICs will be listed if the custom settings option is selected. To configure the adapter, select **NIC1** and click on the **Edit Settings** (pencil-shaped) button. Another NIC can be added by simply clicking on the **+** (plus sign) button. See the following screenshot for what information can be specified:

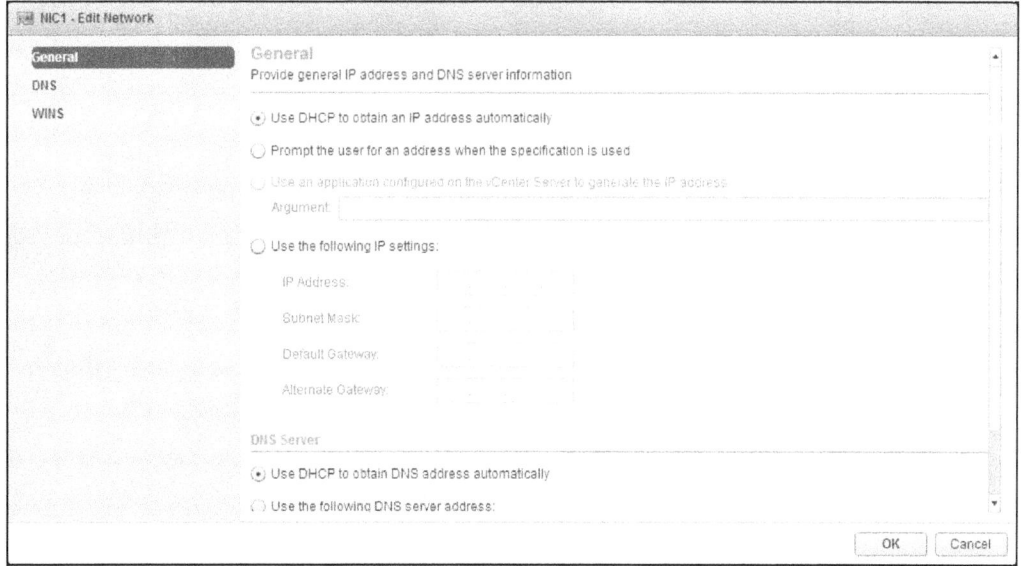

The **Edit Network** dialog box will appear. From here, the specific IP address, subnet mask, default gateway, and WINS and DNS server information can be entered.

Upon configuration of all NICs, click on **Next**.

Set Workgroup or Domain

After configuration, click on **OK** and then click on **Next** on the custom settings pane.

If desired, the virtual machine can be added to a domain upon deployment. The **Workgroup** option is selected by default, but to add to a domain select the **Windows Server Domain** option. Upon specifying the domain, an administrator username and password should be entered in the correct format for the operating system. Make sure that this account entered has the permission to add objects onto the domain. The **Set Workgroup or Domain** pane is shown in the following screenshot:

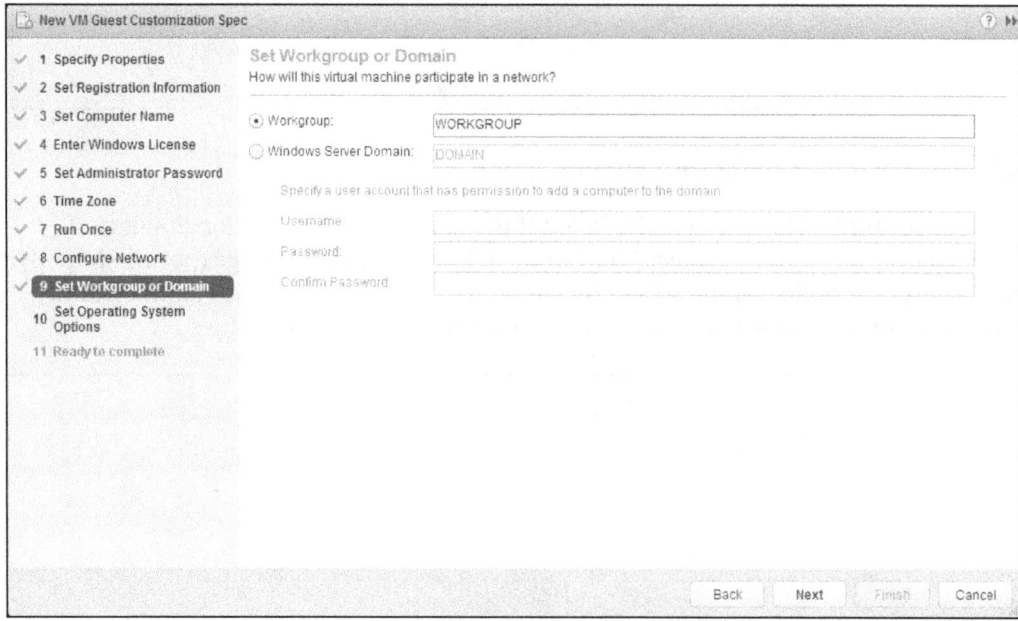

Click on **Next** after entering all the required information.

Set Operating System Options

The next pane, **Set Operating System Options**, allows for deciding whether a new **Security ID (SID)** should be generated or not. Some Windows operating systems use this as the unique identifier for different computer accounts and users. If this option is not selected, the new virtual machines deployed will have the exact SID as the virtual machine or template it was cloned or deployed from. The following screenshot shows the **Set Operating System Options** pane:

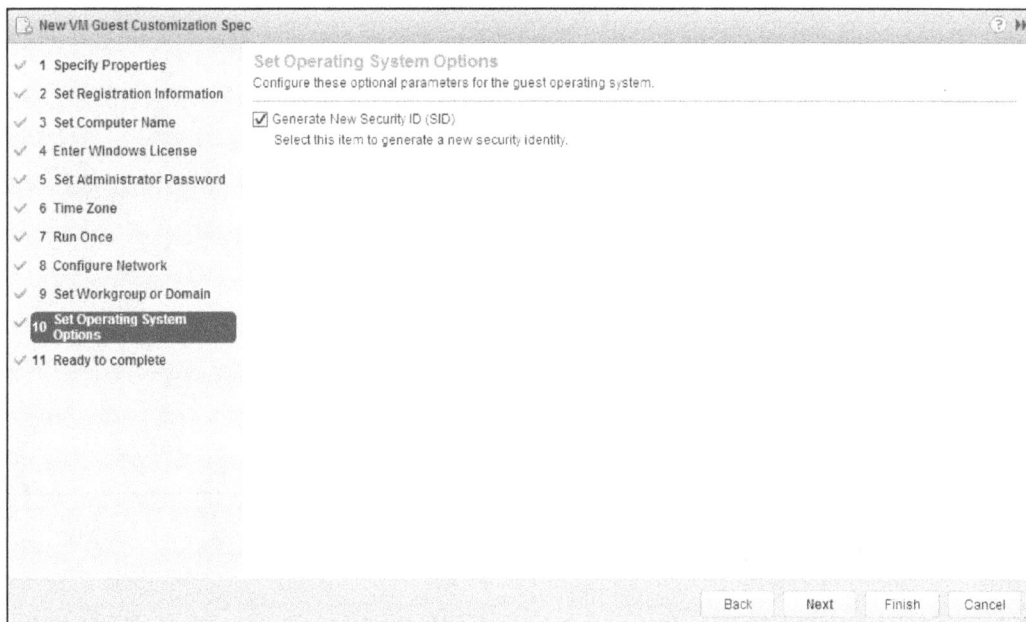

After making a selection, click on **Next**.

Ready to complete

The last pane in the wizard allows for a review of all options selected before creating this customization specification, as shown in the following screenshot:

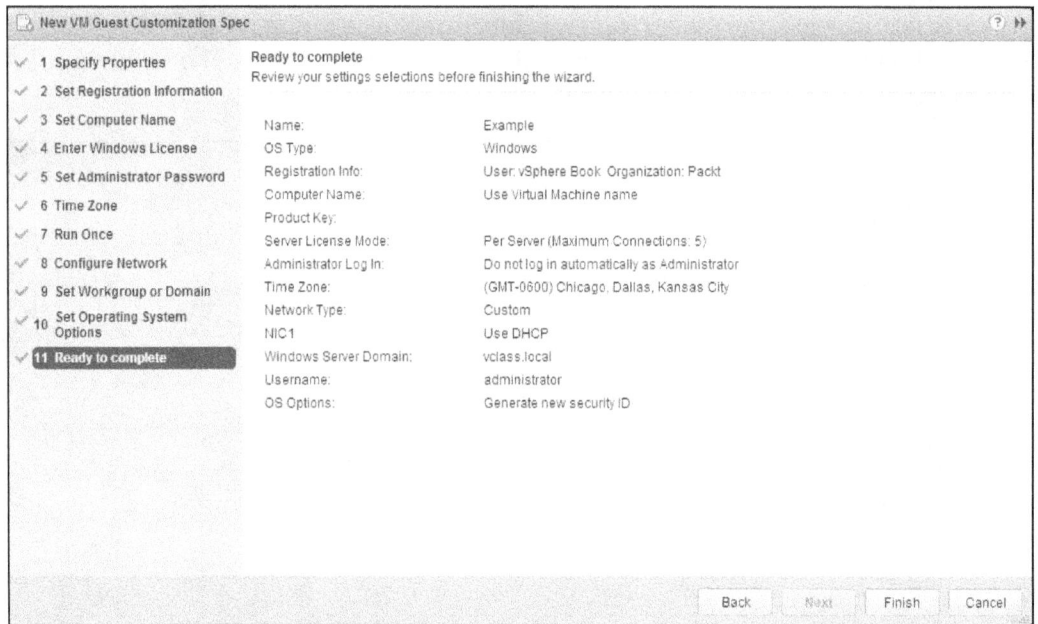

Click on **Finish** if satisfied with all configurations.

Creating a virtual machine from a template

Converting a virtual machine to a template, cloning a virtual machine to a template, or cloning another template can create a template.

Creating a template

A **template** is a preconfigured virtual machine in .vmtx format so that it cannot be powered on. This can either be converted back to a virtual machine (.vmx) or have virtual machines provisioned from it. This template usually includes a hardware configuration, guest operating system, and potentially even applications. Having an image makes creating virtual machines so much faster and makes us less likely to make errors during creation. Another benefit is that a template is a good way to define hardware standards, such as using the VMXNET3 or PVSCSI adapters that should be used with each deployment.

To create a template, first create a virtual machine and configure it, as desired, to be a base image for many more virtual machines. Once this virtual machine is created, there are two options: **Clone to Template...** or **Convert to Template...**. Should the **Clone to Template...** option be selected, the original virtual machine will be retained and a clone will be created of this virtual machine. The cloned copy will be converted from .vmx to .vmtx and will become a template. The second option, demonstrated in the following screenshot, is to convert the virtual machine to a template. This will result in the original .vmx file being converted to a .vmtx file:

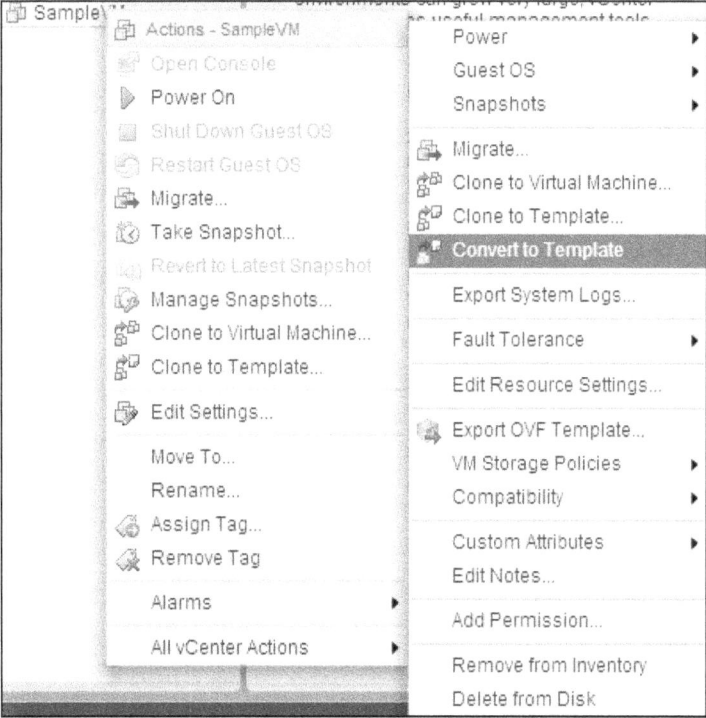

Other Ways to Provision a Virtual Machine

Deploying VMs from the template

To deploy is as simple as a right-click. Right-click on the template (notice the **VM and Template** inventory view) and select the **Deploy VM from this Template** option. This ensures that your template is retained for future use and there will be a new virtual machine with a matching virtual hardware configuration. The other option is **Convert to Virtual Machine...**. This is generally reserved for when updating the template with new patches. It will convert from .vmtx back to .vmx so that the virtual machine can be powered on and updated. Once updates are complete, convert back to the template. The **Deploy VM from this Template** option is shown in the following screenshot:

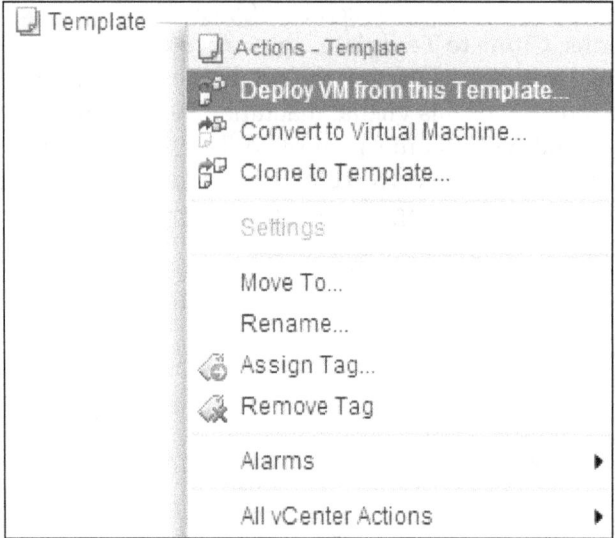

This selection will bring up the **Deploy From Template** wizard.

Select a name and folder

Type the new virtual machine's desired inventory name on this pane and select which folder the virtual machine should be placed in in the **VM and Template** view, as shown in the following screenshot:

Chapter 3

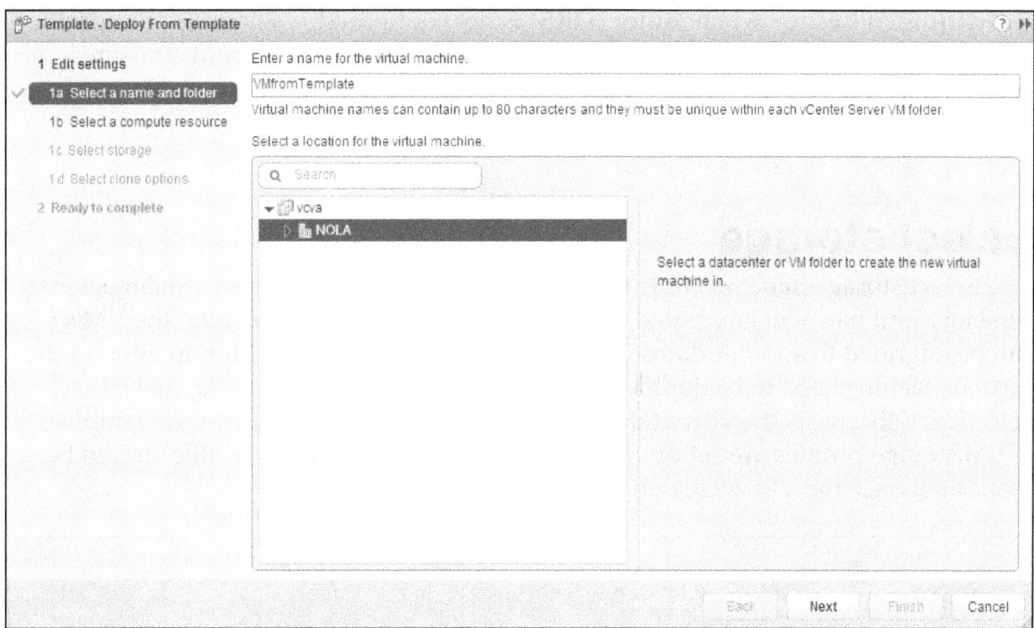

Click on **Next** upon selection.

Select a compute resource

The next pane requires the selection of the cluster that the virtual machine should be placed in to consume compute resources, as shown in the following screenshot:

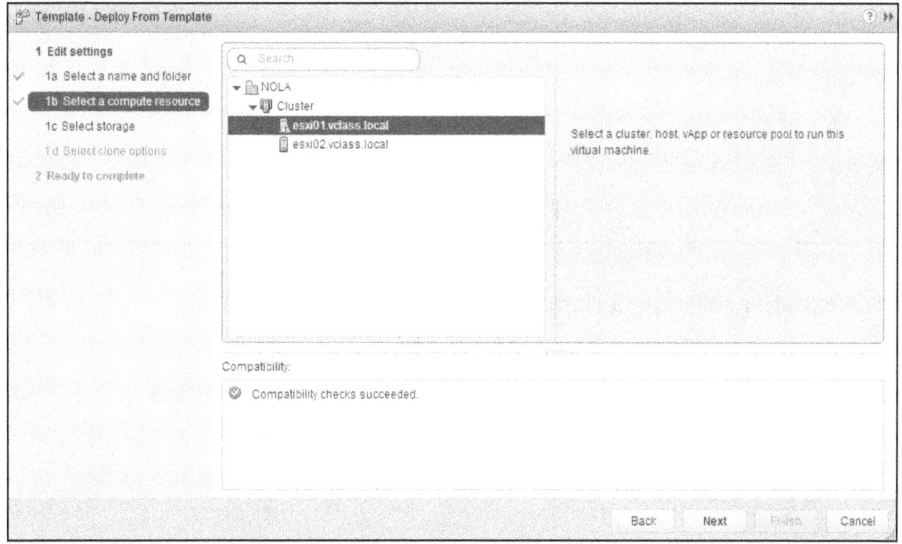

If **Distributed Resource Scheduler (DRS)** is not configured, a selection of a specific ESXi host is required. Choose the host that the virtual machine should consume resources from.

Click on **Next** after selecting the correct cluster.

Select storage

The **Select storage** pane prompts you to select which datastore the virtual machine's directory and files will be created on. This is not a permanent selection; the VM's files can be migrated to another datastore at any time using Storage vMotion. Should the virtual machine need to be deployed as a different virtual disk format, make that selection. Otherwise, the virtual disk will be formatted similar to the base template. If VM storage profiles are set up in vCenter, select which storage profile should be associated once the VM is created:

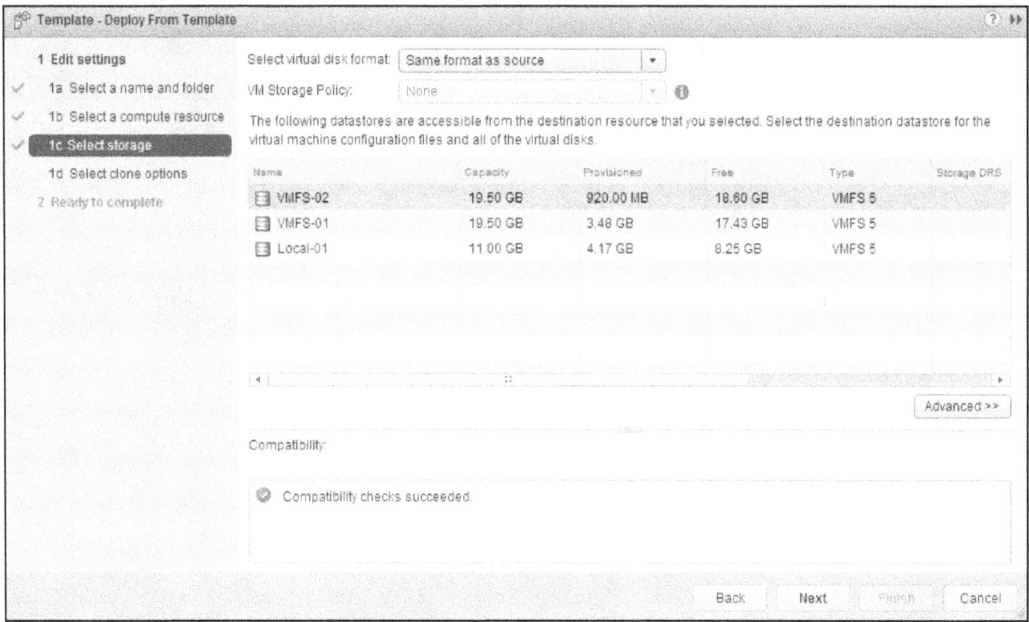

Click on **Next** after selecting a datastore.

Select clone options

Once the correct Sysprep files have been placed in the coordinating directory and customization specifications have been created, the new virtual machine can be customized using an existing customization specification. If it is desired to apply a customization, select the **Customize the operating system** option. The virtual hardware can be reconfigured to meet the newly deployed virtual machine's application requirements by selecting the **Customize this virtual machine's hardware (Experimental)** option. The last option is **Power on virtual machine after creation**; beware of using this option if the newly created virtual machine may cause any kind of IP or MAC conflicts due to a lack of customization. The pane is shown in the following screenshot:

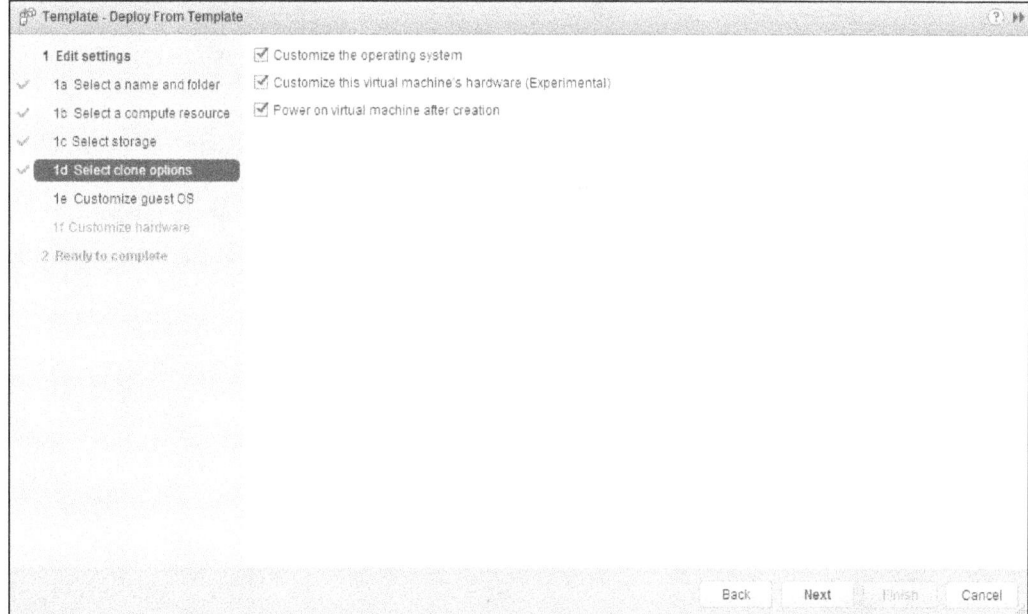

After selecting a customization option, click on **Next**.

The next pane allows you to select an existing customization or create a new one:

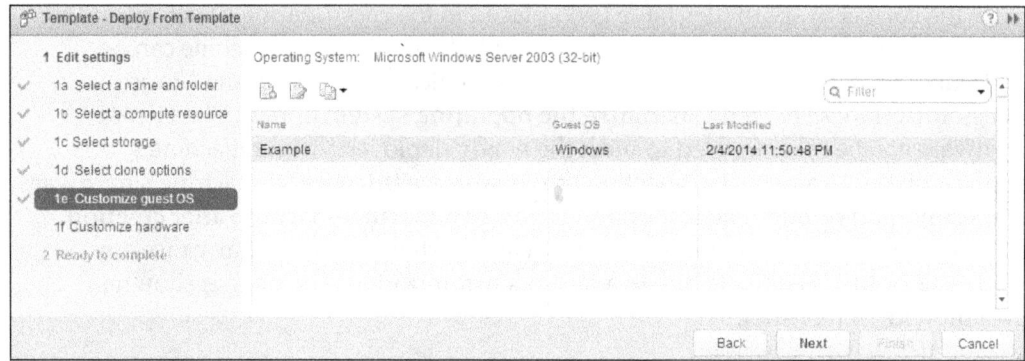

Click on the **Next** button after selecting an existing or creating a new customization specification.

Under the **Customize hardware** pane, you can modify virtual hardware or add new devices to fit the needs of the application that will be installed. For example, you could mount a **Datastore ISO File**, as demonstrated in the following screenshot:

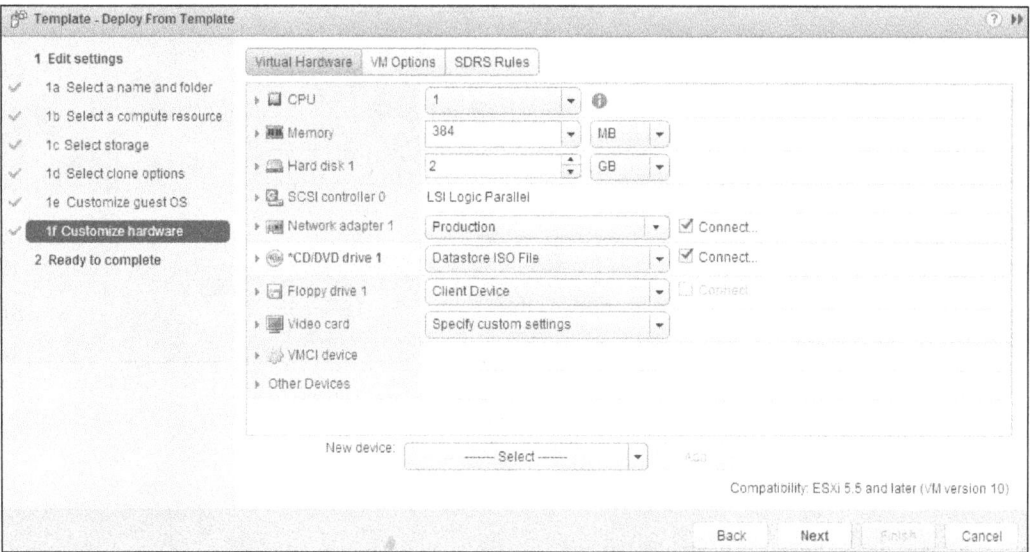

Click on **Next** to review all selections made.

Once all of the configurations have been reviewed, click on **Finish**.

Creating a virtual machine by cloning

If there is a virtual machine that you would like an identical copy of, you can clone it! To clone a virtual machine, simply right-click and select **Clone to Virtual Machine...**. This will clone a whole new VM from an existing one; it will be a duplicate with the same configuration and installed software. Be aware of the fact that a clone results in two identical hostnames, IP addresses, SIDs, and so on; customization specifications should be used to avoid these issues. The **Clone to Virtual Machine...** option is shown in the following screenshot:

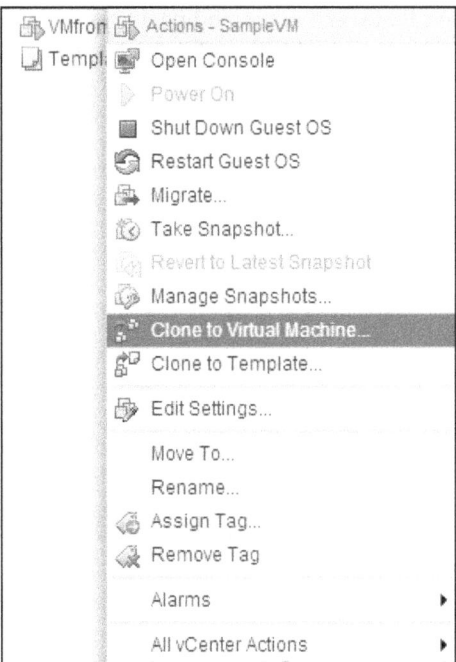

Selecting the **Clone to Virtual Machine...** option will result in the **Clone Virtual Machine Wizard** being launched.

This selection will bring up the Clone Existing Virtual Machine wizard. This will follow the same process outlined in the *Deploying VMs from the template* section.

Creating a virtual machine from an OVF file

Open Virtualization Format (**OVF**) is a cross-platform, open industry standard for packaging and distributing virtual appliances between different virtualization products. VMware has a Virtual Appliance Marketplace from which you can browse and download different virtual appliances.

> While visiting the VMware Virtual Appliance Marketplace, you may have realized that some download packages are available as OVF files while others are available as OVA files. An **Open Virtualization Appliance** (**OVA**) is a single file consisting of a TAR archive for distribution. An OVF file usually consists of multiple files.

Once an OVF file has been downloaded, right-click on an inventory object and select **Deploy OVF Template...**, as shown in the following screenshot:

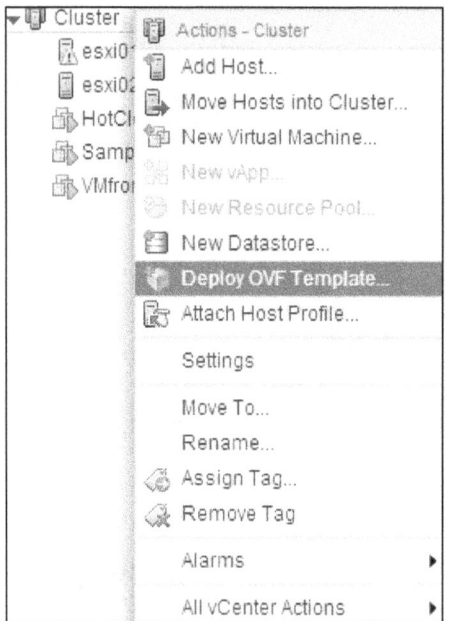

This will launch the **Deploy OVF Template** wizard.

Select source

The first step is to click on the **Browse...** button to search your local computer and select the file that was downloaded. A URL can also be specified so that the OVF package can be downloaded and installed from the Internet:

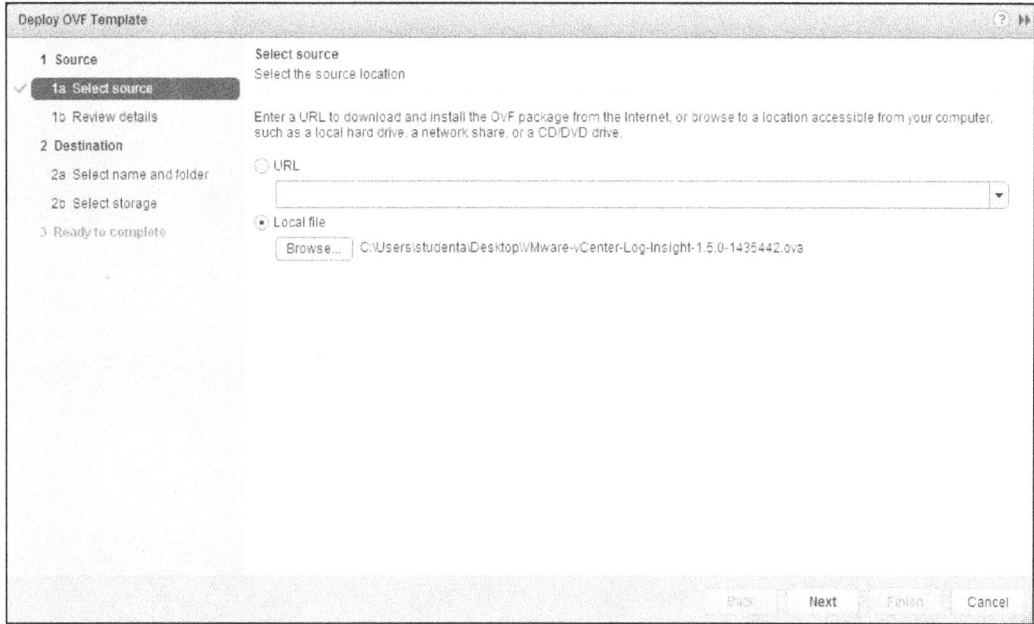

Once the OVF file has been specified, click on **Next**.

Review details

The **Review details** pane previews information relevant to the file selected. Notice which product and version is being deployed and verify that this is the desired OVF template. Also note the disk size required. I have downloaded and am getting ready to deploy VMware vCenter Log Insight.

> VMware vCenter Log Insight provides log management through aggregation, search, and analytics, enabling a wider visibility in dynamic environments.

The **Review details** pane is shown in the following screenshot:

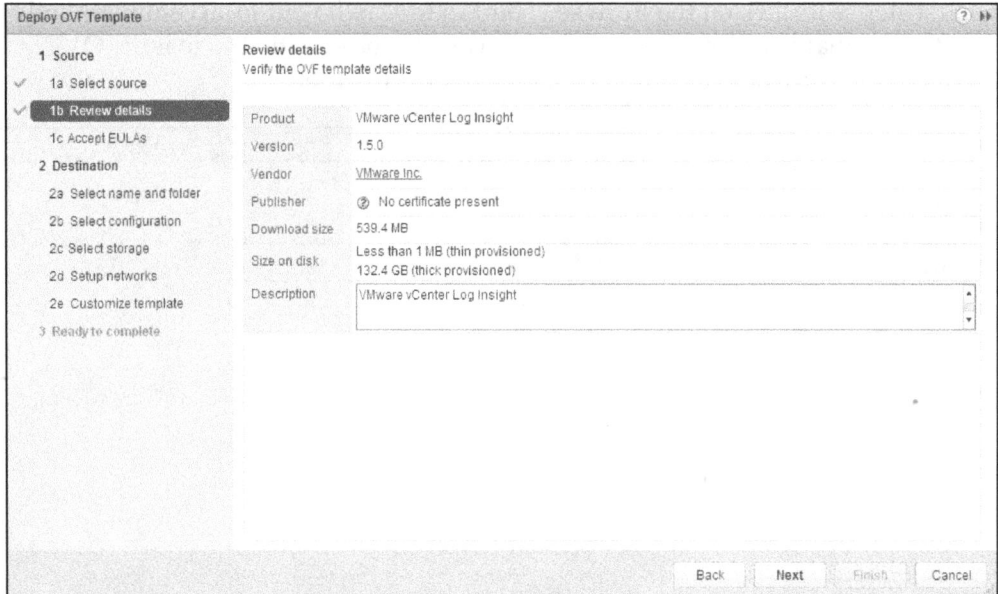

Once the information has been reviewed, click on **Next**.

Accept EULAs

The next pane displays the **End User License Agreement** (**EULA**). Make sure to read through this before moving to the next pane.

If the terms are agreeable, click on the **Accept** button. Click on **Next** to specify your agreement and compliance to this EULA.

Select name and location

On the **Select name and location** pane, type the new virtual machine's desired inventory name and select which folder in the **VM and Template** inventory view the virtual machine should be placed in.

The next pane requires the selection of the cluster that the virtual machine should be placed in to consume computing resources. If DRS is not configured, a selection of a specific ESXi host is required. Choose the host that the virtual machine should consume resources from.

Select the **Next** button after a folder has been selected in the **VM and Template** inventory view, and a cluster or ESXi host selection will be made.

Select storage

The **Select storage** pane prompts you to select which datastore the virtual machine's directory and files will be created in. This is not a permanent selection; the VM's files can be migrated to another datastore at any time using Storage vMotion. If VM storage profiles are set up in vCenter, then select which storage profile should be associated with the VM being deployed from the OVF template. The datastores that are available in the **Select storage** pane are shown in the following screenshot:

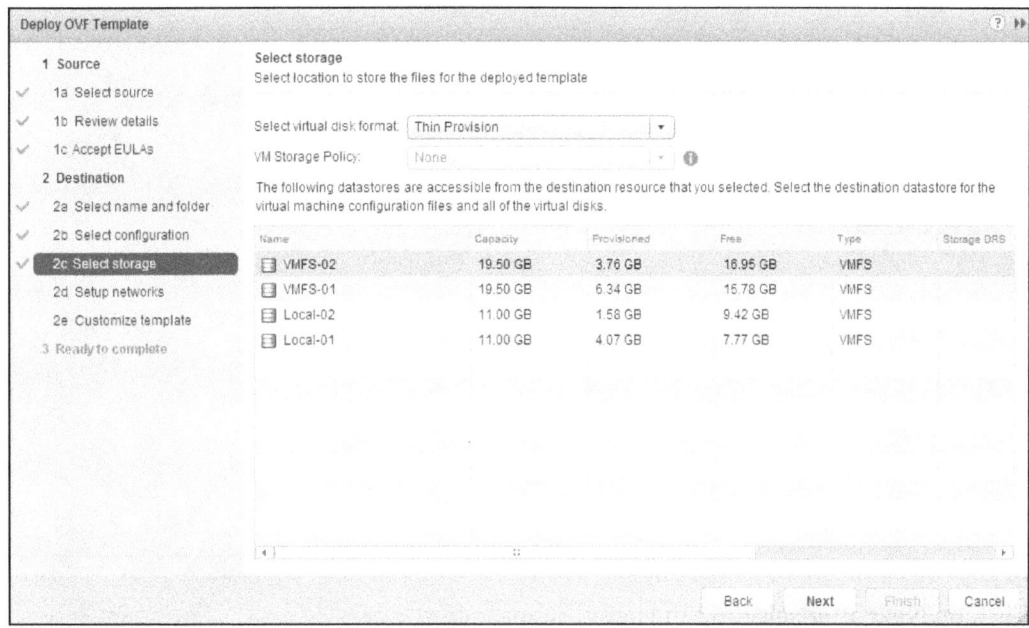

Click on **Next** after selecting a datastore.

Select the virtual disk format that is desired for the OVF template. See *Chapter 2, Creating a Virtual Machine Using the Wizard*, for assistance on the different disk formats available.

Setup networks

The **Setup networks** pane allows for the selection of the network on which the OVF template should be deployed for use. In the following screenshot, there is only one network adapter for the virtual appliance being deployed, but in some cases there can be multiple configured network adapters:

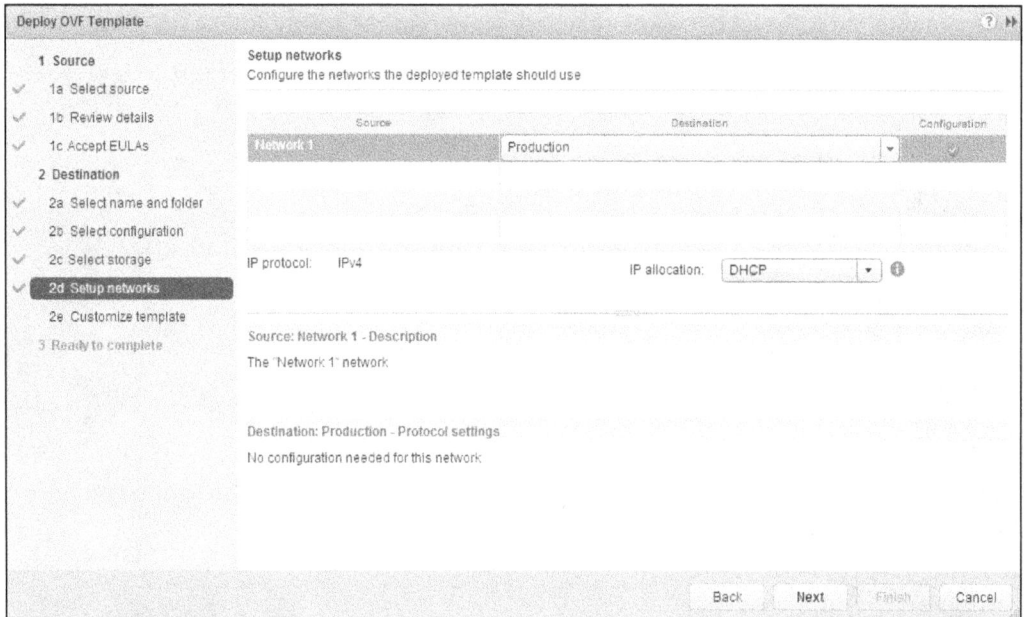

Click on **Next** after selecting the network mapping.

Customize template

The **Customize template** pane allows for any kind of customization needed for the virtual appliance to be deployed. For the VMware vCenter Log Insight virtual appliance that I selected, it is prompting me to enter networking property information, default gateway, DNS, IP address, netmask, and hostname for the virtual appliance, as shown in the following screenshot:

Chapter 3

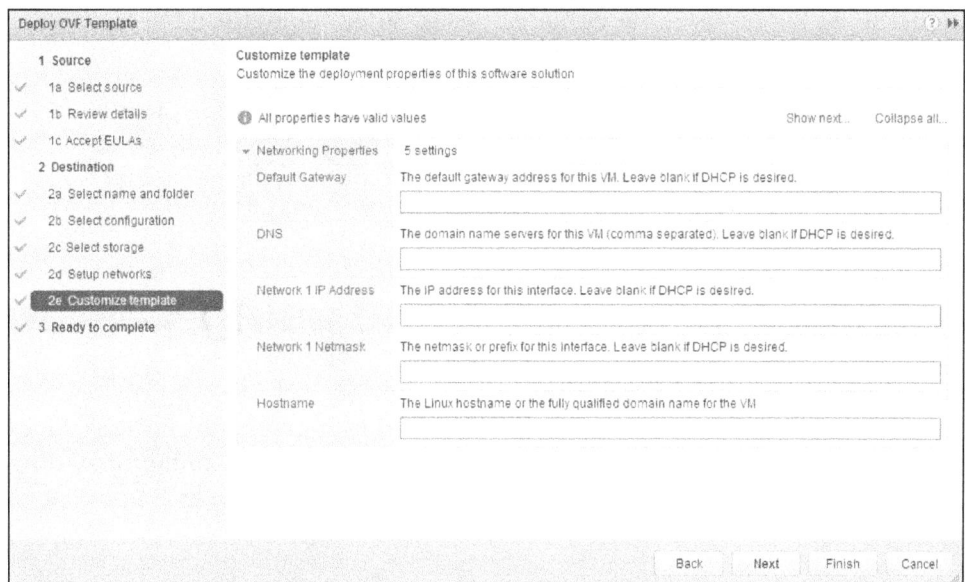

Click on **Next** after entering all required information.

Ready to complete

The last pane allows you to review all options before launching the creation of the virtual machine from an OVF template, as shown in the following screenshot:

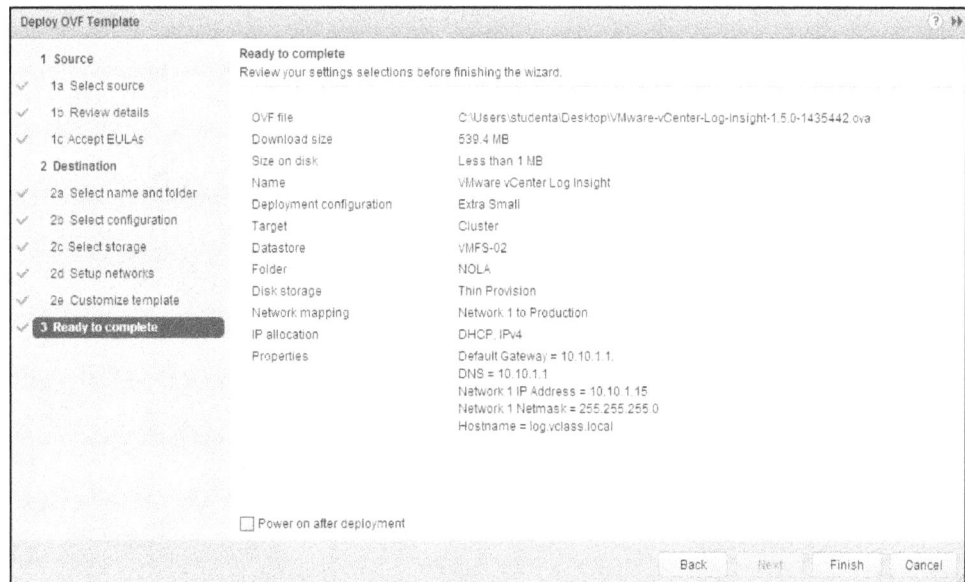

You can choose to power on the virtual appliance after deployment by checking the box and clicking on the **Finish** button.

The screenshot in the following section demonstrates the deploying of an OVF template into the vCenter inventory. The OVF template will appear in the inventory just like any other virtual machine, displaying the name that was specified in the wizard.

Creating a virtual machine using VMware vCenter Converter

VMware vCenter Converter is a solution to convert virtual and physical machines into VMware virtual machines. This product can also be used to configure existing virtual machines within vCenter. VMware vCenter Converter can be found in a standalone version for download on the VMware website.

There is a variety of sources that VMware vCenter Converter allows for conversion to a new VMware virtual machine, including:

- VMware virtual machines (`.vmx`)
- Physical machines
- Microsoft Virtual PC or Virtual Server (`.vmc`)
- Microsoft Hyper-V virtual machines
- Symantec LiveState Recovery image (`.sv2i`)
- Acronis True Image backup (`.tib`)

This is not an exhaustive list. Consult the *VMware vCenter Converter Standalone User's guide* for a complete list.

Chapter 3

Once VMware vCenter Converter is installed and opened, click on the **Convert machine** button to launch the conversion wizard, as shown in the following screenshot:

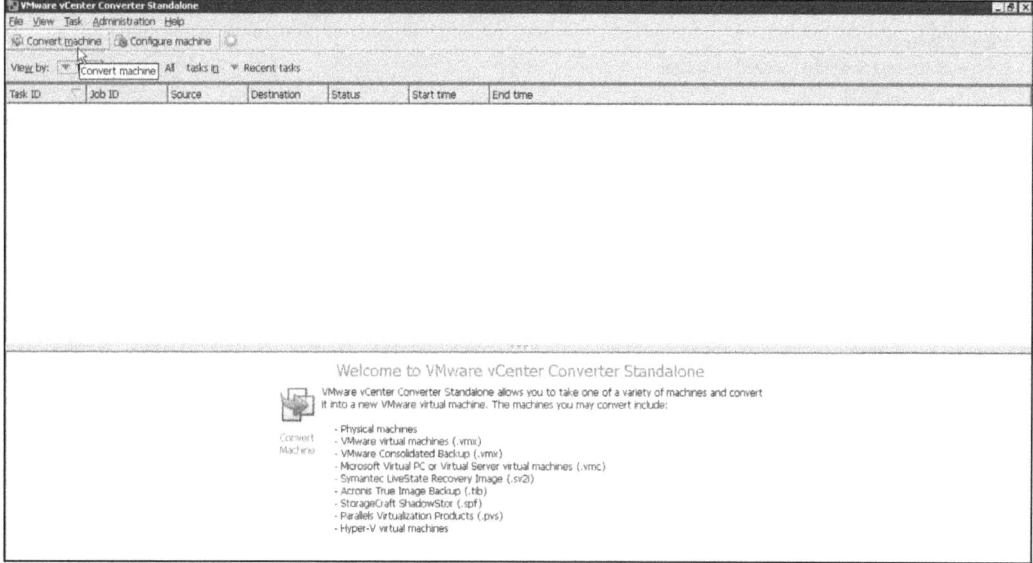

Once the conversion wizard is launched, drop down the menu for the **Select source type** field and choose one of the options. I've selected **VMware Infrastructure virtual machine**, but the situation will dictate the selection. Under the **Specify server connection information** section, enter the server's hostname and user account credentials. In this instance, I have specified my vCenter information since I have selected the **VMware Infrastructure virtual machine** option.

Source System

The following screenshot shows the **Source System** pane:

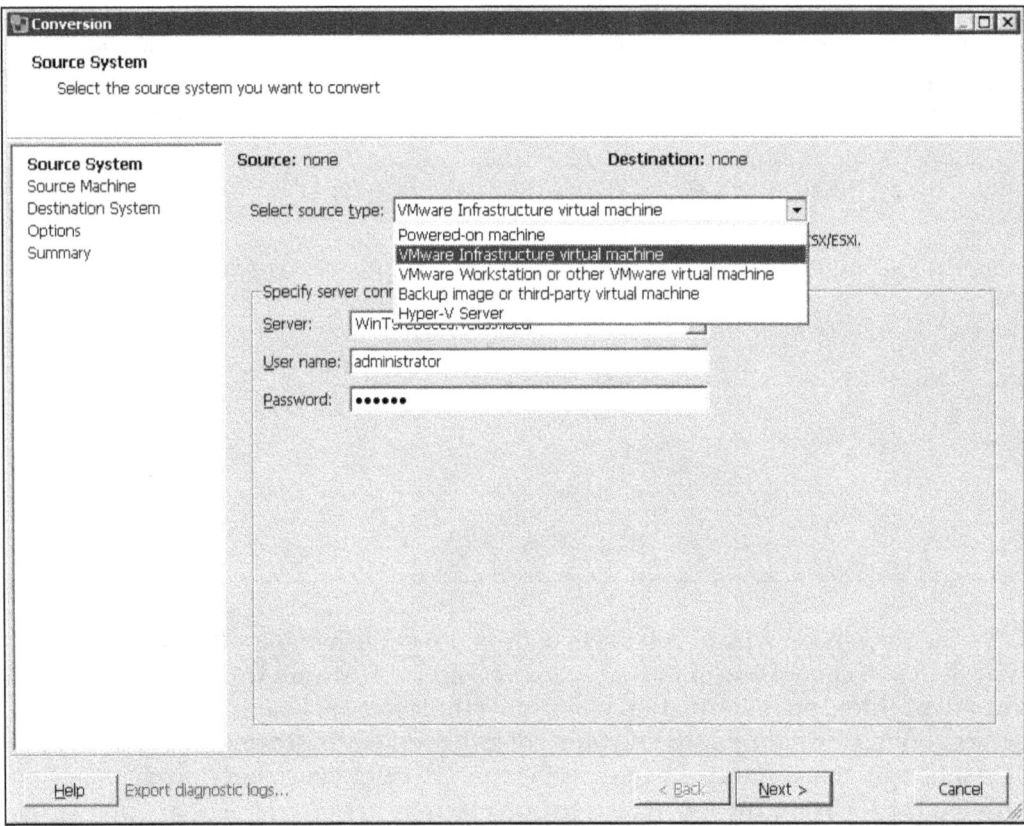

Click on **Next** after completing the **Source System** pane.

Source Machine

On the **Source Machine** pane, notice that **Source** specified at the top is what was entered on the previous pane. Next, browse the inventory to select the host from the box on the left and then the virtual machine to be converted from the box on the right, as shown in the following screenshot:

Chapter 3

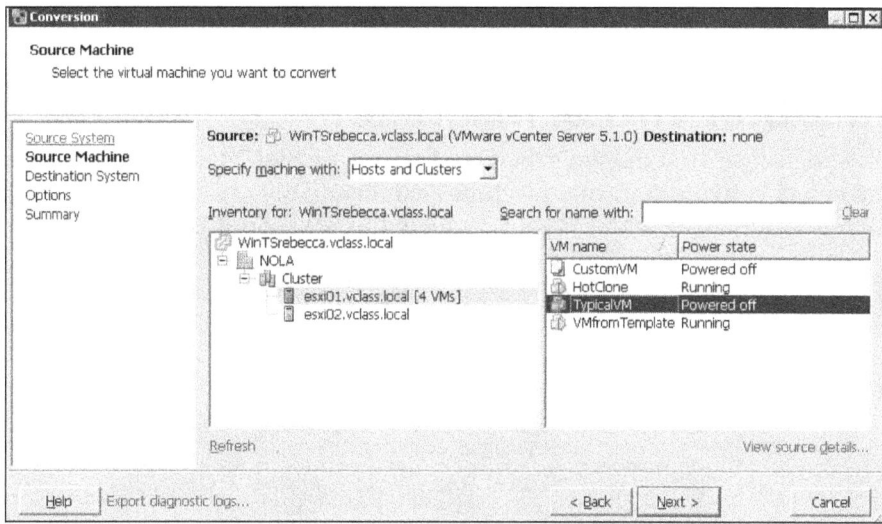

Keep in mind that this pane will vary depending on the type of source machine previously selected. Once the ESXi host and virtual machine have been selected, click on the **Next** button.

Destination System

The **Destination System** pane prompts for the destination type; select either the **VMware Infrastructure virtual machine** option or the **VMware Workstation or other VMware virtual machine** option. Once the type is selected, enter the credential information needed for the destination server, as shown in the following screenshot:

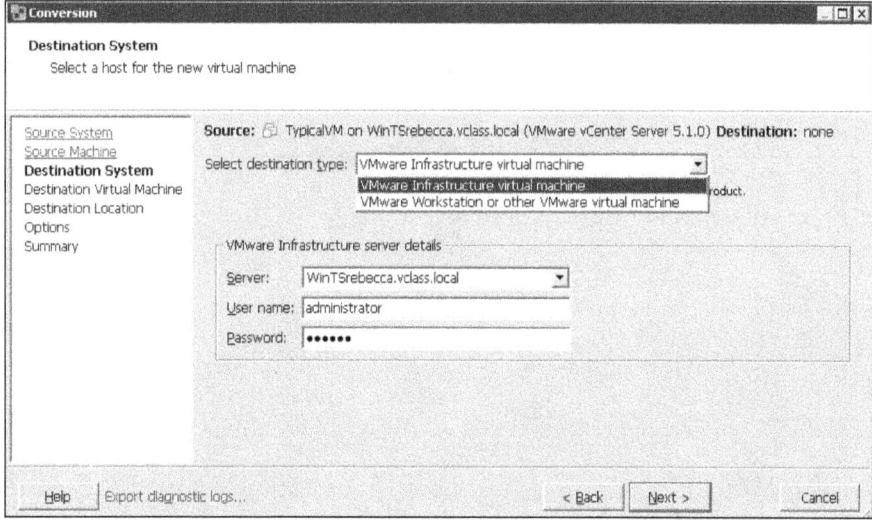

Click on **Next** upon completion of the **Destination System** pane.

Destination Virtual Machine

The following screenshot displays the **Destination Virtual Machine** pane. For this, enter the newly converted virtual machine's name and also select which folder in the **VM and Template** vCenter inventory view this VM should be placed:

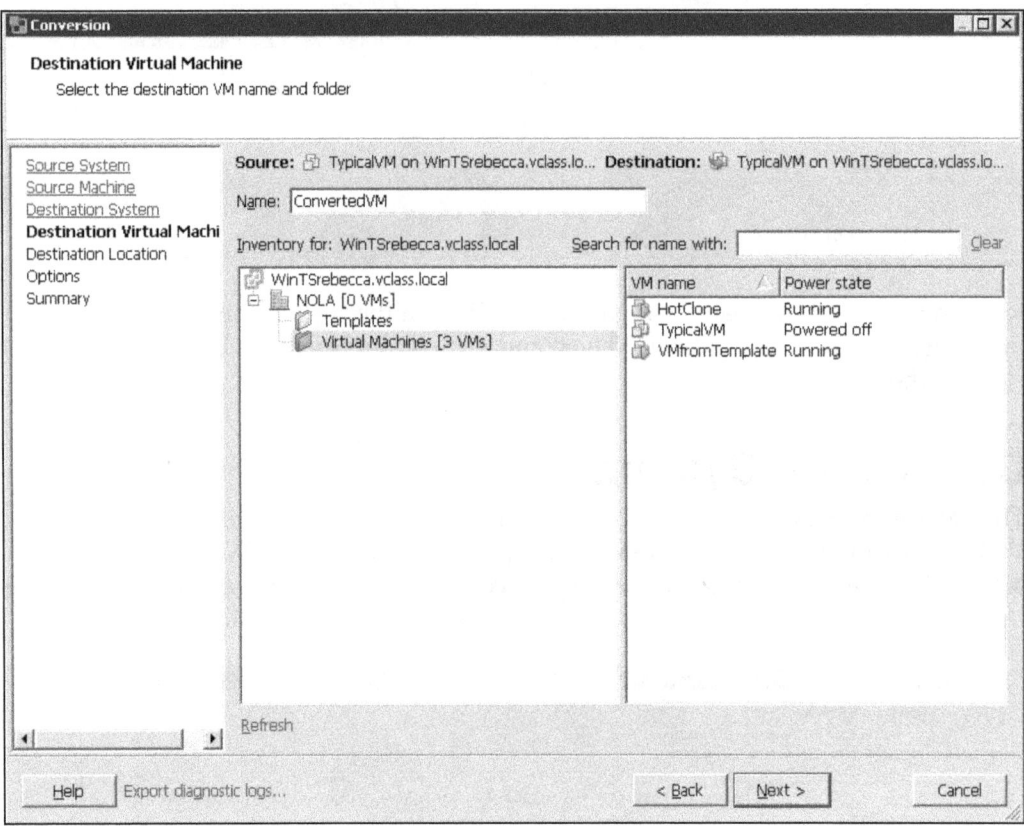

Click on **Next** after making the required selections.

Destination Location

For the **Destination Location** pane, select which ESXi host the virtual machine should consume resources from. Note the **Total source disks size** tab above the **Datastore** box on the right-hand side of the pane. Choose the correct datastore from based off of the source machine's application requirements. Lastly, select the desired virtual machine version. Refer to *Chapter 2, Creating a Virtual Machine Using the Wizard*, for assistance in this selection. The **Destination Location** pane is shown in the following screenshot:

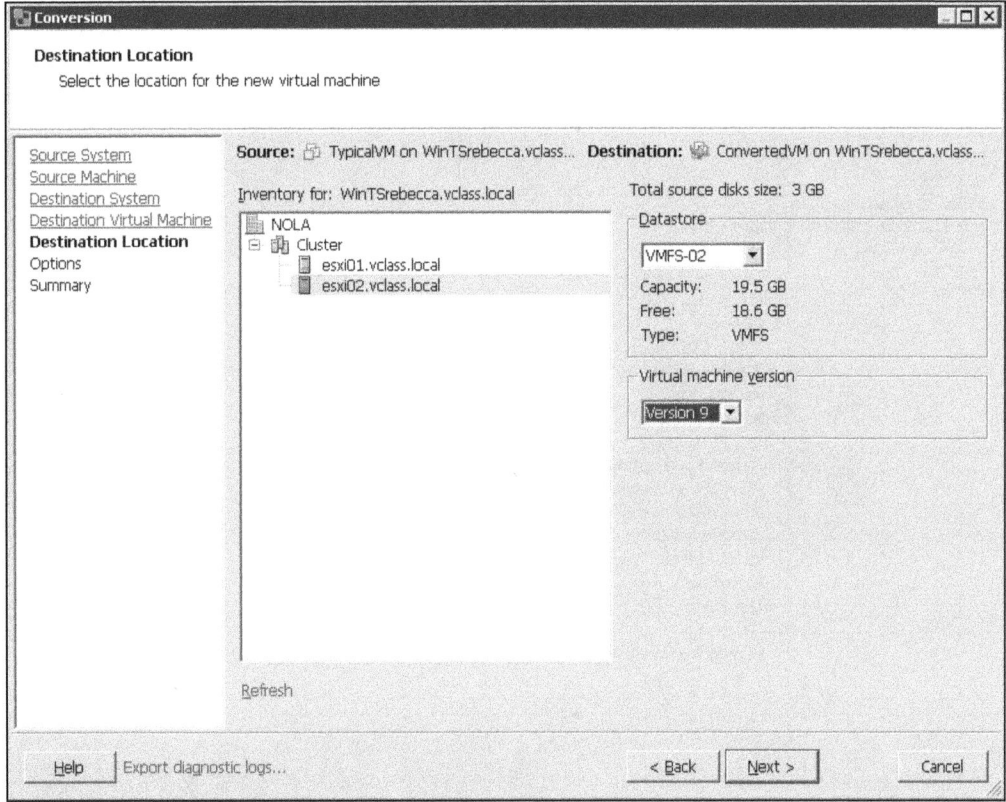

Click on **Next** after selecting the compute and storage resources.

Other Ways to Provision a Virtual Machine

Options

The **Options** pane allows for a reconfiguration of the virtual machine to be converted. If it is desired to adjust the amount of memory or number of vCPUs, editing the devices can do this. The amount of data being copied, the network, and the advanced options can be manipulated as needed. For example, you may decide to not copy any data and use Raw Device Mapping for the virtual machine. Also, notice that the resources can be throttled during the conversion period. The **Options** pane is shown in the following screenshot:

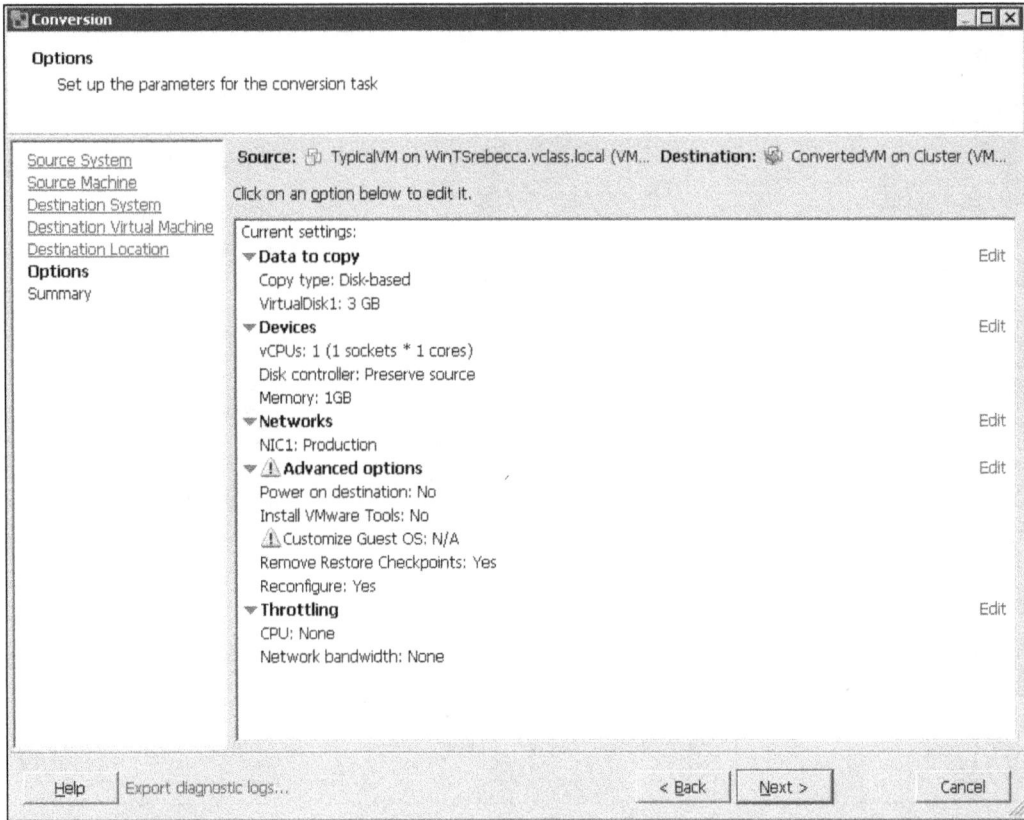

Chapter 3

The following screenshot demonstrates editing the **Devices** section and selecting to modify CPU configuration for the virtual machine to be converted:

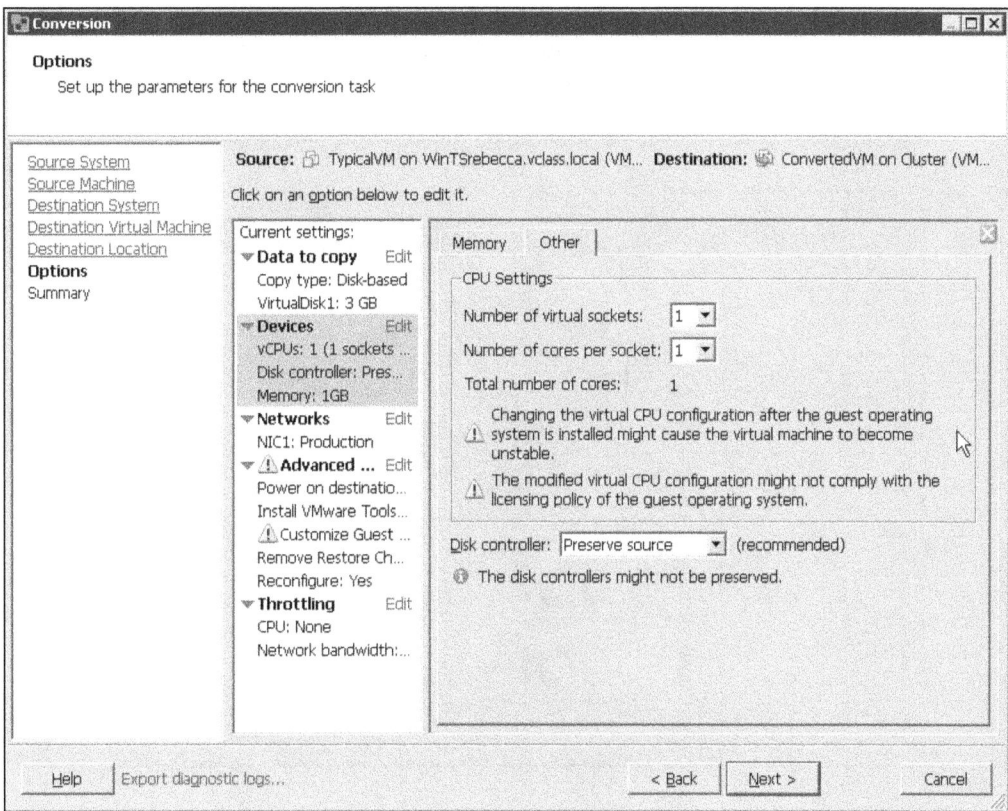

Click on **Next** after configuring the virtual machine as desired.

Summary (pane)

The final pane is **Summary**. It reviews all the information provided and verifies that this is how the virtual machine should be configured. It also verifies the inventory location where the virtual machine should be placed upon completion of the conversion process. The **Summary** pane is shown in the following screenshot:

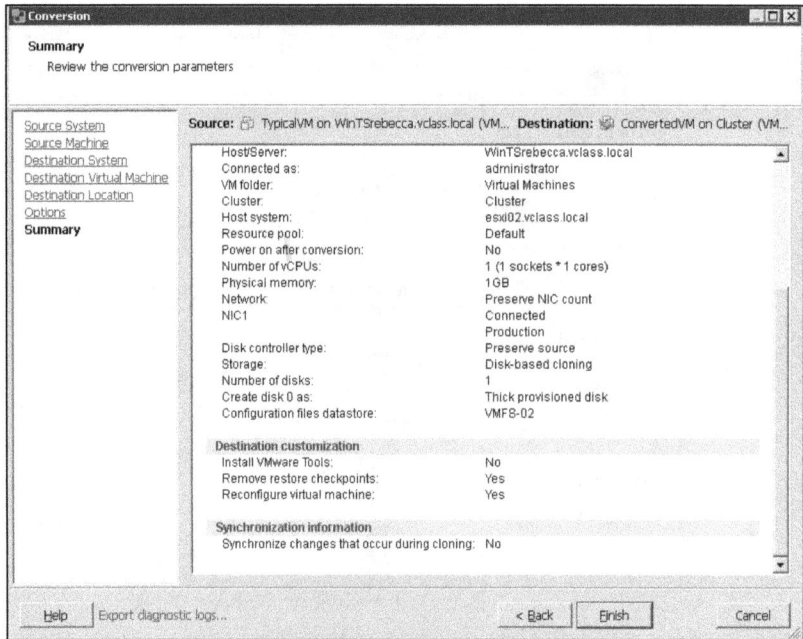

Select the **Finish** button to begin the conversion process.

Summary

Customization specifications can be created to ensure that all hostname, IP addresses, SIDs, and so on are unique to each virtual machine. Virtual machines can be quickly deployed from the template. Use templates to have a base image that is preconfigured and patched, that many virtual machines can be created from, and that can determine a desired configuration for the virtual hardware. A virtual machine can be cloned whether it is powered on or powered off. Preconfigured virtual appliances can be downloaded and easily deployed into the vCenter inventory. Use VMware vCenter Converter Standalone to provision a virtual machine from an existing physical machine or other supported image types.

The next chapter will take a deeper look at some of the advanced virtual machine settings. This will include CPUID, CPU affinity, VMM, and VMware Tools.

4
Advanced Virtual Machine Settings

An administrator can modify many advanced configurations of a virtual machine. These advanced configurations will affect the virtual machine's functionality, compatibility, and performance. This chapter will cover some of these settings, including the virtual machine monitor mode, CPU hot plug, memory hot add, CPUID mask, and CPU affinity. The installation of VMware Tools will also be covered. VMware Tools provide important drivers and performance information to your virtual machines. This should be installed and kept up to date at all times.

In this chapter you will learn the following:

- Virtual machine monitor (VMM)
- CPU hot plug / memory hot add
- CPUID mask
- CPU affinity
- .vswp file location
- Other advanced options
- Installing VMware Tools

Introducing the virtual machine monitor

The **virtual machine monitor** (**VMM**) process runs in the VMkernel and consists of the vCPU and the **memory management unit** (**MMU**). This VMM is responsible for the virtualization of the guest OS instructions and managing memory. The VMM also passes storage and network I/O requests to the VMkernel while passing all other requests to the **Virtual Machine Executable** (**VMX**) process. The combination of techniques used to virtualize the instruction set and memory is known as the **monitor mode**.

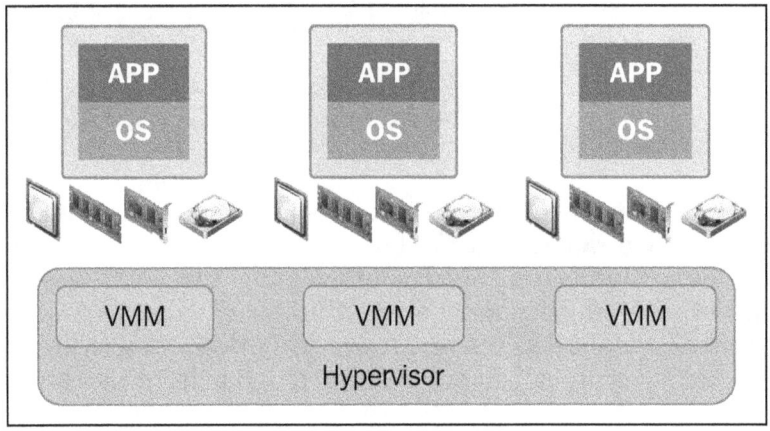

Understanding monitor modes

The VMM can implement the monitor mode with software techniques, hardware techniques, or a combination of both. ESXi can automatically determine whether virtual machines should use hardware support for virtualization based on the processor type and the virtual machine. The virtualization technology is a common feature of modern processors. However, there are some use cases for specific workloads where overriding the automatic selection can provide better performance (for example, Java or Apache servers).

There are three valid monitor mode combinations:

- **BT**: This comprises binary translation and shadow page tables and foundation for VMware virtualization. CPU software virtualization is the traditional method of running a 32-bit guest operating system using an x86 instruction set in a virtualized configuration. The VMM would exist as a software that operates at ring 0 to present the hardware to the guest operating system, which is pushed up to the less privileged ring 1. Direct executions can still occur; the VMM traps all of the guest operating system requests, caches them, and sends them directly to the physical CPU.

- **HV**: This comprises AMD-V or Intel VT-x and shadow page tables (first generation). The execution is offloaded to the physical CPU, but the MMU is done by software using shadow page tables. If an application has several processes to handle, the remapping of the process address space will potentially be slower using hardware virtualization. But running a process tree will be much faster by giving it directly to the physical CPU. The VMM runs at a root mode privileged level. The guest OS operates at ring 0, and it performs direct executions to the physical processor. The VMM allows the CPU to be granted directly to the guest OS's applications. The guest OS owns the physical CPU. The virtual machine filters out special handling requests such as reboots, and it hands these off to the VMM to be handled by the vCPU. Otherwise, this is a case where if the physical processor honored that request, it would reset the entire physical machine.

- **HWMMU**: This comprises AMD-V with RV or Intel VT-x with EPT (second generation). The execution is offloaded to the physical CPU, as described in first generation, but memory is now handled in the hardware using a technique called either Intel **Extended Page Tables** (**EPT**) or AMD **Rapid Virtual Indexing** (**RVI**). There is a cache or table named as **Translation Lookaside Buffer** (**TLB**). The TLB is supposed to take pages from all over the physical memory and make them appear to be contiguous to the virtualized guest OS. This TLB is a component on the CPU whose job it is to translate random physical pages and map them into contiguous pages that look like real and well-organized memory to the guest OS. Every process will have its own memory page table in the TLB, and that's why the TLB should have some measure of cache so it can quickly reference these without having to actually process these things over and over.

x86 operating systems are designed to run directly on physical hardware so they assume full control of this computer hardware. The x86 architecture offers four levels of privilege to operating systems and applications so as to manage access to the computer hardware. These four levels are ring 0, ring 1, ring 2, and ring 3. The operating system needs direct access to hardware and memory, so it must execute its privileged instructions in ring 0. User-level applications generally run in ring 3.

Shadow page tables use virtual memory pages that are contiguous or all lined up next to one another from the view of the guest operating system. But, when we map to the physical memory pages, the real pages of memory may be non-contiguous. This is how the guest operating system maps virtual memory addresses to physical addresses. So, we translate host pages to the guest, and the vMMU translates the physical memory to the guest's virtual memory. The guest operating system has no idea it's accessing the physical memory through guest addresses to host the physical machine's addresses. This is demonstrated in the following diagram:

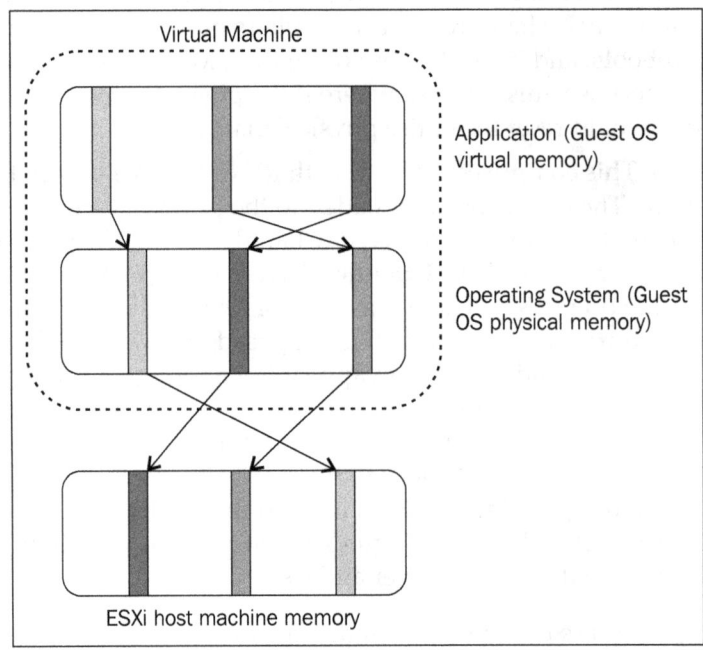

For most of the application workloads, the default monitor mode specified by the VMM is the best. The default monitor mode will be chosen based upon the underlying physical processor features and the guest operating system. Some applications will have better performance when overriding the default monitor mode, but this is not a common configuration. Keep the default, unless there is a reason to override. A few examples include Apache servers can perform better when using hardware virtualization and Java applications will vary based upon the size of the memory pages (with large pages, hardware virtualization generally performs better; with small pages, software virtualization performs better). Some applications are more prone to TLB misses than others.

> A TLB miss occurs when an application that requested a memory address is not present in a TLB cache and the page table has to be consulted instead.

Should it be desired to override the default monitor mode:

1. Right click the virtual machine in the vCenter Server inventory
2. Choose **Edit Settings**.
3. Under virtual hardware, expand **CPU**.

You will see a section called **CPU/MMU Virtualization**, as shown in the following screenshot. From here, click on the dropdown box and make a selection:

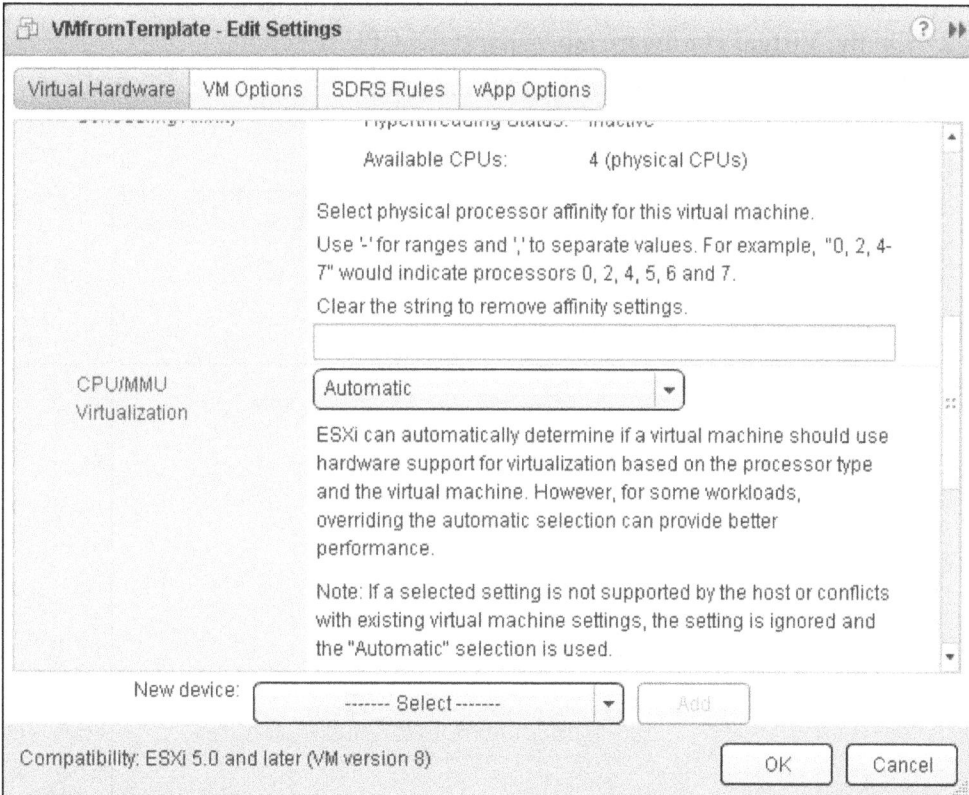

Once the configuration has been made, click on **OK**.

Though the virtual machine can either be powered on or off while changing the monitor mode, it must be restarted, suspended, or migrated using vMotion in order for the change to take effect.

Advanced Virtual Machine Settings

Enabling CPU hot plug / memory hot add

Enabling hot plug and/or hot add allows you to add more CPU and memory resources, respectively, when the virtual machine is powered on.

Virtual machines do not support hot add (adding memory) and hot plug by default. This capability will need to be enabled on a per virtual machine basis in order to utilize it. The virtual hardware version needs to be 7 or greater, so an upgrade may be necessary. Not all guest operating systems support this functionality; make sure to verify compatibility by referring to VMware and the guest operating system documentation before enabling.

To enable this feature, the virtual machine must be shut down. Once powered off:

1. Right click the virtual machine and select **Edit Settings**.
2. On the **Virtual Hardware** tab, expand the **CPU** selection.
3. Check the box next to **Enable CPU Hot Add**.

This is shown in the following screenshot:

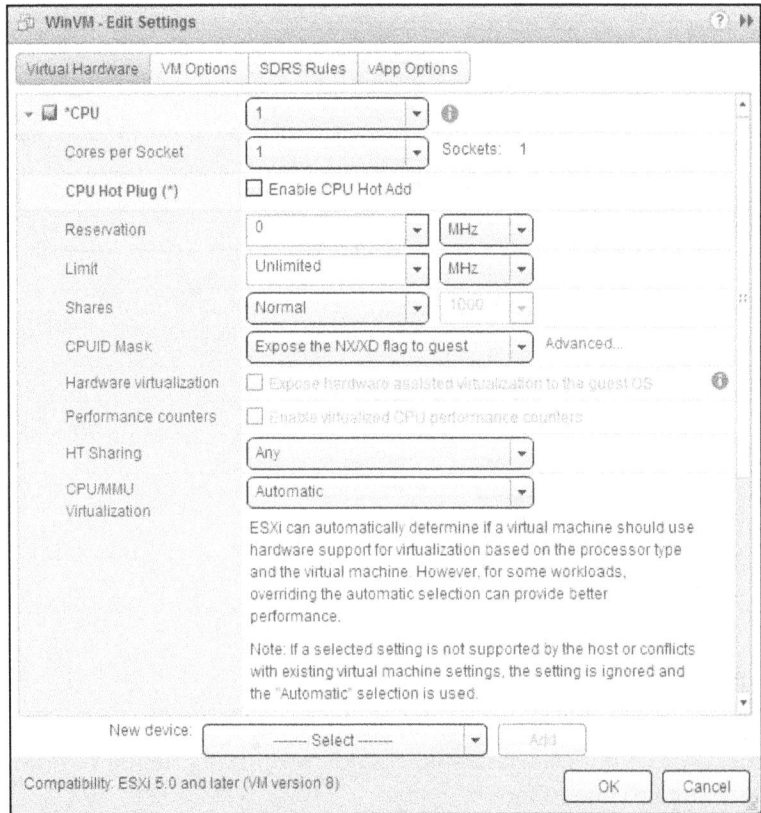

Chapter 4

In order to enable this for memory, expand the **Memory** selection and check the box next to **Memory Hot Plug**.

Once enabled, power on the virtual machine. If more resources are needed, simply right-click on the virtual machine and select **Edit Settings**. Increase the CPU and/or memory as needed while the virtual machine is powered on, as shown in the following screenshot:

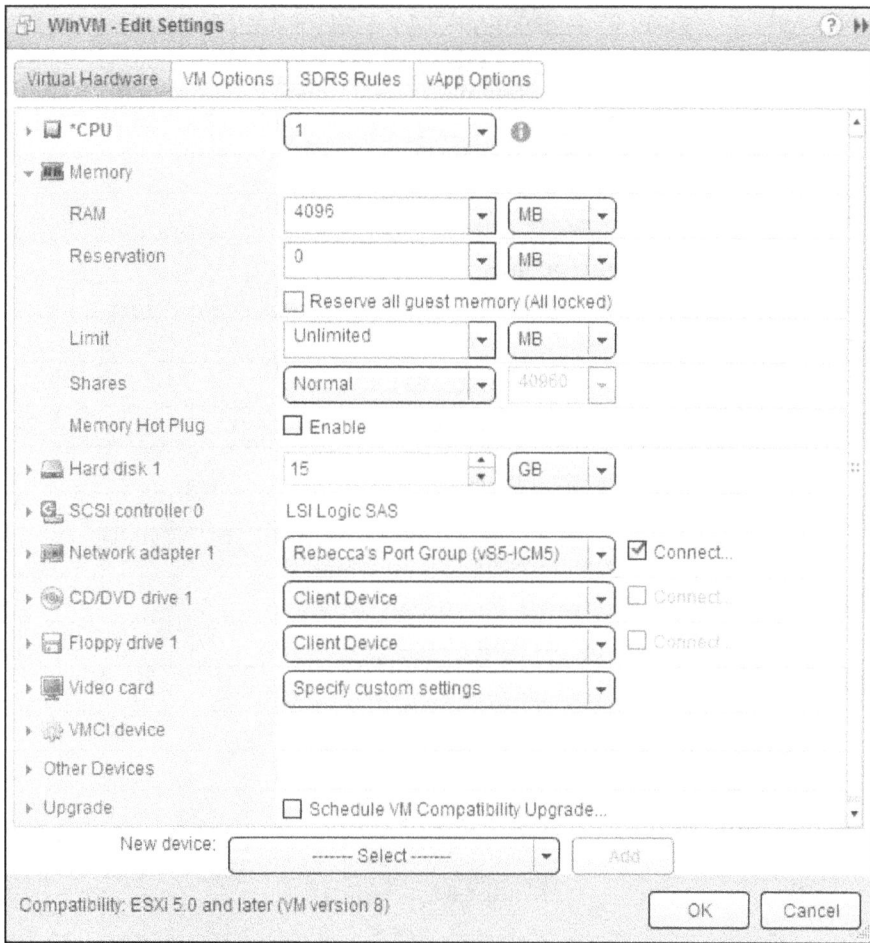

 Keep in mind that even though you will now be able to add memory or CPU resources, resources once added cannot be reduced.

The CPUID mask

CPU identification (CPUID) masks control the CPU features made visible to the guest operating system of the virtual machine. Masking CPU NX/XD bits can make a virtual machine more compatible to migrate to the ESXi hosts. Leaving the CPU NX/XD bit exposed serves the security purpose of marking memory pages as data-only to prevent buffer overflow attacks and malicious software exploits. Check http://vmware.com/kb/1993 for more information. The CPU features are compared with vCenter Server to determine whether to allow or disallow a vMotion migration. Masking the AMD **No eXecute (NX)** and the Intel **eXecute Disable (XD)** bits prevents the virtual machine from using these features, allowing the migration to the ESXi hosts that do not have this capability. If the NX/XD bit is visible, the virtual machine can only be migrated to the ESXi hosts on which the feature is enabled.

To modify the CPUID mask:

1. Shut down the virtual machine
2. Right click the virtual machine in the vCenter Server inventory, selecting **Edit Settings**.
3. On the **Virtual Hardware** tab, expand **CPU**.
4. Make a selection for the **CPUID Mask** configuration.

This is shown in the following screenshot:

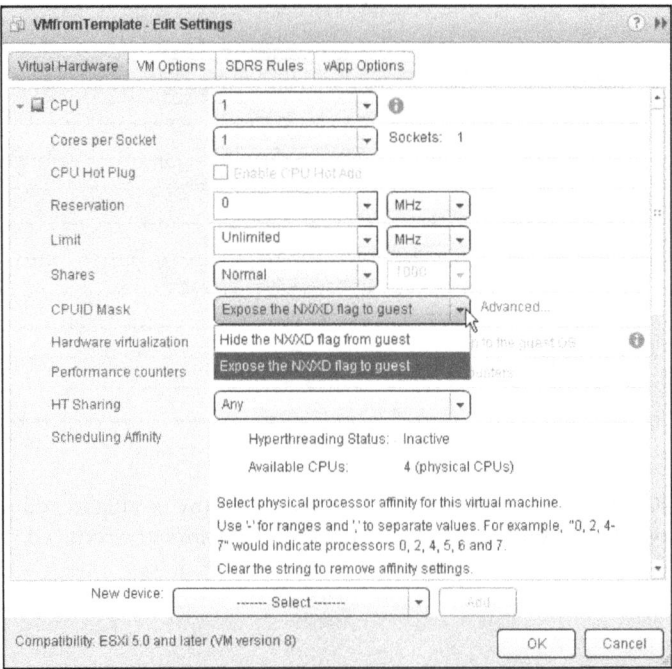

The CPU affinity setting

The CPU affinity setting allows you to restrict the assignment of the virtual machine to a subset of the available processors. This effectively assigns each virtual machine to the processors in the specified affinity set. CPU affinity not only applies to the virtual machines' vCPUs but also all other worlds associated with the virtual machine. A world is similar to a process in a conventional operating system that can be scheduled on a processor. This can include an emulated screen, a keyboard, mouse, CD-ROMs, and so on.

CPU affinity can prevent ESXi systems from performing automatic DRS load balancing across its processors and the host's ability to meet reservations specified for the virtual machine. The CPU scheduler may not be able to manage a virtual machine that is configured using CPU affinity. Use this feature sparingly due to these potential issues.

To configure CPU affinity:

1. Power off the virtual machine.
2. Right click the virtual machine in the vCenter Server inventory and select **Edit Settings**.
3. On the **Virtual Hardware** tab, expand **CPU**.
4. In the **Scheduling Affinity** panel, enter a comma-separated list of hyphenated processor ranges.

Advanced Virtual Machine Settings

For example, 0,2-4 would be CPUs 0, 2, 3, and 4. You must provide as many processor affinities as the number of vCPUs configured. To not use CPU affinity, ensure that nothing is entered in the **Scheduling Affinity** panel, as displayed in the following screenshot:

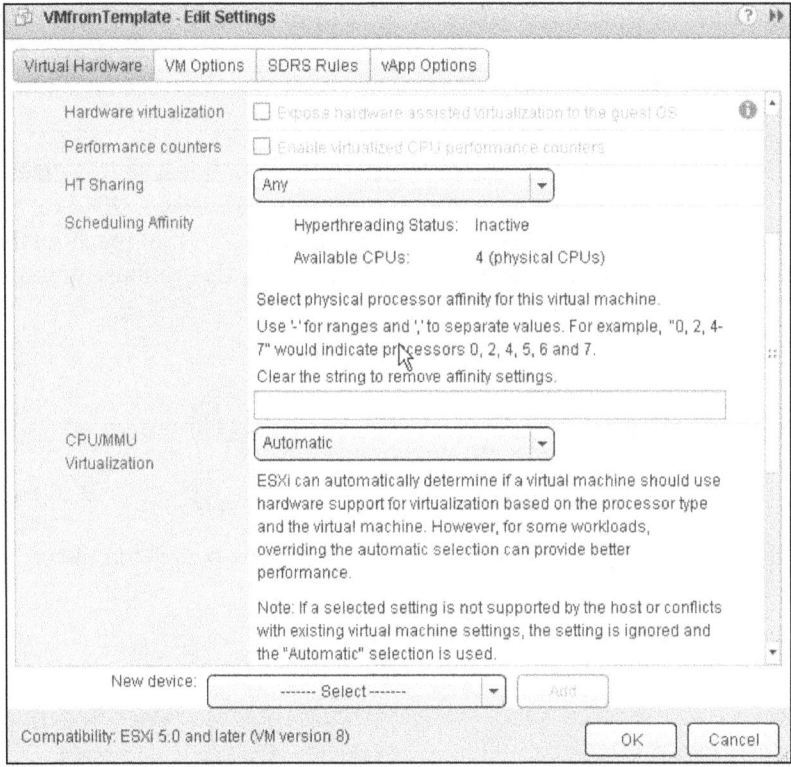

Click on **OK** after checking the configuration.

Setting the .vswp location

The .vswp file can be placed on an alternate location besides the datastore, where all the other files of the virtual machine are stored. An example of this is a high performance database being stored on a datastore other than the .vswp file. This configuration could affect vMotion's performance because the .vswp files may need to be copied between datastores if this is not taken into consideration for the design.

> Remember that the size of the `.vswp` file is the configured memory size minus any memory reservation.

To set the `.vswp` file location at the cluster level:

1. Select the cluster in the vSphere Web Client and go to the **Manage** tab.
2. Under the **Settings** tab, click on **General** underneath the **Configuration** section.
3. Select Edit next to **Swap File Location**.

This brings up the dialogue displayed in the following image. By default, the `.vswp` file will be stored in the same directory as the virtual machine. Alternatively, **Datastore specified by host** could be selected, which will allow for the specification of a datastore location at the ESXi host level.

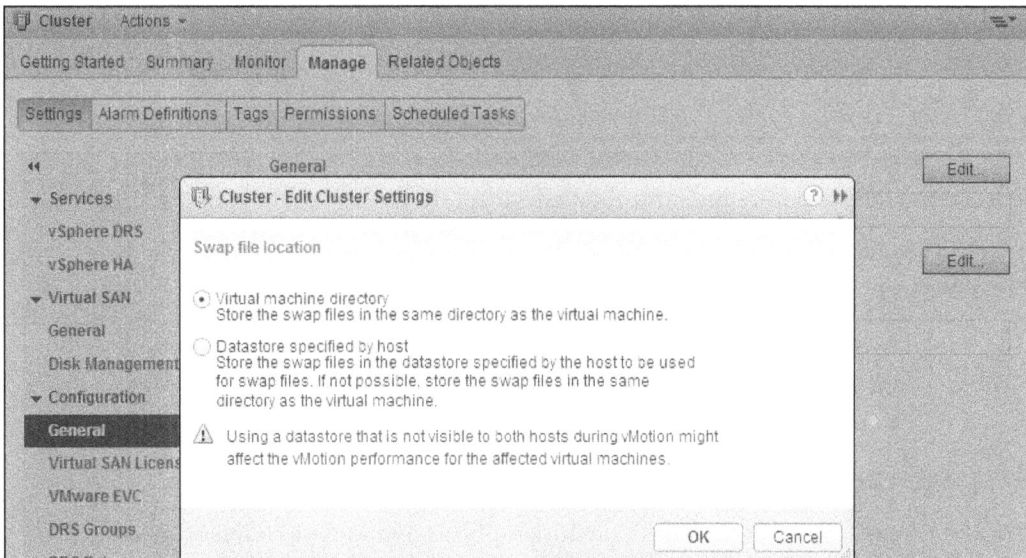

To configure all the virtual machines on an ESXi host to use an alternate `.vswp` file location other than the datastore on which the rest of the virtual machine files are located:

1. Go to the Manage tab of the selected ESXi host.
2. Select the Edit Swap File Location and then choose Use a specific datastore.

This is shown in the following screenshot:

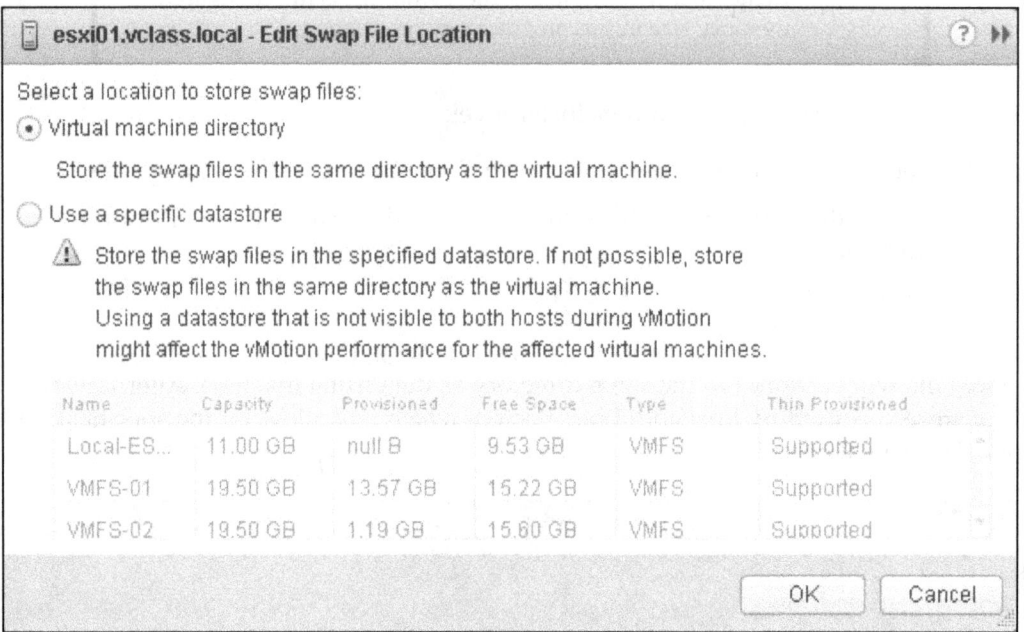

Choose the desired datastore and then click on **OK**.

This setting will take effect once the virtual machines on the ESXi host are power-cycled.

This can also be configured at the virtual machine level, but it can quickly become challenging to manage the different file locations. Use this sparingly.

Viewing other advanced options

There are many advanced virtual machine options available to adjust. This section will go over some of the more common advanced configurations that may be modified.

To modify the virtual machine, right-click in the vCenter Server inventory and select **Edit Settings**.

The General Options section

In the **VM Options** tab, under **General Options**, you will see **VM Name**; this specifies what the virtual machine's name appears as in the vCenter Server inventory, not necessarily what the computer name is in the guest operating system. The **VM Config File** option shows the entire path to reach the .vmx file and which datastore it is located on. The **VM Working Location** option details the location of the virtual machine's directory where its files are located. The **Guest OS** row will show **Windows**, **Linux**, or **Other**; the **Guest OS Version** will display the exact version within that **Guest OS** type, as shown in the following screenshot:

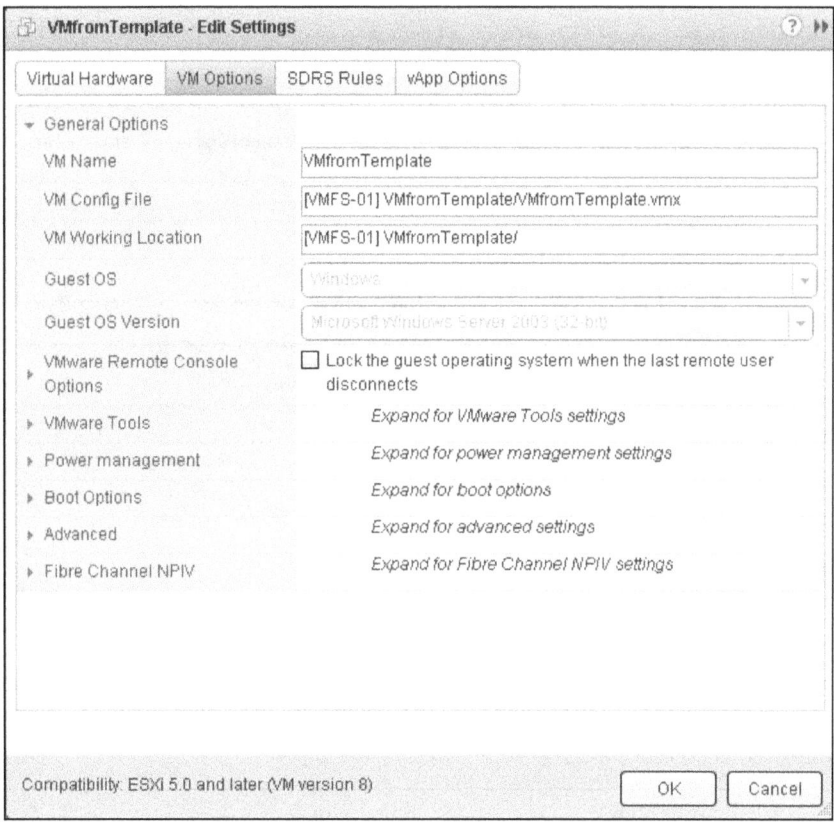

Advanced Virtual Machine Settings

The VMware Remote Console Options section

Under the **VMware Remote Console Options** section, there are two available options: **Guest OS lock** and **Maximum number of sessions**, as shown in the following screenshot. **Guest OS lock** locks the guest operating system upon disconnection of the last remote user. The **Maximum number of sessions** option limits the number of simultaneous connections to this virtual machine.

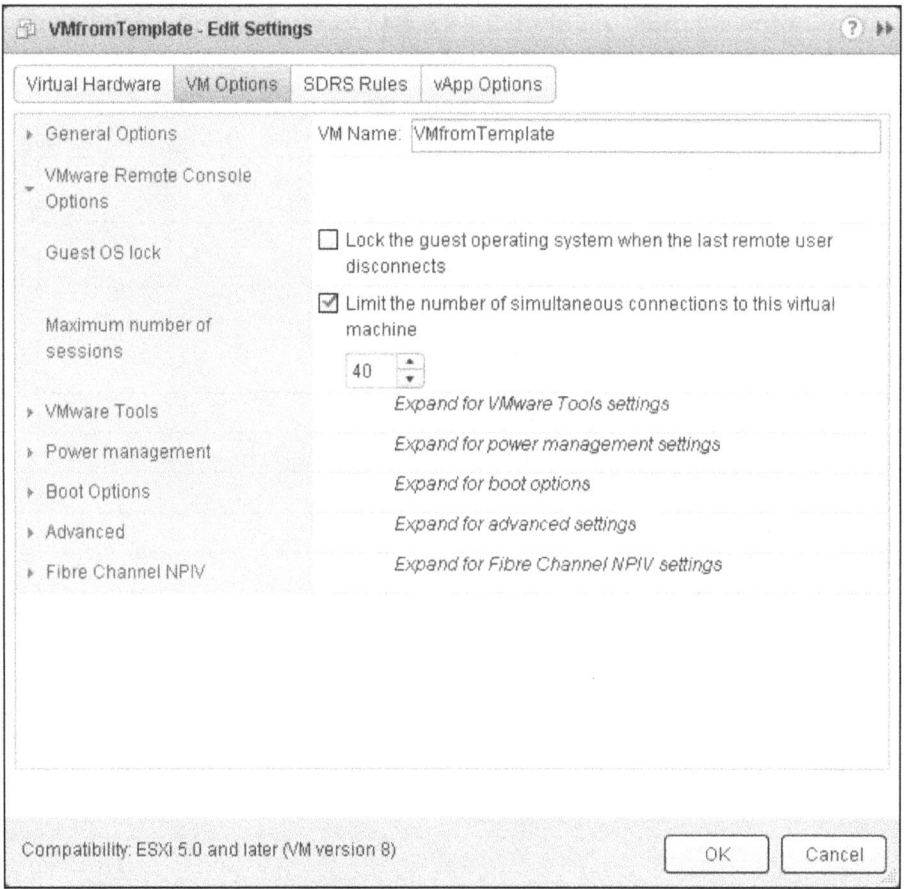

The VMware Tools section

The VMware Tools section controls how VMware Tools in the VMs respond to certain external events such as whether a virtual machine will power off or shut down when the stop button is clicked on. You can use these controls to customize the different power buttons, determining whether clicking on the top button or recycle button will cleanly shut down the guest operating system or a hard power off.

VMware Tools can be set to run certain scripts when specific events occur. Scripts are set in the **VMware Tools** dialog box in the guest OS and then configured to run under **VM Options**.

There is an option to **Check and upgrade VMware Tools before each power on**, as shown in the next screenshot. When selected, this will help keep VMware Tools updated so that the virtual machines always have the newest drivers. This requires VMware Tools to already be installed in the guest operating system. The option checks whether the currently installed version is the most recent of the ESXi host version and, if not, whether it will initiate the upgrade. The final VMware Tools option is **Synchronize guest time with host**, which will use the ESXi host that the virtual machine is residing on for time settings.

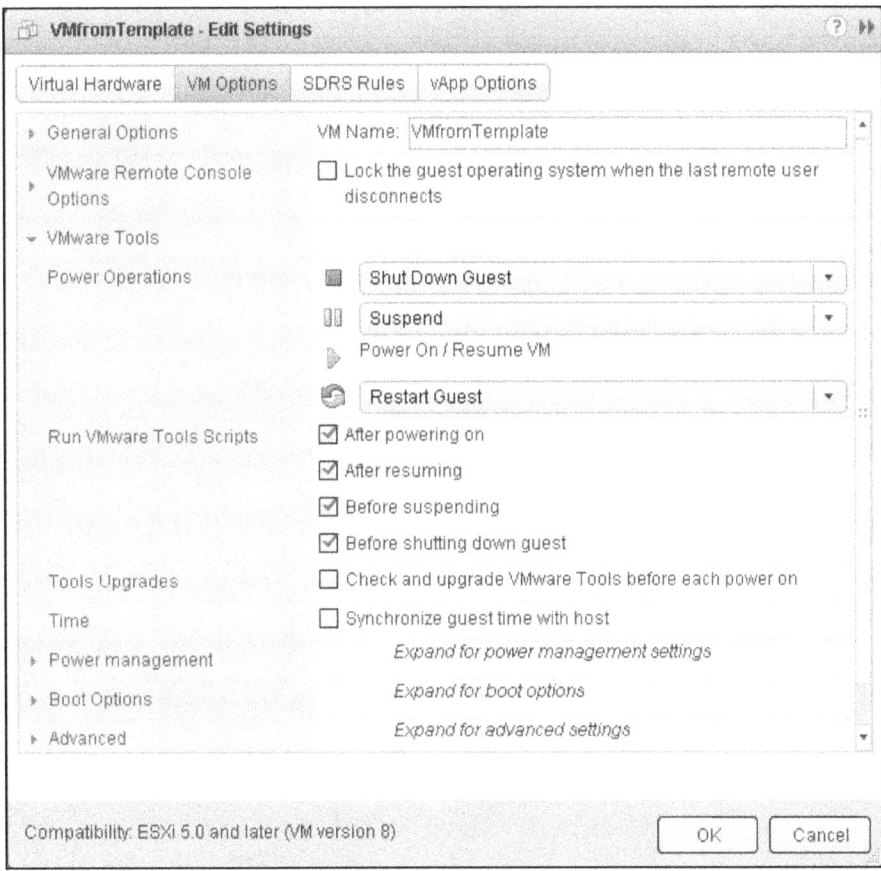

The Boot Options section

When you build a virtual machine and select a guest operating system, a **Firmware** type BIOS or **Extensible Firmware Interface** (**EFI**) is selected by default (depends on firmware supported by the operating system; for example, Mac OS X Server supports only EFI).

Boot Delay allows you to a set a delay before the virtual machine is turned on. This can be useful to stagger VM startups when several VMs are being powered on.

Force BIOS setup is used to change BIOS settings (such as changing the device boot order). The next time the virtual machine boots up, it goes straight into the BIOS.

Failed Boot Recovery has the virtual machine retry booting after 10 seconds if the virtual machine fails to find a boot device, as shown in the following screenshot. Checking the box and then entering the number of seconds before retrying boot can adjust this interval.

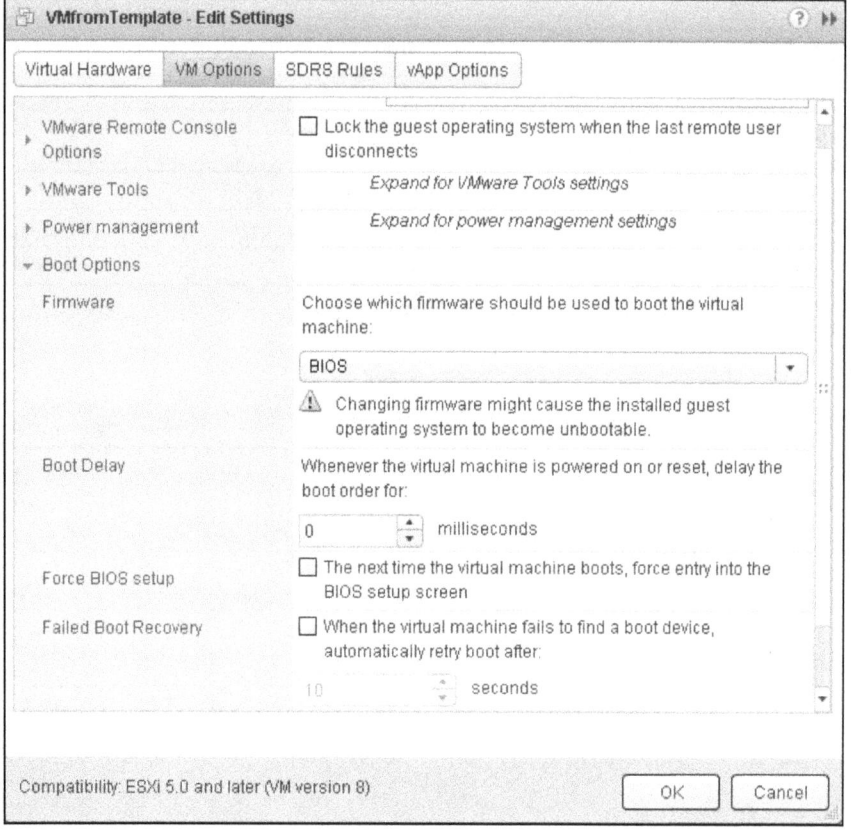

Click on **OK** after making all desired advanced configurations.

Installing VMware Tools

VMware Tools is a utility suite that enhances the performance of a virtual machine's guest OS. If VMware Tools is not installed in the guest operating system, the guest will be lacking in some important functionality. The VMware Tools utility improves virtual machine management by replacing the generic OS drivers with VMware drivers optimized for virtual hardware, as well as with more counters within the performance monitor, the ability to quiesce, and so on.

Installing VMware Tools in a Windows virtual machine

All supported Windows guest operating systems support VMware Tools.

Right-click on the virtual machine in the inventory and navigate to **All vCenter Actions** | **Guest OS** | **Install/Upgrade VMware Tools** within the vSphere Web Client. Alternatively, there is a hyperlink available in the **Summary** tab of a virtual machine. This is demonstrated in the following screenshot:

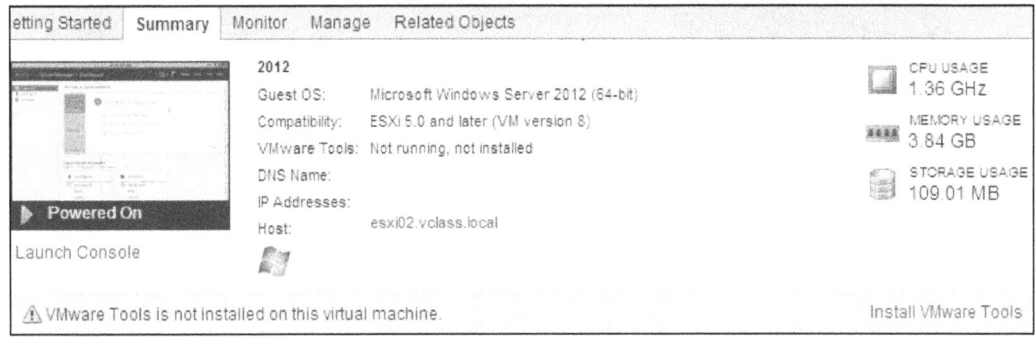

Advanced Virtual Machine Settings

The VMware Tools installer will initialize within the guest operating system, as shown in the next screenshot. This may or may not pop up automatically. This is dependent on whether the auto run functionality is enabled; if disabled, you will need to browse to the CD-ROM and run the setup.

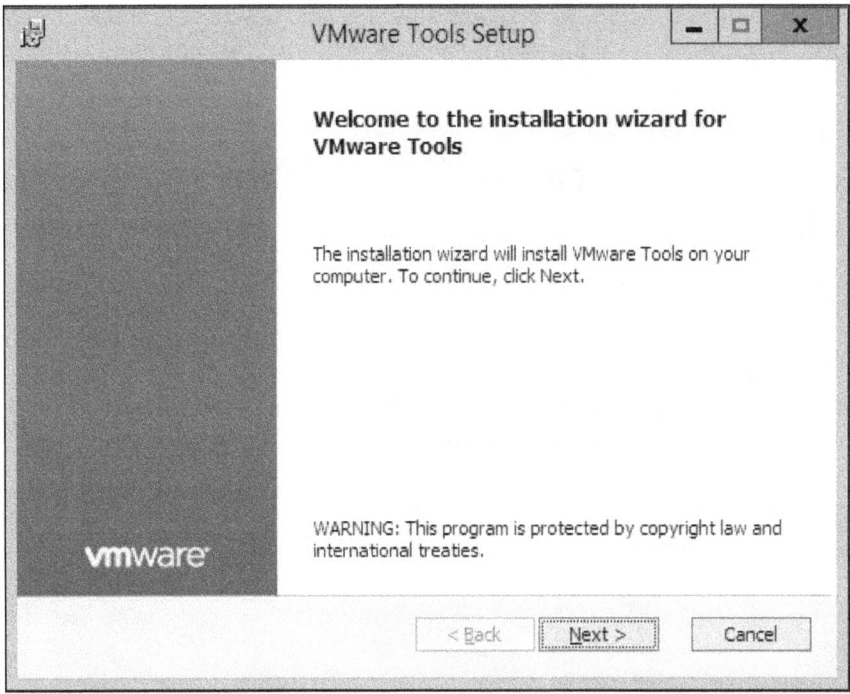

The installer will soon finish the initialization process and you can begin with the installation.

Click on **Next** to get started.

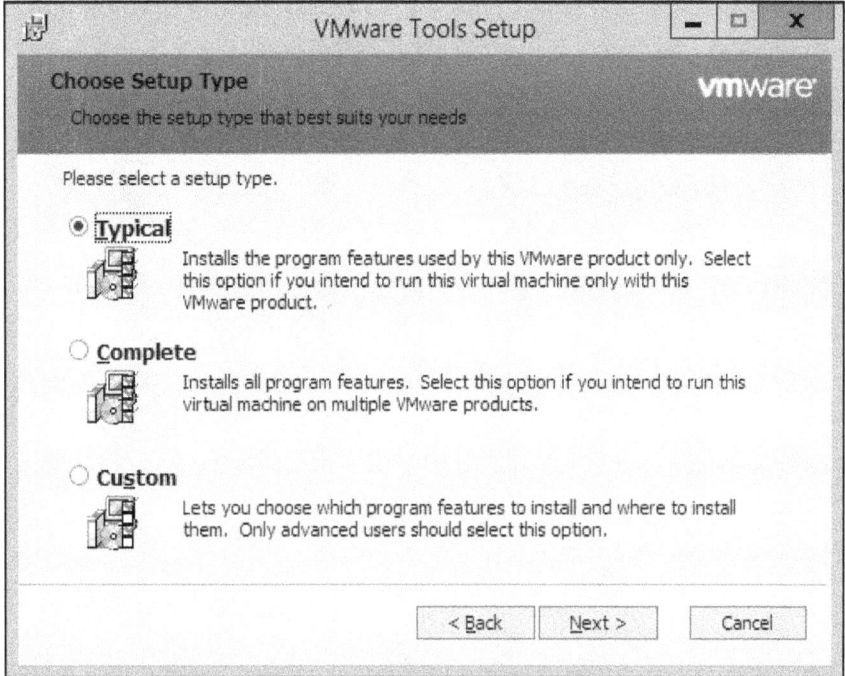

Select the setup type; there are three options available: **Typical**, **Complete**, and **Custom**.

- The **Typical** setup only installs the features that are used by the VMware product in use.
- A **Complete** setup will install all program features used by any VMware product (ESXi, Workstation, and so on).
- With the **Custom** setup, you can choose which features should be installed and where they should be installed.

Click on **Next** after selecting the setup type.

Advanced Virtual Machine Settings

Once all selections have been made, click on the **Install** button to begin the installation process, as shown in the following screenshot:

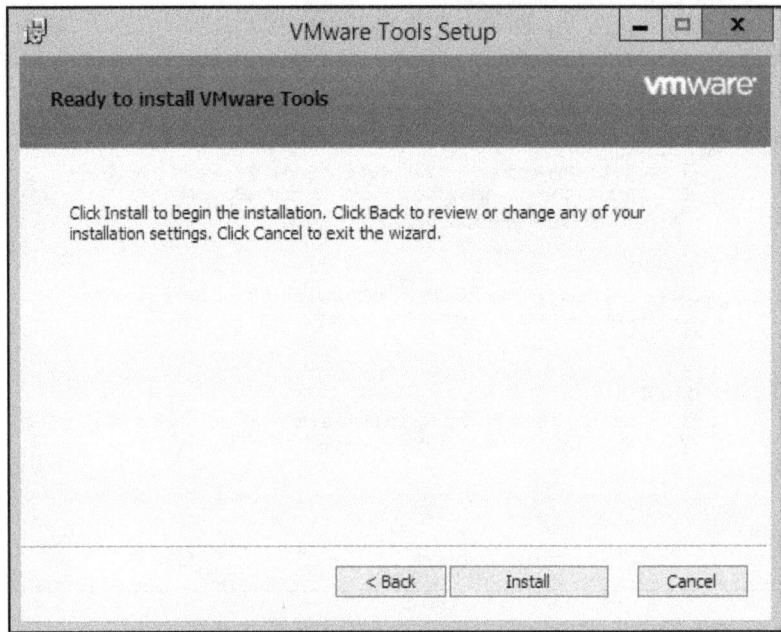

Click on **Finish** once the installation is over, as shown in the following screenshot:

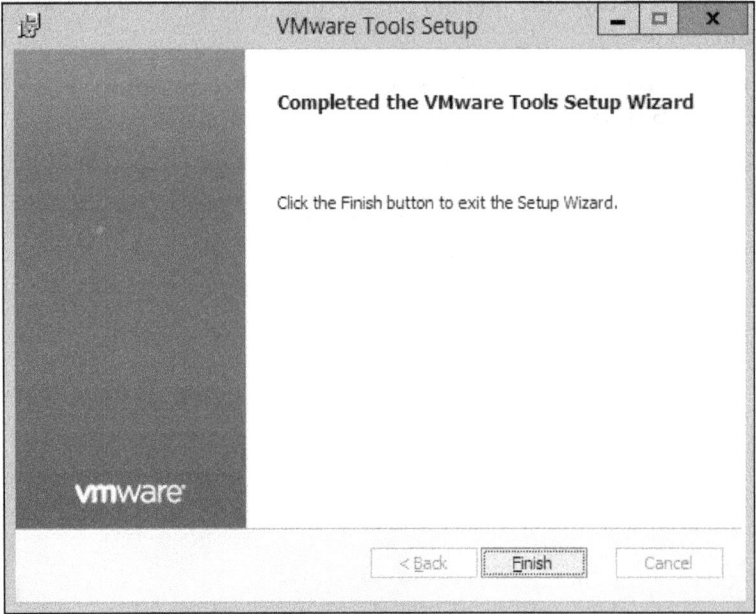

Installing VMware Tools in a Linux virtual machine

Right-click on the virtual machine in the inventory and navigate to **All vCenter Actions** | **Guest OS** | **Install/Upgrade VMware Tools** within the vSphere Web Client. Alternatively, there is a hyperlink available in the **Summary** tab of a virtual machine. This is demonstrated in the following screenshot:

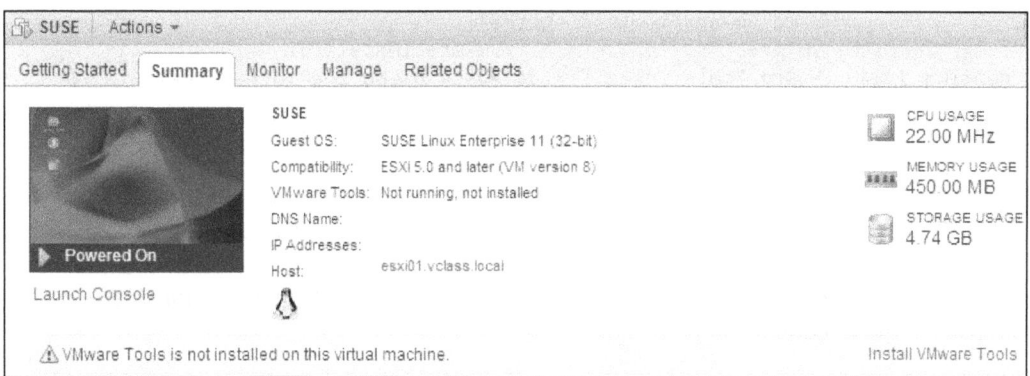

As root, mount the VMware Tools CD-ROM image and check to a working directory, such as `/tmp`, as shown in the following screenshot. Untar the VMware Tools file (this is demonstrated at the bottom of the screenshot) by using the following command:

`tar zxf /mnt/cdrom/VMwareTools-#.#.#-<####>.tar.gz`

```
linux-3fgb:~/Desktop # cd /tmp
linux-3fgb:/tmp # ls
cdrom            orbit-admin              virtual-root.qnVLTq
.esd-0           orbit-gdm                virtual-root.RjkRwa
.esd-1000        orbit-root               vmware-admin
.esd-107         pulse-4SilGIVLhG4J       VMwareTools-9.4.0-1280544.tar.gz
gpg-Plk17f       pulse-BoC73LIA3js3       vmware-tools-distrib
.ICE-unix        pulse-nYrn3ikW8Zn3       .X0-lock
keyring-3COWhv   unique                   .X11-unix
keyring-/root Vd6 virtual-admin.OYbavZ    .X2-lock
keyring   SJq    virtual-admin.TNZrIF     xwlog
linux-3fgb:/tmp # tar zxf /mnt/cdrom/VMwareTools-9.4.0-1280544.tar.gz
```

Unmount the CD-ROM image using the following command:

`umount /dev/cdrom`

Advanced Virtual Machine Settings

Run the installer using the following commands:

```
cd vmware-tools-distrib
./vmware-install.pl
```

Respond to the configuration questions prompted by the installer. Pressing *Enter* will accept the default value, as shown in the following screenshot:

```
linux-3fgb:/tmp # umount /dev/cdrom
linux-3fgb:/tmp # cd vmware-tools-distrib/
linux-3fgb:/tmp/vmware-tools-distrib # ./vmware-install.pl
Creating a new VMware Tools installer database using the tar4 format.

Installing VMware Tools.

In which directory do you want to install the binary files?
[/usr/bin]
```

Once the installation is complete, you will see the message that is demonstrated in the following screenshot:

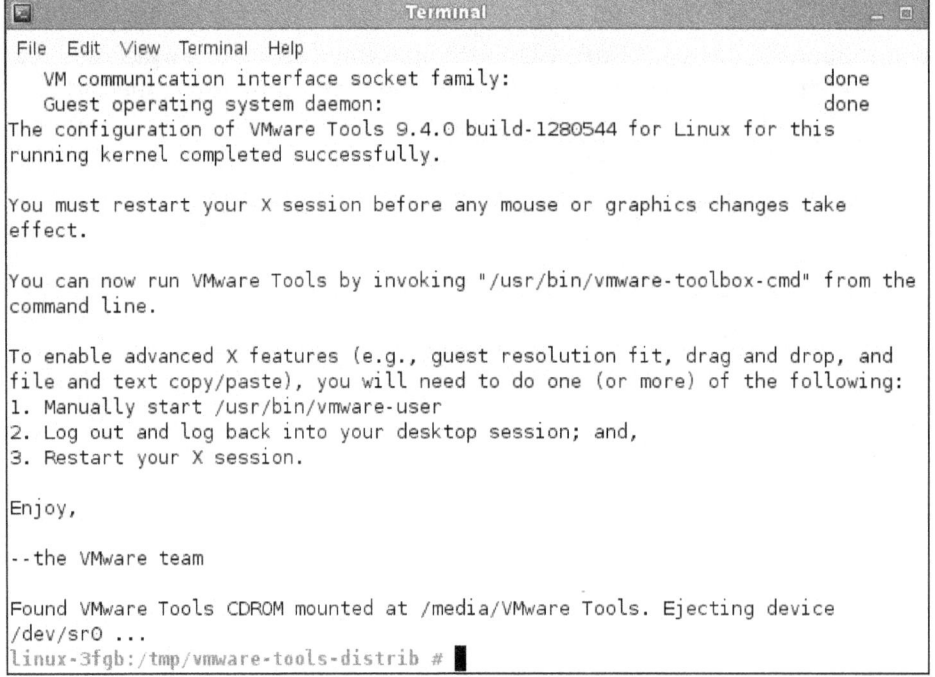

Log off from the root account once finished. View the **Summary** tab of a virtual machine to determine whether or not VMware Tools are installed, running, and up to date. The following screenshot displays this:

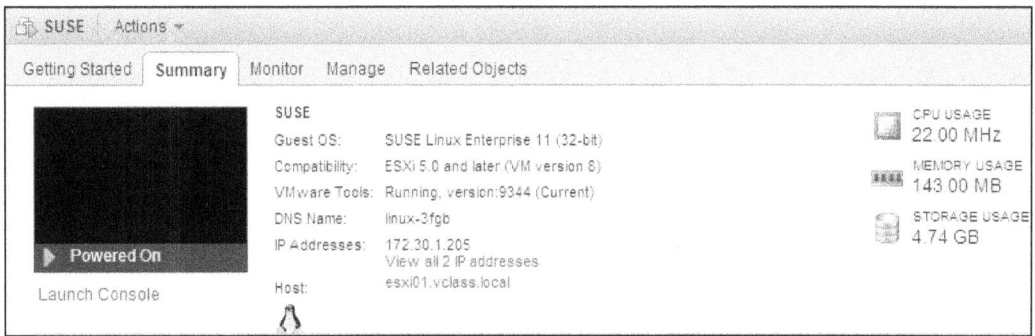

 The installation of VMware Tools may also be scripted. Check http://www.vmware.com/pdf/vmware-tools-installation-configuration.pdf for more information.

Summary

The VMM process runs in the VMkernel and consists of the vCPU and the MMU. The VMM can implement the monitor mode with software techniques, hardware techniques, or a combination of both. CPU hot plug and memory hot add, when enabled, allow for more CPU and memory resources to be added to virtual machines on demand. CPUID masks control the CPU features made visible to the guest operating system of the virtual machine. The CPU affinity setting allows you to restrict the assignment of the virtual machine to a subset of the available processors. The .vswp file can be placed on an alternate location besides the datastore, where all the other files of the virtual machine are stored. Generally, this is done for some sort of performance or storage tiering reason. VMware Tools is a utility suite that enhances the performance of a virtual machine's guest OS, which should be installed in every virtual machine and kept up to date.

The next chapter will discuss how virtual machines running multi-tiered applications can be managed using vApps.

5
Managing Multitiered Applications with vApps

This chapter discovers the power of vSphere vApps. vApps offer amazing functionality and portability that will be desired within your VMware infrastructure. vApps are containers used for holding one or more virtual machines and can be configured as resource pools. Shares, limits, and reservations can be set at the vApp level to dictate how the virtual machines will receive CPU and memory resources. vApps can not only be used as resource pools, but can also be used to share some functionalities with virtual machines. These functionalities include the ability to clone as well as start up and shut down the virtual machines in a specific order. You previously learned how to import an OVF template; this chapter will show you how to export a vApp into an OVF template for distribution.

In this chapter, you will learn:

- How to create a vApp
- vApp options
- Populating a vApp
- Configuring startup and shutdown options

What is a vApp?

A vApp is a container, similar to a resource pool, but with some virtual machine-like functionalities. vSphere is used as a platform for running applications and virtual machines. vApps can be used to package and manage these applications so that they are able to run directly on top of vSphere. Many vendors use vApps as a way to package their applications for quick deployment. For example, VMware has made vCenter Operations Manager available in a vApp format. If you use or administer VMware vCloud Director, then you may be familiar with vApps. Keep in mind that vSphere vApps are slightly different from those available in vCloud.

Since a vApp is a resource pool with extra functionality, it's recommended that resource pools and virtual machines not be made sibling objects within a hierarchy because, by default, resource pools are assigned shares that may not appropriately compare to those assigned to a virtual machine, which can potentially cause performance issues.

vApps offer a multitude of benefits, including:

- Container for one or more virtual machines
- Resource controls (shares, limits, and reservations) for the VMs within the container
- Portability; everything is encapsulated and can be moved to a different virtual infrastructure
- Network information
- Can be started, stopped, or suspended
- Virtual machine startup and shutdown order

> Be aware that the vApp metadata is located in the vCenter Server's database so that the virtual machine in a vApp can be distributed across multiple ESXi hosts. This metadata information could be lost if the vCenter Server database is ever cleared or if the vApp is residing on a standalone ESXi host that is removed from the vCenter Server inventory. Back up the vApps to an OVF package to avoid losing any metadata.

The distribution format for a vApp is **OVF (Open Virtualization Format)**.

Creating a vApp

vApps can be created in folders, on standalone ESXi hosts, within resource pools, other vApps, or in DRS-enabled clusters. To create a vApp, navigate to one of these objects, right-click, and select **New vApp...**. This will launch the **New vApp** wizard.

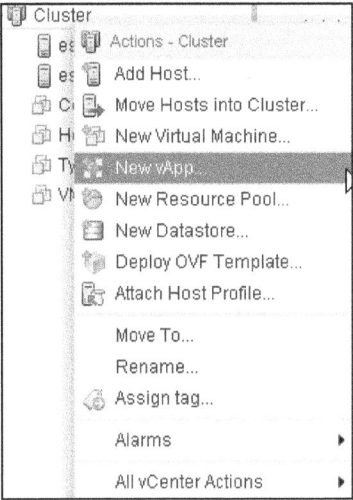

Once the **New vApp** wizard is launched, select **Create a new vApp** to begin the process of creating a vApp from scratch, as shown in the following screenshot:

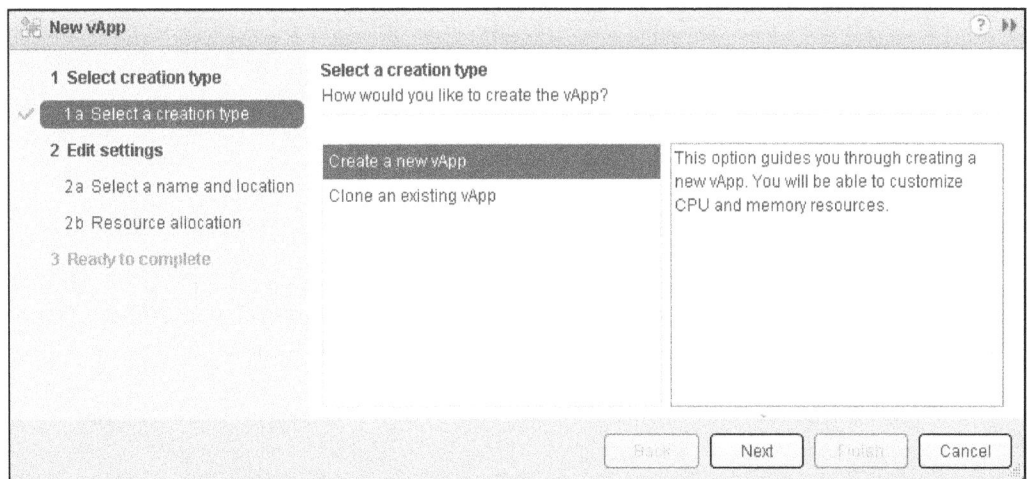

Click on **Next** after making the selection.

Managing Multitiered Applications with vApps

The **Select a name and location** pane allows for the specification of the vApp's name. Make sure to name the vApp appropriately since this will be containing a specific multitiered application. Choose a folder to place the vApp in the **Virtual Machines** and **Templates** inventory views in vCenter.

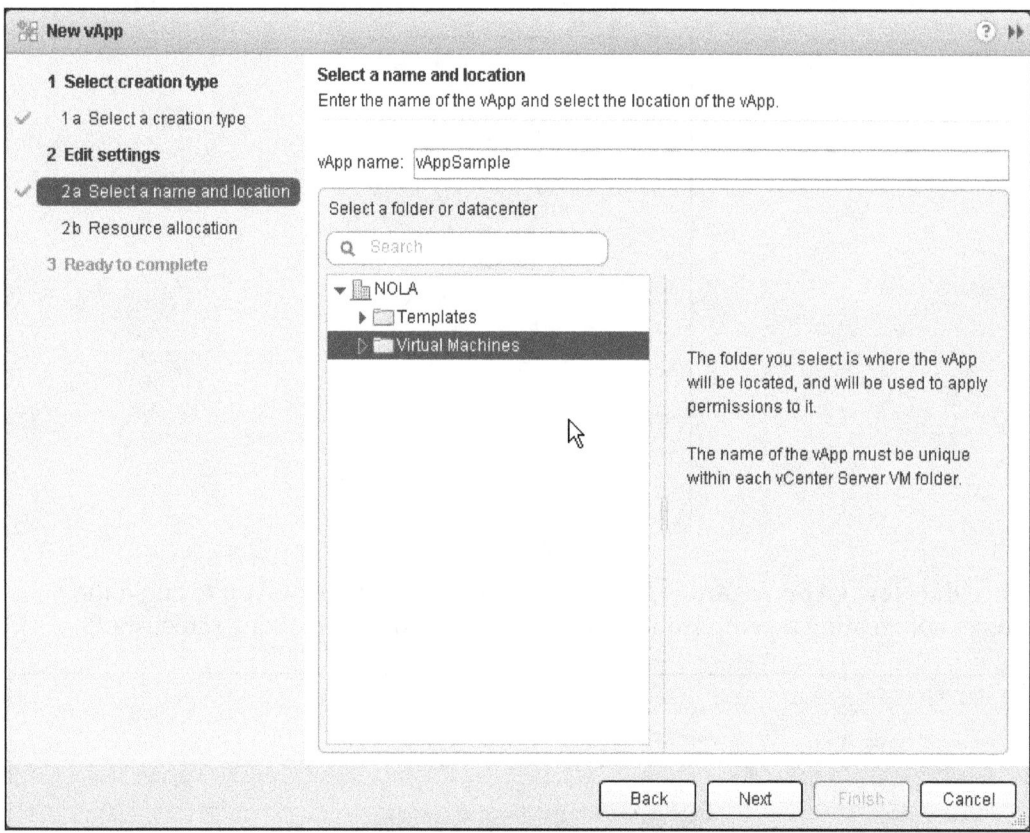

After selecting the correct folder in the **Virtual Machines** and **Templates** views, click on **Next**.

On the **Resource allocation** pane, you are able to apportion memory and CPU resources to the new vApp by using reservations, shares, and limits.

Chapter 5

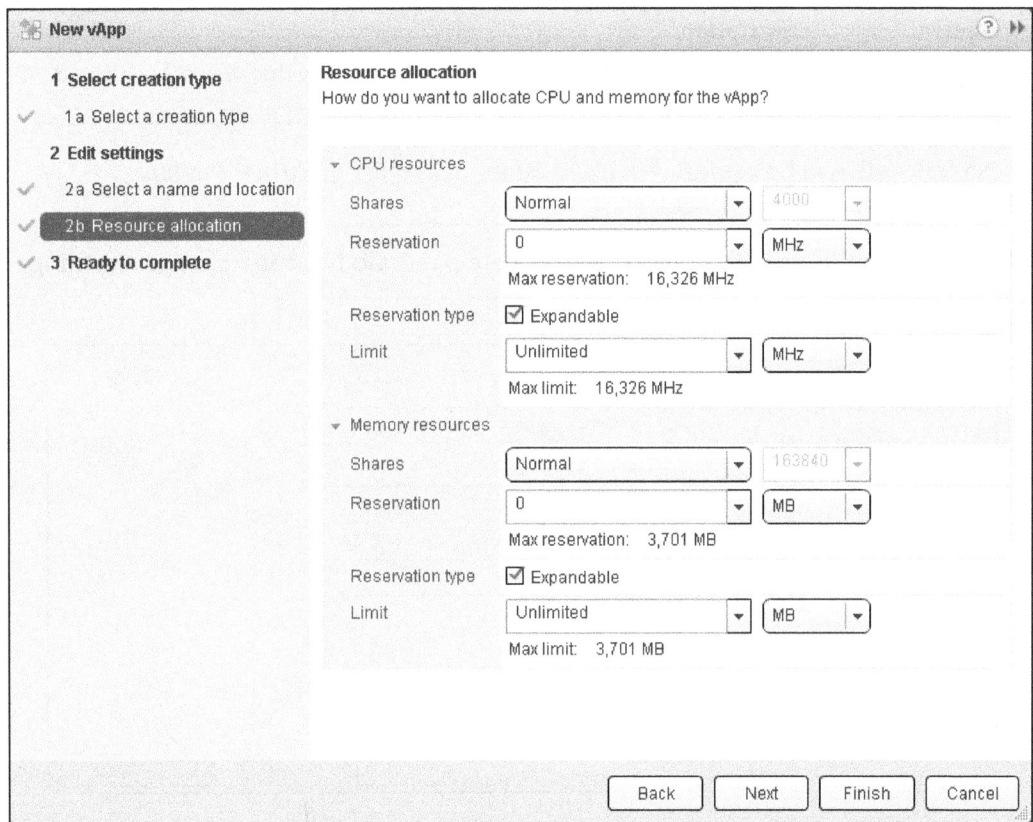

Consult the following table for assistance in making these selections. Click on **Next** after making the selections.

Option	Description
Shares	The value that specifies the relative priority or importance of this vApp's access to a given resource with respect to the parent's total resources. Sibling vApps share resources according to this value. Select **Low**, **Normal**, or **High**; this specifies share values in a 1:2:4 ratio, respectively. Select **Custom** to assign a vApp a specific proportional weight if the default ratio doesn't fit.
Reservation	Guaranteed amount of resource for this vApp. Must be available for the vApp to power on.
Reservation type	If the **Expandable** checkbox is selected, this will make the reservation expandable. This means that if the combined reservations of the virtual machines exceed the reservation of the vApp, the vApp can use resources from its parent resource pools to meet the demand.

[143]

Managing Multitiered Applications with vApps

Option	Description
Limit	Consumption of resources cannot exceed this value. Select **Unlimited** to specify no upper limit.

These concepts will be explored in more detail in *Chapter 6, Virtual Machine Performance and Resource Allocation*.

Check all the settings in the **Ready to complete** pane. Go back and change anything if needed.

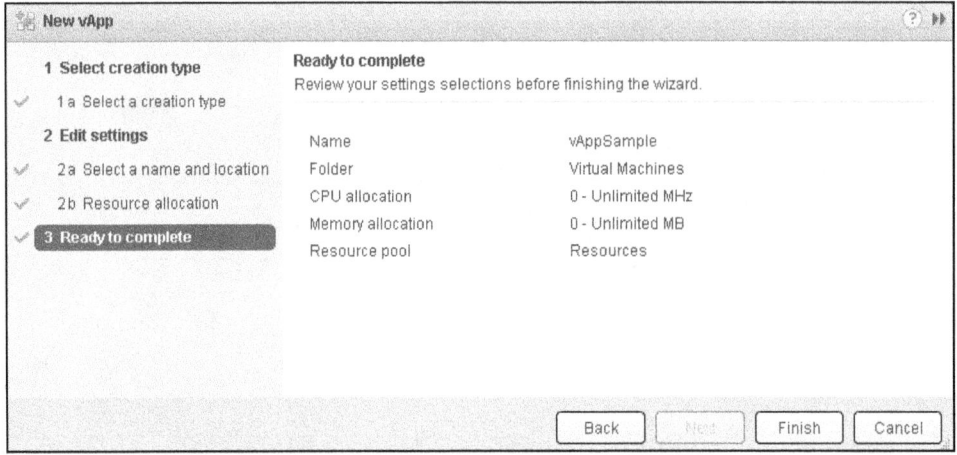

Click on **Finish** when you are done with the vApp settings.

You will now see the vApp that you created in the vCenter Server inventory. To populate this vApp, select an existing virtual machine that isn't already contained in the vApp and drag the object to the target vApp.

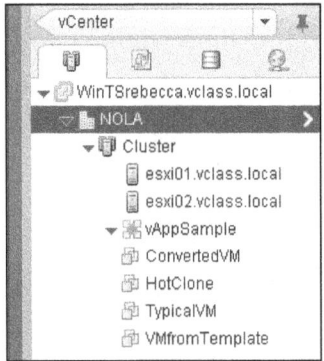

New virtual machines and child vApps may also be created under a vApp.

vApp options

Once the vApp has been created, there are many settings than can be edited as required. To edit the vApp's configuration, right-click on the vApp in the vCenter Server inventory and select **Edit settings**. The **CPU resources** and **Memory resources** sections originally allocated can be adjusted as needed, as shown in the following screenshot:

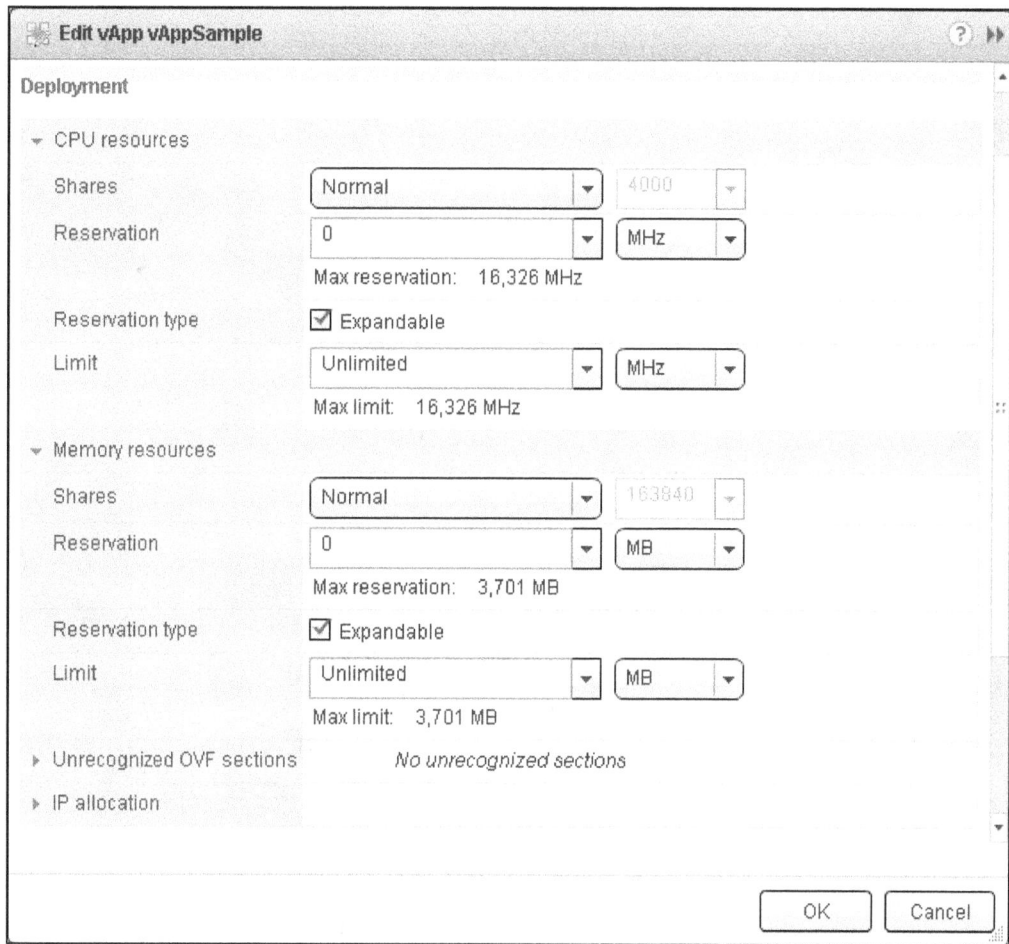

The CPU- and memory-related options can be adjusted at any time after creation. The resource options displayed in the preceding screenshot are the same options that are available when using a resource pool. A vApp is a resource pool with additional features.

IP addressing policies

A setting that everyone should be familiar with is the **IP allocation policy** option. This modifies how IP addresses can be allocated to the virtual machines for the vApp if IP pools are in use. The following screenshot displays that the vApp is using the **Static - Manual** option; there are however multiple options to choose from.

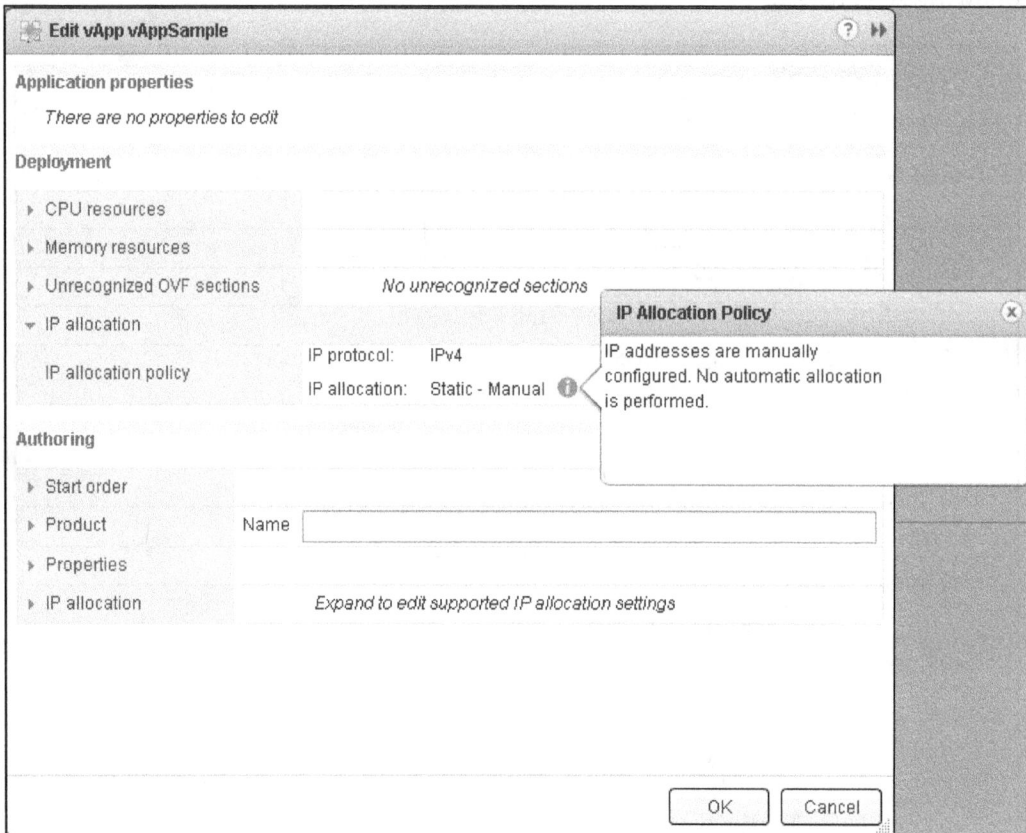

The following options are available for the **IP allocation policy** for a vApp:

- **Static - Manual**: In this option, no automatic allocation is performed; the IP addresses are manually configured.
- **Static - IP Pool**: In this option, the IP addresses are allocated automatically at power-on from a vCenter Server managed IP network range. These IP addresses will remain assigned even at power-off.
- **Transient**: In this option, the IP addresses are allocated automatically from a vCenter Server managed IP network range at power-on. These IP addresses are released when the virtual machines are powered off.
- **DHCP**: In this option, the IP addresses are allocated by using a DHCP server. The leases must be periodically renewed.

If you plan on using the vApp's **IP allocation policy** options, keep in mind that there are a few more steps for this to function properly. An IP Pool must be created at the datacenter level for use by the **Static-IP Pool, Transient**, and **DHCP** options. Check the *Add a Network Protocol Profile* section under VMware's *vSphere Virtual Machine Administration* guide for more information on how to create this pool. The documentation can be found at `https://www.vmware.com/support/pubs/vsphere-esxi-vcenter-server-pubs.html`. The virtual machines within the vApp must also be configured to accept IP addresses; check `http://kb.vmware.com/kb/1031476` for more information.

Select the desired IP allocation policy that best fits the needs of your virtual machines residing in the vApp.

Using the **IP allocation scheme** will determine which IP allocation policy options are enabled. If the **OVF environment** option is selected, then this will allow the IP allocation policy to be determined by the OVF environment. The IP addresses are allocated using DHCP when the virtual machines are powered on if the **DHCP** option is selected.

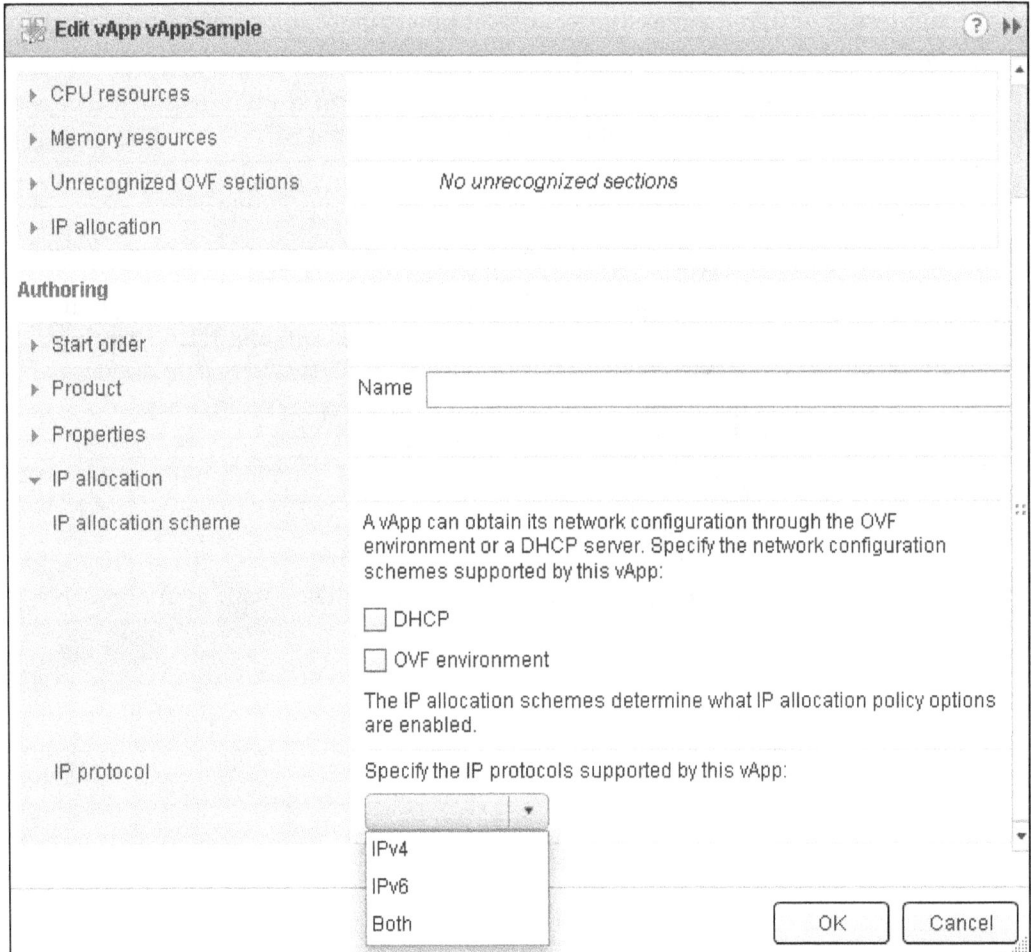

Choose the appropriate vApp-supported IP protocol, either **IPv4**, **IPv6**, or **Both**.

Virtual machine startup/shutdown order

One great feature of vApps is that you can specifically set the order in which virtual machines (and nested vApps) within a vApp start up and shut down. Choose which order to power on by assigning the virtual machines to groups. You can also specify that a virtual machine should wait a specific amount of seconds before powering on or powering off the next virtual machine in the vApp. A different time interval can be placed between each group. Another option is to select **VMware Tools are ready**; choosing this will allow for the virtual machines to wait until the VMware Tools have started and ready on one virtual machine before powering on the next. This way, if you have set the interval to 600 seconds, if the virtual machine is powered on, and if the VMware Tools initialize in 75 seconds, then the next virtual machine will go ahead and power on, and not wait until the entire interval has elapsed.

The **Shutdown Action** operation works similarly, except that you can modify the operation to either conduct **Guest Shutdown**, **Power Off**, or **Suspend** on the virtual machines.

All of these **Start order** settings are contained inside the vApp and are portable when the vApp is transferred.

 Though these settings are contained within the vApp and are portable, keep in mind that High Availability does not follow the startup order configured in the vApp in case of an HA event.

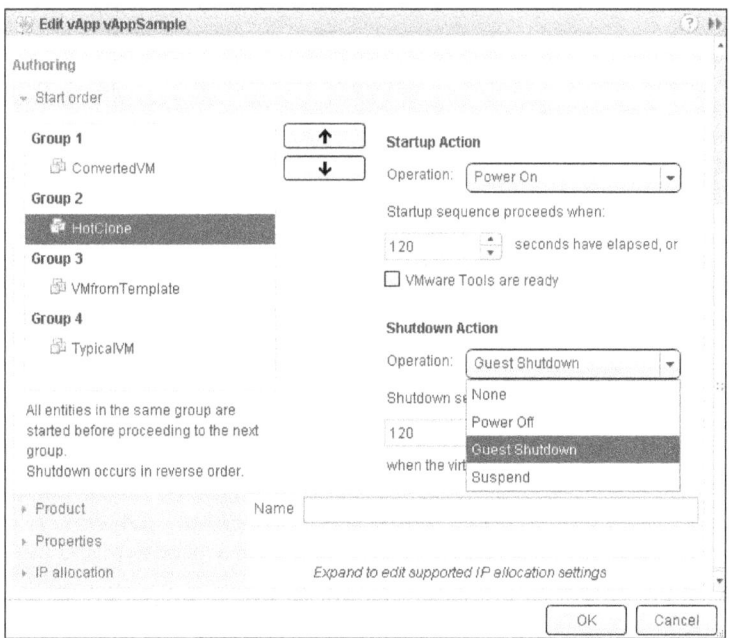

Once the virtual machine's start order has been configured, press **OK**.

For more information regarding startup and shutdown actions, check `http://kb.vmware.com/kb/2012036`.

Also, you can find out more information regarding vApp properties by checking the *vSphere Virtual Machine Administration* guide documentation.

Exporting a vApp

Once this vApp has been deployed, the virtual machines are placed within, and the vApp policies are configured, you can export this vApp as an OVF template. It is greatly beneficial if this multitiered application is to be deployed multiple times or deployed between virtual infrastructures. Create and configure this as a template for all deployments of this application.

To export this vApp, right-click on the desired vApp and select the **Export OVF Template...** option, as shown in the following screenshot:

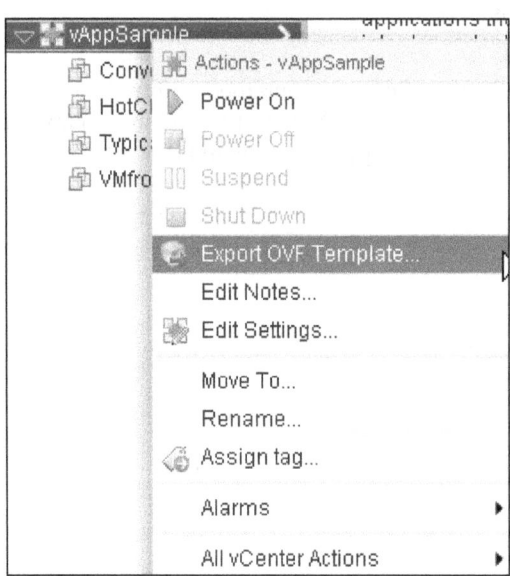

Selecting this option will bring up a menu to complete the export operation.

Enter a value for the **Name** field of the OVF template, and click on the **Choose** button to select the directory that the vApp should be exported to. You can choose whether this should be exported as an OVF or OVA file. The **Annotation** box provides a place to enter any notes as needed.

Selecting **Folder of files (OVF)** will store the OVF template (.ovf, .vmdk, and so on) as a set of files. It is optimal if it is planned whether this OVF will be published on an image library or on a web server.

Selecting **Single file (OVA)** will package the OVF template into a single .ova file, which is convenient if planning to move around using a USB device.

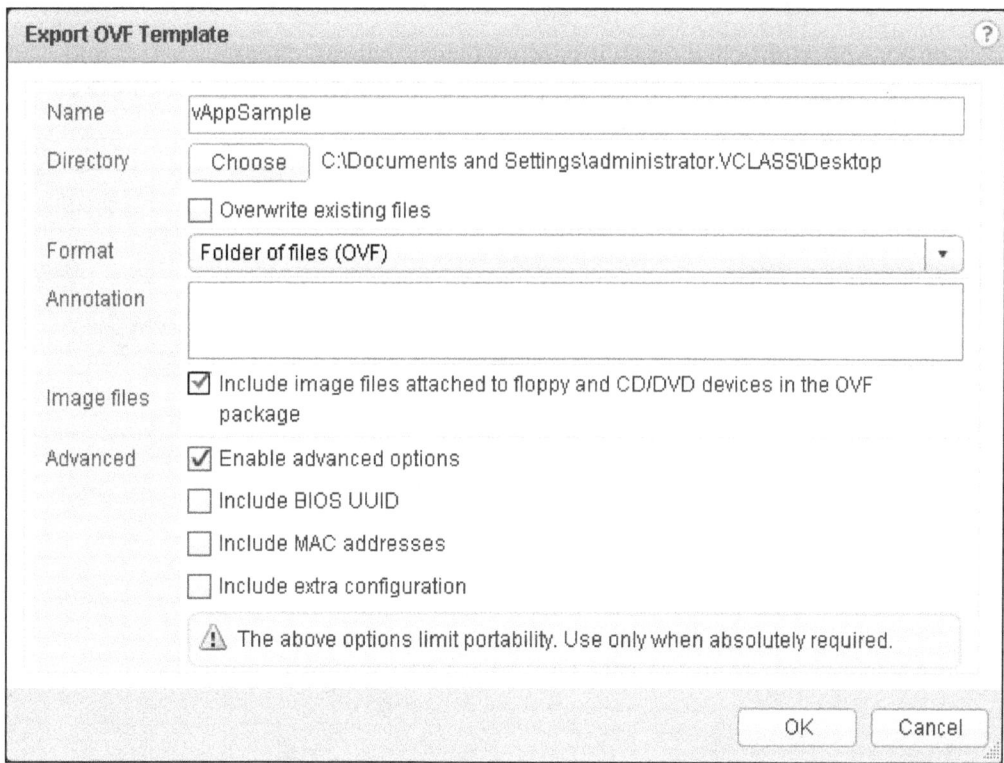

Select the **Enable advanced options** checkbox if it is desired to include other information, such as BIOS UUID, MAC addresses, and any extra configuration, in the exported template. By default, the **Enable advanced options** checkbox is not selected in order to make the vApp more portable by not including information specific to the included virtual machines. If you want to export an exact copy of this vApp to include things like the MAC addresses, select the appropriate options. Be aware that importing this vApp into the same environment that it was exported from can result in issues of duplicate UUIDs and MAC addresses.

Cloning a vApp

Another benefit of the vApp's virtual machine-like functionality is being able to clone a vApp. This is advantageous when you want to duplicate the vApp setup in a test or development environment in order to do something like test or update a new patch. But be aware that you cannot use guest customization specifications, so duplicate names, SIDS, and IP addresses can occur.

To clone a vApp, right-click on an inventory object that can contain a vApp and select **New vApp...**. Once the **New vApp** wizard is launched, select the **Clone an existing vApp** option, as shown in the following screenshot:

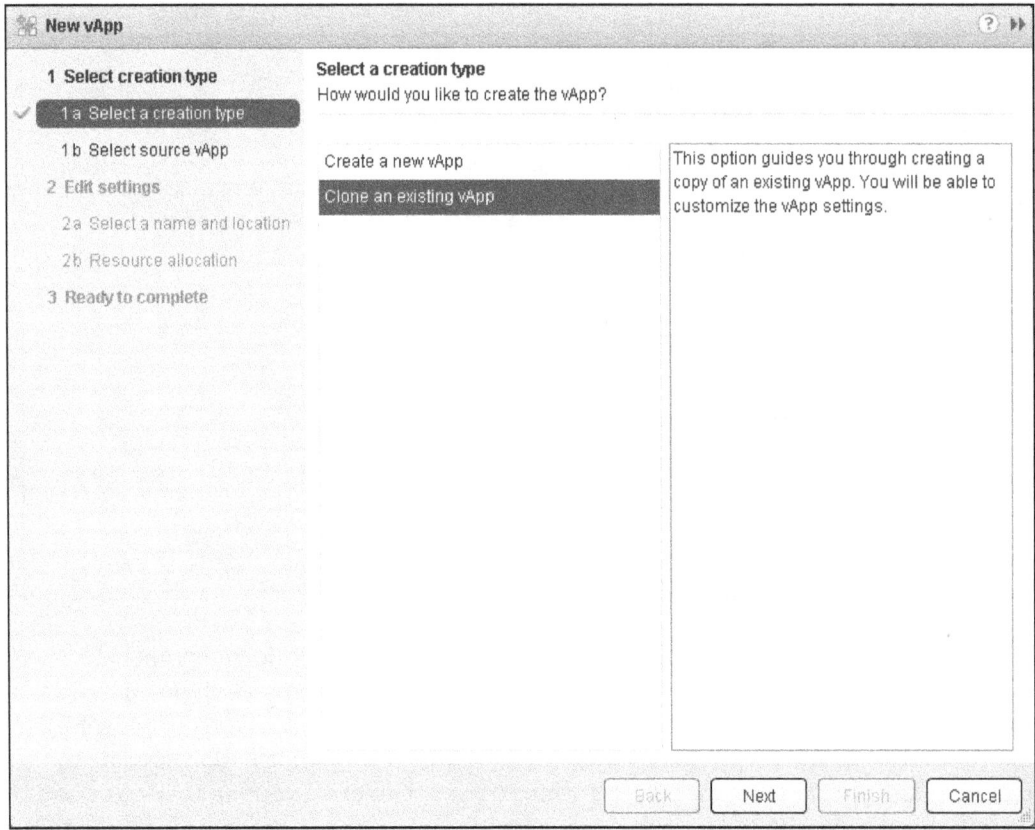

On the next pane, select the source vApp that you would like to clone:

Chapter 5

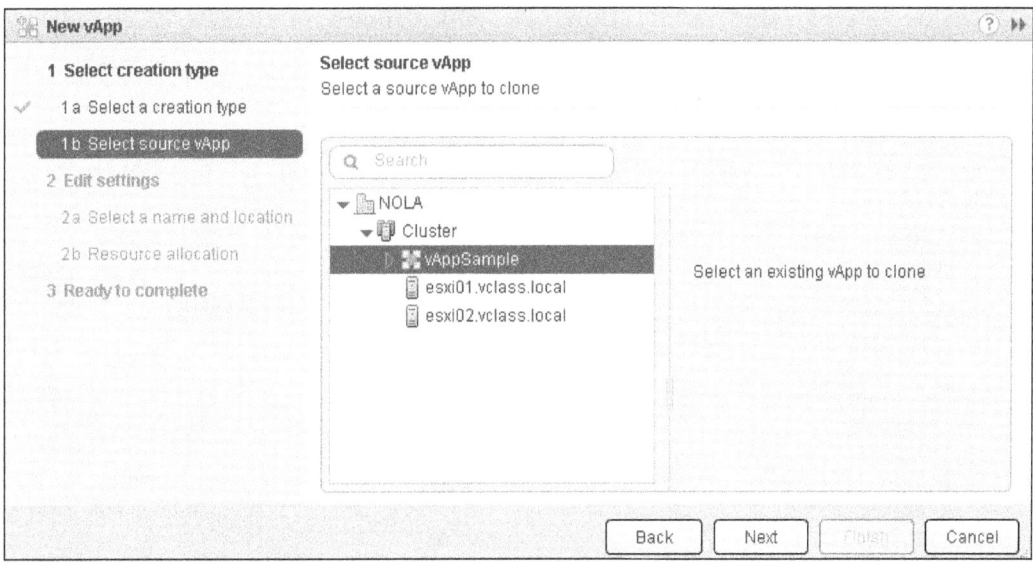

Once the vApp has been selected, click on **Next**.

The **Select destination** pane allows the choice of which object the cloned vApp should be placed under in the Hosts and Clusters inventory view in vCenter.

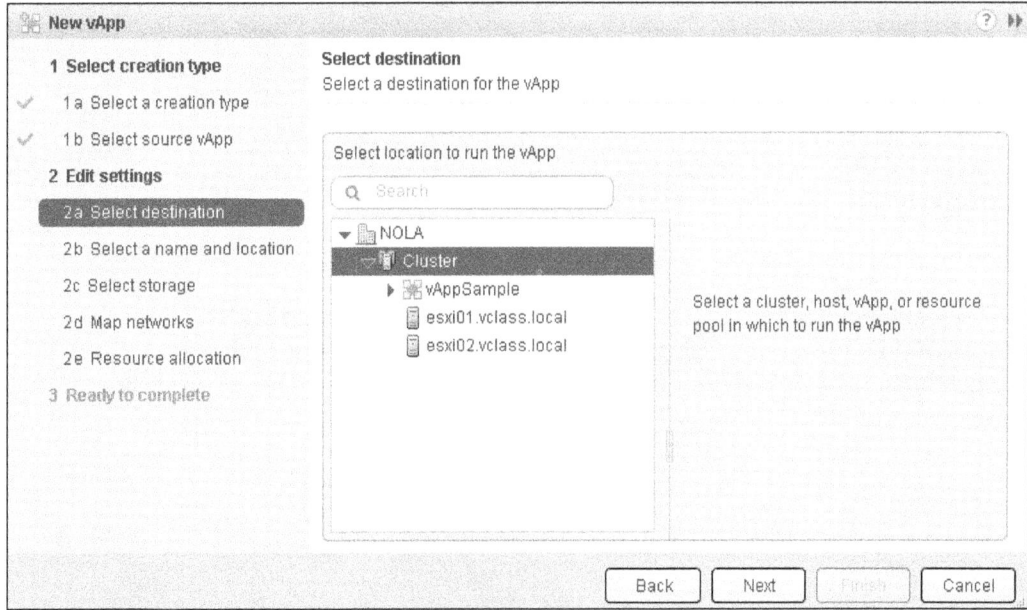

Click on **Next** after making this selection.

Next is the **Select a name and location** pane, which allows for the new vApp to be named. Choose which folder in the VM and Template inventory view the vApp should be placed under.

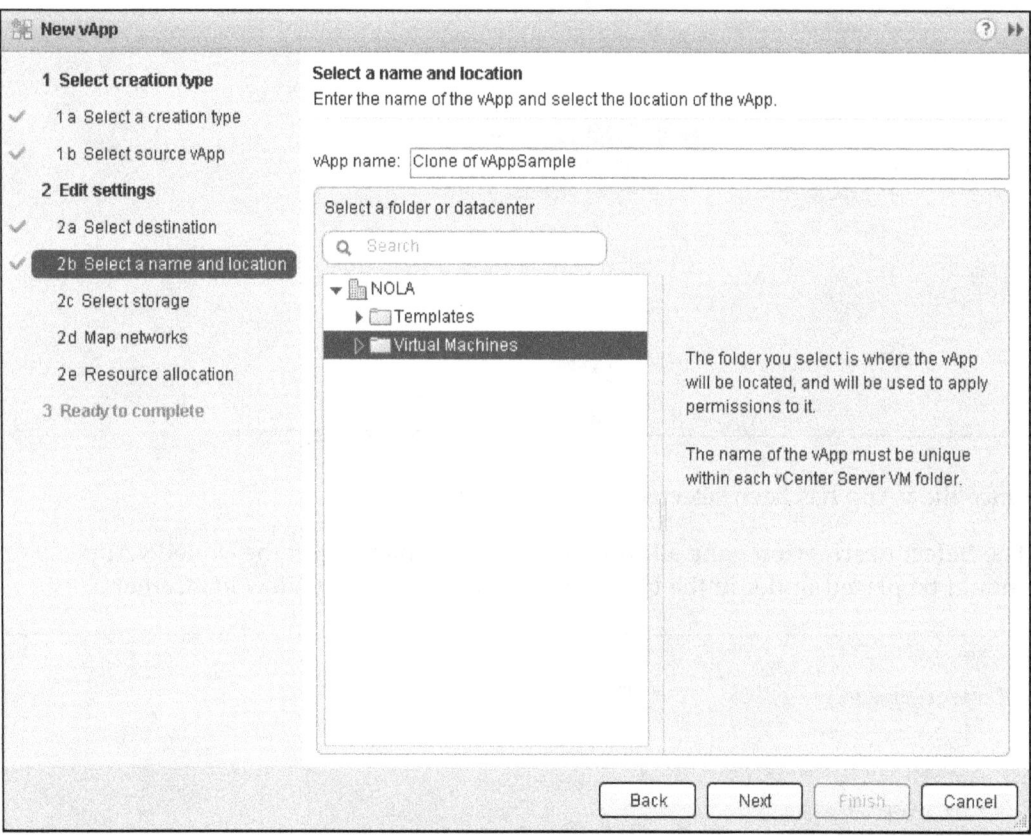

Click on **Next** after making selections.

The next pane will allow you to specify which datastore the new virtual machine files should be placed on. Using the **Select virtual disk format** option will allow the destination vApp's virtual machine to be provisioned differently from the source vApp.

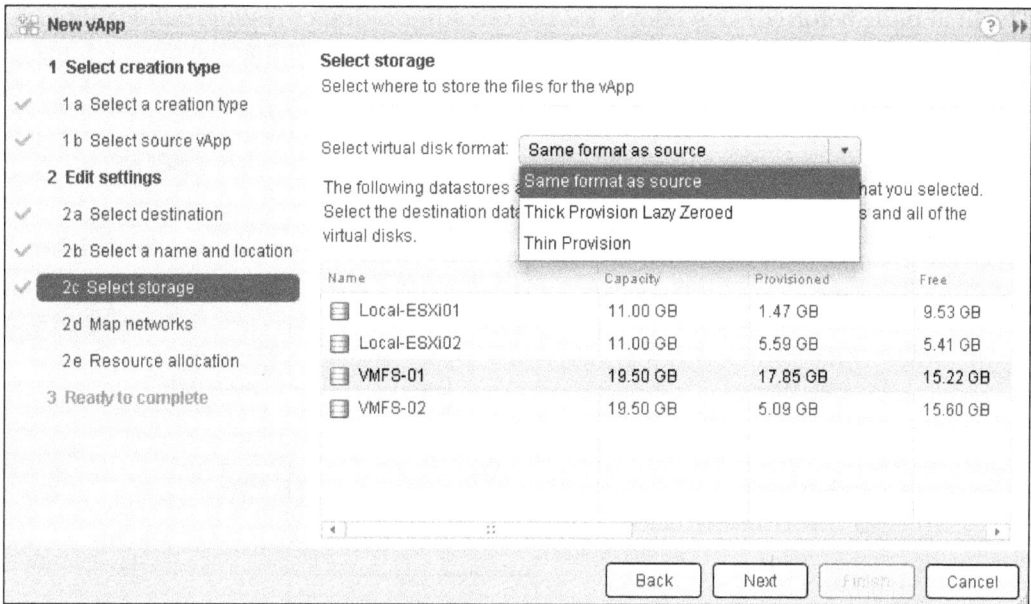

Click on **Next**.

The **Map networks** pane allows for the selection of which network the virtual machines in the cloned vApp should be connected to.

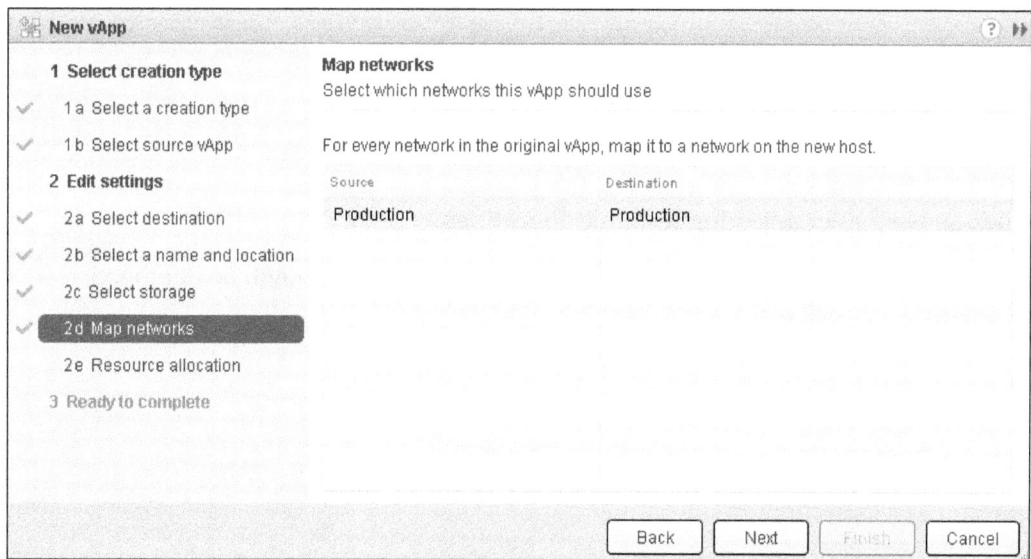

After selecting the vApp network, click on **Next**.

Managing Multitiered Applications with vApps

The final pane before review allows for the reconfiguration of resource allocations. Adjust the **Shares**, **Reservation**, and **Limit** fields as needed so that the destination vApp is configured according to desired expectations.

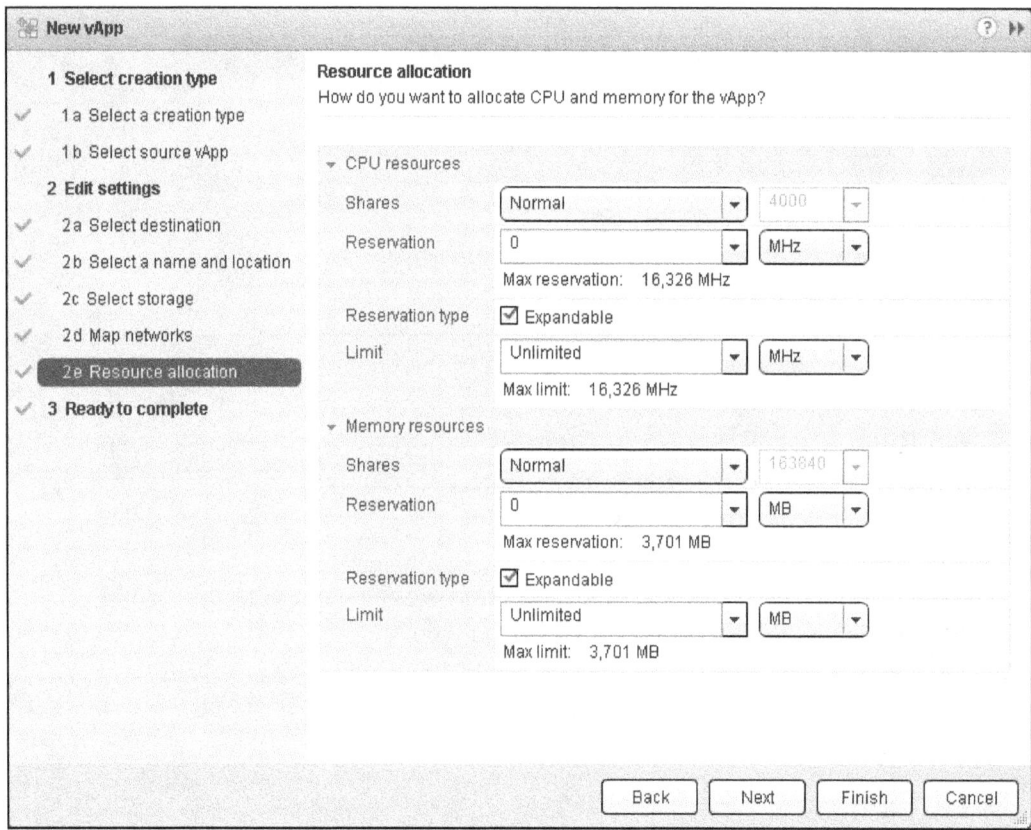

Click on **Next** after adjusting resource allocations.

Review all vApp settings to ensure that the destination vApp will be deployed as desired. Go back and change any setting if needed.

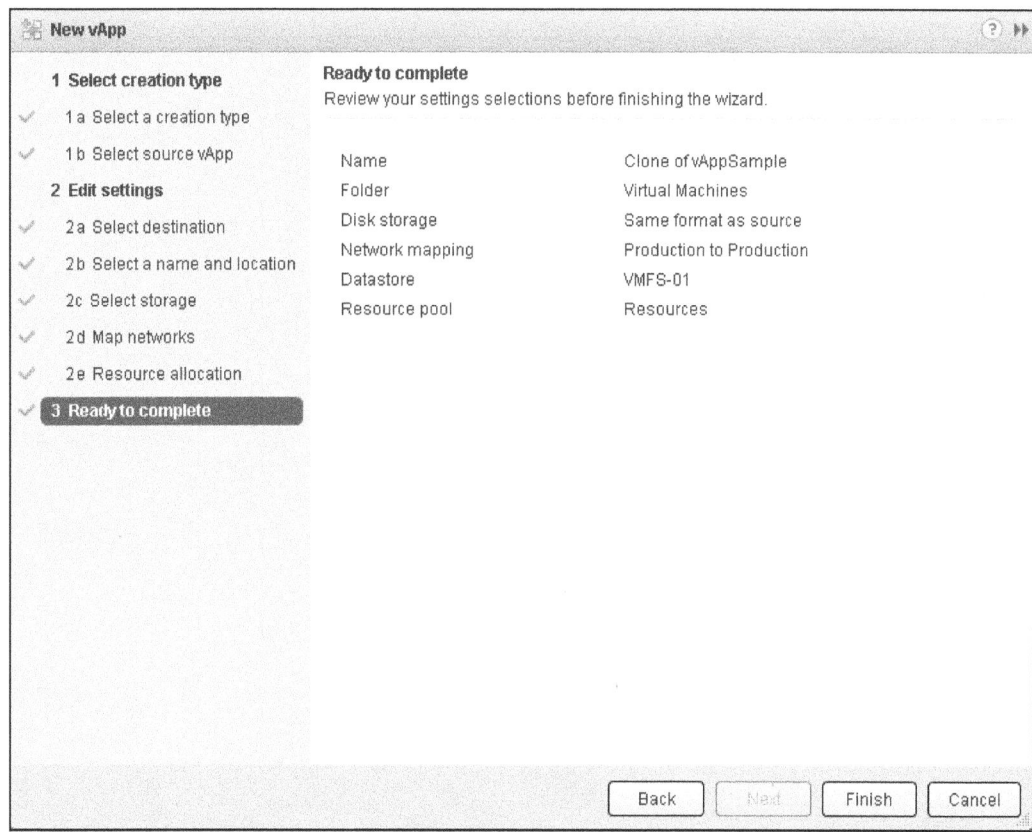

Click on **Finish** upon reviewing the settings.

Summary

A vApp is a container, acting like a resource pool, but with some extra virtual machine-like functionality. The resource pool functionality includes resource allocation settings, such as shares, reservations, and limits, which can be configured for a vApp and a resource pool. Another great benefit of using vApps is that a specific virtual machine startup and shutdown order can be defined. The vApps can be cloned and exported for portability. vApps can be used to package and manage these multitiered applications so that they are able to run directly on top of vSphere. Many vendors are using vApps to allow for applications to be deployed more easily.

The next chapter will discuss virtual machine performance and resource allocation.

6
Virtual Machine Performance and Resource Allocation

This chapter explores different settings that may improve a virtual machine's resource allocation and performance, if needed. These resource allocation settings affect the amount of resources given to a virtual machine and how virtual machines compete when in contention. These settings include shares, limits, and reservations and can be applied to CPU and memory resources. Shares and limits may also be configured for storage and network resource access, depending on your vSphere licensing tier.

In this chapter, you will learn about:

- CPU scheduler
- Memory reclamation techniques
- Shares, limits, and reservations
- Resource pools
- Network I/O Control
- Storage I/O Control
- Disk alignment
- Performance tuning

Resource performance concepts

Resource contention is a conflict over access to a shared resource. Oversubscription can lead to contention, if not properly managed and monitored. Each of the primary four resources (CPU, memory, network, and disk) can experience contention.

CPU virtualization

CPU virtualization emphasizes performance and will run directly on the available processors when possible. Whenever possible, the underlying physical resources are used. The virtualization layer runs instructions only when needed to make sure that the virtual machines continue running as if directly accessing hardware on a physical server. A virtual machine can be configured with up to 64 **virtual CPUs (vCPUs)** as of vSphere 5.5. Keep in mind that a virtual machine cannot have more vCPUs than logical CPUs available on the ESXi host. The VMkernel includes a CPU scheduler that dynamically schedules vCPUs on the ESXi host's physical processor.

The CPU scheduler can use each logical processor independently to execute VMs, providing capabilities similar to traditional **symmetric multiprocessing** (**SMP**) systems. Symmetric multiprocessing is simply the act of having more than one vCPU on a single physical CPU. The VMkernel intelligently manages processor time to guarantee that the load is spread smoothly across processor cores in the system. After every 2 to 40 milliseconds, the VMkernel looks to migrate vCPUs from one logical processor to another to keep the load balanced. If a logical processor has no work, it is put into a halted state. This action frees its execution resources and allows the VMs running on the other logical processor on the same core to use the full execution resources of the core.

The VMkernel scheduler considers socket-core-thread topology when making scheduling decisions. A **socket** is a single package that can have one or more physical processor cores, where each core has one or more logical processors or threads.

If hyperthreading is enabled on the host system, then ESXi can execute two threads or sets of instructions at the same time. The benefit of hyperthreading is that it provides more scheduling options. Hyperthreading is enabled by default. To ensure that it is functioning, consult the hardware documentation to see if the BIOS includes support for hyperthreading, and then enable hyperthreading in the system BIOS, if necessary.

Coscheduling allows the execution of a set of threads or processes simultaneously to achieve high performance. Since multiple cooperating threads or processes often synchronize, not allowing for concurrent execution would increase the latency of synchronization. Operating systems require synchronous progress on all CPUs and malfunction may occur if this requirement is not met. When these operating systems run within a virtual machine, ESXi must maintain this synchronous process on the vCPUs.

Since ESXi 3.x, VMware has been using relaxed coscheduling to meet the challenge presented. Only vCPUs that are skewed must be co-started; this makes sure that when any vCPU is scheduled, a vCPU that is deemed "behind" will also be scheduled, thus reducing skew. Relaxed coscheduling allows for a subset of a virtual machine's vCPUs to be simultaneously scheduled after skew is detected.

Memory reclamation

Memory overcommitment happens when the physical memory installed on an ESXi host is less than the sum of memory allocated to all virtual machines on the ESXi host. The virtual machine's overhead memory is extra host physical memory that is required by the VMkernel beyond the memory allocated to the virtual machine. So why overcommit memory resources? Overcommitment allows for a more effective use of physical resources by raising the consolidation ratio, lowering the total cost of operating virtual machines, and increasing operational efficiency. Memory overcommitment does not necessarily lead to performance loss in a guest OS or its applications, but may cause performance loss when much of a virtual machine's memory has to be reclaimed due to contention.

Memory overcommitment allows the VMkernel to reclaim memory that is not actively used by virtual machines in order to meet the demands of other virtual machines and the hypervisor. It is important to understand that the VMkernel is not aware of the guest operating system's internal memory management mechanisms. Guest operating systems commonly use an allocated memory list and a free memory list. Whenever a guest operating system requests a page of memory, the VMkernel will back that "virtual" page with physical memory. Eventually, the guest operating system stops using the page internally, but it does not remove the data; the guest OS just removes the address space pointer from the allocated memory list and places this pointer on the free memory list. Since the data itself has not changed, the ESXi host will continue keeping this data in physical memory.

A virtual machine cannot be powered on if the minimum memory isn't available or the swap file size doesn't equal the difference between allocated and reserved memory. This means the virtual machine will not power on if the datastore on which the swap files will be created does not have sufficient space.

Transparent page sharing (TPS)

Transparent page sharing allows pages of memory that are identical to be stored in the same place. This is the only memory reclamation technique that occurs at a regular interval; the other options that will be discussed are used when the ESXi host experiences memory contention. During periods of idle CPU time, the hypervisor looks for identical memory pages located across multiple virtual machines. Once these pages are matched, they are shared in the physical RAM. ESXi systems use a proprietary page sharing technique to securely eliminate redundant copies of memory pages so as to allow for a more efficient support of overcommitment.

Transparent page sharing is basically a deduplication method applied to memory rather than storage. For organizations that tend to use the same operating system or very similar operating systems for many virtual machines, the memory impact can provide substantial savings.

The following diagram demonstrates transparent page sharing. The top half of the diagram is indicative of virtual machine memory and the bottom half is the physical host memory. Notice that each virtual machine contains a green page of memory that is shared by all three virtual machines:

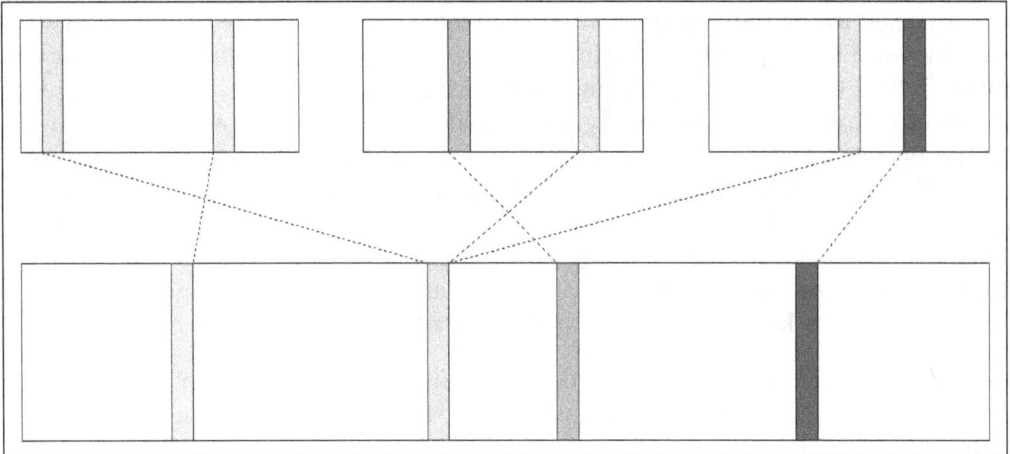

Remember that transparent page sharing occurs always, whereas the next topics only occur during memory contention.

Ballooning

Ballooning occurs before using the .vswp file during memory contention. VMware Tools must be installed for this mechanism to function; part of this driver package is the memory balloon driver (vmmemctl). The memory balloon driver works with the hypervisor to reclaim pages of memory that are considered to be the least valuable to the virtual machine's guest operating system; these are generally page-marked as free or idle but can reclaim active pages if absolutely necessary. If the ESXi server begins to run low on physical memory, it will communicate with the memory balloon driver to reclaim memory inside the guest operating system that is no longer valuable to the operating system. Essentially, the hypervisor will grow the memory balloon driver within the guest operating system so as to increase memory pressure. The pressure caused by the increase of the memory balloon driver will cause the guest operating system to use its own native memory management algorithm. Ballooning will utilize the guest operating system's own virtual disk (for Windows this is the page file, while for Linux OSes it is a swap partition).

The real beauty of ballooning is that it is intelligent memory management, because it allows the guest operating system to make the hard decision of which pages of memory will be paged out without any hypervisor involvement. The guest operating system is fully aware of the memory state. Therefore, the virtual machine will keep performing well as long as it has idle or free pages of memory to balloon. When ballooning is engaged in a guest operating system, it can only force virtual machines to page up to 65 percent of their memory; the VMkernel is responsible for determining which virtual machines will be ballooned and which will not. The goal is to balloon idle virtual machines memory before active virtual machine memory.

This process reduces the change of the physical ESXi host memory being swapped; swapping causes greater performance degradation than ballooning.

Compression

The physical pages of memory can be compressed and then decompressed by the ESXi host. If pages of memory that would normally be swapped can be compressed and stored in the compression cache, then the next page access would result in decompression. Decompression is much faster than disk access. If memory compression were taking place, there may be a few noncompressible pages (cannot be compressed to 2 KB or smaller) that would need to be swapped out even if the compression cache is not full. Otherwise, pages that would normally be swapped to disk are chosen as candidates for memory compression. This only occurs during memory contention and will not occur if unnecessary.

Compression is preferred to swapping because the page compression technique used is much faster than the normal page swap-out operation, which involves using disk I/O.

This feature can be disabled or the maximum size of the compression cache can be specified using the **Advanced System Settings** option in the vSphere Web Client.

This is a per-ESXi host setting and would need to be adjusted on each ESXi host. Consider using host profiles as a means to apply a desired configuration across multiple ESXi hosts.

> Host profiles are an Enterprise Plus level feature that allow for governing and ensuring compliance to a standard ESXi configuration. Think of host profiles as a template of sorts for your ESXi hosts.

To adjust the settings of the ESXi host, perform the following steps:

1. Open up the vSphere Web Client and browse to an ESXi host.
2. Select the **Manage** tab and click on the **Settings** tab; select **Advanced System Settings** from here.
3. Locate the specific key and click on the **Edit** button.
4. Enter the desired value.
5. Click on **OK**.

This is demonstrated in the next screenshot.

Compression is enabled by default; it is rarely disabled. However, more often, the size of the compression cache is modified if contention is not a possibility in an environment due to lack of overcommitment. This is shown to demonstrate how to size the cache; disabling is also conducted the same way. The **Advanced System Settings** screen is shown in the following screenshot:

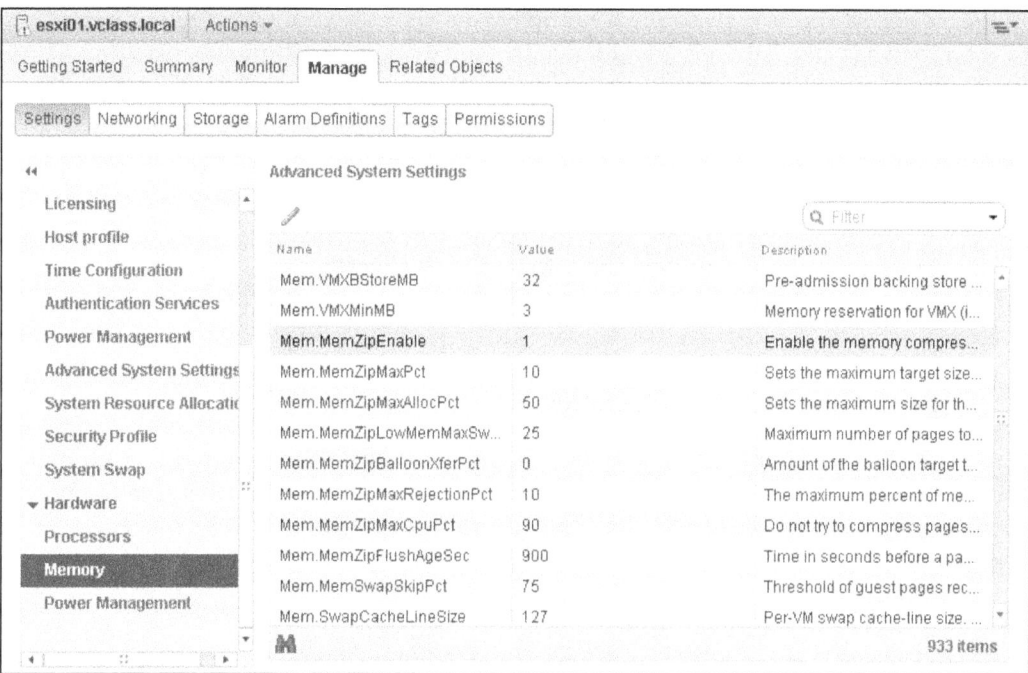

When enabling or disabling the memory compression cache, select the **Mem.MemZipEnable** key. Entering 1 and 0 will enable and disable the memory compression cache, respectively.

To set the maximum size, use the **Mem.MemZipMaxPct** key. This value is the size of the virtual machine's compression cache in comparison to the virtual machine's size. This must be between 5 and 100 percent. By default, the cache size is 10 percent.

Swapping to host cache

If an ESXi host has **solid-state drives** (**SSD**), then these can be used for a VMFS datastore where it can be specified for use as a host cache. An SSD is a type of storage drive that stores data on solid-state flash memory. This cache is on a low-latency disk that is being used by ESXi that has a write back cache for virtual machine swap files. All virtual machines running on the ESXi host will share this cache. The host will still create regular swap files on a datastore even if a host cache is enabled; the virtual machines will swap to this host cache until the limited SSD space is depleted, at which point the virtual machines will use their regular swap files on the datastore.

Virtual Machine Performance and Resource Allocation

In most cases, swapping to an SSD is much faster than swapping to regular swap files on the hard disk storage. The idea is that as SSDs come down in price, this is a feature that will be more widely used. Another possibility is that a datastore is backed by a storage array with SSDs and the .vswp files are stored on that specific datastore.

To configure a host cache, perform the following steps:

1. Browse to an ESXi host in the vSphere Web Client.
2. Click on the **Manage** tab.
3. Select the **Storage** tab.
4. Select **Host Cache Configuration**.

You must have an SSD-backed datastore in the inventory. If this prerequisite is met, then you will select the datastore in this list and click on the **Allocate space for host cache** button and configure a size for the allocation. The **Host Cache Configuration** screen is shown in the following screenshot:

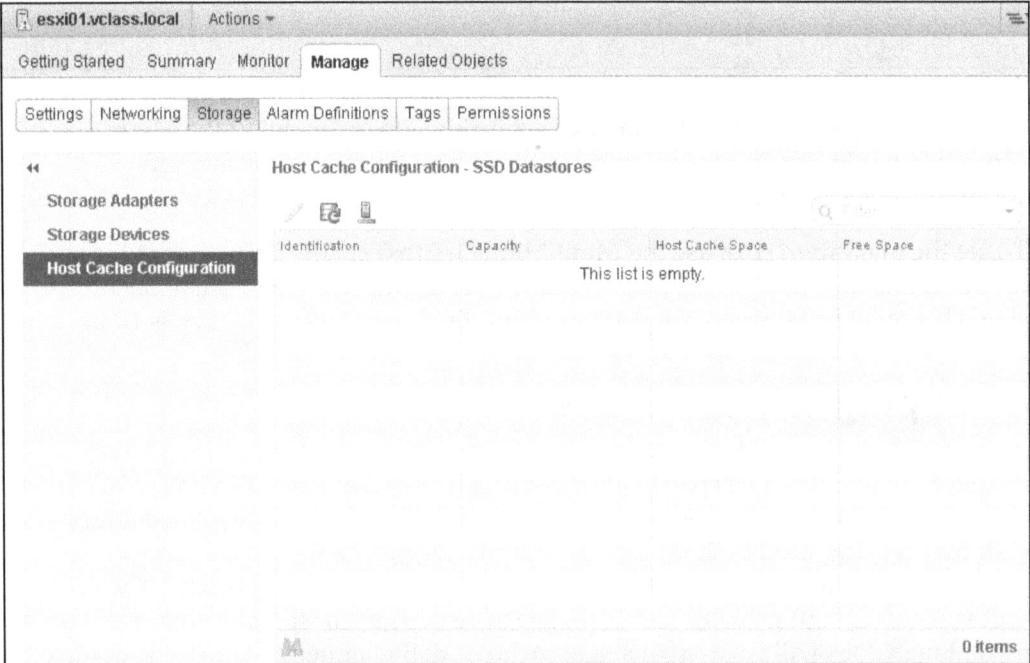

Once the host cache has been configured:

1. Click on the **Settings** tab under the **Manage** tab.
2. Choose **System Swap**.

If the ESXi host is not configured to use the host cache, then click on the **Edit** button, as shown in the following screenshot:

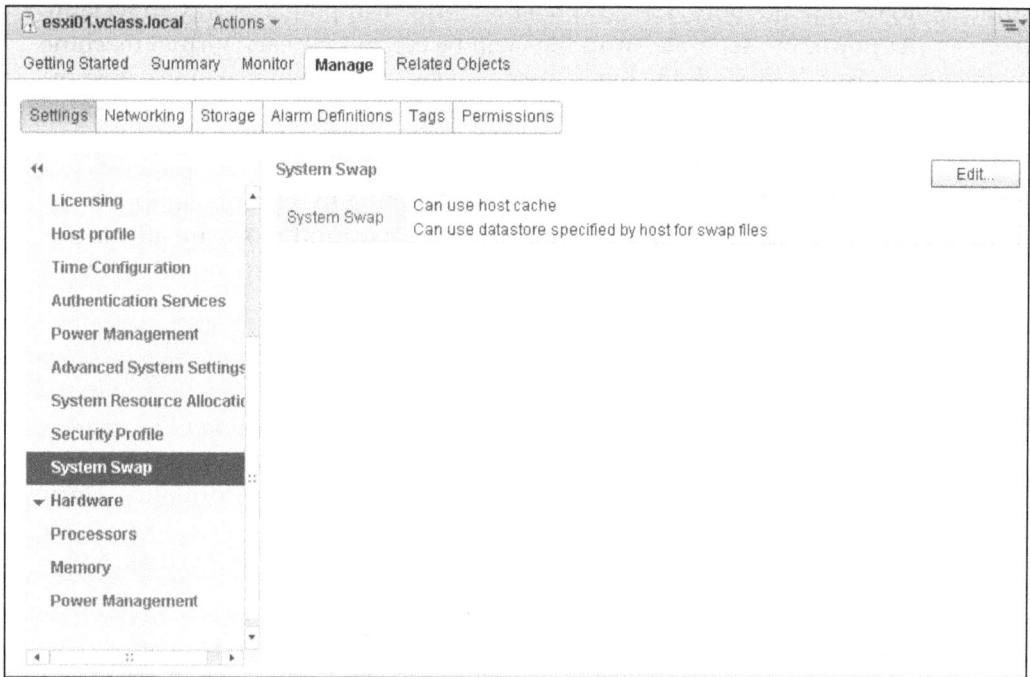

This will bring up a dialog box, which will allow you to check the box **Can use host cache**, as shown in the following screenshot:

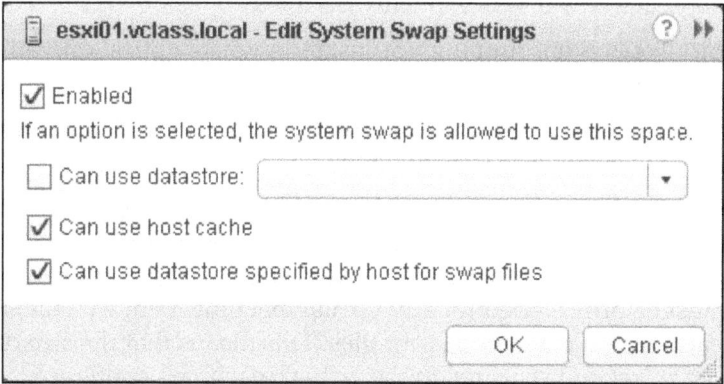

Once this selection has been made, click on **OK**.

Hypervisor swapping

In the cases where ballooning, compression, and transparent page sharing are not sufficient to reclaim memory, the ESXi host will use swapping as a way to reclaim memory. At power on, separate swap files will be created for each virtual machine by the hypervisor. If needed, the hypervisor will swap a virtual machine's memory to the swap file in order to free up physical memory for the hypervisor and other virtual machines.

It takes time for transparent page sharing and ballooning to reclaim memory from virtual machines. The page scan rate and the opportunity to share affects the transparent page sharing speed. Reclamation by ballooning is dependent on the response time of a virtual machine's guest operating for memory allocation. Don't forget that there is a 65 percent memory size limitation on how much ballooning can reclaim.

Hypervisor swapping, on the other hand, guarantees the reclamation of memory within a specified time. However, hypervisor swapping is used as a last resort to reclaim memory from the virtual machine due to its impact on performance. During swapping, the hypervisor will arbitrarily steal pages from the guest. It doesn't care what memory it takes, it just forces the guest operating system to go to disk, as needed, with its remaining sum of memory.

Memory will be forcibly reclaimed using swapping as a last resort. However, there are times that swapping may occur before ballooning. These instances include:

- The vmmemctl driver (memory balloon driver), or VMware Tools, was not installed
- The vmmemctl driver was explicitly disabled
- VMware Tools is not running, for instance, when a guest operating system is booting up
- The memory balloon driver is unable to reclaim memory fast enough to satisfy the current system demands

Otherwise, if the memory balloon driver is properly functioning, but the maximum balloon size has been reached, then swapping will occur.

Swap space must be provisioned for any virtual machine memory that is not reserved for each virtual machine's swap files. This means that the size of the virtual machine's .vswp file is equal to the virtual machine's configured memory minus any memory reservation. These files are created at the virtual machine's power on to ensure that the ESXi host can preserve the virtual machine's memory under any circumstance.

By default, the virtual machine's swap files are created in the same datastore location as the rest of the virtual machine files. If the default configuration is not desired, this can be changed at the virtual machine level or at the ESXi host level.

To change the datastore used to store the virtual machine swap files at the host level, perform the following steps:

1. Use the vSphere Web Client and browse to the ESXi host.
2. Choose the **Manage** tab and select **Swap file location** under the **Settings** tab. By default, the swap file location is the virtual machine's directory where the rest of its files are located.
3. To change this, choose the **Edit** button, as shown in the following screenshot:

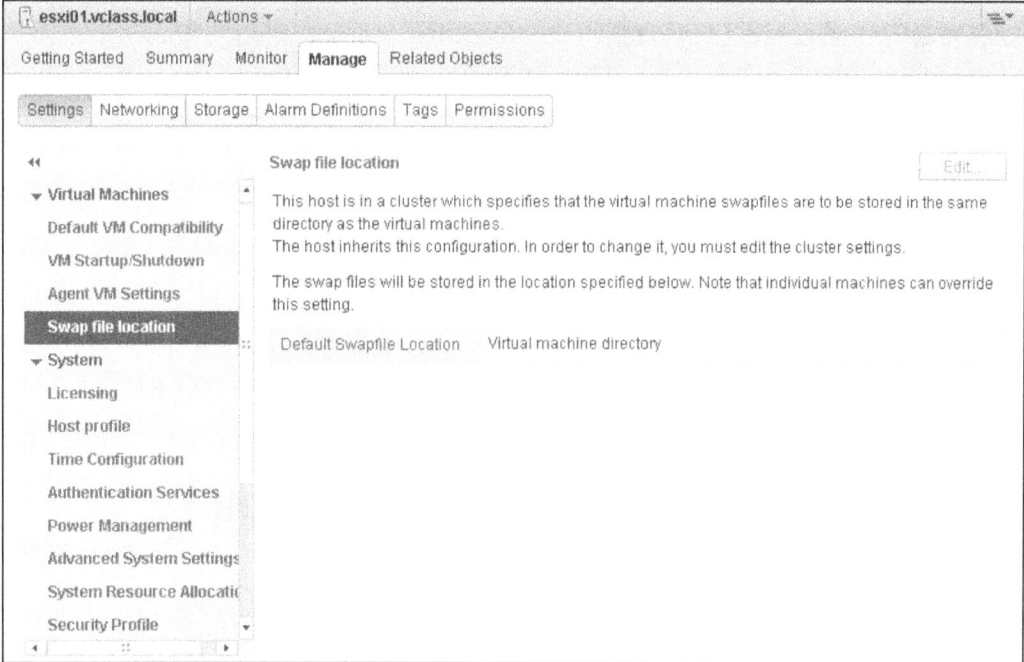

Once modified, the next time the virtual machines residing on this ESXi host are power cycled, their swap files will be created in the specified datastore.

Network constraint

Network performance issues are typically caused by the saturation of a network link between the clients and servers. vSphere 5.x supports 1 Gigabit and 10 Gigabit Ethernet, and vSphere 5.5 now also supports 40 Gigabit Ethernet. These higher bandwidth networks reduce the chance of having network bottlenecks, but it is always a possibility. The network performance will be dependent on application workload as well as the network configurations. Network intensive applications can result in oversubscribed network links, which may lead to network contention. Ensure that the infrastructure bandwidth is sufficient for all traffic types. Network I/O Control, discussed later in the chapter, can be configured to prioritize network access for the different traffic types.

Storage constraint

Saturating the underlying storage hardware often causes storage performance issues. Disk intensive applications could saturate the storage and/or the path. To determine whether your vSphere environment is experiencing storage issues, monitor disk latency. *Chapter 7, Monitoring Virtual Machines*, details this process. Storage I/O Control is also discussed in this chapter and can be used to determine if a latency threshold is exceeded. Ensure that your storage can meet the I/O demands of the virtual machines. Consider using SSD solutions as a means of removing the disk spindle from the equation. Using a disk cache approach can increase the IOPS that your storage is capable of. **Input/Output Operations Per Second (IOPS)** is a common metric used to judge overall storage performance. Shares may also be used to prioritize virtual machine access to storage resources.

Understanding resource controls

An administrator can customize the amount of resources allocated to a virtual machine, or to the resource pool in which those virtual machines reside, by modifying resource controls. Each of the primary four resources (CPU, memory, network, and storage) can be controlled, but network and storage require the use of the advanced features of Network I/O Control and Storage I/O Control. There are three resource controls that are available to determine how resources are provided to a virtual machine; these are shares, limits, and reservations. When an ESXi host's memory or CPU resources are overcommitted, a virtual machine's allocation target is somewhere between its specified reservation and specified limit, depending on the VM's share and the system load. This is something that we will explore later in this chapter.

Shares

A **share** is a value that specifies the relative priority or importance of a virtual machine (or resource pool) in regards to its access to a given resource. Keep in mind that shares only operate in times of contention, meaning that if a virtual machine has twice the share value of another virtual machine, then it is entitled to twice as much of that resource when these two virtual machines are competing for resources. If there is no competition and contention is also not occurring, share values are irrelevant and a virtual machine can consume up to its limit if available.

Generally speaking, share values are designated as **High**, **Normal**, or **Low**, and these values specify a 4:2:1 ratio, respectively. This is demonstrated in the next screenshot. A **Custom** value can also be selected to assign a specific number of shares, or proportional weight, to the virtual machine if the default values are not desired. Be careful when using **Custom** values; don't lose track of the ratio because doing so will potentially result in disproportioned resources.

By default, virtual machines are assigned a **Normal** share value. To modify this configuration, perform the following steps:

1. Right click the virtual machine and select **Edit Settings**.
2. Under the **Virtual Hardware** tab, expand either the **CPU** or **Memory** fields.
3. Modify the drop-down box next to the **Shares** field.

The following screenshot provides an example of memory resource controls that are available to be configured:

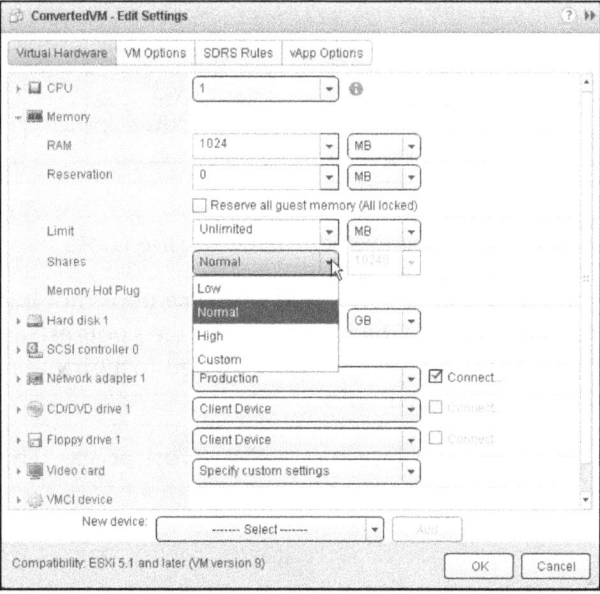

These share values can be assigned individually for memory and CPU resources. For example, a virtual machine may be configured for a **High** share value for CPU but a **Normal** value for memory resources.

Shares make more sense when it is considered that they work at the same level when compared to other virtual machines or resources pools. This means that shares are used to compete against sibling objects (virtual machines or resource pools) while in contention within the same parent in a resource pool hierarchy.

The following diagram demonstrates a three virtual machine scenario when share values are being enforced (during contention). The total share values equal 9000; this means that, during contention, VM1 receives 3000/9000 or 33 percent of resources, VM2 receives 1000/9000 or 11 percent of resources, and VM3 receives 5000/9000 or 56 percent of resources:

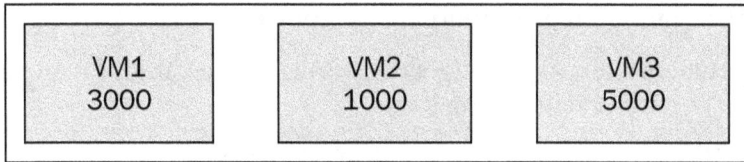

Keep in mind that this is all relative, so should another virtual machine power on at this level, then the total amount of shares change. If a fourth virtual machine brought the share values total 14,000, VM1 would receive 21 percent, VM2 would receive 7 percent, and VM3 and VM4 would receive 36 percent each, as shown in the following diagram:

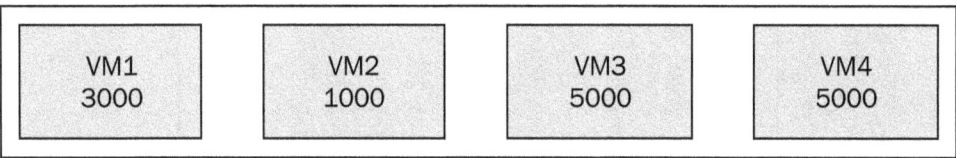

Do not forget that share values are only enforced during contention.

It is recommended that virtual machines and resource pools not be made sibling objects within a hierarchy because, by default, resource pools are assigned shares that may not appropriately compare to those assigned to a virtual machine. This can potentially cause performance issues.

Shares can also be configured for datastore and network access. This is discussed later in the chapter.

Limits

A limit specifies the ceiling of CPU cycles or amount of host physical memory that a virtual machine can consume. By default, a virtual machine is set to unlimited for both CPU and memory resources, but this is a bit misleading. A limit is specified in megahertz or megabytes. A virtual machine can only consume up to its configured amount plus overhead; if a virtual machine is configured for 8 GB of memory, then it cannot exceed 8 GB plus memory overhead even though the memory limit is set to unlimited. In this scenario, 8 GB plus memory overhead is the virtual machine's inherent and effective limit since that is the configured amount.

Limits can be used to manage user expectation in a small environment and are especially great for use in test environments to continually lower the amount of resources in order to determine how much should be configured in production. The drawback to configuring a limit is that the guest operating system believes that it has the configured amount of the resource, but the limit is already configured. Let's say a virtual machine is configured for 8 GB of memory and a limit was set at 4 GB. If you look at the system properties of the guest operating system, it will display that 8 GB of memory is available and that it is unaware that a limit was set and the virtual machine cannot exceed 4 GB of physical host memory. When a limit is reached, the guest operating system can still request new pages of memory but because of the configured limit, the VMkernel will not allow the guest operating system to consume more physical memory. The virtual machine will be treated as though it were under contention. Memory reclamation techniques will be used to allow the virtual machine to consume more memory resources as requested. First, the VMkernel will inflate the memory balloon driver to let the guest operating system memory manager decide which to page out, then compression will occur, and in a worst-case scenario swapping can occur. If swapping is possible in your environment, consider placing the .vswp files on Tier 1 storage for better performance when in contention.

If a CPU limit is set on a virtual machine, then the virtual machine is deliberately restrained from being scheduled on a physical processor once the allocated CPU resources are consumed. For a symmetric multiprocessing virtual machine, this means that the sum of all vCPUs cannot exceed the specified limit. For example, a virtual machine with four vCPUs and a limit of 1600 MHz with an equal vCPU load cannot exceed more than 400 MHz per vCPU. If only one vCPU is under stress, then the load will be distributed across the rest of the vCPUs.

This can cause certain applications to have undesirable behavior and performance degradation. Use limits sparingly.

Virtual Machine Performance and Resource Allocation

To set a resource limit for a virtual machine, perform the following steps:

1. Right-click on the virtual machine in the vSphere Web Client.
2. Select **Edit Settings**.
3. Under the **Virtual Hardware** tab, expand the desired resource and modify the **Limit** field as needed.

An example of this is demonstrated in the following screenshot:

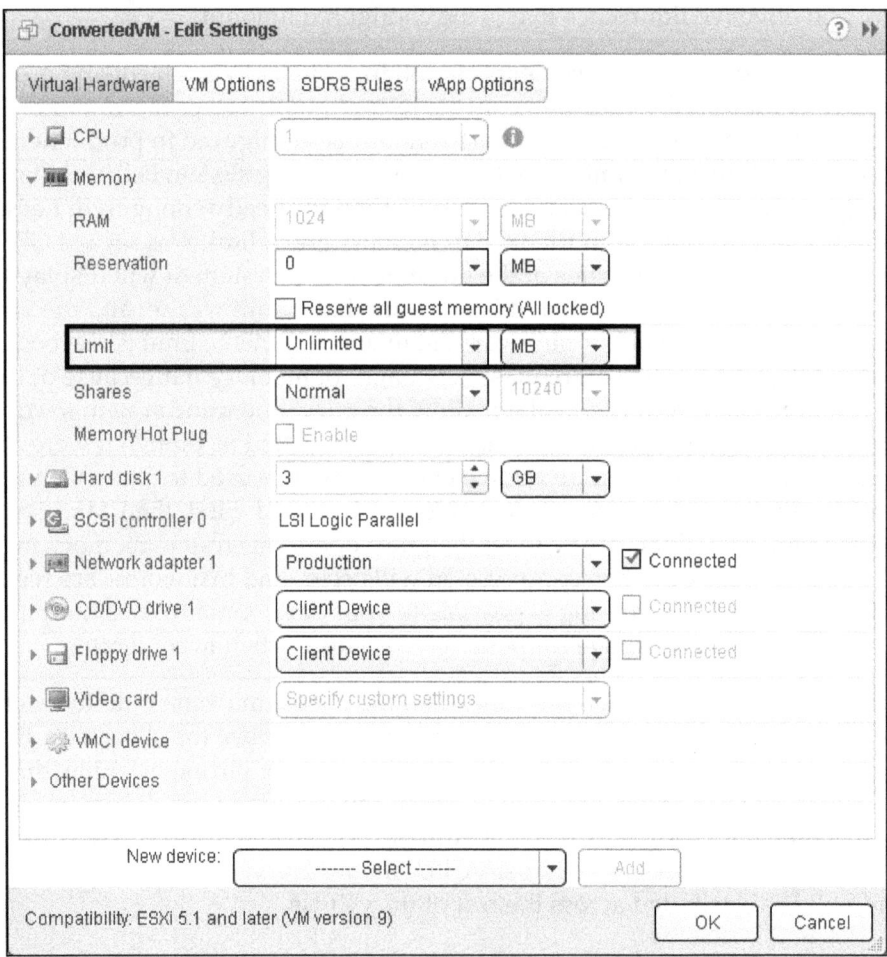

A CPU limit can be configured using the same process outlined previously, except that the **CPU** field will be expanded. Once set, click on **OK**.

Reservations

A reservation specifies the guaranteed minimum resource allocation for a virtual machine. If a virtual machine has a reservation, then the full reservation must be satisfied in order for the virtual machine to power on. A virtual machine will not power on if a reservation is not met. A reservation is specified in megahertz or megabytes. The reservation is guaranteed, even when the server is heavily loaded, meaning that the VMkernel does not reclaim physical memory if it is protected by a reservation, even if there is contention. This physical memory will be available to that specific virtual machine at all times. If a memory reservation is configured for a virtual machine, this is always guaranteed even when in contention, as memory reclamation techniques cannot take away that portion of memory. Since this memory cannot be taken away from a virtual machine during contention, it means that it will not be swapped; a memory reservation changes the size of the .vswp file. Without a reservation, the virtual machine's swap file will be the size of configured memory. However, if a reservation is configured, then the swap file will be the size of configured memory minus any memory reservation. This means that if a virtual machine is configured for 4 GB of memory, then the .vswp file will be 4 GB unless there is a reservation. If a reservation of 1 GB is configured, then the .vswp file will be sized at 3 GB.

Reservations should be used for business critical virtual machines in order to guarantee a specific minimum amount of CPU and/or memory resources.

To set a resource reservation for a virtual machine, perform the following steps:

1. Right-click on the virtual machine in the vSphere Web Client and select **Edit Settings**.

Virtual Machine Performance and Resource Allocation

2. Under the **Virtual Hardware** tab, expand the desired resource and modify the **Reservation** field as needed, as shown in the following screenshot:

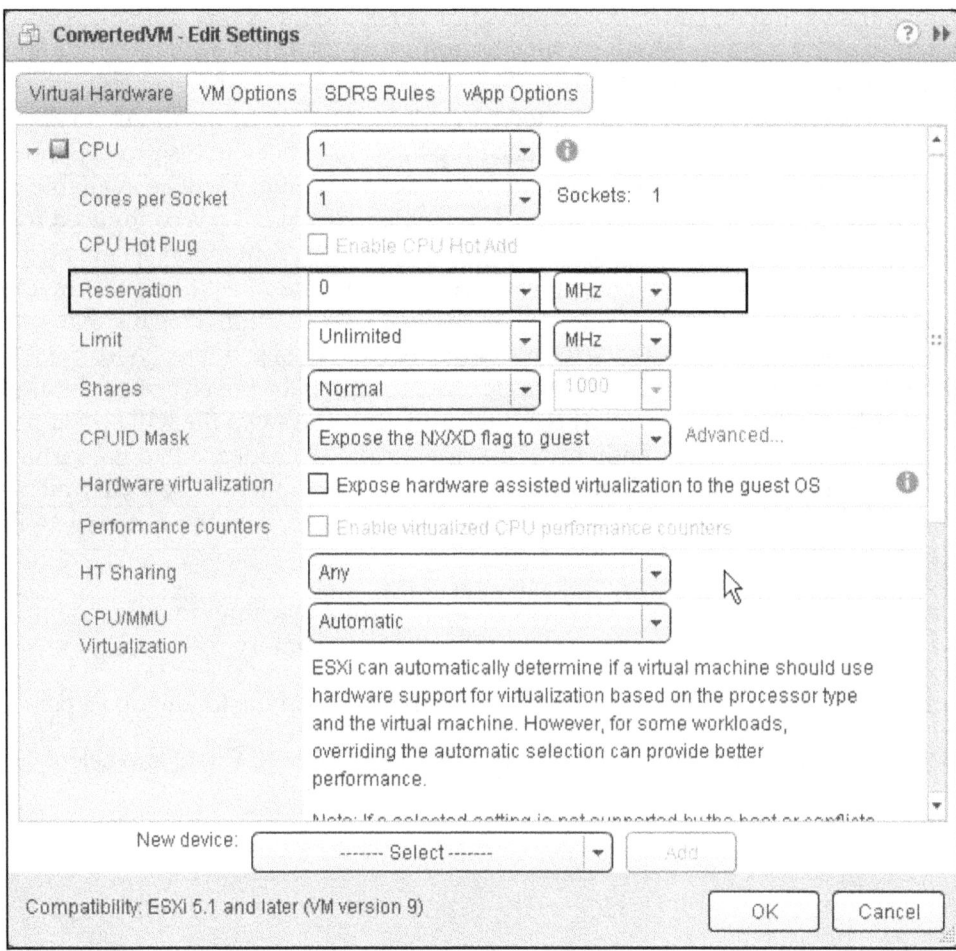

Memory reservation can be configured using the same process outlined previously, except that the **Memory** field will be expanded. Once set, click on **OK**.

Resource pools

A resource pool is a logical abstraction of resources from the root, the root being a standalone ESXi host or a DRS-enabled cluster. The **Distributed Resource Scheduler** (**DRS**) feature is used to load balance virtual machines across a cluster based on CPU and memory utilization. DRS is discussed further in *Chapter 9, Balancing Resource Utilization and Availability*. These resource pools are managed hierarchically using a parent-child relationship. Resource pools divide and allocate resources to virtual machines, child resource pools, or vApps.

Why use resource pools?

- **Organization**: Resource pools are created and organized hierarchically and resource allocations are modified as needed.
- **Separation of resources from hardware**: This is a good thing. Resource management can be performed independently of the cluster and ESXi hosts that are contributing the resources. This will allow for more aggregate computing capacity and less worry regarding the individual ESXi hosts. This allows for an aggregate approach for resources rather than a single ESXi host.
- **Isolation between resource pools and sharing within resource pools**: Resource pools can be used to isolate performance. Virtual machines can be grouped together and have resource controls placed upon them as a group so as to isolate them from another group of virtual machines to avoid unfairly affecting other pools. This means that resource allocations can be made for one set of resources and not affect the other set, potentially representing different departments.
- **Access control**: Permissions can be placed on a resource pool. Resource pools can be used for delegation of privileges.

> VMware vSphere vApps are not only containers for virtual machines running multi-tiered applications but also serve as a resource pool for its virtual machines.

It's recommended that resource pools and VMs not be made sibling objects within a hierarchy, because resource pools are by default assigned shares that may not appropriately compare to those assigned to a VM, which can potentially cause performance issues.

Virtual Machine Performance and Resource Allocation

Creating a resource pool

To create a resource pool, right-click on a parent object for the resource pool (a standalone ESXi host, a DRS enabled cluster, or another resource pool) and select **New Resource Pool...**, as demonstrated in the following screenshot:

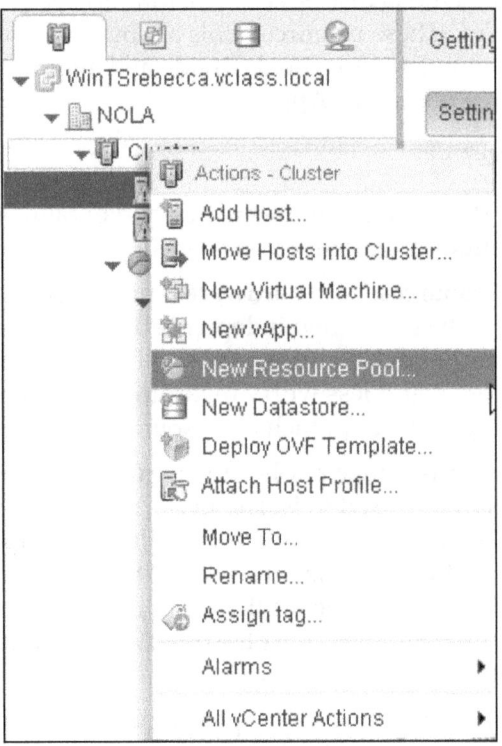

This will launch the resource pool creation dialog box.

Enter the desired name of the resource pool and the allocation of CPU and memory resources to the new resource pool by using the **Shares**, **Reservations**, and **Limit** fields. If the resource pool's reservation should be expandable, select the **Expandable** checkbox (shown in the following screenshot):

Chapter 6

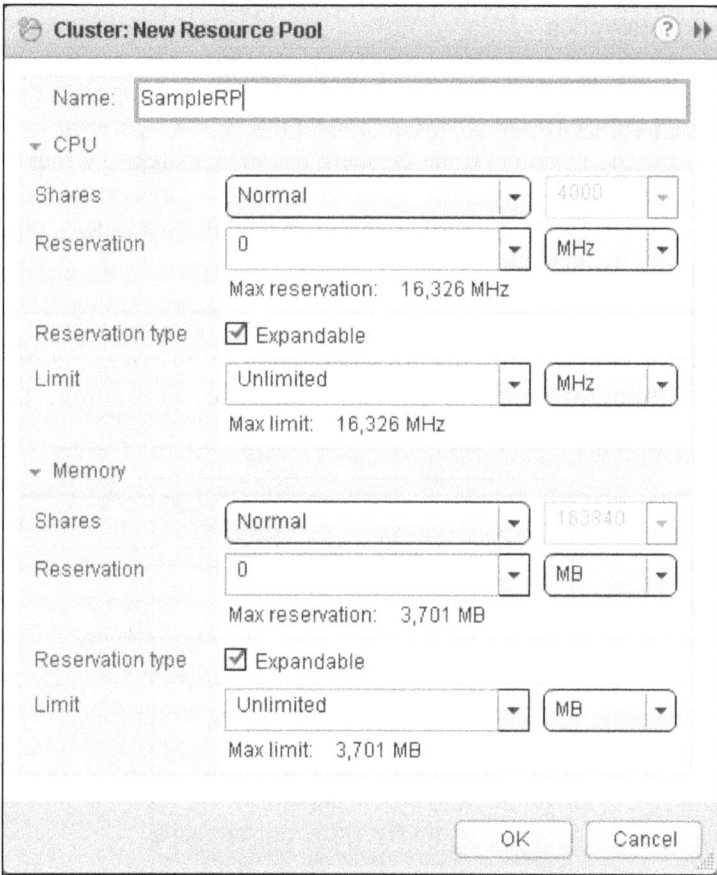

Consult the following table for assistance in making these selections. Click on **OK** after configuration is complete.

The following table depicts the different resource control options available at the resource pool or vApp level:

Option	Description
Shares	Value that specifies the relative priority or importance of this resource pool's access to a given resource with respect to the parent's total. Sibling vApps share resources according to this value. Select **Low**, **Normal** or **High**; this specifies share values in a 1:2:4 ratio, respectively. Select **Custom** to assign resource pools a specific proportional weight if the default ratio doesn't fit.
Reservation	Guaranteed amount of resource for this resource pool.

Virtual Machine Performance and Resource Allocation

Option	Description
Reservation type	If the **Expandable** checkbox is selected, this will make the reservation expandable. This means that if the combined reservations of the virtual machines exceed the reservation of the resource pool, the resource pool can use resources from its parent resource pools or the root to meet the demand.
Limit	Consumption of resources cannot exceed this value. Select **Unlimited** to specify no upper limit.

Once the resource pool is created, populate the pool by moving virtual machines into the pool. Alternatively, child resource pools or vApps can be created within the parent pool. After creation, your inventory pane may look similar to the following screenshot:

Expandable reservations

The following example demonstrates how a resource pool with an expandable reservation works. In this example, the parent resource pool has a single child resource pool and virtual machine; the child resource has two virtual machines. Let's imagine, in this example, that the child resource pool was configured for an expandable reservation and that the numbers associated with each object are reservations. In this scenario, creating a child resource pool with a 3 GHz reservation would leave the parent pool with 5 GHz available. Once VM1 powers on, 3 GHz is still available at the parent pool level. The child resource pool is configured for a 3 GHz reservation, which is not enough to meet the reservations of the virtual machines within. If VM2 powers on, then there is only 1 GHz left; since it was stated at the beginning of this scenario that the child pool was configured for an expandable reservation, this means VM3 can consume 1 GHz from the child pool and 1 GHz from the parent pool. Everything can successfully power on. This example is demonstrated in the following diagram:

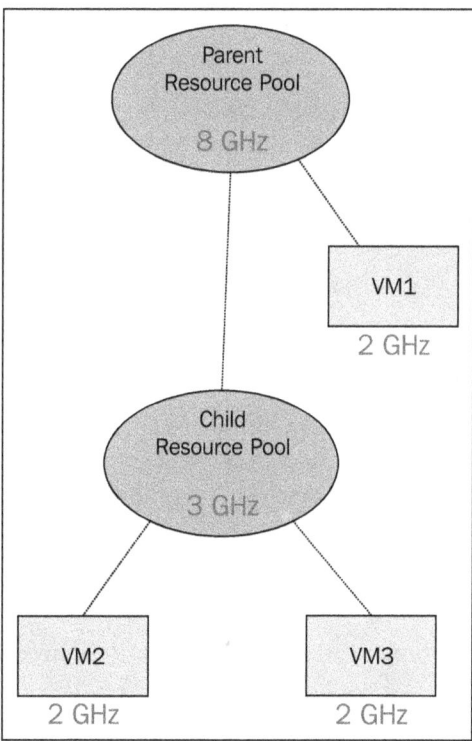

Consider that the child pool may not have been configured for an expandable reservation. If this were the case, then VM1 would be able to power on, but only one virtual machine within the child pool could power on. If VM2 were powered on first, then VM3 would present an error stating that the reservation could not be met and is unable to power on. In order to resolve this, the reservation of the child pool must be increased and be made expandable, or the reservation of the VM3 must be decreased.

Network I/O Control

A distributed virtual switch is similar to a standard virtual switch, except that it operates at the virtual datacenter level and has far more features. Distributed virtual switches are managed by and configured in vCenter. The configuration is consistent across all ESXi hosts configured for use by a distributed virtual switch. vCenter stores the state of the distributed virtual switch, port groups, and ports in its database so that networking policies and performance statistics migrate with the virtual machines when migrated to a different ESXi host. Check http://kb.vmware.com/kb/1010555 and http://kb.vmware.com/kb/1010557 for more on the creation of configuration of distributed virtual switches.

vSphere 4.1 introduced the **Network I/O Control**, a distributed virtual switch feature that gives an administrator the ability to make bandwidth guarantees for different types of network traffic. In an environment where multiple types of traffic are sharing the same network pipe, as where 10 GigE network cards are common, this really becomes an important feature. Network I/O Control can be used to guarantee different service levels in order to prioritize the various types of network traffic.

Network I/O Control is not available for standard virtual switches, only using distributed virtual switches, which requires the vSphere Enterprise Plus license.

Network I/O Control allows an administrator to configure network resource pools. Similar to resource pools for CPU and memory, network resource pools use shares and limits to control bandwidth utilization of various traffic types.

To set up Network I/O Control, perform the following steps:

1. Browse to the distributed virtual switch in the vSphere Web Client.
2. Select the **Manage** tab and then click on the **Resource Allocation** button.

The system-defined pools are created by default; this is demonstrated in the following screenshot. These can be modified as desired or custom (user-defined) pools can be created:

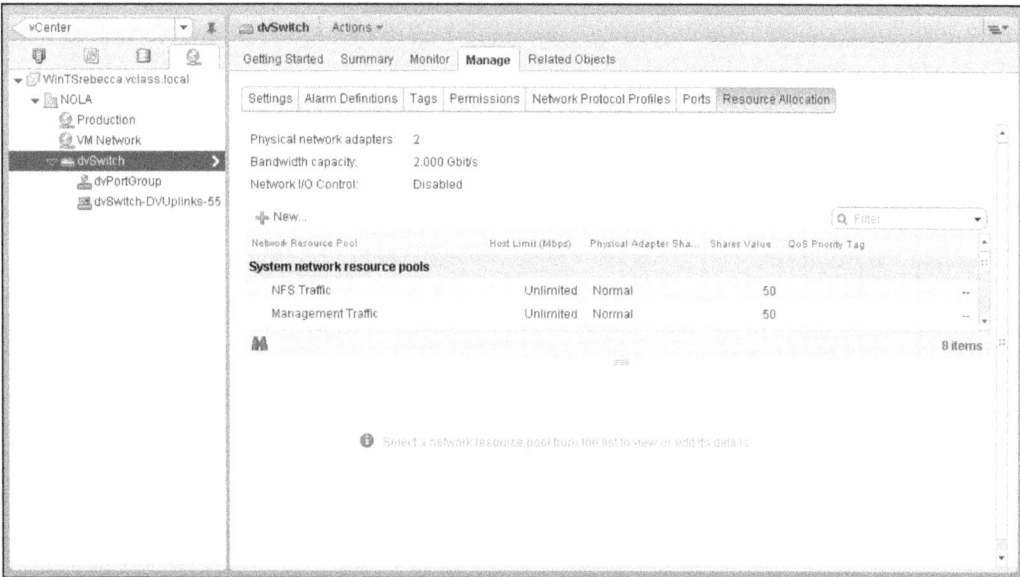

To create a user-defined network resource, click on the **New** button. When the dialog box is launched, specify a name and description. Adjust the settings for the **Physical adapter shares**, **Host limit (Mbps)**, and **QoS tag** fields. This is demonstrated in the following screenshot.

When editing or creating a new network resource pool, the following three settings are configurable:

- **Physical adapter shares**: This allows for prioritization of physical NIC access during times of contention. Four different configurations are possible: **High**, **Normal** (default), **Low**, and **Custom** values.

- **Host limit (Mbps)**: This caps the network bandwidth, in Mbps, that this specific network resource pool can access. By default, this is set to **Unlimited**.

- **QoS tag**: **Quality of Service** (802.1p) tags are placed on all outgoing frames. Any upstream network device that is compatible with this feature will continue to apply to the QoS tags. By default, this is set to **(none)**, but values between **1** and **7** can be configured. See the preceding table for configuration assistance.

These three settings are shown in the following screenshot:

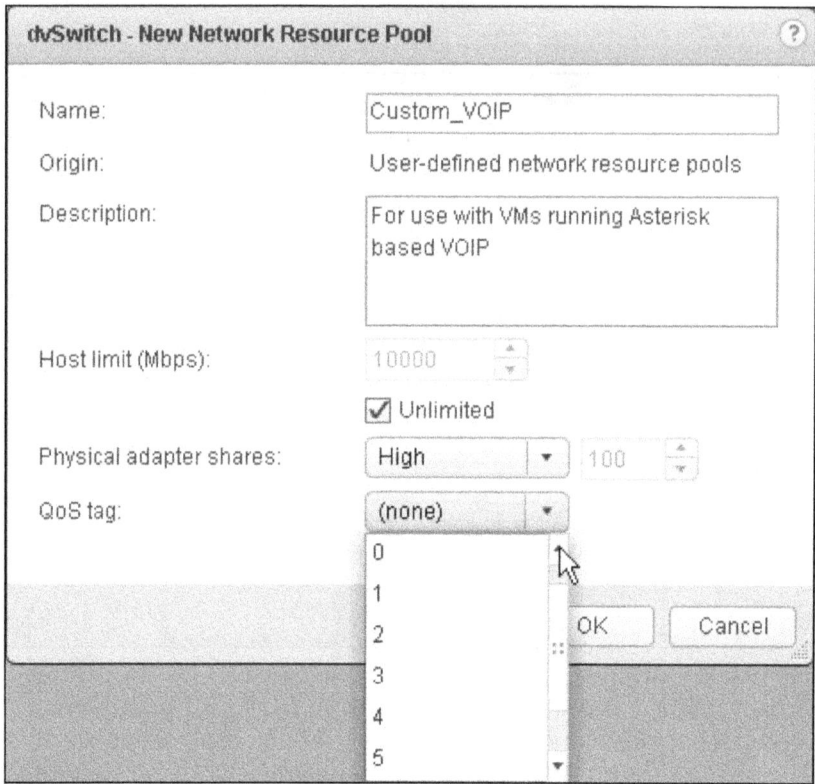

Use the following table to aide in selecting the correct value for a **QoS tag**:

QoS Priority tag	Description
(none)	Best effort
1	Background
2	Excellent effort
3	Critical applications
4	Video, <100 milliseconds latency
5	Voice, <10 milliseconds latency
6	Internetwork control
7	Network control

Chapter 6

Click on **OK** after the network resource pool is configured as desired.

To assign this network resource pool to a distributed port group, perform the following steps:

1. Use the vSphere Web Client to browse to a distributed virtual switch.
2. Right-click on the distributed virtual switch and select **Manage Distributed Port Groups**; this will bring up the wizard presented in the next screenshot.
3. Select the checkbox next to **Resource Allocation**, as shown in the following screenshot:

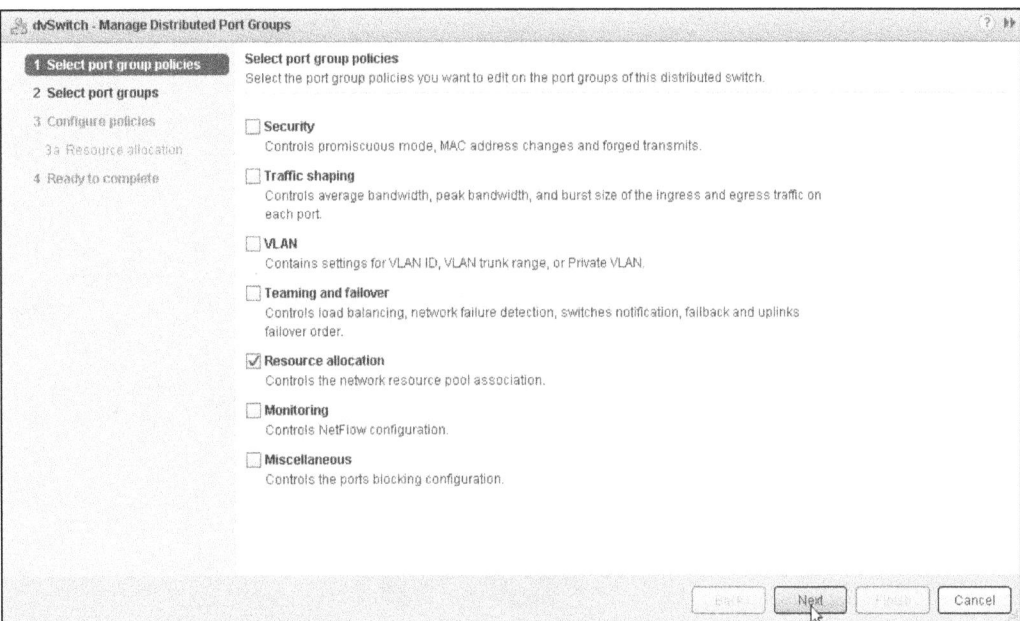

Click on **Next**.

Virtual Machine Performance and Resource Allocation

Select the distributed port group that you would like to associate with this network resource pool.

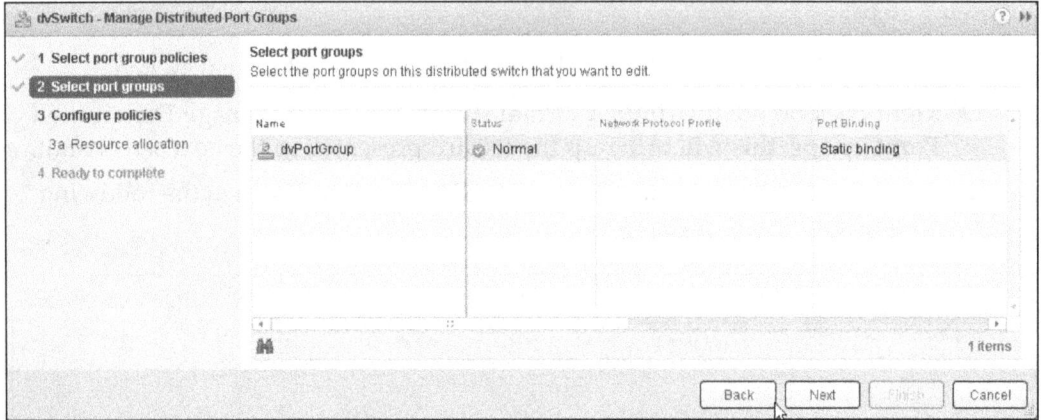

Click on **Next** after making a selection.

On the next pane, click on the drop-down list associated with **Network resource pool**, and select the appropriate resource pool for this specific distributed port group, as shown in the following screenshot:

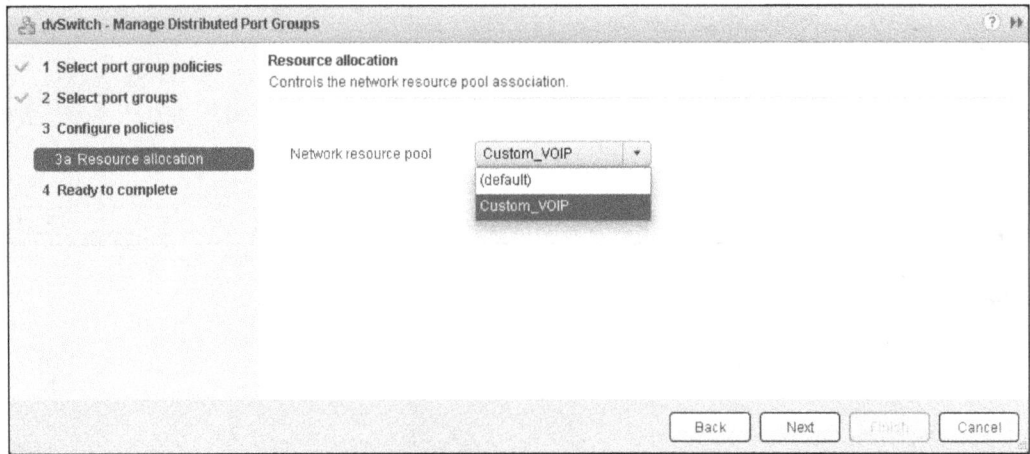

After making the selection, click on **Next**.

Review all of the policies configured in the **Ready to complete** pane:

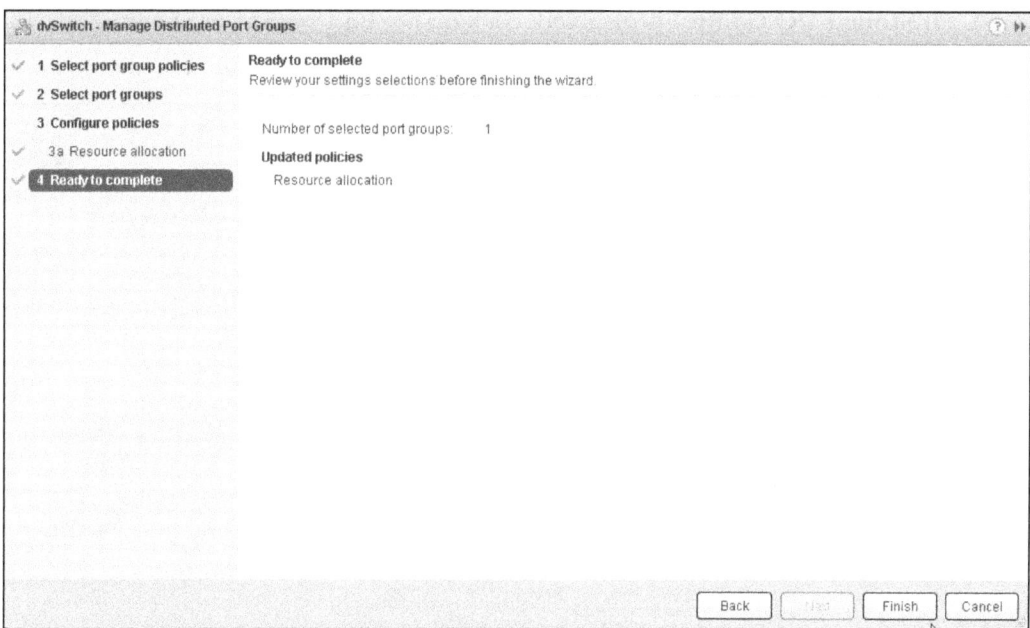

Click on **Finish** when satisfied with the configuration.

Storage I/O Control

With VMware Storage I/O Control, you can configure rules and policies to specify the priority of each virtual machine's storage access by using shares and limits. When I/O congestion is detected, Storage I/O Control dynamically allocates the available I/O resources to VMs according to your rules, enabling you to improve service levels for critical applications and reduce the amount of active performance management required. We can use this feature with or without Storage DRS. Datastore clusters and storage DRS are further discussed in *Chapter 9, Balancing Resource Utilization and Availability*. This feature does require vSphere Enterprise Plus licensing.

To enable this feature, perform the following steps:

1. Browse to a datastore in the vSphere Web Client.
2. Go to the **Manage** tab and select **General** under the **Settings** tab.

Virtual Machine Performance and Resource Allocation

3. If **Storage I/O Control** is disabled, click on the **Edit** button, as shown in the following screenshot:

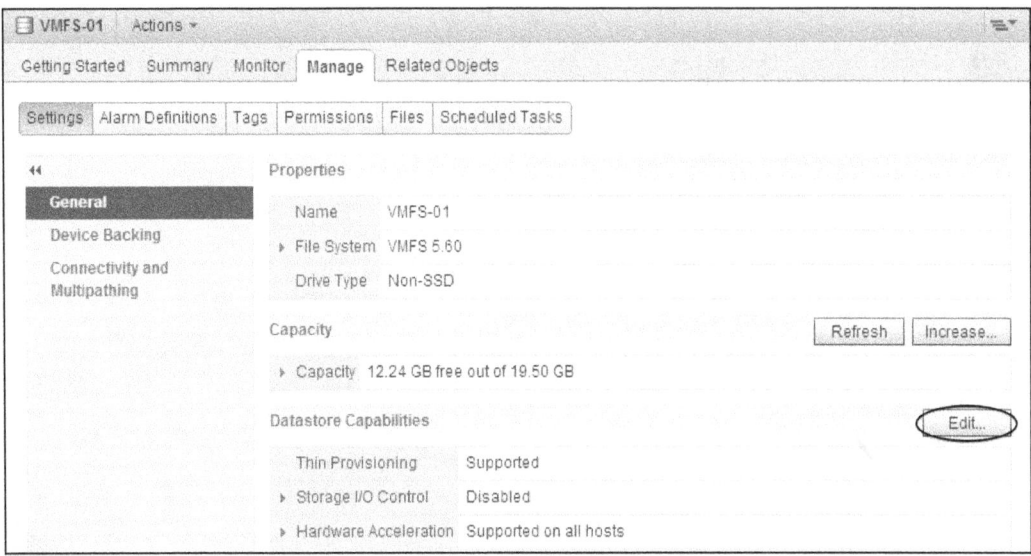

This will bring up the settings dialog box for the selected datastore. Check the box to enable Storage I/O Control (shown in the upcoming screenshot).

Storage I/O Control's default latency threshold is 30 milliseconds with the **Manual** option, which may be fine for some storage but not all. Storage I/O Control can be used to automatically figure out an optimal latency by using an injector-based model. For this selection, choose **Percentage of peak throughput**, which is set to **90** percent by default. The injector is part of Storage I/O Control and is a mechanism used to characterize each of the datastores by injecting random (read) I/O. Before you get worried, the injector only injects I/O when the datastore is idle. Even when the injector is busy, it will back down and retry later when it notices other activities on the datastore. Then in order to characterize the datastore, the injector uses different amounts of outstanding I/Os and measures the latency for this I/O. Using the injector model, Storage I/O Control can determine the peak throughput of a datastore and use it to determine the peak latency of a datastore. Storage I/O Control is then able to set latency thresholds to 90 percent. The **Configure Storage I/O Control** dialog box is shown in the following screenshot:

Chapter 6

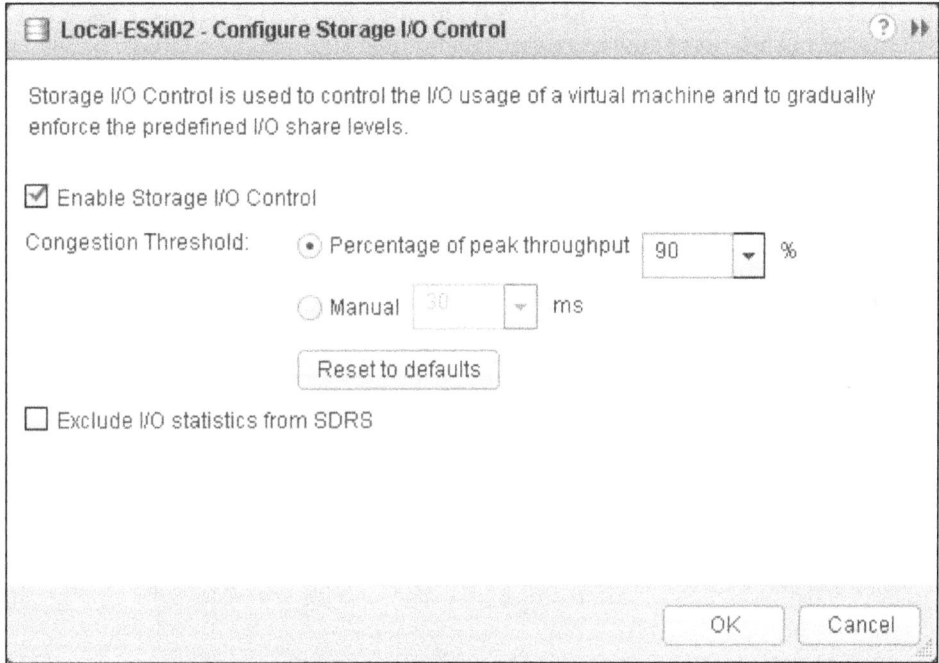

Click on **OK** after configuring this feature.

To set the storage I/O shares and limits for the individual virtual machine, perform the following steps:

1. Browse to a virtual machine in the vSphere Web Client.
2. Right-click on the virtual machine and select **Edit Settings**.

3. In the virtual machine properties dialog box, expand the **Hard disk 1** field under the **Virtual Hardware** tab. By default, all virtual machine shares are set to **Normal (1000)**, with unlimited IOPS, as shown in the following screenshot:

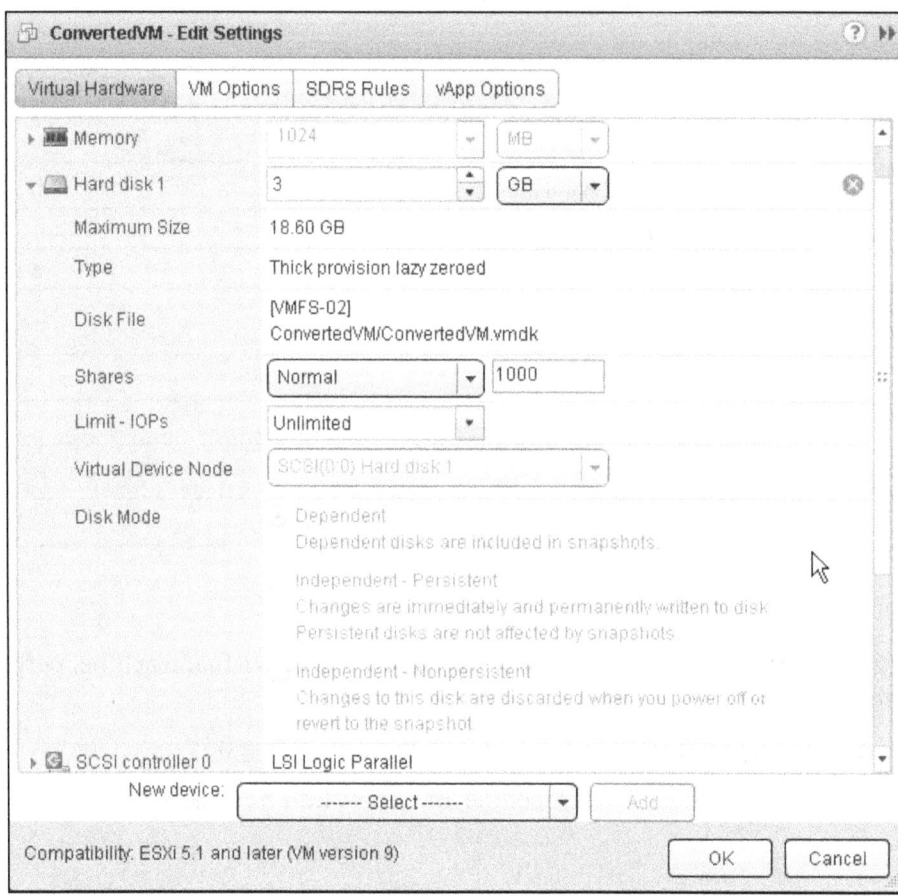

When this feature is enabled on a datastore, our hosts begin to monitor that device's latency when communicating with it. If the latency exceeds the threshold, then it is considered congested and each VM's share values will kick in and be able to access the datastore proportionally.

vSphere Storage APIs

vStorage API is a generic term that covers multiple individual APIs, including Array Integration, Storage Awareness, Multipathing, and Data Protection.

- **VMware vSphere Storage APIs for Array Integration (VAAI)**: Its goal is to assist in providing hardware assistance to accelerate I/O operations, which can be more efficiently accomplished using the storage hardware rather than the ESXi host resources. This can offload different tasks such as cloning, deploying from template, and snapshot operations. This can provide better performance, making these common tasks faster and more efficient. Check `http://kb.vmware.com/kb/1021976` for more information.

- **VMware vSphere Storage APIs for Storage Awareness (VASA)**: This is a software API that provides information to vCenter regarding topology, storage capabilities, and the current state of the storage devices. This essentially gives a vSphere administrator management oversight for storage. vCenter pulls its information from a VASA provider, which is written and distributed by the array vendor. Check `http://kb.vmware.com/kb/2004098` and your storage vendor documentation for more information.

- **VMware vSphere Storage APIs for Multipathing**: This relies on **Pluggable Storage Architecture (PSA)**. The PSA is an extensible framework that allows for and regulates the use of more than one multipathing plugin. This architecture allows for third-party vendors to design failover mechanisms and load balancing techniques for a specific storage array type, and then inject the code directly into ESXi's storage I/O path. For more information, check `http://kb.vmware.com/kb/1011375` and your array vendor's documentation.

- **VMware vSphere Storage APIs for Data Protection (VADP)**: This is a set of APIs that allows for a centralized backup and recovery of virtual machines without needing to install and use backup agents in the guest operating system. Check your backup software vendor documentation for VADP support and check `http://kb.vmware.com/kb/1021175` for more information.

Disk alignment

Performance impacts can be caused by the misalignment of the filesystem partitions. VMFS, like other filesystems, can suffer a penalty when the partition is not properly aligned. An unaligned guest operating system partition can result in the I/O crossing a boundary, causing additional I/O. This can negatively affect throughput and latency.

Use vCenter Server to create VMFS partitions; this issue is avoided because it will automatically align the partitions along the boundaries. However, if your storage vendor does not give you a specific recommendation, make sure to use a starting block that is a multiple of 8 KB. The esxtop utility can be used to monitor storage I/O impact.

The guest operating system data filesystem boundaries within the virtual machines must also be aligned once the VMFS partitions are aligned. It is not necessarily recommended to align the boot disk for a virtual machine; the data disks are the focus of alignment. This issue does not affect many of the newer guest operating systems, such as Windows 2008, Windows 7, and Red Hat Enterprise Linux 6, because these are automatically aligned. Utilities like `diskpart.exe` may be used to create a disk partition using an offset of 2048 sectors or 1 MB. This is a destructive process that would require you to back up and then restore the data.

> Do this as a part of the virtual machine template so that it is done correctly once and is not a worry for each virtual machine running an older guest operating system.

Performance tuning

Performance tuning for virtual machines and ESXi hosts is complicated due to virtual machines sharing the underlying primary four physical resources: storage, networks, CPU, and memory. Overcommitment of resources can cause performance bottlenecks. Not only should physical hardware resources be considered, but software settings also need to be optimized. The **virtual machine monitor** (**VMM**), virtual machine settings, resource controls, and application configurations can also affect performance.

Traditional performance practices

Always use common sense in any design to achieve good performance. Some traditional practices include the following:

- Know the physical resource (primary four) requirements for each virtual machine's applications and guest operating systems, so the virtual machine is correctly configured and capable of providing the resources the applications will demand.
- Configure the virtual machines with the correct virtual hardware for the guest operating system.
- When possible, use the latest hardware available for the ESXi hosts. Newer hardware platforms can have features that can be used to improve hypervisor performance.
- Always consider the bottlenecks related to shared storage. Benchmark these devices so there are no surprises when you run your designed environment in production.
- Never just build out ESXi hosts and dump virtual machines on them. Plan and design to accommodate the workload of your virtual machines and your hosts.

An important step in performance tuning is to closely monitor the workloads in order to discover any potential bottlenecks. vCenter Operations Manager may be used to monitor the health of your infrastructure. vSphere environments are typically dynamic; it is important to keep an eye on the behavior of virtual machines and ESXi hosts. vSphere monitoring tools are available and allow you to monitor your workloads. This will be discussed in *Chapter 7, Monitoring Virtual Machines*.

Performance problems

What is a performance problem? It is a matter of perception; it really depends on whom you ask. Your users will always tell you that it is not fast enough. Management may tell you that you must achieve what the sales guys want or recommend. Using the human factor is not the best way to determine performance design.

Ideally, use some kind of ongoing performance management process, such as a baseline or a **service level agreement** (**SLA**). A performance problem can now be defined as when an application fails to meet a predetermined SLA or deviates negatively from a baseline anytime.

SLAs are used to ensure that requirements of a given contract or job are met. If an SLA is not available, then baseline measurements may be used. Baseline measurements measure your performance, maintain baselines, and try to achieve those as goals for performance.

Finally, as a last resort, use the human factor. Make sure to define a clear statement of the problem and set a target for performance before beginning the troubleshooting process.

Troubleshooting performance

We not only need to define the problems but also a logical way to approach them. Here are a few things to consider when troubleshooting a performance issue:

- What are the symptoms of the performance problem?
- How will you approach fixing the issues?
- Where do you start looking for issues?
- Which tools do you prefer to use for troubleshooting?
- How do you identify where you will look for problems?
- Where do you go from there to find the root cause?
- Where do you go once you've identified what you think the root cause is? What do you change?
- What criterion constitutes a successful resolution for this issue?

In a virtualized environment, you always need to consider the many possible points of constraint: cluster configuration, ESXi host configuration, virtual machine configuration, guest operating system configuration, and application configuration. Do not consider the vSphere-related configurations only; don't forget the other physical networking and storage resources. Use baselines and SLAs to establish performance goals and to determine whether or not you are meeting those performance goals.

Many performance problems in vSphere environments are caused by a few common causes. Check the *vSphere Troubleshooting* guide for more information.

Summary

There are three resource controls that are available to determine how resources are provided to a virtual machine; these are shares, limits, and reservations. Limits, shares, and reservations can also be set on a resource pool and/or a vApp. A resource pool is a logical abstraction of resources from the root pool and is managed hierarchically using a parent-child relationship. Memory overcommitment happens when the physical memory installed on an ESXi host is less than the sum of memory allocated to all virtual machines as well as overhead. vSphere uses multiple memory reclamation techniques to prevent an ESXi host from crashing when physical memory is low. Transparent page sharing allows pages of memory that are identical to be stored in the same place. Ballooning requires VMware Tools to be installed. If necessary, the hypervisor can directly swap out guest physical memory to the swap file, which frees host physical memory for other virtual machines as well as the hypervisor.

With VMware Storage I/O Control, you can configure rules and policies to specify the priority of each virtual machine's storage access by using shares and limits. Network I/O Control allows an administrator to configure network resource pools. Filesystems, including VMFS, can suffer a penalty when the partition is not properly aligned.

Virtual machine performance is affected by hardware and software configurations. Due to the sharing of underlying physical resources, performance tuning can be very complicated. Use a common sense approach when it comes to configuring virtual machines and designing for performance.

The next chapter will discuss monitoring of virtual machines.

7
Monitoring Virtual Machines

In this chapter, we will discover how vSphere administrators can monitor the resource usage of different inventory objects. It is important to monitor the vSphere infrastructure to determine if there is a resource bottleneck or if a virtual machine or ESXi host is experiencing constraint. There are many tools that are available within vSphere that can assist VMware administrators to monitor resources and detect any potential bottlenecks. Both esxtop and performance charts are natively available within vSphere for monitoring. Alarms may also be configured to alert administrators when specific events occur or when thresholds are exceeded.

In this chapter, you will learn to:

- Use performance charts
- Use esxtop
- Configure condition-based alarms
- Configure event-based alarm

Performance charts

Performance charts can be displayed using the vSphere Client connected to either an ESXi host directly or a vCenter Server or by using the vSphere Web Client. Throughout this chapter we will be discussing tools that are natively available within vCenter and ESXi, but keep in mind that the vCenter Operations Manager may also be used to monitor the health of your infrastructure. These performance charts can provide a great deal of useful information for an administrator to analyze performance. There are two types of charts available: overview and advanced.

Overview performance charts

Overview performance charts display the performance statistics that are most useful to quickly diagnose problems and monitor performance.

To view an overview performance chart:

1. Select a virtual machine or ESXi host in the vCenter inventory pane within the vSphere Web Client.
2. Click on the **Monitor** tab.
3. Choose the **Performance** button and click on the **Overview** link on the left pane.

Depending on what target object is selected from the inventory pane, using this process will provide a quick view of the ESXi host or virtual machine's health and its performance. The following screenshot provides a partial view of the overview performance charts for an ESXi host; to view more, you would typically just scroll down in the vSphere Web Client. Overview performance charts should be used when you are just seeking a quick view of the most common metrics for the selected inventory objects.

The following screenshot displays the CPU usage of an ESXi host; notice that the CPU (% is very low as there is currently not much running on the selected host. There are many different Overview performance charts that may be viewed, such as CPU ready time, memory ballooning, swap activity, and so on. Continue scrolling down to see more charts.

Advanced performance charts

An advanced performance chart provides a more granular graphical display of an object's statistical data. For example, the performance data can be displayed over multiple time periods. You can use an advanced performance chart to examine a variety of objects in more detail, including

- Datacenters
- Clusters
- ESXi hosts
- Resource pools
- Virtual machines
- vApps
- Datastores

Monitoring Virtual Machines

The following are the steps to view an advanced performance chart:

1. Select an object in the vCenter inventory pane within the vSphere Web Client.
2. Click on the **Monitor** tab.
3. Click on the **Performance** button.
4. Click on the **Advanced** link on the left pane.

The following screenshot provides an example of the advanced performance charts for an ESXi host. To customize the advanced performance chart, click on the **Chart Options** hyperlink, as shown in the following screenshot:

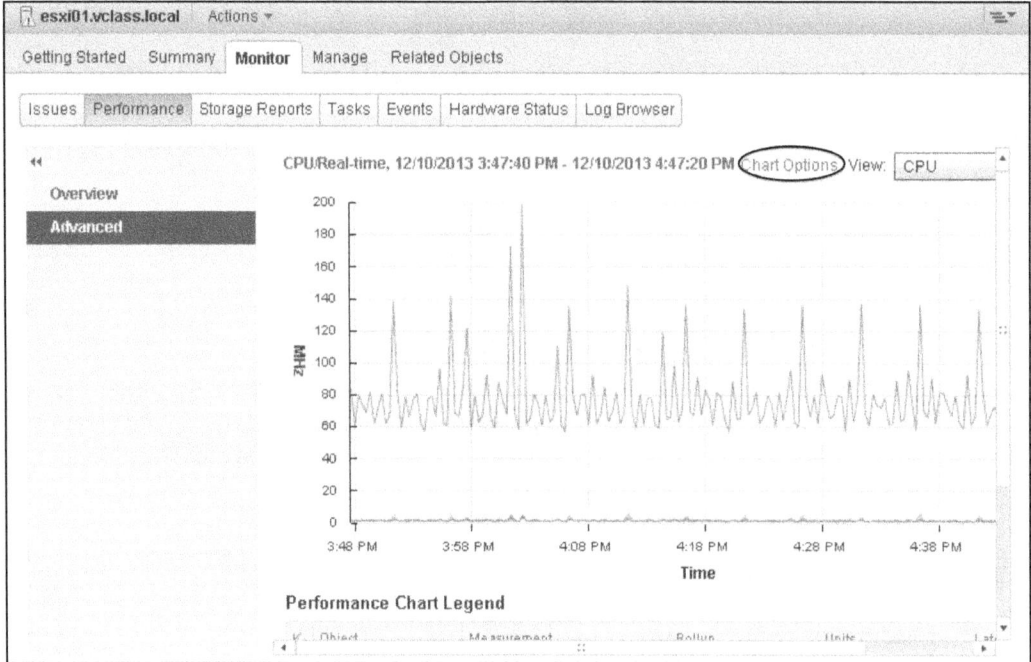

There are many options that are available when using an advanced performance chart. Clicking on the **Chart Options** hyperlink will present a dialog box allowing the administrator to customize the advanced performance chart. The following screenshot displays the many chart options available using this type of chart:

Chapter 7

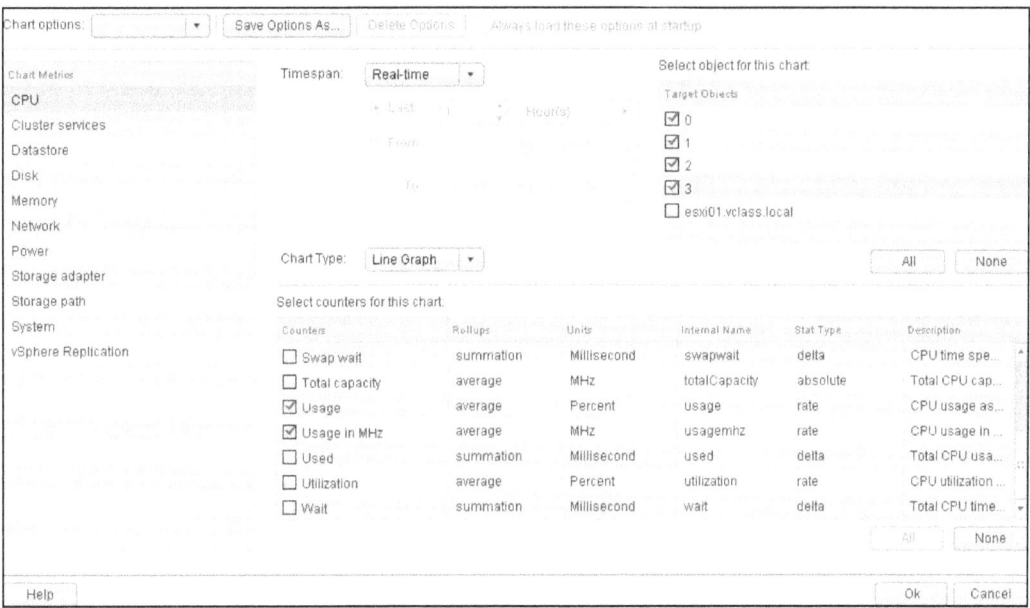

The options available using the advanced performance chart include the following:

- **Chart Metrics**: This option allows you to select the resource or object to view its available metrics.
- **Timespan**: Historical information can be used to see the past day, week, month, and year at varying granularity. There is no option for true real-time results; real time is generated at a 20 second interval for an hour. After an hour, those values get stored into 5-minute rollups. The weekly results get rolled up into 30-minute samples. Monthly results are rolled up into 2-hour samples. Annual samples are rolled up into daily samples so the charts don't inundate the vCenter Server database.
- **Select object for this chart**: Objects are instances or aggregations of devices such as physical cores, vCPUs, HBAs, NICs, and so on. Select the object(s) for which you are trying to view performance information.
- **Chart Type**: This option allows you to choose a line graph or stacked graph. A line graph shows the monitored instances independently, each plotted on a separate line in the chart. The stacked graph option shows each monitored instance stacked atop each other for comparison purposes. There are other chart types available depending on which **Chart Metric** was chosen

[201]

- **Select counters for this chart**: The counters identify which statistics to collect with regard to the selected objects, for example, the ready time for the selected vCPUs or packets dropped for the selected NIC. In case you are unsure which counter to select, a description is provided in order to assist in this process. Refer to the *vSphere Monitoring and Performance* guide for more information regarding available counters at http://pubs.vmware.com/vsphere-55/topic/com.vmware.ICbase/PDF/vsphere-esxi-vcenter-server-55-monitoring-performance-guide.pdf.

The selection of the counter determines what the unit of measurement is, the rollup, and the statistic type. Depending on which counter is selected, there are a few different statistic types that may be used. These are as follows:

- **Rate**: This is the value over a current interval, for example, CPU usage
- **Delta**: This is a change from a previous interval, for example, CPU ready
- **Absolute**: This is a completely independent value, for example, active memory

The unit of measurement dictates the standard in which the statistic quantity is measured. Another value that is determined by the counter select is the rollup. Rollup is the conversion between our statistic intervals. The past hour statistics are shown at a 20 second granularity, for instance. The rollup is the type of statistical values returned for that particular counter. There are a few different ways that the data can be rolled up. These are as follows:

- **Average**: This is the collected data during an interval that is gathered and averaged.
- **Latest**: This represents the current value
- **Minimum**: This is the minimum value that is rolled up
- **Maximum**: This is the maximum value that is rolled up
- **Summation**: This indicates the data is collected and summed, and the measurement displayed is the sum of the data collected during the set interval

After this advanced performance chart has been customized as desired, the options can be preserved for future use by clicking on the **Save Options As** button.

Use advanced performance charts to gain a more granular view of an object's performance. An overview performance chart gives very limited information for common counters. If anything appears abnormal when viewing the overview performance chart, then use an advanced performance chart to gain more insight with what is occurring. Once a bottleneck or constraint is identified, a solution can be formulated to resolve the issue.

For information regarding data collection intervals and levels, view the *vSphere Monitoring and Performance* guide.

Using esxtop

The `esxtop` and `resxtop` commands enable command-line monitoring for real-time ESXi host resource usage for each of the core four resources: CPU, memory, network, and disk. When this tool is used interactively, the data is viewed on different types of screens, one for each of the resources. The data presented includes some metrics that are not accessible using the overview or advanced performance charts. The fundamental difference between `resxtop` and `esxtop` is that `esxtop` can only be started through the local ESXi Shell of the ESXi host (through the DCUI or SSH) whereas `resxtop` can be used remotely.

There are three modes of execution available for `esxtop` and `resxtop`:

- **Interactive mode**: This is the default mode. This option provides real-time statistics that can be viewed by navigating throughout the different resource screens.
- **Batch mode**: This mode allows the collection of data in order to save the resource utilization statistics in a file. To do this, use the command `esxtop -b > filename.csv`. Alternatively, `resxtop` can be used.
- **Replay mode**: This mode uses data collected by the `vm-support` command, interprets it, and plays it back as `esxtop` statistics.

The `resxtop` utility is a vSphere CLI command, thus requiring the use of a vSphere CLI package or the **vSphere Management Assistant** (**vMA**).

The following image displays an example of running the `esxtop` utility directly in the ESXi Shell. First open an SSH application, for example, PuTTY, and connect to an ESXi host. SSH would need to be enabled for the target ESXi host prior to beginning this process.

When connecting to the ESXi Shell using an SSH application, ensure SSH is enabled on the desired ESXi host. For steps on how to enable SSH, visit `http://vmware.com/kb/1017910`.

Once authenticated, type `esxtop` to begin running this utility.

Monitoring Virtual Machines

There are several statistics that appear on all the available views within `esxtop` (or `resxtop`) while running in the interactive mode:

- The top line is the Uptime line; this displays the current time, the time since the last restart, the number of currently running worlds, and load averages. A world is an ESXi VMkernel schedulable component, like a process on a guest operating system. Worlds, just like processes, are scheduled by the VMkernel.

- Underneath that, the load averages over the past one-minute, five minutes, and fifteen minutes are displayed. These load averages take the running as well as the ready-to-run worlds into consideration. A load average of 1.00 means that there is full utilization of all physical CPUs; likewise, a load average of 2.00 means that the ESXi host system may need double as many physical CPUs as are currently available. A 0.50 load average would mean that the physical CPUs are half-utilized.

These are demonstrated at the top of the following screenshot:

```
6:37:53am up 2 days 11:04, 422 worlds, 2 VMs, 2 vCPUs; CPU load average: 0.01
0.01, 0.01
PCPU USED(%):  1.2 1.3 2.4 1.0 AVG: 1.5
PCPU UTIL(%):  1.4 1.5 2.5 1.2 AVG: 1.6

      ID NAME                NWLD    %USED    %RUN    %SYS    %WAIT %VMWAIT    %RDY
 1095285 esxtop.592421          1     1.74    1.41    0.00    98.80       -    0.00
  494761 SampleVM               7     1.30    1.27    0.02   700.00    0.24    0.07
  494954 SUSE                   7     0.85    0.84    0.01   700.00    0.16    0.10
       2 system                70     0.62    0.62    0.00  7000.00       -    0.37
       8 helper               156     0.19    0.19    0.00 15600.00       -     0.0
    3027 sh.34389               1     0.17    0.17    0.00   100.00       -    0.02
    1779 hostd.33757           13     0.09    0.08    0.00  1300.00       -    0.03
    3209 vpxa.34485            10     0.08    0.07    0.01  1000.00       -    0.04
    2669 logchannellogge        1     0.05    0.04    0.00   100.00       -    0.02
    2745 rhttpproxy.3424        9     0.04    0.04    0.00   900.00       -    0.04
    1274 net-lacp.33404         3     0.02    0.02    0.00   300.00       -    0.01
    1298 vmkiscsid.33419        2     0.01    0.01    0.00   200.00       -    0.01
 1095172 sshd.592364            1     0.01    0.01    0.00   100.00       -    0.00
    3529 openwsmand.3465        3     0.01    0.01    0.00   300.00       -    0.01
    1853 net-lbt.33797          1     0.01    0.01    0.00   100.00       -    0.00
     882 vmsyslogd.33178        3     0.00    0.00    0.00   300.00       -    0.00
       9 drivers               13     0.00    0.00    0.00  1300.00       -    0.01
    1527 vmware-usbarbit        2     0.00    0.00    0.00   200.00       -    0.01
```

Monitoring CPU

The default view in esxtop is the CPU pane. In this utility, a group refers to a running virtual machine, a resource pool, or a non-virtual machine world. These groups will be assigned a **group ID (GID)**.

Some of the common CPU statistics are as follows:

- **%USED**: This is the percentage of physical CPU core cycles used
- **%SYS**: This is the percentage of time spent in the VMkernel to process interrupts and other system activities
- **%WAIT**: This is the percentage of time spent in the block or busy wait state including the idle time
- **%RDY**: This is the percentage of time the vCPU is ready to run but is not provided CPU resources on which to execute
- **%CSTP**: This is the percentage of time spent in a ready, co-schedule state
- **%MLMTD**: This is the percentage of time not running due to a limit
- **NWLD**: This is the number of worlds that are associated with a given group

The CPU pane is shown in the previous screenshot.

Monitoring memory

To view the memory statistics, press the *M* key (upper or lowercase). This panel will display host-wide and group memory utilization information. The top line is the Uptime line; this displays the current time, the time since the last restart, the number of currently running worlds consuming memory, and over commitment averages. Underneath this line are multiple useful fields regarding ESXi host memory utilization; all are displayed in **megabytes** (**MB**):

- **PMEM**: This is memory information for the server
- **VMKMEM**: This is memory statistics for the ESXi VMkernel
- **PSHARE**: This is the amount of memory being shared using transparent page sharing
- **SWAP**: This is the swap usage statistics
- **ZIP**: This is memory compression information
- **MEMCTL**: This is memory balloon data

Monitoring Virtual Machines

The following screenshot displays `esxtop` in the memory view:

```
 6:40:10am up 2 days 11:07, 422 worlds, 2 VMs, 2 vCPUs; MEM overcommit avg: 0.00
, 0.00, 0.00
PMEM    /MB:   4095    total:   1018       vmk,    844 other,   2232 free
VMKMEM/MB:     4076  managed:    244   minfree,   2872 rsvd,    1204 ursvd,   high state
PSHARE/MB:      175   shared,     20    common:    155 saving
SWAP    /MB:      0     curr,      0   rclmtgt:                0.00 r/s,      0.00 w/s
ZIP     /MB:      0   zipped,      0     saved
MEMCTL/MB:        0     curr,      0    target,    814 max

      GID NAME               MCTL?    MCTLSZ   MCTLTGT   MCTLMAX     SWCUR     SWTGT
     3218 nssquery.34494       N        0.00      0.00      0.00      0.00      0.00
   494761 SampleVM             Y        0.00      0.00    249.21      0.00      0.00
     3763 sfcb-sfcb.34764      N        0.00      0.00      0.00      0.00      0.00
     3162 sh.34462             N        0.00      0.00      0.00      0.00      0.00
     1282 busybox.33413        N        0.00      0.00      0.00      0.00      0.00
      896 sh.33187             N        0.00      0.00      0.00      0.00      0.00
  1096326 sleep.592949         N        0.00      0.00      0.00      0.00      0.00
     2926 dcbd.34339           N        0.00      0.00      0.00      0.00      0.00
     4685 sfcb-ProviderMa      N        0.00      0.00      0.00      0.00      0.00
     3000 smartd.34376         N        0.00      0.00      0.00      0.00      0.00
     4107 sh.34940             N        0.00      0.00      0.00      0.00      0.00
     2879 sh.34316             N        0.00      0.00      0.00      0.00      0.00
  1095269 sh.592413            N        0.00      0.00      0.00      0.00      0.00
     3082 nscd.34416           N        0.00      0.00      0.00      0.00      0.00
```

There are a few more notable memory counters. These include:

- **MEMSZ**: This is the amount of memory allocated to the group
- **GRANT**: This is the amount of memory actually mapped to the group
- **SZTGT**: This is the amount of memory that the ESXi VMkernel wants to allocate to the group
- **MCTL?**: This lets us know whether or not the memory balloon driver is installed; **Y** means yes, **N** means no
- **MCTLSZ**: This is the memory amount reclaimed by ballooning
- **SWCUR**: This is the current swap usage
- **SWR/s**: This is swap reads per second, or the rate that ESXi swaps memory in from disk
- **SWW/s**: This is swap writes per second, or the rate that ESXi swaps memory out to disk
- **ZIP/s**: This is the compressed memory per second.
- **UNZIP/s**: This is the decompressed memory per second

`esxtop` often shows more information than what is needed for a specific problem you are troubleshooting. To display only virtual machine instances, type V (uppercase V) and this will shift the view to only virtual machine resource utilization. The following screenshot demonstrates the memory view but filters the information to only virtual machines:

```
6:40:16am up 2 days 11:07, 422 worlds, 2 VMs, 2 vCPUs; MEM overcommit avg: 0.00
, 0.00, 0.00
PMEM    /MB:  4095    total:    1018      vmk,    844 other,    2232 free
VMKMEM/MB:    4076  managed:     244  minfree,   2871 rsvd,     1204 ursvd,     high state
PSHARE/MB:     175   shared,      20   common:    155 saving
SWAP    /MB:     0      curr,      0 rclmtgt:                   0.00 r/s,       0.00 w/s
ZIP     /MB:     0    zipped,      0    saved
MEMCTL/MB:       0      curr,      0   target,    814 max
View VM only
         GID NAME            MCTL?    MCTLSZ    MCTLTGT    MCTLMAX    SWCUR    SWTGT
      494954 SUSE                Y      0.00       0.00     564.79     0.00     0.00
      494761 SampleVM            Y      0.00       0.00     249.21     0.00     0.00
```

Monitoring network

The network panel will display server-wide network utilization statistics. To view the network pane, press the *n* key (upper or lowercase). The statistical information is arranged by port ID for each virtual network device configured as shown in the following screenshot:

```
6:43:25am up 2 days 11:10, 422 worlds, 2 VMs, 2 vCPUs; CPU load average: 0.01
0.01, 0.01
   PORT-ID           USED-BY  TEAM-PNIC   PKTTX/s   MbTX/s   PKTRX/s   MbRX
   33554433       Management        n/a      0.00     0.00      0.00    0.
   33554434           vmnic0          -      2.96     0.01      1.58    0.
   33554435 Shadow of vmnic0        n/a      0.00     0.00      0.00    0.
   33554436             vmk0     vmnic0      2.96     0.01      0.99    0.
   33554437             vmk1     vmnic0      0.00     0.00      0.00    0.
   50331649       Management        n/a      0.00     0.00      0.00    0.
   50331650           vmnic1          -      0.00     0.00     25.88    0.
   50331651 Shadow of vmnic1        n/a      0.00     0.00      0.00    0.
   50331652           vmnic3          -      0.00     0.00     25.88    0.
   50331653 Shadow of vmnic3        n/a      0.00     0.00      0.00    0.
   50331654  285312:SampleVM     vmnic3      0.00     0.00      0.40    0.
   50331655      285420:SUSE     vmnic3      0.00     0.00      0.40    0.
```

Some helpful network statistics are as follows:

- **PORT-ID**: This is the virtual network device port ID
- **USED-BY**: This is the user of a virtual network device
- **TEAM-PNIC**: This is the physical NIC used for the team uplink
- **PKTTX/s**: This is packets transmitted per second
- **PKTRX/s**: This is packets received per second
- **MbTX/s**: This is megabits transmitted per second
- **MbRX/s**: This is megabits received per second
- **%DRPTX**: This is the transmit packets dropped percentage
- **%DRPRX**: This is receive packets dropped percentage

More network counters can be added by pressing the *F* key (upper or lower case).

Monitoring storage

The following screenshot displays the statistics that are available in the storage adapter view. Press *D* (upper or lowercase) to see the disk adapter information:

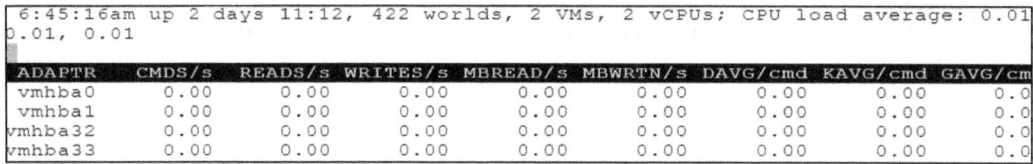

Pressing the *U* key (upper or lowercase) will display the storage device view. This view displays server wide storage device information, demonstrated by the following screenshot:

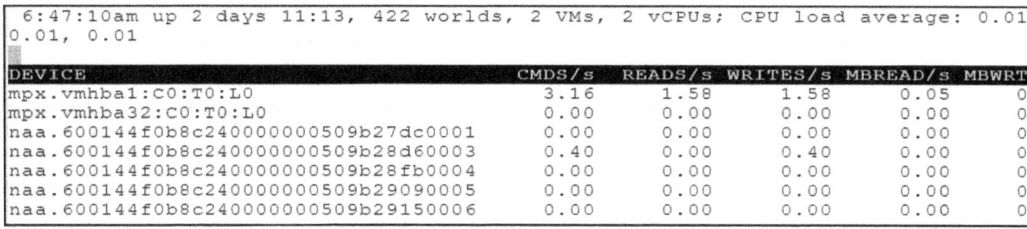

A few common storage statistics include:

- **CMDS/s**: This is the number of commands per second
- **READS/s**: This is the number of read commands per second
- **WRITES/s**: This is the number of write commands per second
- **MBREAD/s**: This is megabytes read per second
- **MBWRTN/s**: This is megabytes written per second
- **DAVG/cmd**: This is the average device read latency per command (in milliseconds)
- **KAVG/cmd**: This is the average ESXi VMkernel latency per command (in milliseconds)

Once again, don't forget that the storage information for the virtual machines can be displayed by pressing *V* (uppercase V) in the disk device view.

The esxtop options

If at any point you are unsure of which options are available to you, press either *H* (upper or lowercase) or *?* to print out all available interactive mode commands. The following screenshot demonstrates how the help option can be used to give a brief summary of available choices and list the `esxtop` displays:

```
^L        - redraw screen
space     - update display
h or ?    - help; show this text
q         - quit

Interactive commands are:

fF        Add or remove fields
oO        Change the order of displayed fields
s         Set the delay in seconds between updates
#         Set the number of instances to display
W         Write configuration file ~/.esxtop50rc
k         Kill a world
V         View only VM instances
L         Change the length of the NAME field
l         Limit display to a single group

Sort by:
          M:MEMSZ          B:MCTLSZ          N:GID
Switch display:
          c:cpu            i:interrupt       m:memory         n:network
          d:disk adapter   u:disk device     v:disk VM        p:power mgmt

Hit any key to continue:
```

To change views, simply press the key listed in the help menu.

Press *f* (upper or lowercase) to display all available statistics that can be added or removed from the current view. The following screenshot displays all statistics available in the memory pane by pressing *f*.

```
Current Field order: aBcDefghiJKlmnopq

   A:   ID = Id
*  B:   GID = Group Id
   C:   LWID = Leader World Id (World Group Id)
*  D:   NAME = Name
   E:   NWLD = Num Members
   F:   MEM ALLOC = MEM Allocations
   G:   NUMA STATS = Numa Statistics
   H:   SIZE = MEM Size (MB)
   I:   ACTV = MEM Active (MB)
*  J:   MCTL = MEM Ctl (MB)
*  K:   SWAP STATS = Swap Statistics (MB)
   L:   LLSWAP STATS = Llswap Statistics (MB)
   M:   CPT = MEM Checkpoint (MB)
   N:   COW = MEM Cow (MB)
   O:   OVHD = MEM Overhead (MB)
   P:   CMT = MEM Committed (MB)
   Q:   ZIP = MEM Compression (MB)

Toggle fields with a-q, any other key to return:
```

Monitoring Virtual Machines

To add or remove fields, simply press the specified letter.

For information on all counters available within `esxtop` and `resxtop`, refer to the *vSphere 5.5 Monitoring Performance* guide.

Using alarms

An alarm is a notification in response to a selected condition or event for an object in the vCenter Server inventory. There are many predefined alarms for most objects within the vCenter Server inventory. The predefined alarms are configurable to an extent, but if the alarm doesn't address a specific event or condition that you want to monitor, then a custom alarm can be defined.

Custom alarms can be created as either condition-based or event-based. **Condition-based alarms** monitor the current condition or state of an object whereas **event-based alarms** monitor events that occur within vCenter.

Some examples of condition-based alarms include:

- An ESXi host gets disconnected from vCenter
- A virtual machine is using 90 percent of its total memory
- A datastore's total space is 85 percent provisioned

Some examples of event-based alarms include:

- A vSphere license has expired
- SSH was enabled on an ESXi host
- A virtual machine was migrated

What you are trying to monitor will dictate which type of alarm should be chosen.

Creating condition-based alarms

Use condition-based alarms to monitor a specific state or condition of an object.

The steps to create an alarm are as follows:

1. Browse to an object in the vCenter Server inventory using the vSphere Web Client.
2. Go to the **Manage** tab.
3. Click on the **Alarm Definitions** button.
4. To create a new custom alarm, press the green **+** icon.

This process is demonstrated in the following screenshot:

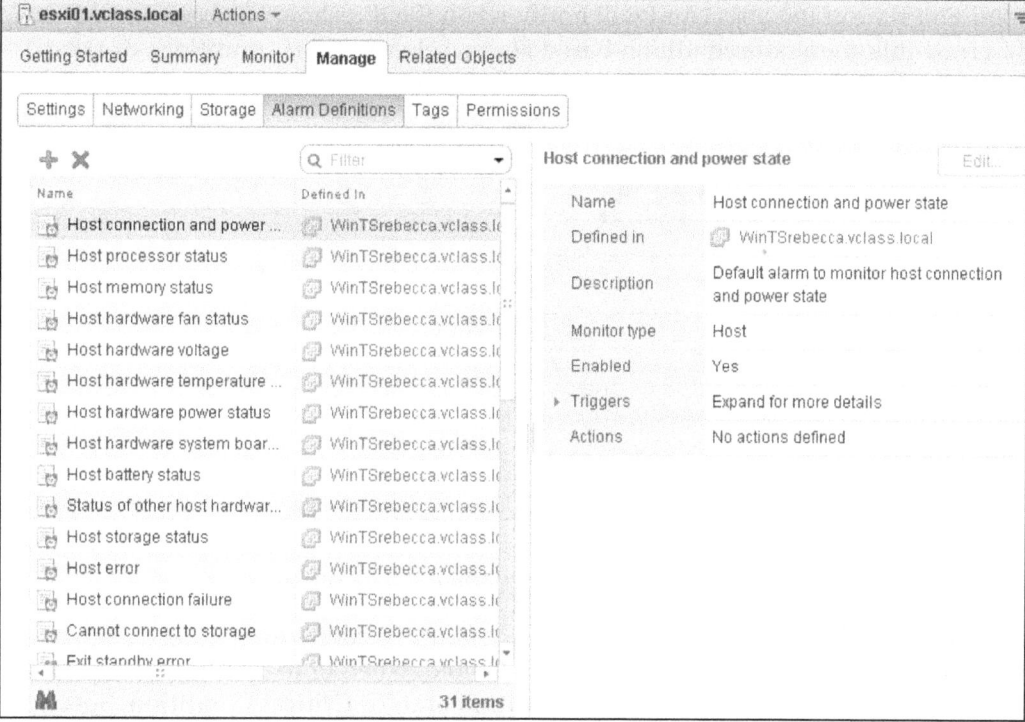

Pressing the green + icon will result in a dialog allowing the creation of a custom alarm.

Enter a **Name** and **Description** for this alarm. For **Monitor**, select what object should be monitored by this alarm. The available choices are as follows:

- Datacenters
- Clusters
- ESXi hosts
- Virtual machines
- Datastores
- Networks
- Distributed switches
- Distributed virtual port groups

Monitoring Virtual Machines

The **Monitor for** choice allows for the specification of a condition-based alarm or an event-based alarm. A condition-based alarm trigger will monitor the current condition state of the object and will notify when the threshold has been exceeded. To create this alarm as a condition-based alarm, select **specific conditions or state, for example CPU usage**, as shown in the following screenshot:

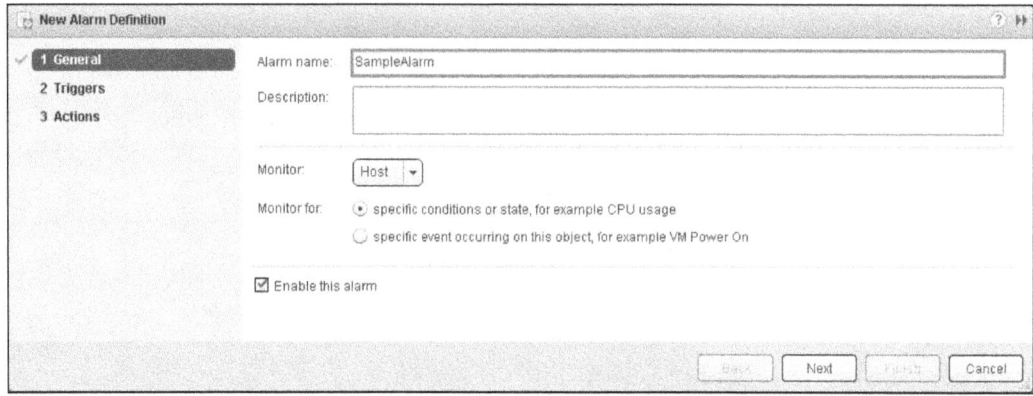

Leave the box checked for the alarm to be enabled. Click on **Next**.

Alarms do not have triggers configured by default. To configure a trigger, click on the **+** button. Specify what value **Trigger** will hold, whether to monitor for a state above, below, or equal to a **Warning Condition** and/or **Critical Condition**. Specify what the **Warning Condition**, **Critical Condition**, and the condition length will be. Warnings mean getting concerned, whereas critical signifies that you need to take action immediately. The length should be set to an appropriate amount so that you are not notified of very temporary issues, such as a short CPU spike.

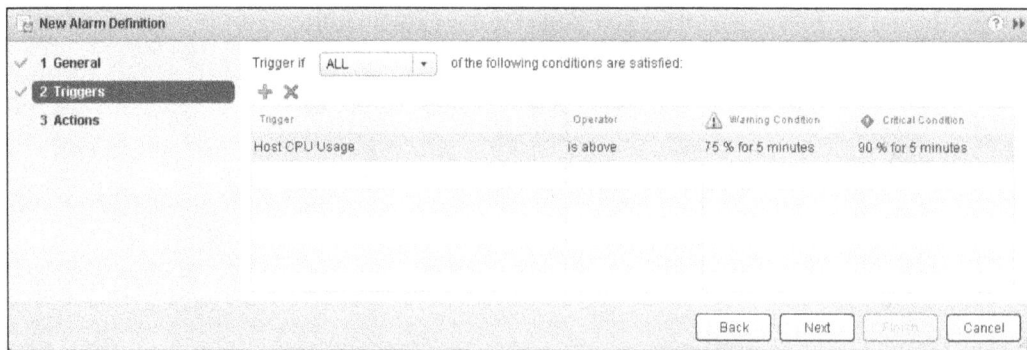

Towards the top of the screen, specify whether all conditions should be met (in a case where multiple triggers are specified) or any condition met will be enough to generate an alarm. Once configured, click on **Next**.

An action can be configured in response to an alarm. There are three configurable actions available:

- Notification emails
- SNMP notification trap
- Run a command within vCenter

These colors and shapes signify an alarm's severity: a red diamond is a critical alert, a yellow triangle is a warning, and a green circle is normal.

These actions can be triggered when the state changes as follows:

- From a green circle to a yellow triangle
- From a yellow triangle to a red diamond
- From a red diamond to a yellow triangle
- From a yellow triangle to a green circle

For each action, it can be specified to do nothing (leave empty), have vCenter Server do the action only one time (specify **Once**), or have vCenter Server repeat the action until a state change occurs (specify **Repeat**).

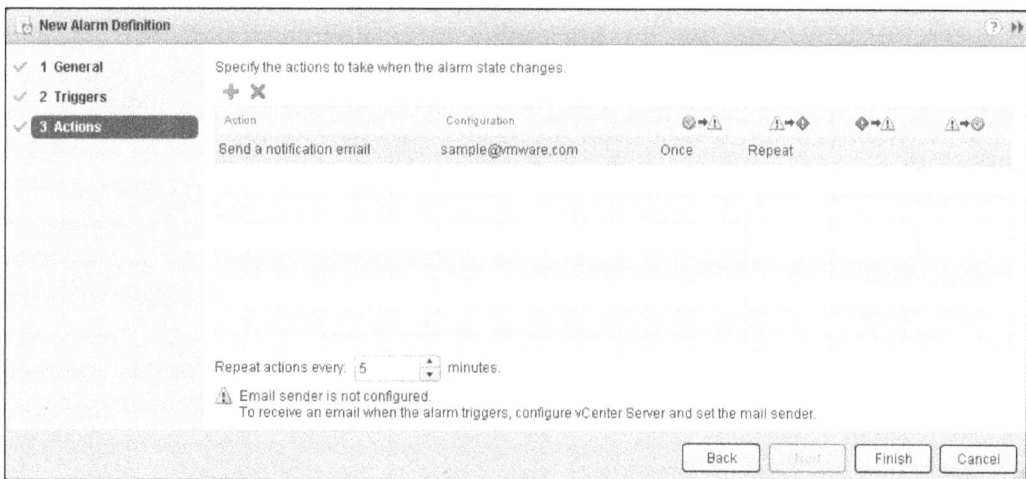

Monitoring Virtual Machines

Specify the minutes desired for **Repeat actions every**, which is **5** minutes by default. For the notification email or SNMP trap, this must be set up in the advanced vCenter Server settings prior to configuring an alarm action. Click on **Next** after configuration.

Creating event-based alarms

The process of creating an event-based alarm is similar except that in the **General** pane, under **Monitor for,** select **specific event occurring on this object, for example VM Power On**. Click on **Next,** as shown in the following screenshot:

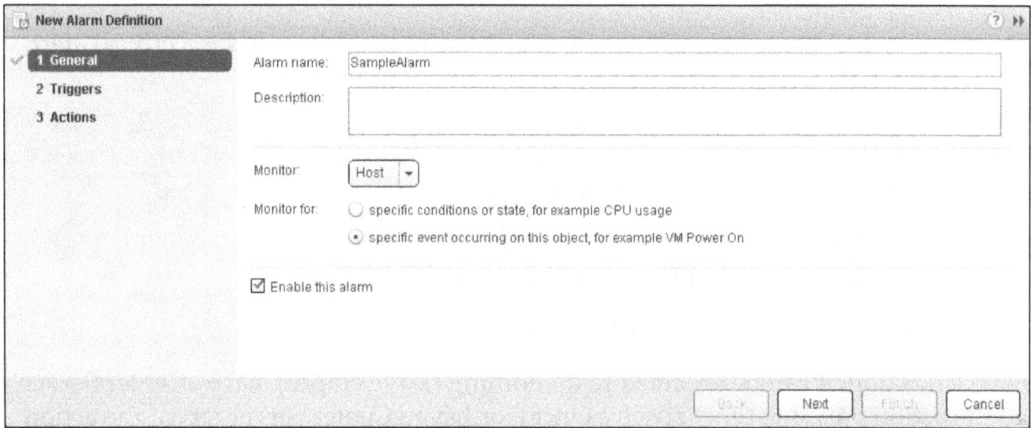

Event-based alarms do not rely on any kind of threshold or duration. This type of alarm uses **Arguments**, **Value**, and **Operator** to identify a triggering event. The **Event** specified in the following image is **vSphere HA detected a host failure**. The **Argument** and **Operator** specifies that the datacenter name should be equal to the **Value** of **NOLA**. So, for this alarm to be triggered, any host residing in the NOLA datacenter would have to be detected as failed by vSphere HA.

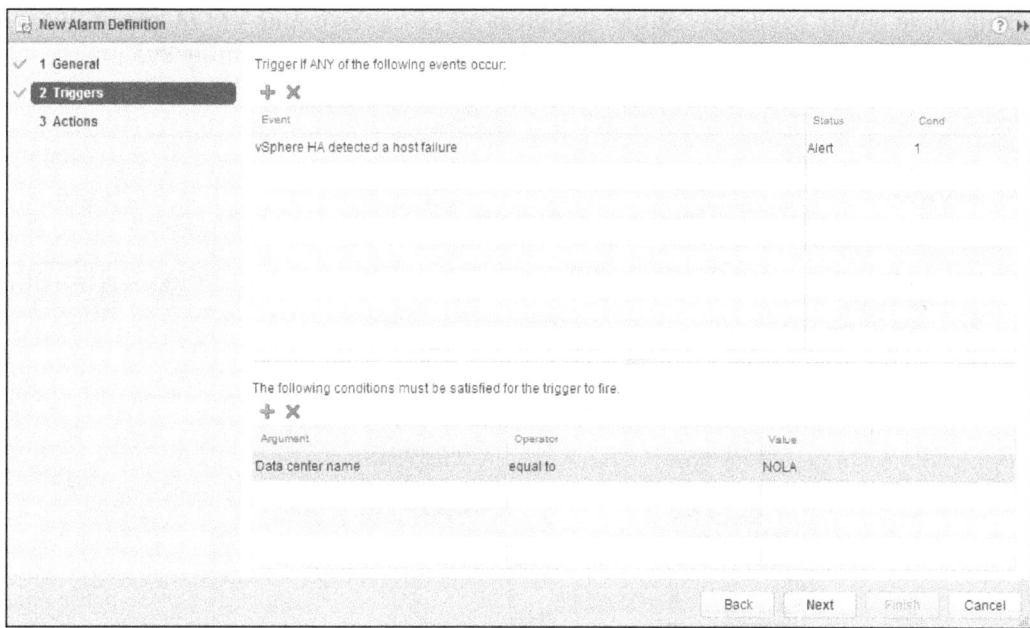

Upon configuring the triggers, click on **Next**. After specifying the Actions, click on **Finish**.

Other places to find information

There are many places where you can find performance and resource usage information besides the places we've discussed so far.

For example, consider using a guest operating system such as Perfmon. VMware Tools includes a Perfmon DLL providing additional counters, which gives the guest operating system some visibility into the ESXi host memory and CPU usage. Perfmon is an SNMP-based tool for Windows operating systems that is used to monitor performance.

Using these newly available counters, such as VM Processor and VM Memory, enables the administrator to view actual use within the guest operating system, which can be compared to the statistics viewed in the vSphere Web Client.

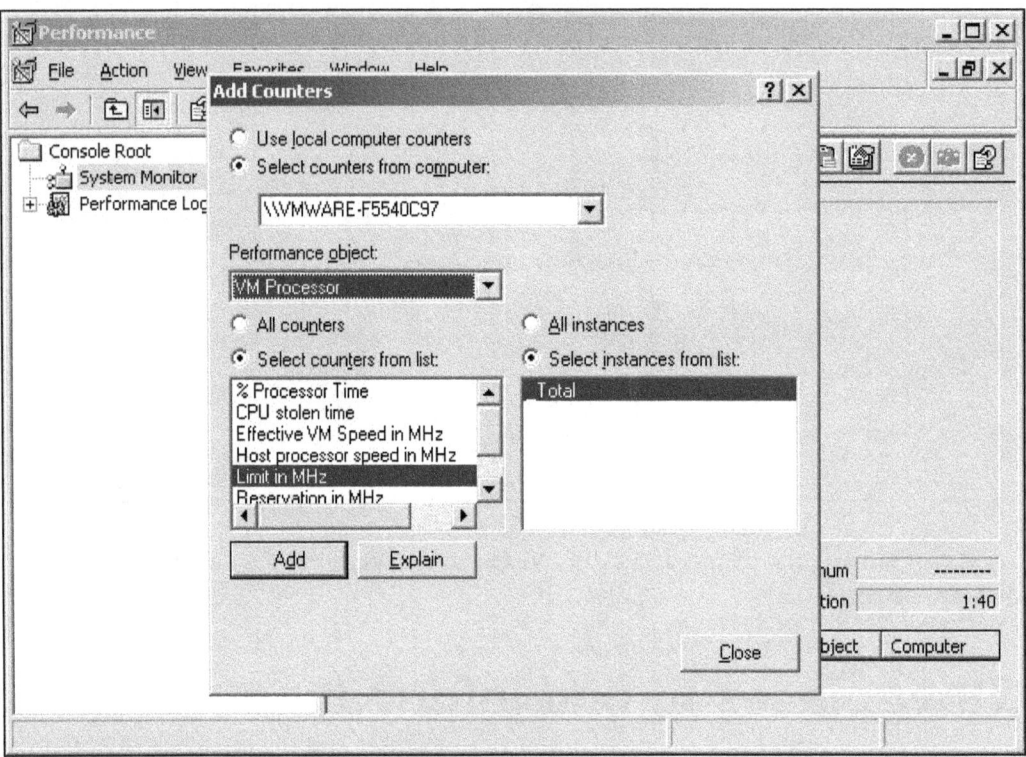

Without VMware Tools, the Perfmon counters are inaccurate because the guest operating system is unaware of virtualization.

Also, consider using an object's **Summary** tab. The **Summary** tab can provide useful information for objects such as an ESXi host (demonstrated in the following screenshot), a virtual machine, resource pool, or a vApp. At the top right of the image, there are a few bars signifying the **CAPACITY**, **FREE** amount, and **USED** amount of the **CPU**, **MEMORY**, and **STORAGE** resources.

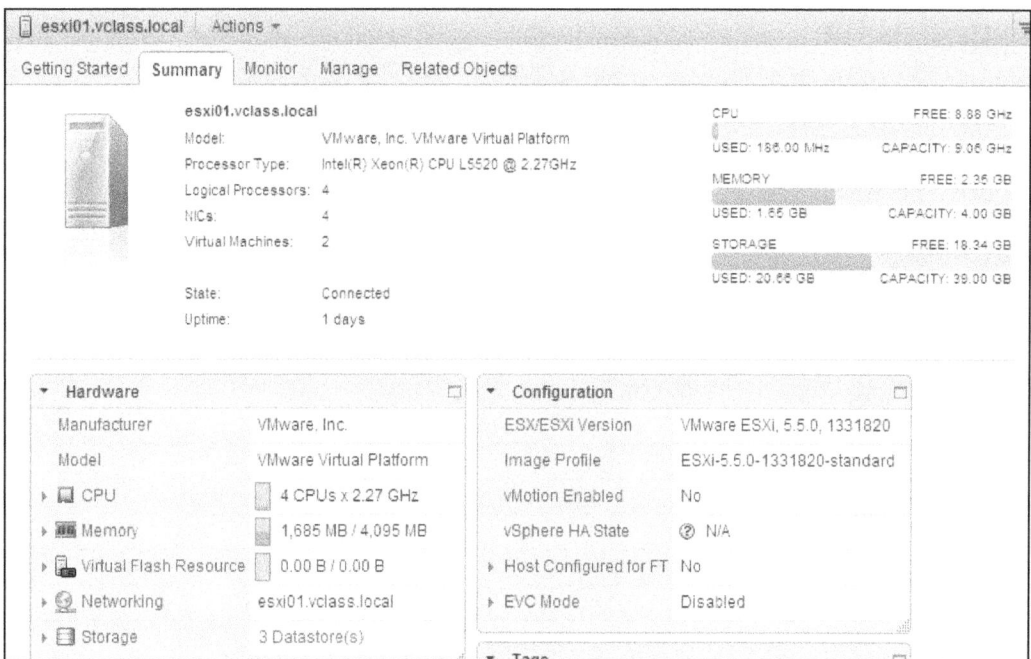

The **Hardware** pane shows the ESXi host information for the physical server. The **Configuration** pane provides the software information regarding the ESXi configuration. For example, **ESX/ESXi Version** and **Image Profile** denote the specific ESXi build that is currently installed.

Another good place to view information is the **Monitor** tab. The **Resource Allocation** button will be discussed in *Chapter 9, Balancing Resource Utilization and Availability*. The following screenshot shows the **Utilization** button on a resource pool. One of the more useful pieces of information is the **Guest Memory** pane. This demonstrates the amount of **Private** and **Shared** guest memory, which shows Transparent Page Sharing in action. The **Shared** memory is the amount of memory currently being shared using TPS.

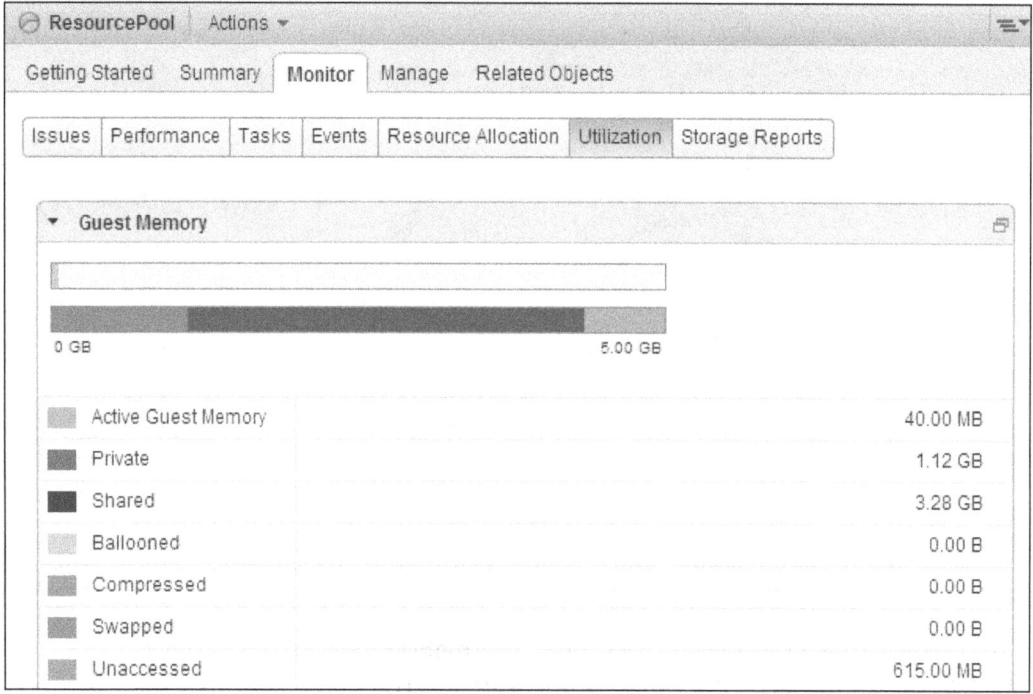

Here, you can also see the amount of memory within this resource pool being **Ballooned**, **Compressed**, and **Swapped** during memory reclamation.

Summary

Performance charts can be displayed using the vSphere Client connected to either an ESXi host directly or a vCenter Server or by using the vSphere Web Client. Overview performance charts display performance statistics that are most useful to quickly diagnose problems and monitor performance. An advanced performance chart provides a more detailed graphical display for an object's statistical data. The `esxtop` and `resxtop` commands enable command-line monitoring for real-time ESXi host resource usage for each of the core four resources: CPU, memory, network, and disk. The `esxtop` and `resxtop` utilities are available in interactive, batch, and replay modes.

An alarm is a notification in response to a selected condition or event for an object in the vCenter Server inventory. A condition-based alarm trigger will monitor the current condition state of the object and will send a notification when the threshold is exceeded. Event-based alarms use arguments, values, and operators to identify a triggering event. Alarms can be configured to perform an action of either running a command, sending a notification email, or an SNMP notification trap.

The next chapter will discuss migrating virtual machines.

8
Migrating Virtual Machines

Virtual machines can be nondisruptively migrated to different ESXi hosts, datastores, or both. This chapter explores how to configure a vMotion network as well as how to conduct the migration using vMotion, Storage vMotion, or cross-host Storage vMotion. Being able to move a virtual machine without interruption changes how a datacenter operates. Now, an ESXi host may have maintenance conducted during the work day without any disruption to the end user. Cluster features, such as **Distributed Resource Scheduler (DRS)** and **Storage Distributed Resource Scheduler (SDRS)**, discussed in later chapters, leverage vMotion and Storage vMotion technologies, respectively.

In this chapter, you will learn:

- Configuring a vMotion network
- How to use vMotion
- How to use Storage vMotion
- Cross-host Storage vMotion

vMotion

A virtual machine can be migrated to a different ESXi host while it is powered on (vMotion), powered off (cold migration), or suspended. vSphere vMotion migrates virtual machines from one ESXi host to another without any kind of downtime or disruption. Using this feature, the entire state of a virtual machine is moved from one ESXi host to another while the actual virtual machine files remain in the same datastore.

The state information includes the current memory content and the information that defines a virtual machine. This includes information such as BIOS, devices, CPU, and MAC addresses for Ethernet cards.

vSphere DRS leverages vMotion technology to migrate the virtual machine workload across a cluster. This idea is further explored in *Chapter 9, Balancing Resource Utilization and Availability*.

So how does vMotion work? A vMotion migration consists of the following actions:

- The memory state of a virtual machine is copied over the vMotion network from one host to another. Our users will continue to access the virtual machine and possibly even update the pages of memory. Any page that is modified during this period is kept in a memory bitmap on the source ESXi host.
- After most of the virtual machine's memory is copied to target, the virtual machine is quiesced, meaning that no additional activity will occur on the virtual machine. The virtual machine's device state and memory bitmap will be transferred to the destination ESXi host during this quiesced period.
- The virtual machine is initialized and begins running on the target ESXi host as the virtual machine on the source is quiesced. A **Reverse Address Resolution Protocol** (**RARP**) request notifies the subnet that the virtual machine's MAC address is now located on a new switch port.
- Users begin accessing the virtual machine on the target ESXi host instead of the source.
- The pages of memory that the virtual machine was using on the source are marked as free.

VMware customers have used vMotion since 2004, setting the standard for a dependable live migration. vMotion is an important technology because it allows for an ESXi host to be evacuated (all running virtual machines migrated off) so that it may have maintenance performed on it without affecting the virtual machines.

Configuring for vMotion

The source and destination ESXi host have to meet certain requirements for a vMotion migration to be successful. These requirements are as follows:

- Shared storage. (As of vSphere 5.1, administrators are able to take advantage of migrating virtual machines without shared storage. See the *Cross-host Storage vMotion* section for more information.)
- Gigabit Ethernet (or better) interconnection.
- Consistent network configuration, both physical and virtual, to include the names of VMkernel ports for vMotion and virtual machine port groups.
- Source and destination ESXi hosts' CPUs from the same compatibility group.

CPU compatibility is a vMotion requirement that must be met. The manufacturer and family must be compatible and similar instruction sets must be present. **AMD No eXecute** (**NX**) and **Intel eXecute Disable** (**XD**) is a security feature of processors that marks memory pages as data-only to prevent malicious software exploits and buffer overflow attacks. If NX/XD is exposed on source, then it must be exposed on the destination (hiding would increase vMotion compatibility). This was previously discussed in *Chapter 4*, *Advanced Virtual Machine Settings*.

One of the prerequisites for vMotion is a vMotion network. To create a VMkernel port for vMotion, perform the following steps:

1. Browse to an ESXi host in the inventory using the vSphere Web Client.
2. Go to the **Manage** tab and select **Virtual switches**.
3. From there, select the icon signifying **Add host networking**, as shown in the following screenshot:

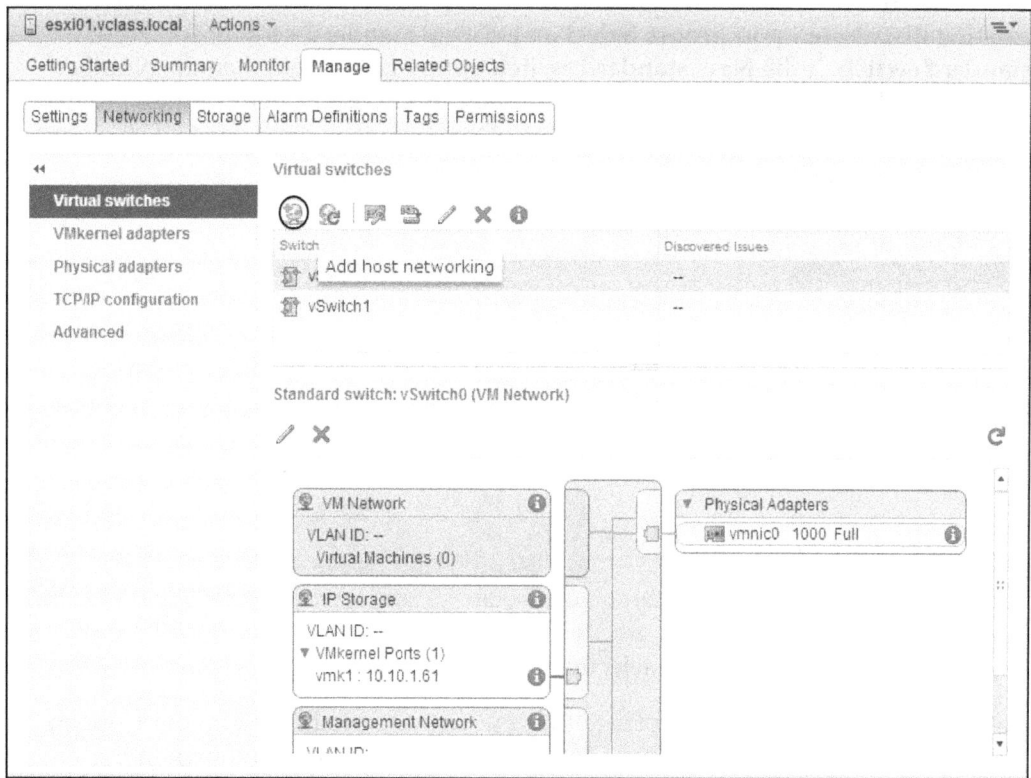

Migrating Virtual Machines

This will launch the **Add Networking** wizard. Select the **VMkernel Network Adapter** option and click on **Next**, as shown in the following screenshot:

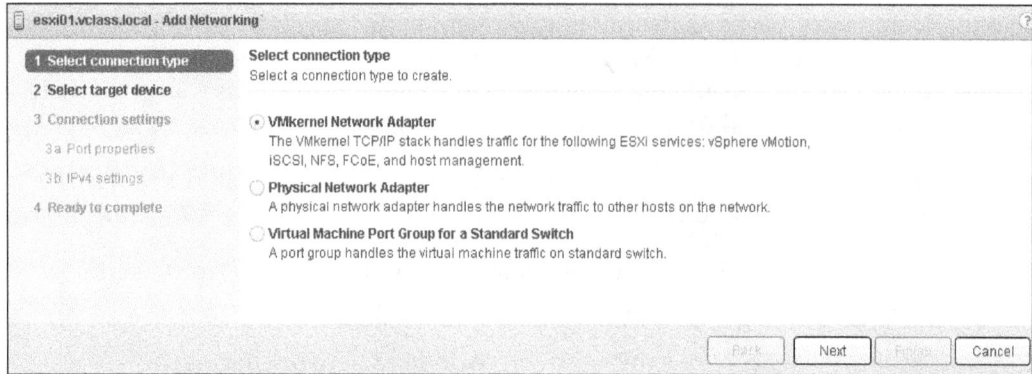

Under the **Select target device** pane, there are three options available: **Select an existing distributed port group**, **Select an existing standard switch**, and **New standard switch**. If the **New standard switch** option is selected, then the **Number of ports** field must be selected. The default selection is **128**, as demonstrated in the following screenshot:

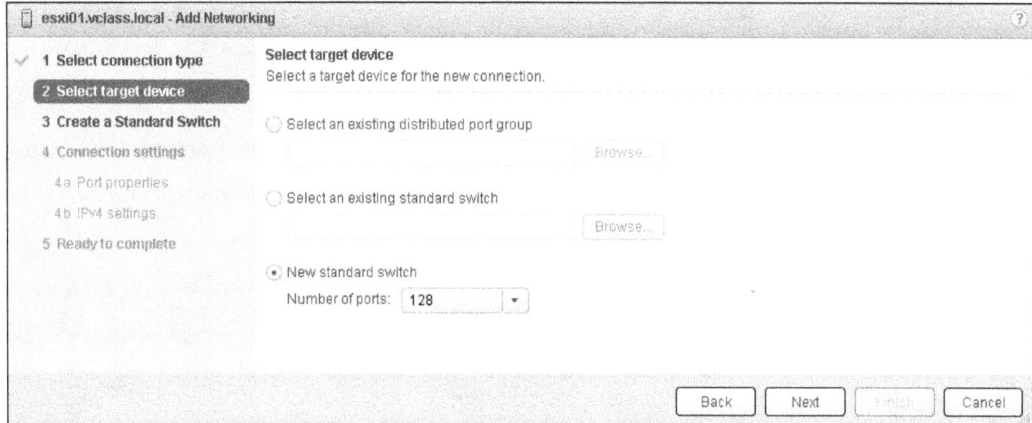

Click on **Next** after making the selections.

To add a physical network adapter to the new virtual switch, click on the **+** (green plus sign) button while the **Active adapters** option is selected, as shown in the following screenshot:

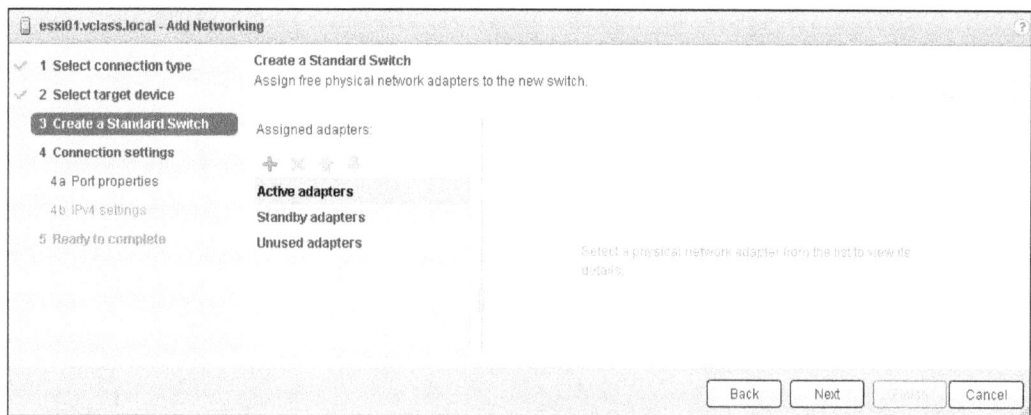

Clicking on the **+** (green plus sign) button will open a dialog box to add physical adapters to the switch. Select which vmnic will be an uplink for the newly created standard switch, as shown in the following screenshot:

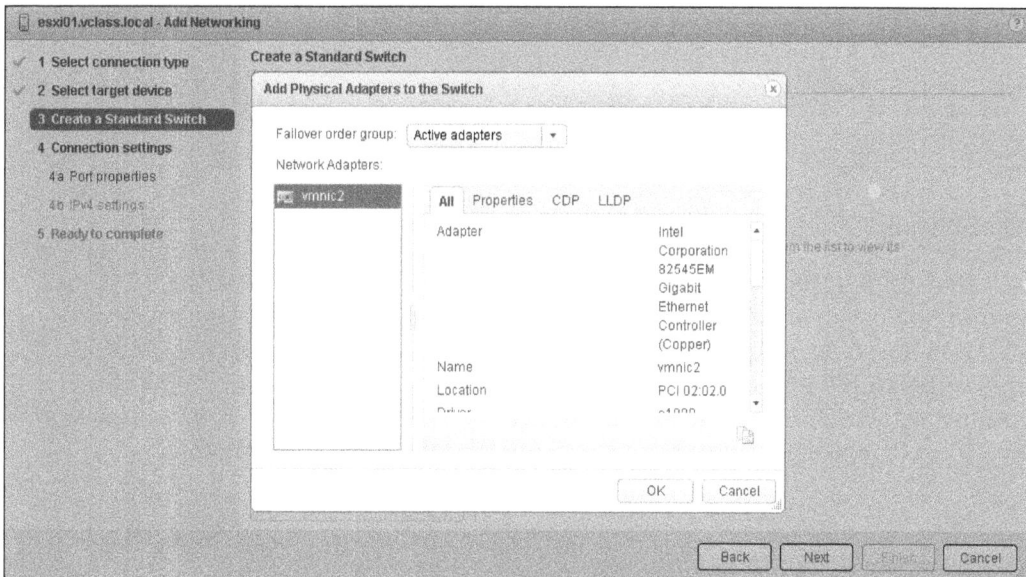

vMotion performance increases with additional bandwidth, so make sure to dedicate, at minimum, a physical 1 GigE NIC for vMotion use.

Click on **OK** after making the selection.

Migrating Virtual Machines

On the **Port properties** pane, specify the **Network label** and **VLAN ID** fields (if applicable). Under the **Available services** section, make sure to select the **vMotion traffic** option, as demonstrated in the following screenshot:

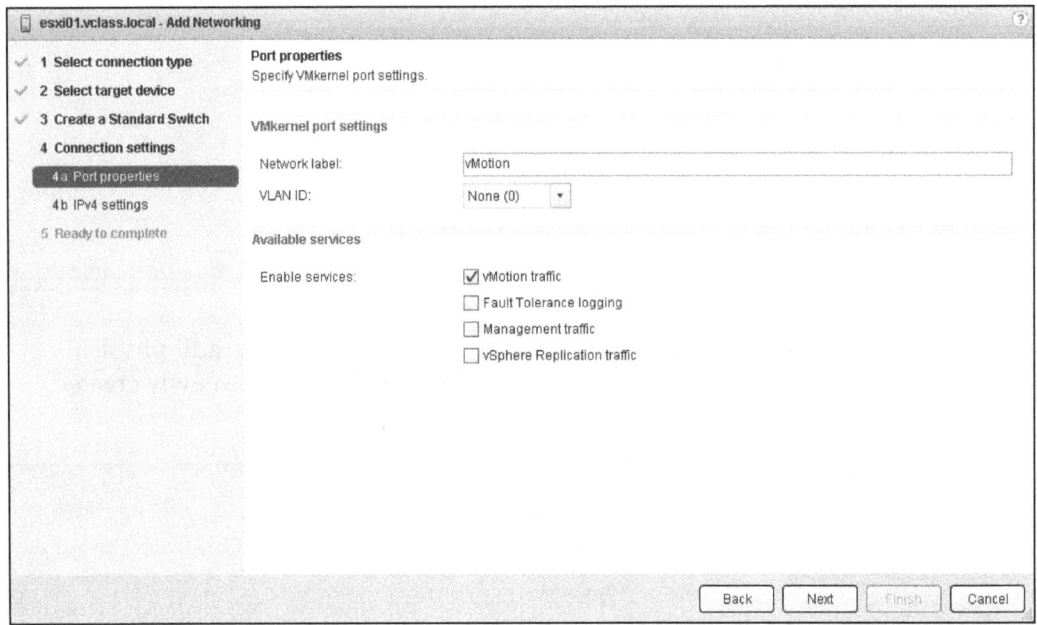

Click on **Next** after making the selections.

A VMkernel port requires an IP address since it is an IP interface for the ESXi host to communicate over a specific network. In this case, the network will be used for vMotion traffic. Supply an IPv4 address and subnet mask. An interface should be created on each ESXi host that will be configured for vMotion. Keep in mind that routing vMotion traffic is neither recommended nor supported by VMware at this time. The **IPv4 settings** pane is displayed in the following screenshot:

Chapter 8

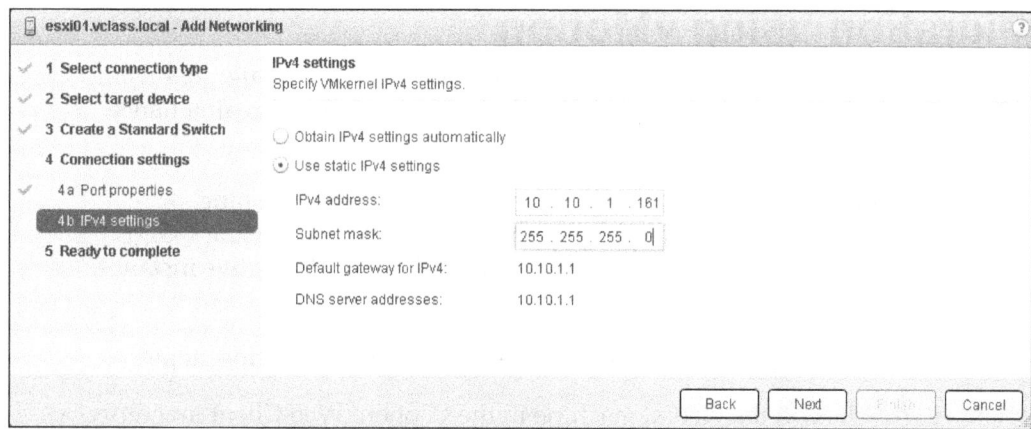

Click on **Next** after completing the **IPv4 settings** pane.

Review all information given during the **Add Networking** wizard, which is shown in the following screenshot:

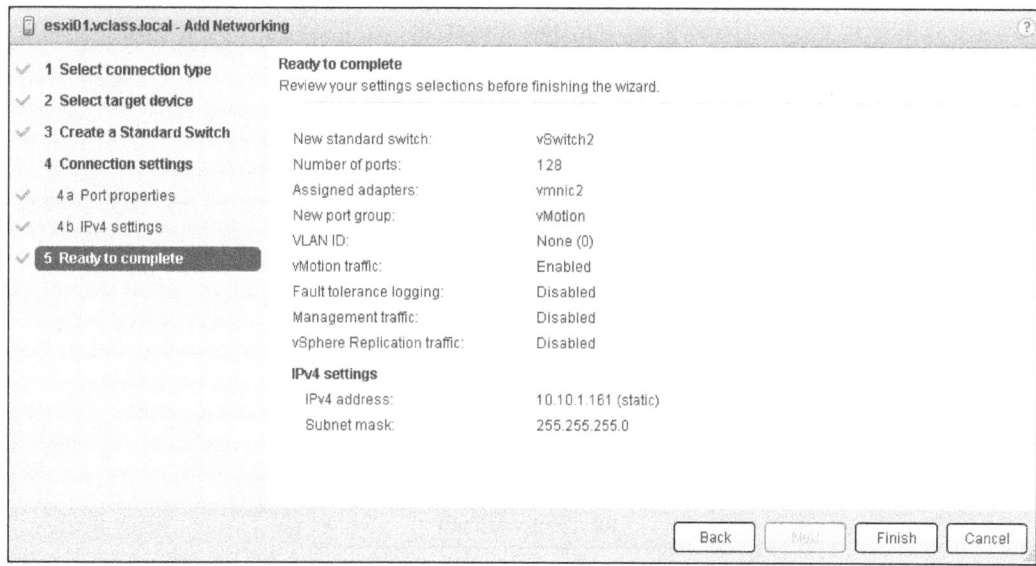

Click on **Finish** once you are done reviewing the information.

Migrating Virtual Machines

Migration using vMotion

There are many reasons why a virtual machine may need to be migrated using vMotion, including evacuating an ESXi host in order to conduct maintenance, load balancing, and so on.

A maximum of four simultaneous vMotion, Storage vMotion, cloning, or deployments from templates are allowed for a single ESXi host using 1 GigE." Any further attempted instance will be queued until one of the active instances is completed.

To use vMotion to migrate a virtual machine, perform the following steps:

1. Right-click on the virtual machine in the vSphere Web Client inventory and select **Migrate...**, as shown in the following screenshot:

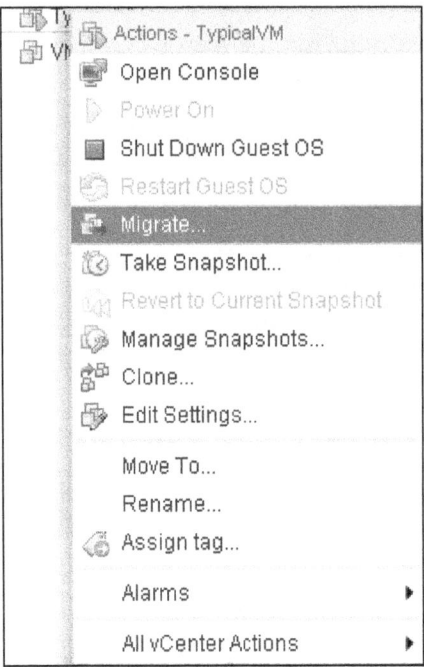

2. Once the **Migrate** wizard is launched, select the **Change host** migration option to perform a vMotion migration, as shown in the following screenshot:

Chapter 8

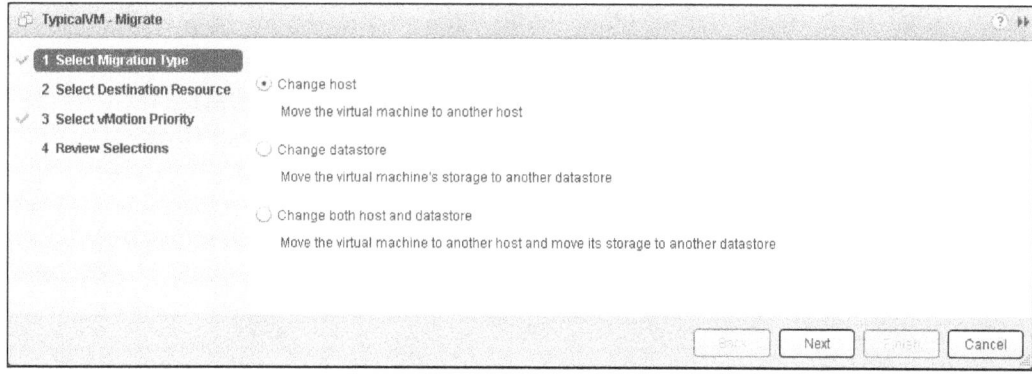

3. Click on **Next**.
4. Make a selection for the destination resource.

   When you select the ESXi host and the cluster as the destination resource, a validation check is performed to verify that most of the vMotion requirements have been met. If validation succeeds, then the wizard will allow you to continue by clicking on **Next**. If validation is not successful, a list of vMotion warnings and errors will be displayed in the **Compatibility** section. No errors are shown in the following screenshot.

   Errors have red diamonds and the warnings have yellow triangles. A warning will allow you to continue with the vMotion migration whereas an error will not. If an error is displayed, then you must exit from the wizard and fix the errors before attempting a retry. The **Compatibility** section is shown in the following screenshot:

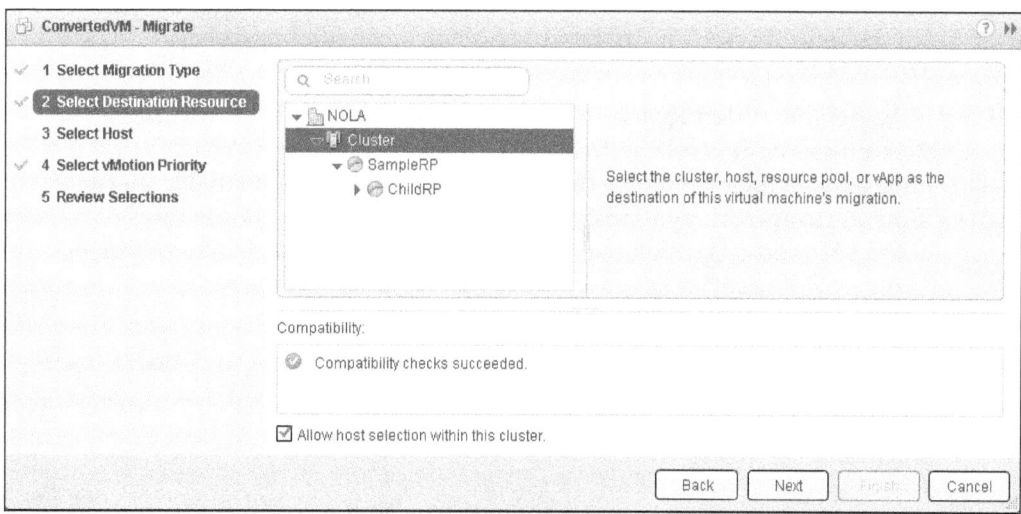

5. Click on **Next** after verifying compatibility.
6. Select which ESXi host the virtual machine should be moved to.

   This screen will be available if the option **Allow host selection within this cluster** is selected in the previous screenshot. The **Select Host** pane is shown in the following screenshot:

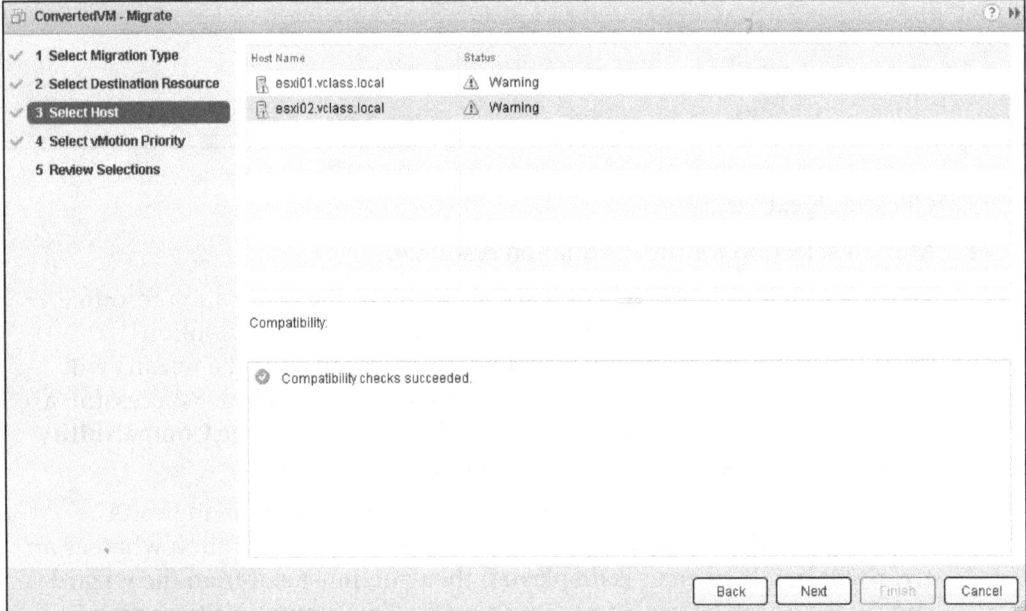

7. Click on **Next** after selecting the ESXi host.
8. On the **Select vMotion Priority** pane, choose whether to reserve CPU for optimal vMotion performance or perform with available CPU resources.

   If the default option **Reserve CPU for optimal vMotion performance (Recommended)** is selected, then the vMotion migration can only be initiated if sufficient CPU resources are immediately available. Otherwise, if the **Perform with available CPU resources** option is chosen, the length of the vMotion migration may be extended due to lack of CPU resources. These options are displayed in the following screenshot:

Chapter 8

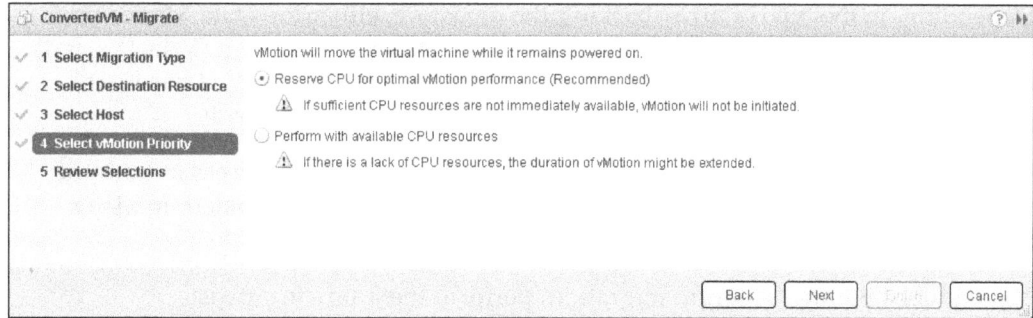

9. Click on the **Next** button after making the selection.

   The **Review Selections** pane will allow you to take a look at all the migration settings. It is shown in the following screenshot:

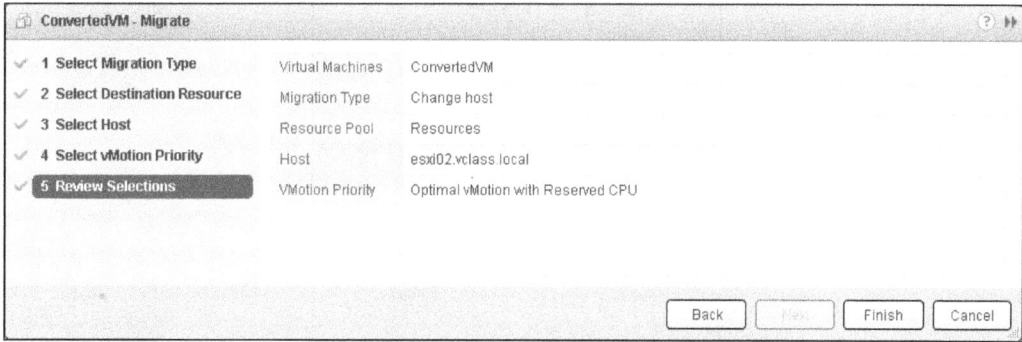

10. Click on the **Finish** button to initiate the vMotion migration.

Migration using Storage vMotion

Storage vMotion involves moving a virtual machine's files from one datastore to another. Using this technology, you can move a virtual machine between storage devices to allow for maintenance or reconfiguration of the original storage device without any kind of virtual machine downtime.

Outwardly, everything in Storage vMotion looks identical to what it used to look like in the case of the administrator; however, it operates differently under the hood in vSphere 5.x. Now, when a Storage vMotion migration is initiated, a new process, known as **mirror driver**, runs on the ESXi host. The mirror driver ensures that, as blocks change at the source datastore during Storage vMotion migration, it writes the changes to both datastores simultaneously.

Migrating Virtual Machines

Depending on the type of array backing the datastore, either the **Data Mover** built into the VMkernel or the **vSphere Storage APIs — Array Integration (VAAI) —** will be used to copy the blocks to the destination. VAAI, sometimes called hardware acceleration, can be used to offload the operations to the storage array.

The ESXi host that the virtual machine is running on must have access to both the source and destination datastore. The VMDKs must be in the persistent mode or be RDMs.

To conduct a Storage vMotion migration, perform the following steps:

1. Right-click on the virtual machine in the inventory of the vSphere Web Client and select **Migrate...**, as shown in the following screenshot:

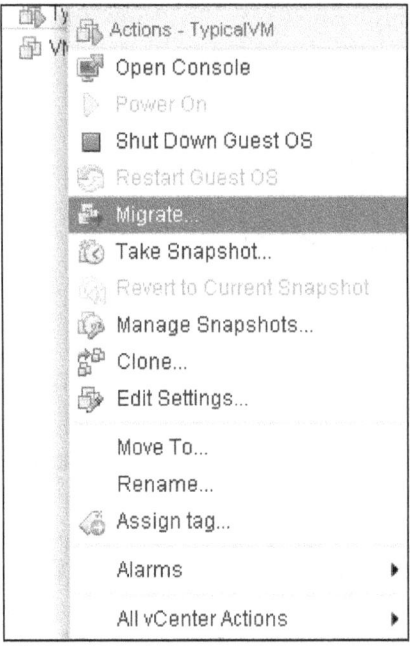

Chapter 8

2. Select the **Change datastore** option.

   This will allow the selection of Storage vMotion options. The **Select Migration Type** pane is displayed in the following screenshot:

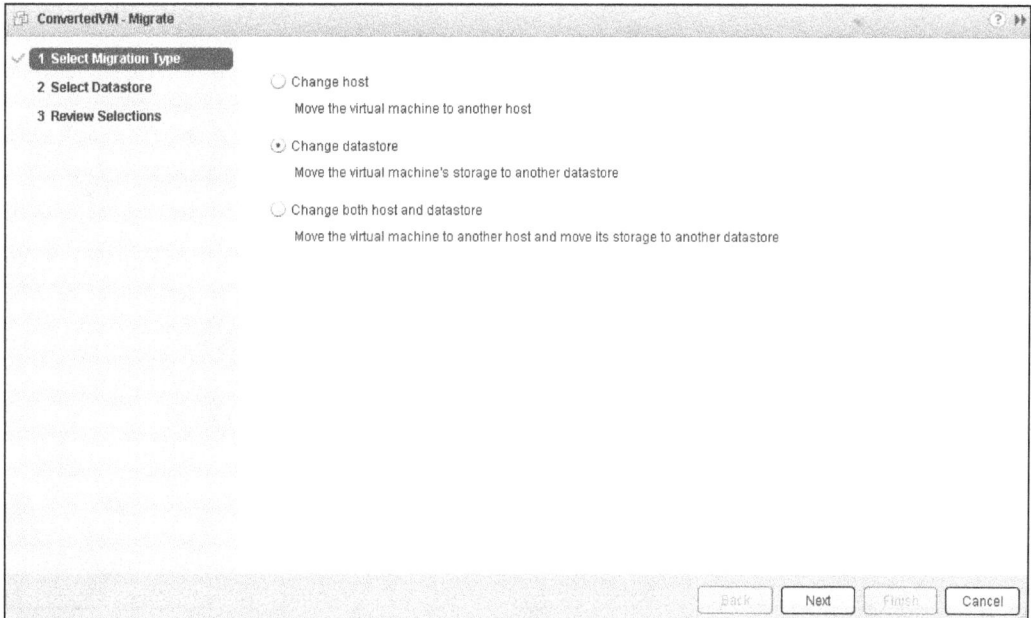

3. Click on **Next** after selecting the migration type.
4. On the **Select Datastore** pane, choose the destination datastore where the virtual machine files should reside after the Storage vMotion migration is complete.

Migrating Virtual Machines

A **VM Storage Profile** may also be selected from its drop-down list if configured in your environment. The **Select Datastore** pane is shown in the following screenshot:

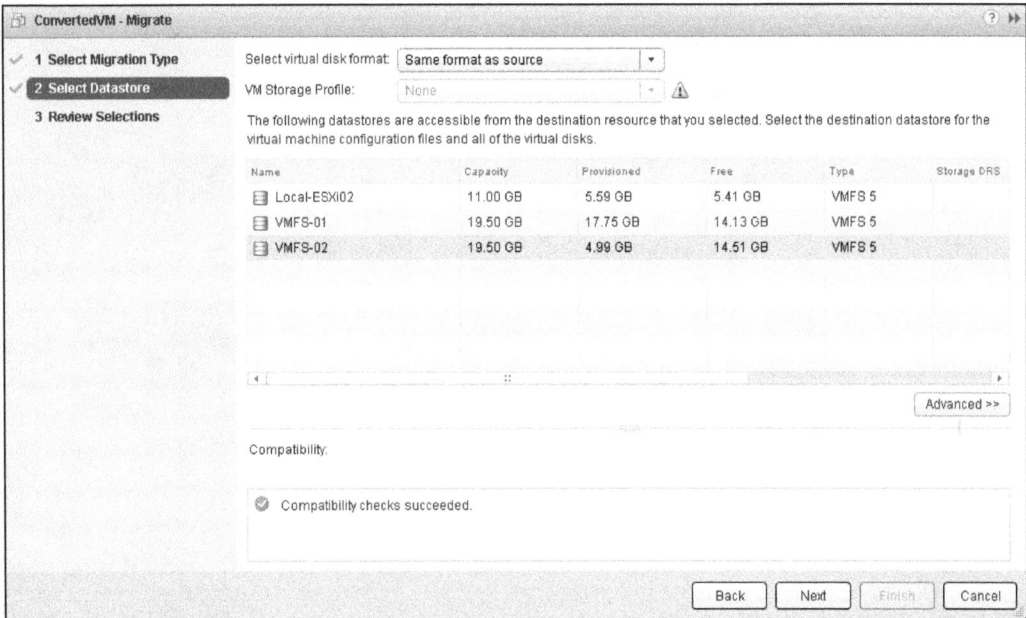

Another option on the **Select Datastore** pane is **Select virtual disk format**. This will allow for the selection of the following options:

- **Same format as source**
- **Thick Provision Lazy Zeroed**
- **Thick Provision Eager Zeroed**
- **Thin Provision**

The **Same format as source** option is selected by default; this will result in the same provisioning type for the virtual disk at the destination as at the source. Use the Storage vMotion technology to change the virtual disk provisioning type as needed while the virtual machine is powered on. Make sure to choose the destination datastore before making this selection. Selecting a different datastore later will result in this option being reset. The **Same format as source** option is shown in the shown screenshot:

Chapter 8

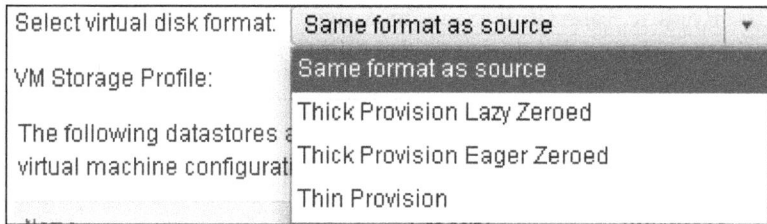

Clicking on the **Advanced** button on the **Select Datastore** pane will allow for datastore specification for individual virtual disks and the configuration file. This means that if a virtual machine has multiple virtual disks, you can choose to migrate each disk to a distinctly different datastore. To make this specification, click on the datastore name in the **Storage** column and dropdown to make a selection, as shown in the following screenshot:

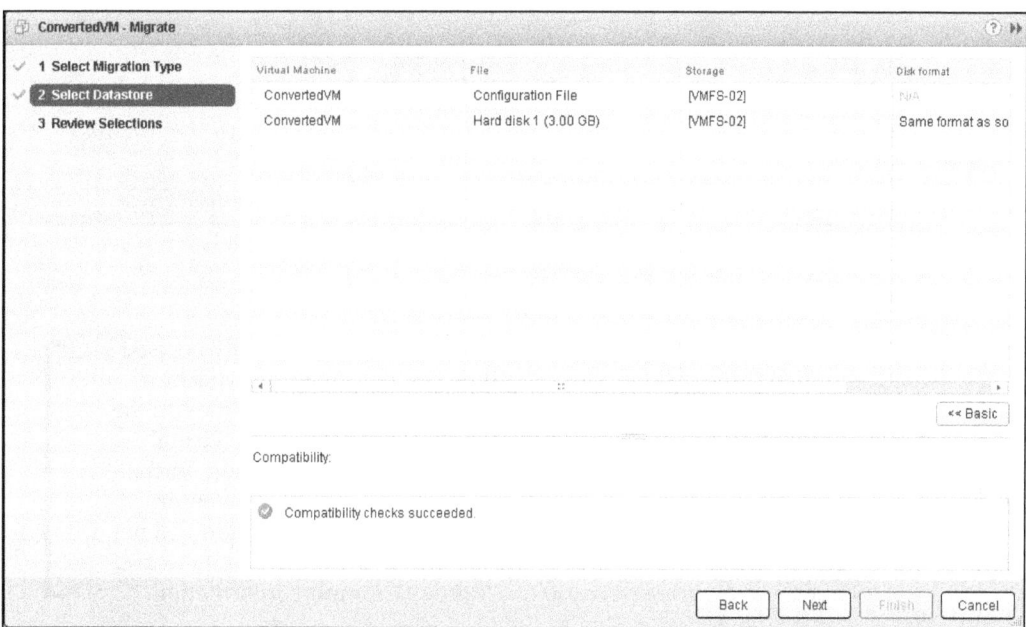

5. Once the selections have been made, click on **Next**.

[235]

Migrating Virtual Machines

On the **Review Selections** pane, look over all the choices for the Storage vMotion migration, as shown in the following screenshot:

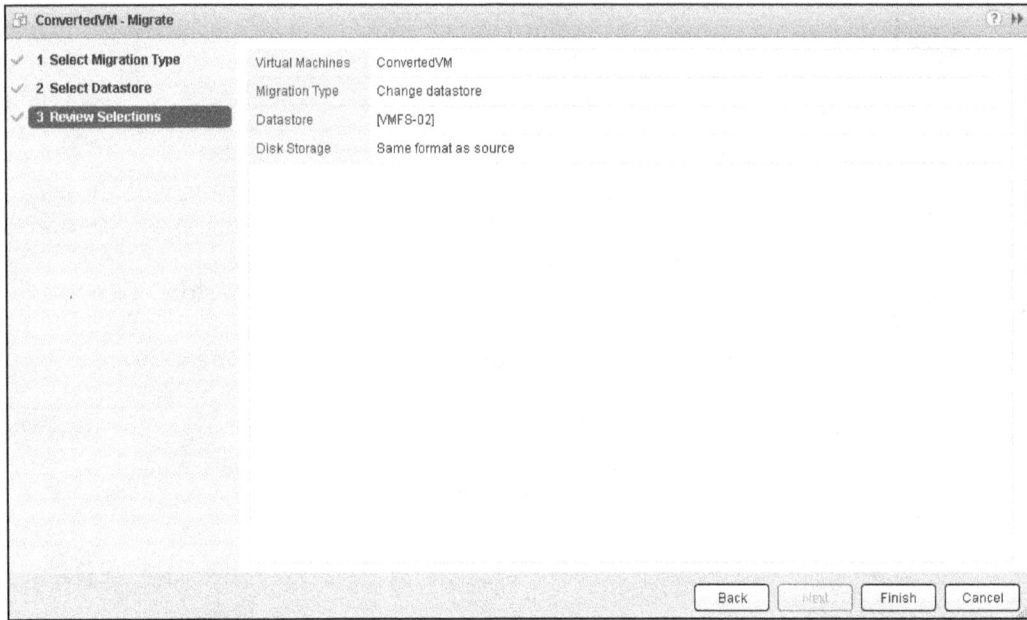

6. Once satisfied, click on **Finish**.

>
> In vSphere 5.5, migration by Storage vMotion can not only be used to change the disk provisioning type but also the virtual machine filenames. Storage vMotion changes the virtual machine files on the destination datastore to match the inventory name of the virtual machine. This migration type will rename all configuration, virtual disk, snapshot, and .nvram files. However, if the new inventory name exceeds the maximum filename length, the migration will not be successful. Check http://kb.vmware.com/kb/1029513 and http://kb.vmware.com/kb/2008877 for more information.

Cross-host Storage vMotion

vMotion can be used to migrate a virtual machine to a different host and datastore simultaneously; this is commonly known as a **cross-host Storage vMotion** or an **Enhanced vMotion**. In vSphere 5.1 and later, vMotion does not require environments with shared storage; virtual machines can now be migrated across storage accessibility boundaries.

This option is only available using the vSphere Web Client for a powered on virtual machine; a virtual machine can only simultaneously change host and datastore while powered off using the vSphere Client. This is useful when performing cross-cluster migration whenever the target cluster's ESXi hosts may not have access to the source cluster's storage.

Cross-host Storage vMotion is a manual process; DRS and Storage DRS do not leverage this feature.

No more than two concurrent cross-host Storage vMotion instances are allowed at a time on an ESXi host. Any further attempted instances will be queued until one of the active instances is complete.

To use cross-host Storage vMotion to migrate a virtual machine, perform the following steps:

1. Right-click on the virtual machine in the vSphere Web Client inventory and select **Migrate...**, as shown in the following screenshot:

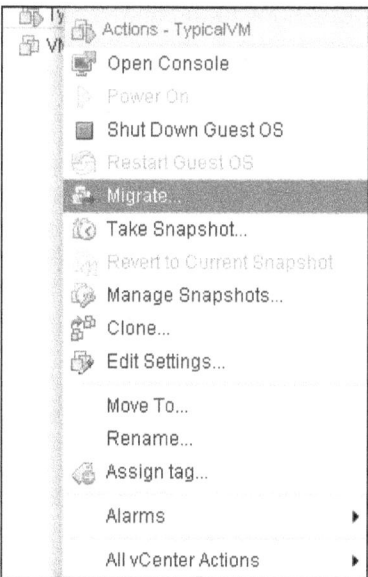

2. Select the **Change both host and datastore** option to perform this migration type.

   Making this selection will result in a cross-host Storage vMotion.
   The **Select Migration Type** pane is shown in the following screenshot:

   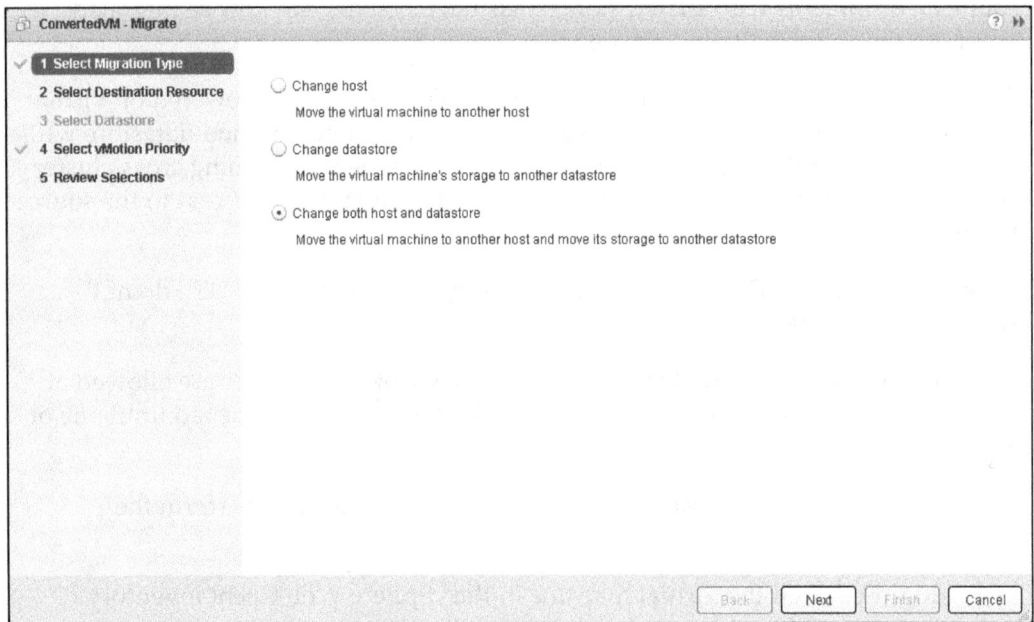

3. After choosing this option, click on **Next**.

   When you select the ESXi host and the cluster as the destination resource, a validation check is performed to verify that many of the vMotion requirements have been met. If validation succeeds, then the wizard will allow you to continue by clicking on **Next**. If validation is not successful, a list of vMotion warnings and errors will be displayed in the **Compatibility** section. No errors are shown in the following screenshot.

Errors have red diamonds and warnings have yellow triangles. A warning will allow you to continue with the vMotion migration whereas an error will not. If an error is displayed, then you must exit from the wizard and fix the errors before attempting to retry vMotion migration. The **Compatibility** section is shown in the following screenshot:

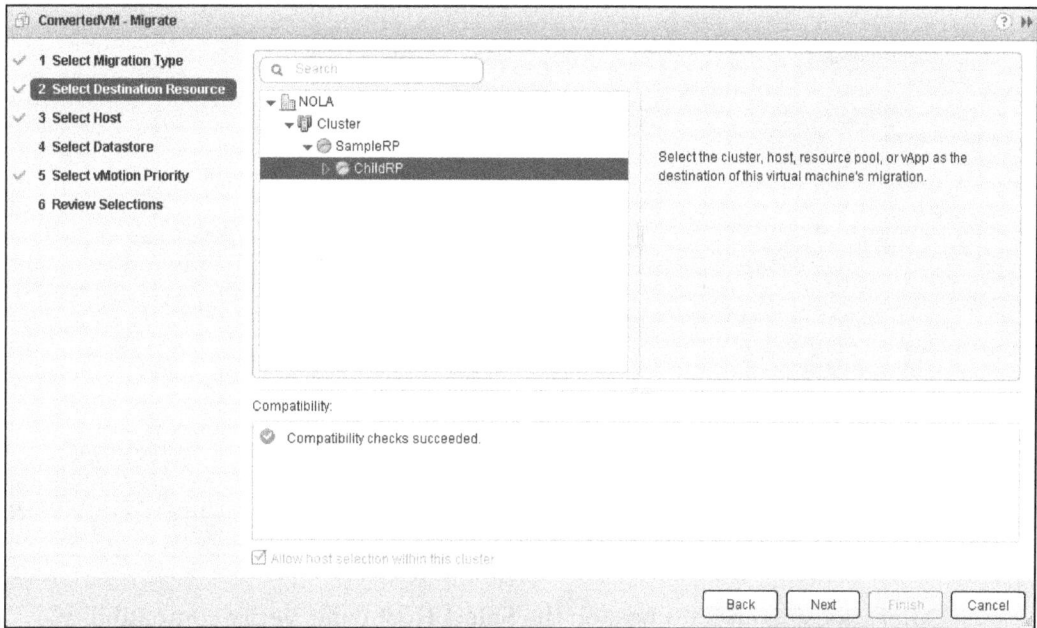

4. Select the cluster or resource pool in the **Select Destination Resource** pane.
5. Click on **Next** after verifying that the compatibility checks have succeeded.
6. Select which ESXi host the virtual machine should be moved to.

Migrating Virtual Machines

This screen will be available if the option **Allow host selection within this cluster** is selected, which is shown in the previous screenshot. The **Select Host** pane is shown in the following screenshot:

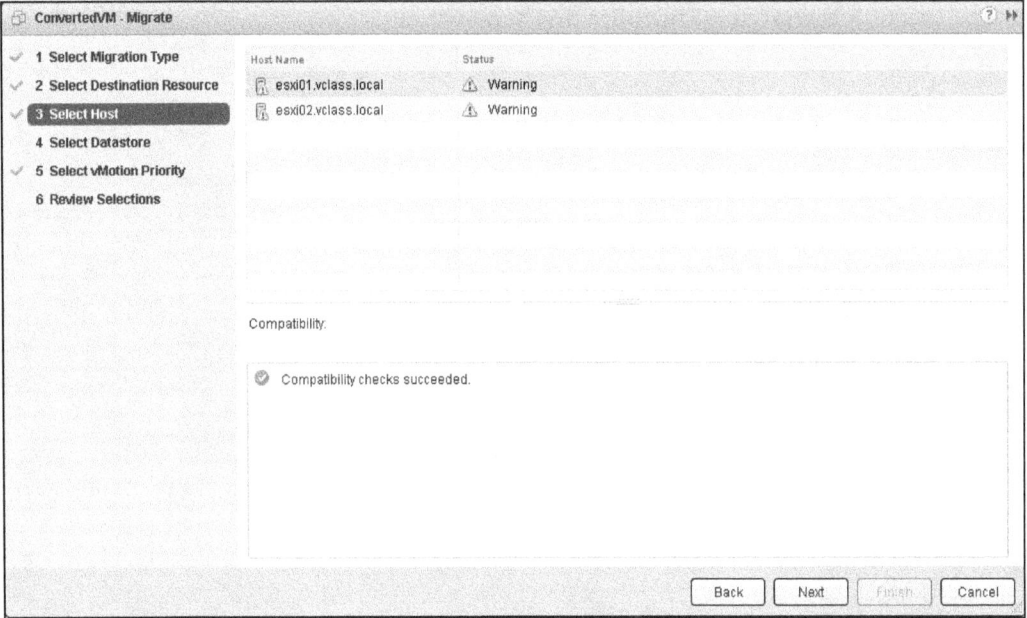

7. After choosing an ESXi host on the **Select Host** pane, verify compatibility and then click on **Next**.

8. On the **Select Datastore** pane, choose the destination datastore where the virtual machine files should reside after the cross-host Storage vMotion migration is complete.

The **VM Storage Profile** option may also be selected from its drop-down list if configured in your environment. The other option is **Select virtual disk format**; by default, the destination files will be the same disk provisioning type as the source virtual disk. Otherwise, choose a different disk provisioning type. The **Select Datastore** pane is shown in the following screenshot:

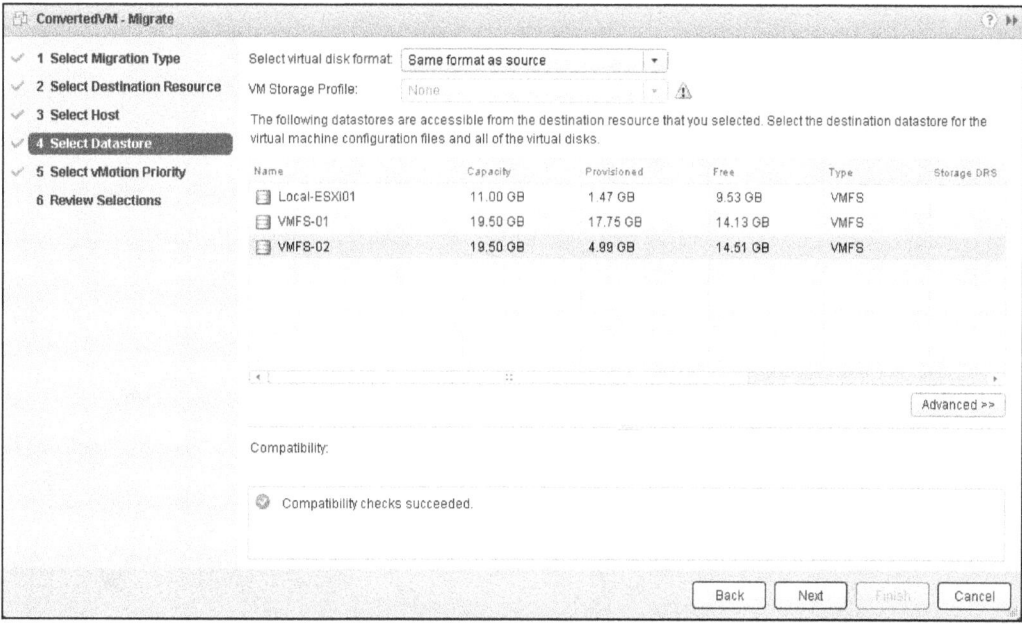

9. Click on **Next** after completing the **Select Datastore** pane.
10. On the **Select vMotion Priority** pane, choose whether to reserve CPU for optimal vMotion performance or perform with available CPU resources.

Migrating Virtual Machines

If the default option **Reserve CPU for optimal vMotion performance (Recommended)** is selected, then the vMotion migration will only be initiated if sufficient CPU resources are immediately available. If the **Perform with available CPU resources** option is chosen, then the length of the vMotion migration may be extended due to a lack of CPU resources. The **Select vMotion Priority** pane is shown in the following screenshot:

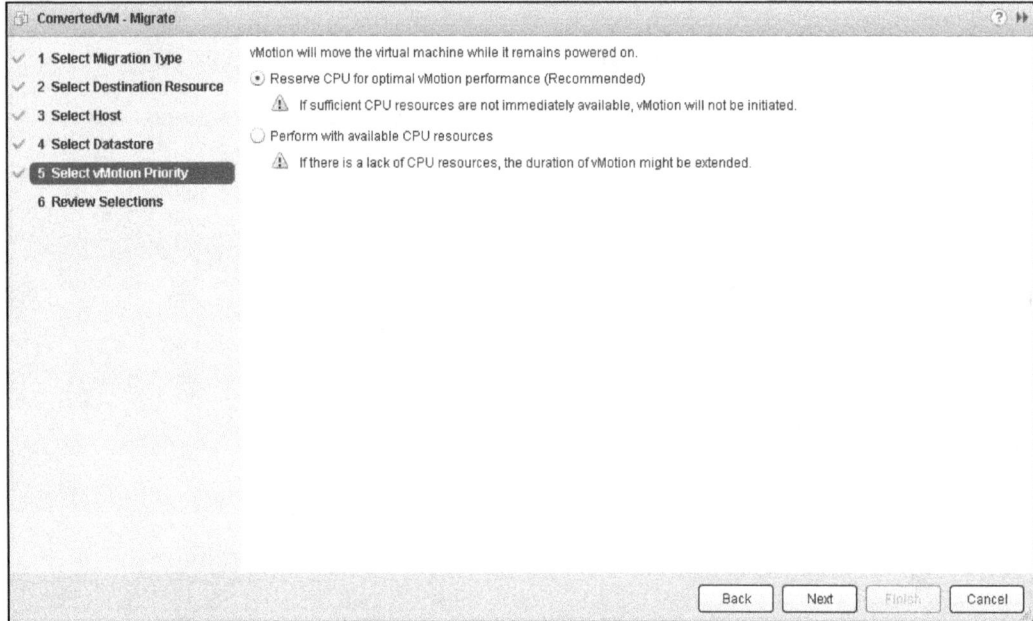

11. Click on the **Next** button after making the selection.

    The **Review Selections** pane will allow for you to look over all the migration settings, as shown in the following screenshot:

Chapter 8

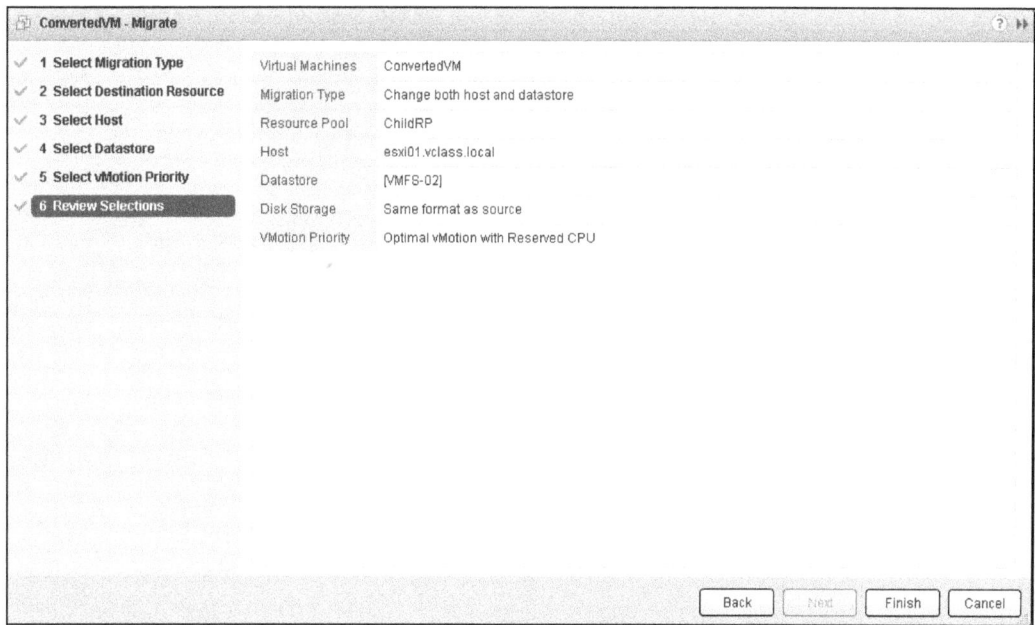

12. Click on **Finish** after looking over all the migration settings on the **Review Selections** pane.

This will initiate the cross-host Storage vMotion migration.

Summary

A vMotion network is required for vMotion and cross-host Storage vMotion. Configuring a VMkernel port on each ESXi host for vMotion traffic creates this network. Migration using vMotion moves a virtual machine's state to a different ESXi host with no downtime while the virtual machine is actively running. Migration using Storage vMotion moves a virtual machine's files to a different datastore with no downtime while the virtual machine is actively running. A virtual machine can change host and datastore simultaneously while powered on using a cross-host Storage vMotion. Cross-host Storage vMotion is only available using the vSphere Web Client with platform Version 5.1 or newer.

The next chapter will discuss cluster features such as DRS, Storage DRS, and High Availability.

9
Balancing Resource Utilization and Availability

A vSphere administrator may choose to automate the process of balancing the virtual machine workload using DRS and Storage DRS. High Availability provides vital protection against ESXi host failure and certain types of virtual machine failure. It is important to understand how these features work and how they are configured.

In this chapter, we will cover the following topics:

- DRS overview
- DRS configuration
- HA overview
- HA configuration
- SDRS overview
- SDRS configuration

Clusters

A **cluster** is a collection of ESXi hosts with shared CPU and memory resources. Clusters not only are helpful in organizing your environment but also provide many advanced features. Some of these are as follows:

- **Distributed Resource Scheduler (DRS)**
- **High Availability (HA)**
- **Distributed Power Management (DPM)**
- **Enhanced vMotion Compatibility (EVC)**
- **Virtual SAN (VSAN)**

Balancing Resource Utilization and Availability

We will discuss the DRS and HA features in this chapter.

EVC can help alleviate CPU compatibility issues across a cluster. See `http://kb.vmware.com/kb/1003212` for more information.

When DPM is enabled, DRS places, or recommends that you place, ESXi hosts in the standby power mode if sufficient excess capacity is found. It will also power on, or recommend that you power on, ESXi hosts if additional capacity is needed. For more information on DPM, see `http://kb.vmware.com/kb/2007560`.

VSAN is a directly attached software-defined product that creates shared storage. For more information on VSAN, see `http://www.vmware.com/products/virtual-san`.

Creating a cluster

Generally, clusters consist of ESXi hosts with compatible CPUs. For example, you may have separate clusters for ESXi hosts with Intel processors than those with AMD processors. See *Chapter 8, Migrating Virtual Machines*, for more information on CPU compatibility.

To create a cluster, perform the following steps:

1. Use the vSphere Web Client to browse to the **Hosts and Clusters** inventory view.
2. Right-click on the datacenter object.
3. Select **New Cluster...**.

   This is demonstrated in the following screenshot:

   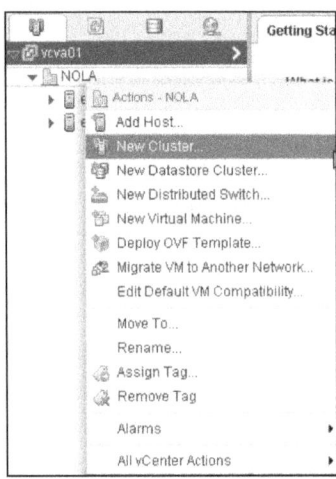

The **New Cluster** window will open; type in a name in the **Name** field for the cluster. If you wish to simply create the cluster object without enabling any feature, click on **OK**. This window is demonstrated in the following screenshot:

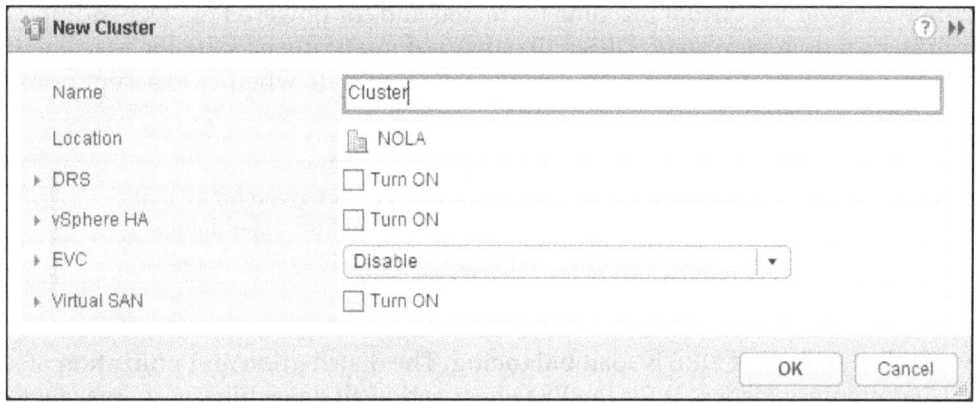

However, to enable any cluster feature, simply select the respective checkboxes next to **Turn ON** and perform the following steps:

1. Enter all the required information for the **New Cluster** dialog box.
2. Click on **OK**.

Once the cluster is created, simply drag-and-drop the ESXi hosts into the new object.

Your environment may already have an existing cluster with multiple features enabled. If this is the case, then you may not need to create a new ESXi cluster. The following sections will discuss the relevant settings for DRS and HA.

Distributed Resource Scheduler (DRS)

To obtain the full benefit of cluster-level resource management, you must first enable the DRS feature. DRS provides the functionalities of initial placement and automated load balancing for the virtual machines in the cluster. DRS uses CPU and memory usage as its metrics to determine imbalances and requires the vSphere Enterprise Edition or a higher license.

Overview of DRS

DRS has two functions: initial placement and dynamic load balancing. **Initial placement** generates a recommendation of which ESXi host a virtual machine should run on whenever the virtual machine is created and/or powered on. Depending on the cluster's automation level, DRS will either automatically execute the placement recommendation or display it, allowing the user to decide whether to accept or reject the recommendation.

 Initial placement recommendations are not given for virtual machines running in a non-DRS cluster or on a standalone ESXi host. The virtual machines will continue to run on the same ESXi host when powered on.

Another key feature of DRS is **load balancing**. The distribution and utilization of CPU and memory resources for the ESXi host and virtual machines within a cluster are continuously monitored. DRS takes the metrics and compares them to ideal resource utilization based on the configuration of virtual machines and resource pools, the current resource demand, and the imbalance target. Migrations (or recommendations for migration) will be performed accordingly. Remember that DRS leverages vMotion technology to migrate the virtual machines.

There are certain requirements that must be met for DRS to properly function, which are as follows:

- Shared storage (All virtual machines' files need to be placed on storage volumes that are accessible by all ESXi hosts in the cluster.)
- Gigabit Ethernet (or better) interconnection configured for vMotion traffic
- Consistent network configuration, both physical and virtual, to include the names of VMkernel ports for vMotion and virtual machine port groups
- Cluster ESXi hosts must have CPUs from the same compatibility group

Enabling and configuring DRS

DRS may be enabled once the prerequisites have been met. To enable DRS on an existing cluster, perform the following steps:

1. Use the vSphere Web Client to navigate to the cluster's **Manage** tab.
2. Under the **Settings** tab, choose **vSphere DRS**.
3. Click on the **Edit** button.

Chapter 9

This is demonstrated in the following screenshot:

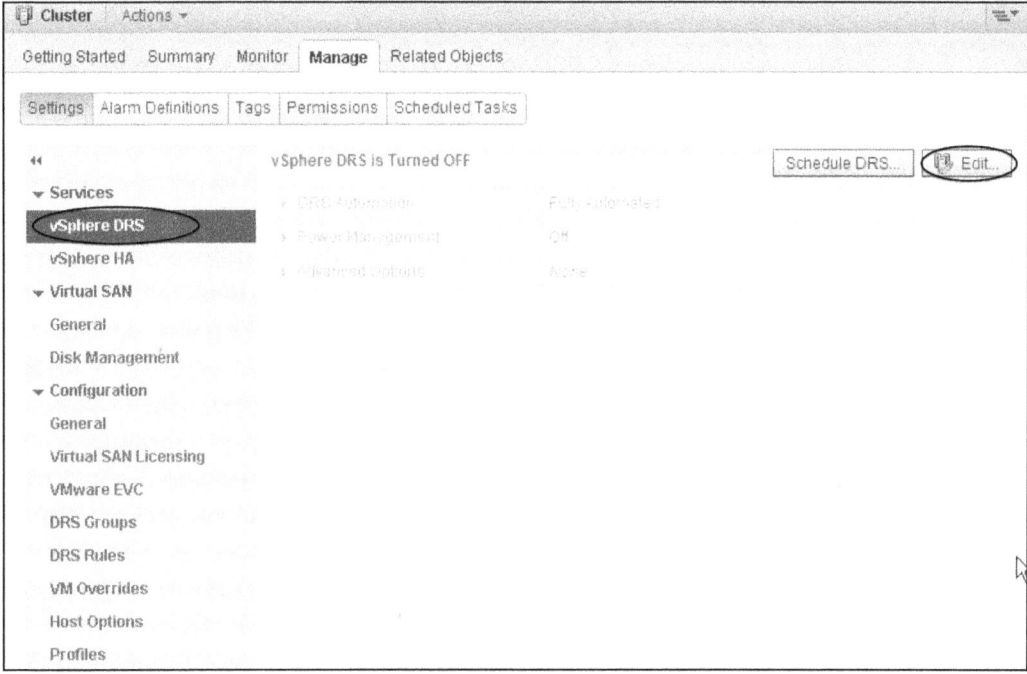

4. Select the checkbox next to **Turn ON vSphere DRS** as shown in the following screenshot:.

   This will allow further configuration of the feature. See the upcoming screenshot as an example.

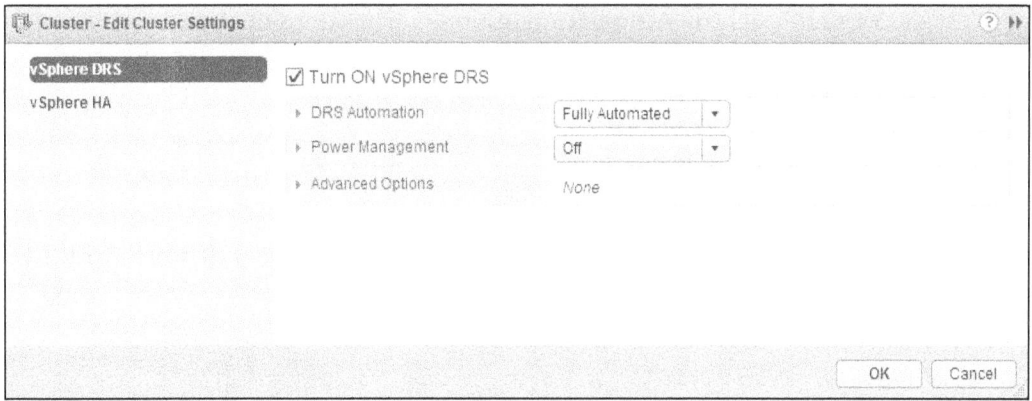

Expanding the **DRS Automation** option will unveil the different configuration options. The **Automation Level** option provides you with three more options:

- **Manual**: By selecting this option, recommendations will be made for initial placement and load balancing. The administrator must accept the recommendations.
- **Partially Automated**: By selecting this option, initial placement is automatic but load-balancing recommendations are made. The administrator must manually accept the recommendations.
- **Fully Automated**: By selecting this option, initial placement and load balancing is automatic and can be controlled by managing the migration threshold.

The **Migration Threshold** option allows you to specify which priority levels of recommendations are generated and then applied (if fully automated) or shown (if partially automated or manual). The slider can be set to one of the five settings, from **Conservative** to **Aggressive**; each setting allows for one or more priority levels:

- **Conservative** generates priority one recommendations (mandatory; critical imbalance).
- The next level to the right generates priority one and priority two recommendations. The priority one recommendation is mandatory and indicative of a critical imbalance, but the priority two recommendation is slightly less critical.
- This continues all the way to **Aggressive**, which generates all recommendations, from priority one through priority five.

The **Virtual Machine Automation** option, when selected, allows you to customize the virtual machine automation levels to override the cluster's automation level, as shown in the following screenshot:

Chapter 9

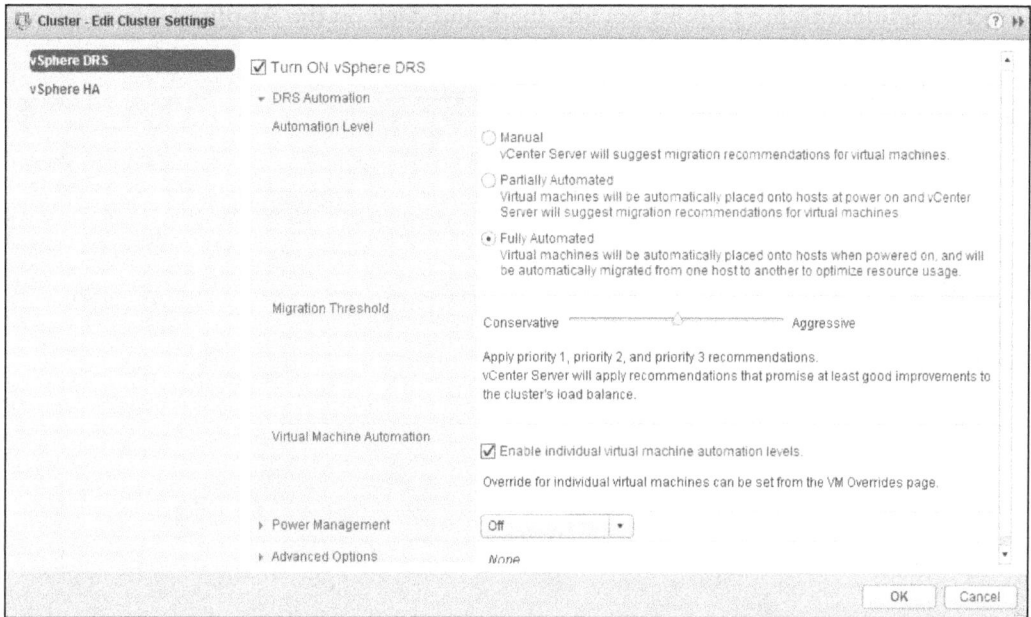

5. Select the **Automation Level** and **Migration Threshold** options, and select whether to enable the **Virtual Machine Automation** option.

6. Click on **OK** once you have finished configuring vSphere DRS.

The preceding screenshot demonstrates these selections.

DRS recommendations and monitoring DRS

If DRS is configured for anything less than **Fully Automated** and **Aggressive**, then an administrator will need to check for and apply the remaining DRS recommendations.

To view DRS recommendations, perform the following steps:

1. Browse to the cluster using the vSphere Web Client.
2. Click on the **Monitor** tab and then on the **vSphere DRS** button.
3. Select **Recommendations** to view any current DRS recommendation.
4. Click on the **Run DRS Now** button to refresh the list of recommendations.

If recommendations are present, review them and click on the **Apply Recommendations** button as shown in the following screenshot:

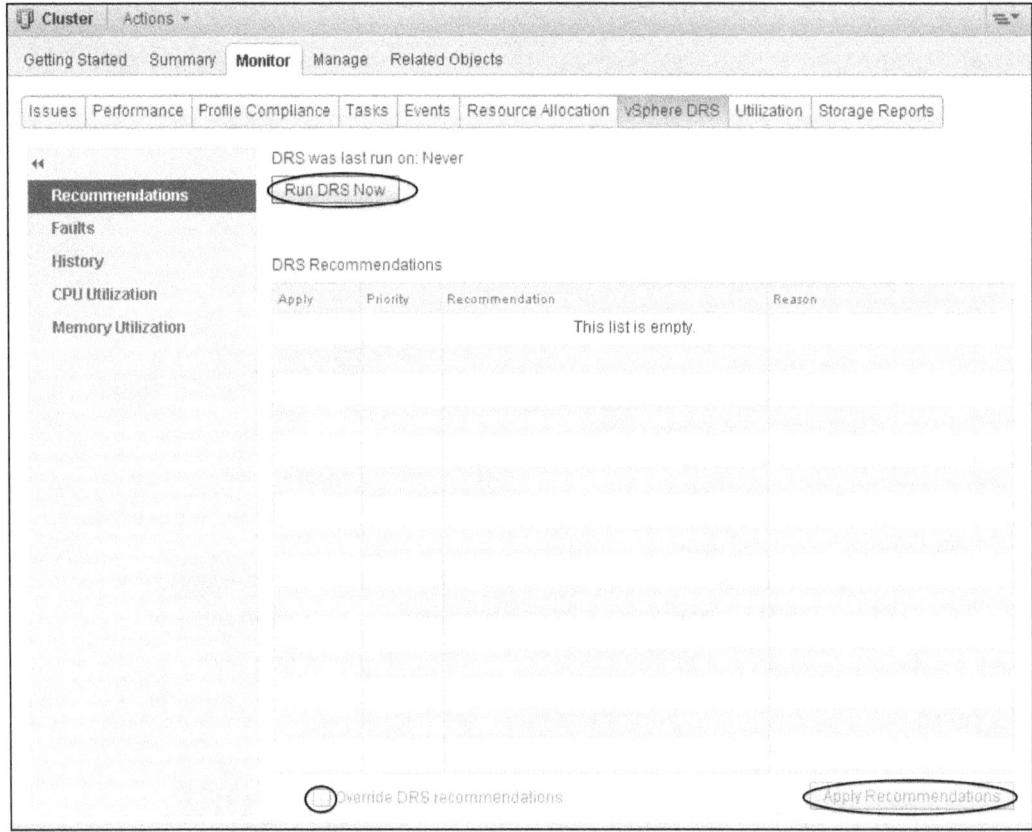

If multiple recommendations are made and you wish to apply only a subset of recommendations, then select the checkbox next to **Override DRS recommendations**. Deselect the recommendations that are not desired and click on the **Apply Recommendations** button. This is demonstrated in the preceding screenshot.

I often use resource distribution charts to demonstrate whether a cluster is load balanced. Keep in mind that the resource distribution will vary based on the selection of the migration threshold during the DRS configuration.

Chapter 9

To view the CPU and memory distribution across the ESXi hosts in the cluster, perform the following steps:

1. Click on the **Monitor** tab.
2. Click on the **vSphere DRS** button.
3. Select either **CPU Utilization** or **Memory Utilization**.

Memory utilization can be displayed in either percent or MB, whereas CPU utilization can be displayed as percent or MHz. You can select either from the drop-down list next to **Show as**, as displayed in the following screenshot:

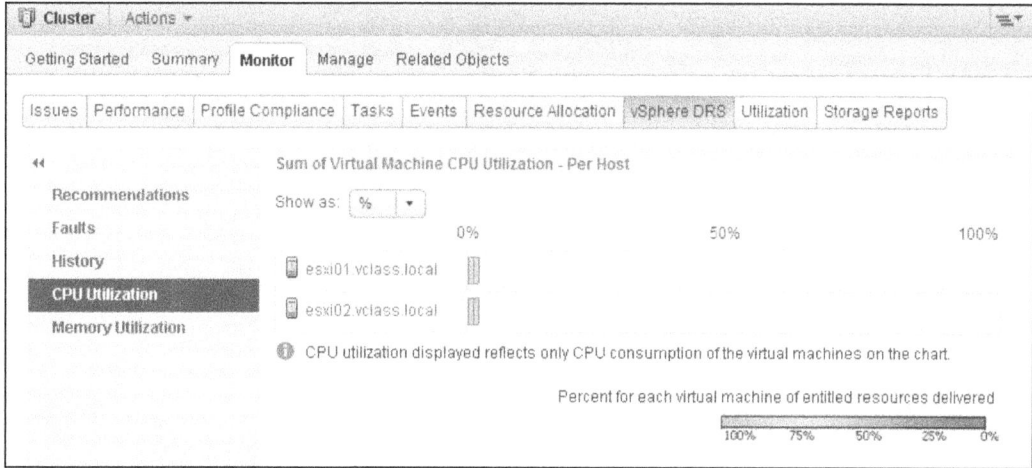

Using the **Monitor** tab will help identify any load distribution issues in the cluster.

Balancing Resource Utilization and Availability

In the **Summary** tab of the cluster, click on the **vSphere DRS** button. There is a cool level image that depicts whether the cluster is balanced. Also, note that you can determine the automation level and the threshold of priority levels that are applied automatically. This is shown in the following screenshot:

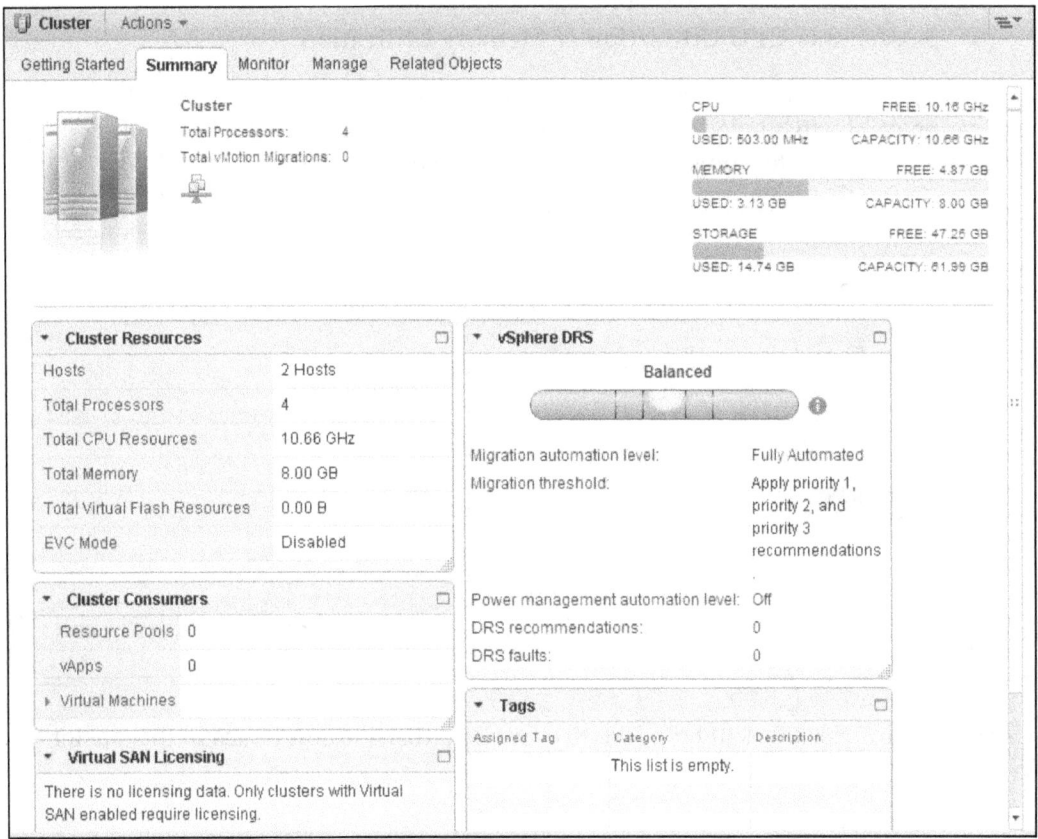

The **Summary** tab is a nice place to quickly gather information regarding the configuration of the vSphere DRS cluster.

Affinity/Anti-affinity rules

After a vSphere DRS cluster is created, the DRS rules can be created to specify affinity or anti-affinity rules:

- **Keep Virtual Machines Together**: This is an option under the affinity rules. DRS should try to place certain virtual machines together on the same host, possibly for performance reasons. For example, you may choose to place a web frontend and its database on the same host because of the performance gain using VMCI.
- **Separate Virtual Machines**: This is an option under the anti-affinity rules. DRS should try to place the specified virtual machines on different ESXi hosts, possibly for availability reasons.
- **Virtual Machines to Host**: DRS should try to place virtual machines on a specific ESXi host or DRS group, possibly for licensing reasons. For example, only a portion of a cluster may be licensed for Oracle.

If two rules conflict, then you are prevented from enabling both.

One or more DRS groups can be created for use in a vSphere DRS cluster. Groups can be created for virtual machines and ESXi hosts. These groups help define the DRS rules without having to make specifications for each individual virtual machine.

A virtual machine can belong to more than one virtual machine DRS group; likewise, an ESXi host can belong to one or more host DRS groups.

Because this is cluster based, the virtual machines and ESXi hosts included in the rule must reside in the same cluster.

To configure DRS rules, perform the following steps:

1. Go to the **Manage** tab of the cluster.
2. Under the **Settings** tab, select **DRS Rules**.
3. To add a DRS rule, click on the **Add** button.
4. Specify a name for the rule and the type of the DRS rule.

    If the **Virtual Machines to Host** option is selected, then the DRS groups must first be created and configured. Choosing this option will require the selection of a VM group and host group. However, if **Keep Virtual Machines Together** or **Separate Virtual Machines** is selected, then choose the specific virtual machines.

5. Click on **Add...** to choose what virtual machines or DRS groups this rule will apply to. This is shown in the following screenshot:

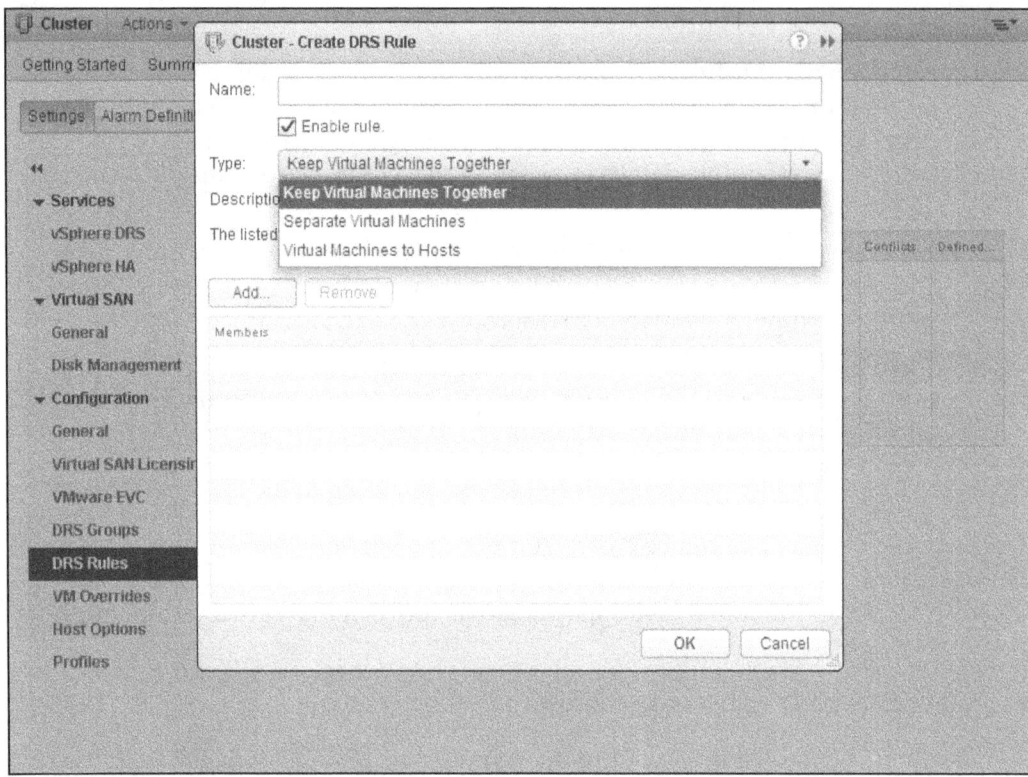

6. Click on **OK** after specifying a DRS rule.

High Availability

vSphere HA clusters enable a group of ESXi hosts to work together so that a higher level of availability is provided for virtual machines, which is more than what a single ESXi host can provide. vSphere HA pools ESXi hosts and virtual machines into a cluster. These ESXi hosts in the cluster are monitored and in the event of a failure, the virtual machines are restarted on an alternate ESXi host.

Overview of HA

vSphere HA has recently undergone a complete overhaul and operates very differently from previous versions in vSphere 5.x.

An agent, **Fault Domain Manager** (**FDM**), is uploaded to the ESXi hosts as they are added to a vSphere HA cluster. This agent is configured to communicate with other agents within the vSphere HA cluster. An ESXi host can function as either a master host or a slave host.

When a cluster is enabled for vSphere HA, all active ESXi hosts participate in a process known as **election**. The election will determine the master host in the cluster; there is one master host and every other host is a slave. The master is typically the ESXi host in the cluster that has the most LUNs mounted. If all cluster ESXi hosts have the same amount of LUNs mounted, then **Managed Object ID** (**MOID**) is used. MOID is a unique ID assigned to each host by vCenter, and the host with the lexically highest MOID will win the role of the master host.

The master host in the vSphere HA cluster has multiple responsibilities. These include the following:

- It monitors the state of the slave hosts in the HA-enabled cluster. Should a slave host fail or become unreachable, the master host identifies which virtual machines require a restart.
- It monitors the state of protected virtual machines. If a virtual machine fails, the master host makes sure that it is restarted.
- It manages the lists of vSphere HA cluster ESXi hosts and protects the virtual machines.
- It acts as a management interface to the vSphere HA cluster for vCenter Server and reports the cluster's health status.

The slave hosts are responsible for locally running virtual machines, monitoring virtual machine runtime states, and reporting status updates to the master host.

The master host monitors the slaves through an exchange of network heartbeats (ICMP pings) per second. If the master host stops receiving these heartbeats from a slave host, it will try to identify whether the host is alive before declaring a failure. This check of being alive involves the master host determining whether the slave is exchanging heartbeats with a datastore, as well as the response to the ICMP pings sent to the management network IP interface.

 **Datastore heartbeating** is a new vSphere HA feature as of vSphere 5.0. It is used to determine whether a slave host has failed and is either isolated from the network or in a network partition.

If a master host is unable to communicate with the slave host's agent—that is, the slave host had not replied to the ICMP pings and has not issued heartbeats to the datastore—the master host will declare the slave host as failed. The failed host's virtual machines will be restarted on a different ESXi host.

Host network isolation occurs when an ESXi host is still up and running, but no longer exchanges traffic from the HA agents on the management network. In other words, a master host will be unable to communicate with the slave host's agent and the slave will not reply to the ICMP pings. However, the heartbeats will continue to be exchanged with a datastore. At this point, the master host will assume that the slave host is in a network isolated or network partition state and will continue to monitor the host and the virtual machines. The slave host will attempt to ping the cluster isolation address once it has stopped exchanging traffic on the management network. If this ping fails, the slave host will declare itself isolated from the network, at which time it will conduct the host isolation response.

In the event a vSphere HA cluster has a management network failure, a portion of the ESXi hosts may not be able to communicate with other ESXi hosts over that management network. This may result in a **network partition**, sometimes called a "split-brain". This can lead to degraded cluster management and virtual machine protection. A network partition needs to be resolved quickly. Since not all of the ESXi hosts are able to communicate with each other, configuration changes cannot be made to all ESXi hosts. This is because the cluster only recognizes a single master and the partitioned ESXi hosts will not be able to communicate with the master that orchestrates the changes. A network partition could result in a portion of the vSphere HA cluster using old configurations while the rest use newer configurations. Make sure to resolve a network partition as soon as possible to avoid any vSphere HA configuration issues.

For more information on vSphere HA, see the *VMware vSphere High Availability* guide. Duncan Epping (VCDX #7) also has a great guide to HA on his blog (http://www.yellow-bricks.com/vmware-high-availability-deepdiv/).

Configuring HA

To configure vSphere High Availability, perform the following steps:

1. Navigate to the cluster using the vSphere Web Client.
2. Go to the **Manage** tab, click on the **Settings** tab, and then choose **vSphere HA**.
3. Click on the **Edit** button to enable and configure this feature as shown in the following screenshot:

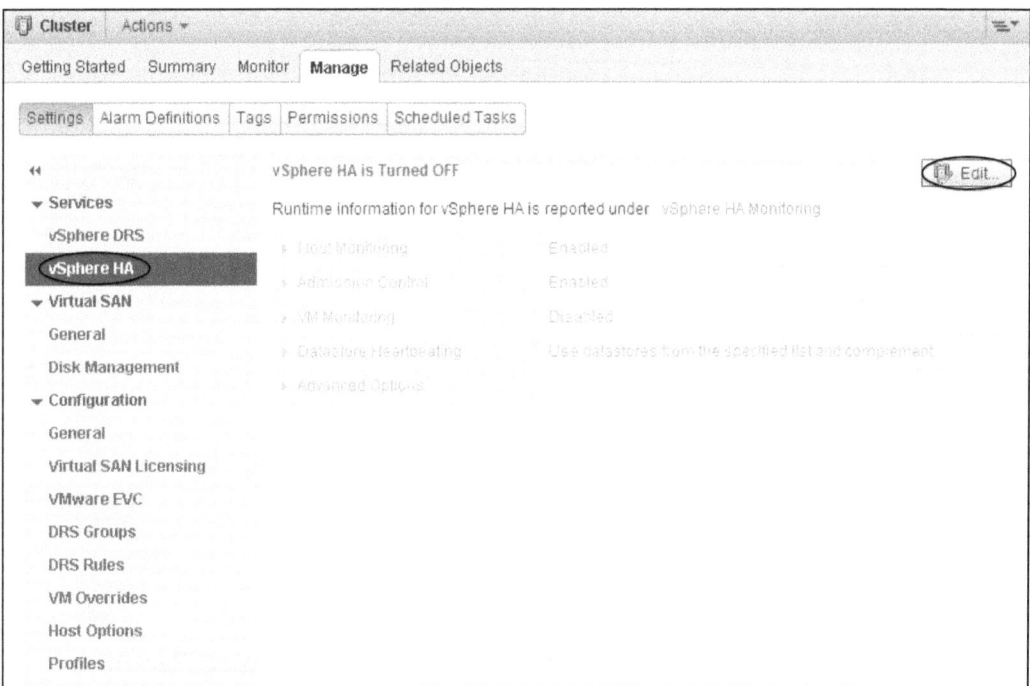

If the **Host Monitoring** option is selected, then vSphere HA will actively monitor and respond to host failures. This is enabled by default.

The **VM restart priority** option determines the relative order that virtual machines are restarted on new hosts after an ESXi host failure. vSphere HA will try to restart the virtual machines of the highest priority level first and then progress to the lower priority ones until all virtual machines are restarted or there are no more cluster resources. By specifying this at the cluster level (as shown in the following screenshot), all virtual machine will inherit the policy. However, it is possible to explicitly define the **VM restart priority** option at the virtual machine level.

The **Host isolation response** option is used by the ESXi host to handle its virtual machines when the management network connectivity is lost but the host continues to run. The default selection is **Leave powered on**; the other options are **Shut down** or **Power off**, both of which will result in a failover. The **Shut down** option requires VMware Tools to be installed in the guest operating system of the virtual machines. The **vSphere HA** pane is shown in the following screenshot:

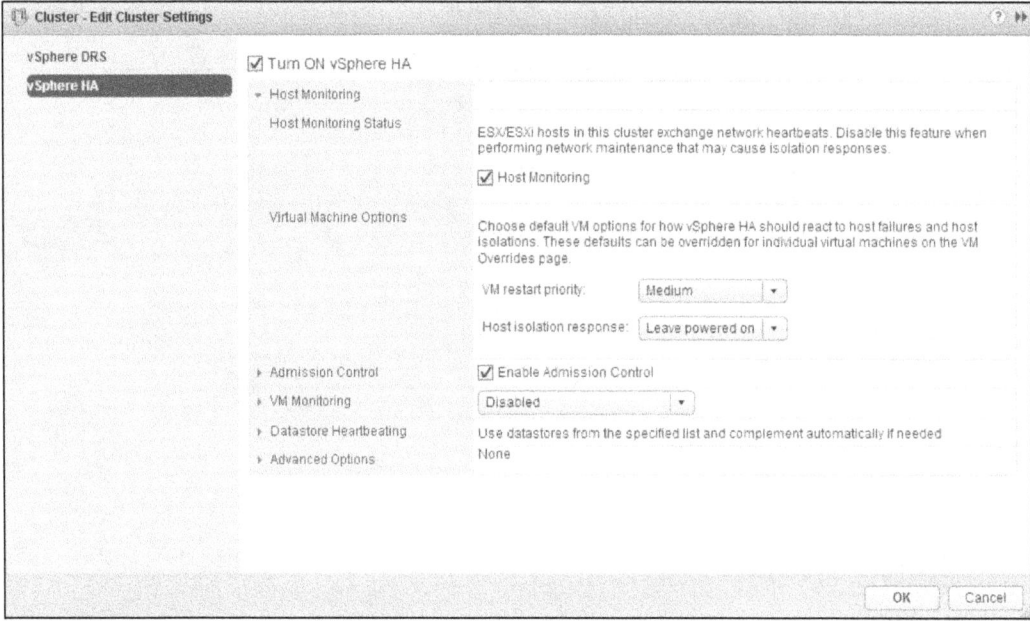

4. Select the required **Host Monitoring** options.

5. To continue configuring vSphere HA, expand the **Admission Control** pane. The **Enable Admission Control** option is selected by default.

   Admission Control is a policy that it will enforce availability constraints to preserve the ability to failover when enabled. If you attempt to power on a virtual machine that will violate this constraint, then a generated message will inform you that this isn't allowed due to a violation of the admission control. This is done to ensure that enough resources are available in case of an HA event.

The first **Admission Control** option is **Define failover capacity by static number of hosts**. This uses a slot size policy—a **slot** is the logical representation of memory and CPU resources that the cluster must provide to a virtual machine in the worst case failure scenario. The slot size is determined by the largest virtual machine CPU and memory reservations in the cluster. If no reservations are configured, then the default values are used; the default values are 32 MHz for CPU and memory overhead.

Depending on the specified number of hosts that the cluster can tolerate failing (**Reserved failover capacity**), a coordinating number of slots are reserved for use only during a vSphere HA event. This means that if the option is configured to reserve failover capacity for **1** host (shown as the example in the following screenshot), then half of the slots would be reserved in a 2-host cluster, one-third of the slots would be reserved in a 3-host cluster, and so on.

Keep in mind that the slot size is variable unless the **Fixed slot size** option is selected. Choosing this will allow for an explicit definition of the slot size. Otherwise, the slot size will vary based on the largest configured reservations or memory overhead for the powered on cluster virtual machines.

Another available option is **Define failover capacity by reserving a percentage of the cluster resources**. The percentage specified indicates the portion of resources that will remain unused and reserved in case of a vSphere HA failover. This applies to both CPU and memory. The **Admission Control** pane is shown in the following screenshot:

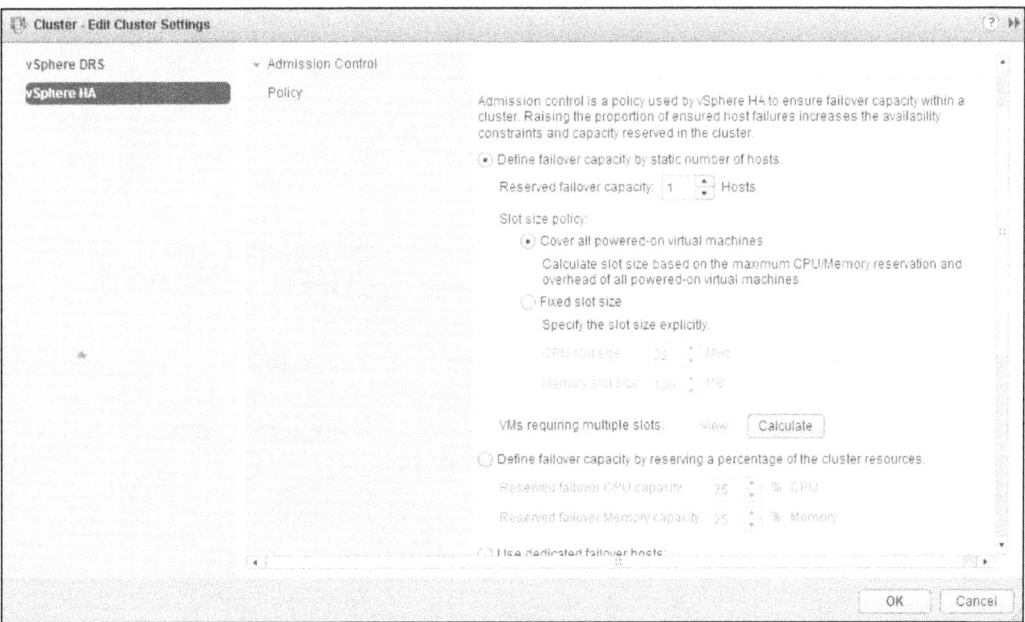

Balancing Resource Utilization and Availability

Scrolling further down the **Admission Control** pane will take you to the third option, **Use dedicated failover hosts**. This selection permits the specification of one or more ESXi hosts as a standby failover host. When this option is selected, vSphere HA will attempt to restart the virtual machines on any of the specified failover hosts. However, if this is not possible, then the virtual machines will be restarted on other ESXi hosts in the cluster.

The last option, **Do not reserve failover capacity**, will not reserve any cluster resources for use during a vSphere HA event. This allows virtual machines that violate availability constraints to power on. This is shown in the following screenshot:

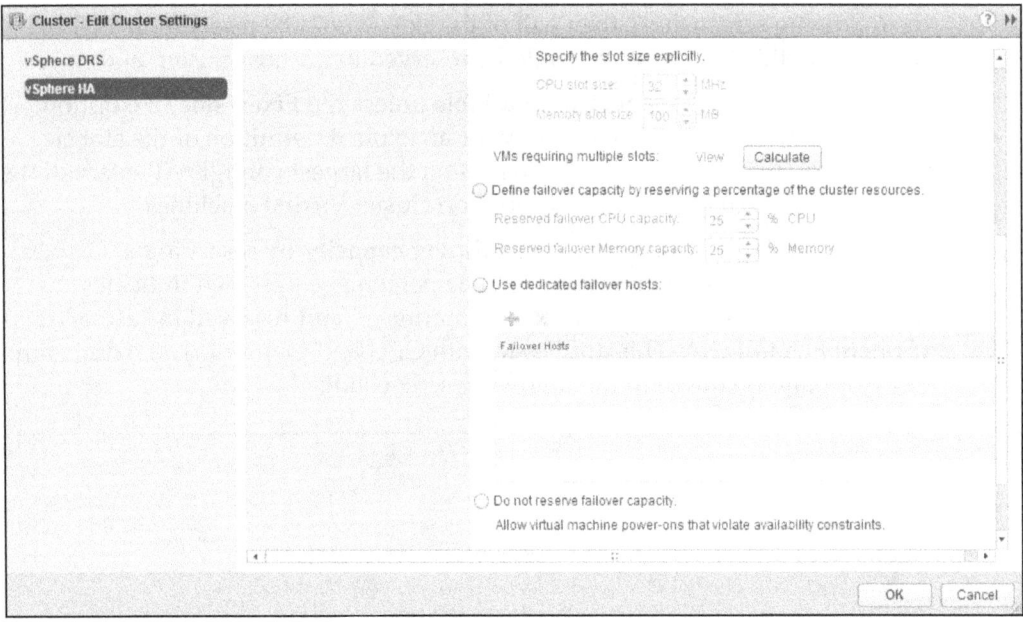

Each option of the **Admission Control** option has a recommended use that depends on how heterogeneous or homogenized the virtual machines are within a cluster.

In a heterogeneous cluster, the **Define failover capacity by static number of hosts** option can be too conservative in defining a slot size. This is because it considers the largest virtual machine reservations and assumes the largest host failures while computing the failover capacity.

Resource fragmentation generally happens when there are sufficient resources for virtual machines to be failed over, except those resources are fragmented across multiple ESXi hosts. A virtual machine can only run on a single ESXi host at a time. The **Define failover capacity by reserving a percentage of the cluster resources** option does not address this issue. The **Use dedicated failover hosts** option mitigates this issue by reserving hosts for failover, and the **Define failover capacity by static number of hosts** option avoids this issue by defining a slot as a virtual machine reservation.

6. Select the desired **Admission Control** options.
7. Expand the **VM Monitoring** option to continue configuring vSphere HA.

    The **VM Monitoring Status** option, when enabled, restarts individual virtual machines if their VMware Tools heartbeats are not received or if the guest OS hasn't issued I/O for a set interval.

    Under the **Monitor Sensitivity** option, a **Preset** value can be used to determine when a virtual machine should be restarted due to a failed interval. **High** will restart the virtual machine if heartbeats are not received for 30 seconds, whereas **Low** will restart after 2 minutes of no heartbeats. If the **Preset** values do not meet the desired intervals, use the **Custom** option to specify the **Failure interval** option, as shown in the following screenshot:

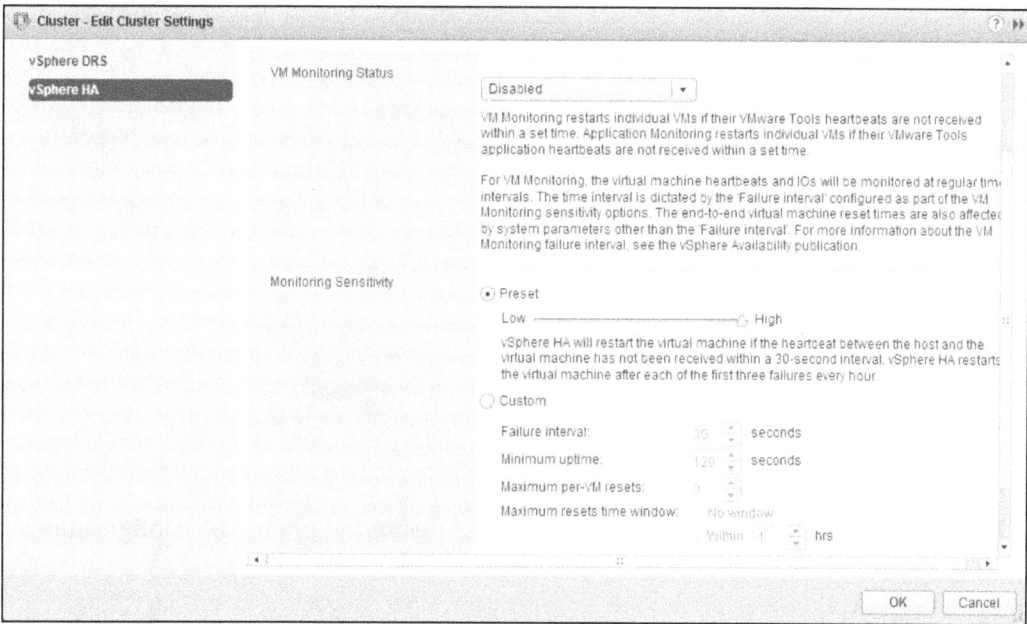

8. Select the necessary **VM Monitoring** options.//
9. Expand the **Datastore Heartbeating** section to continue configuring vSphere HA.

    Datastore Heartbeating is used as a secondary mechanism to detect whether an ESXi host has failed or is isolated due to a management network failure. I recommend that you use two to four datastores to accomplish this; these datastores should be shared across all ESXi hosts in the cluster. The **Heartbeat datastore selection policy** options will determine how the datastores are chosen for use.

    vSphere HA creates a directory, .vSphere-HA, at the root of each datastore. This directory is used for both datastore heartbeating and the protected list, which specifies the set of virtual machines safeguarded by vSphere HA. Do not delete or modify this directory or the files stored in this directory. Doing so can negatively affect the vSphere HA operations. The **Datastore Heartbeating** section is shown in the following screenshot:

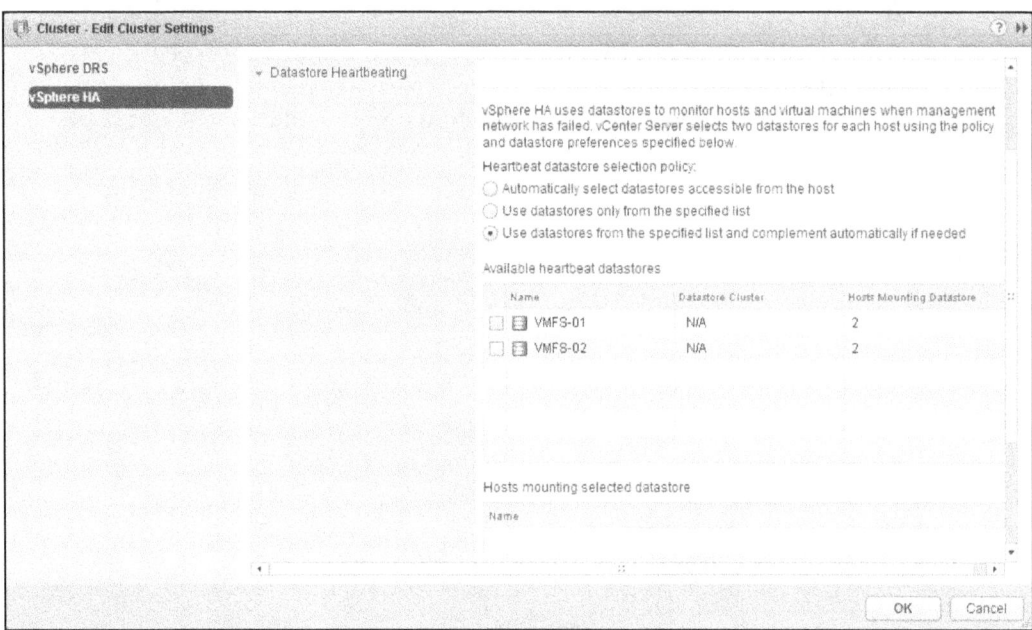

10. Click on **OK** after you have made all the desired vSphere HA configurations.

A nice place to get a quick overview of the vSphere HA status can be found by browsing to the cluster using the vSphere Web Client. Select the **Monitor** tab and then the **vSphere HA** tab, and from there select **Summary**. The **Summary** pane is shown in the following screenshot:

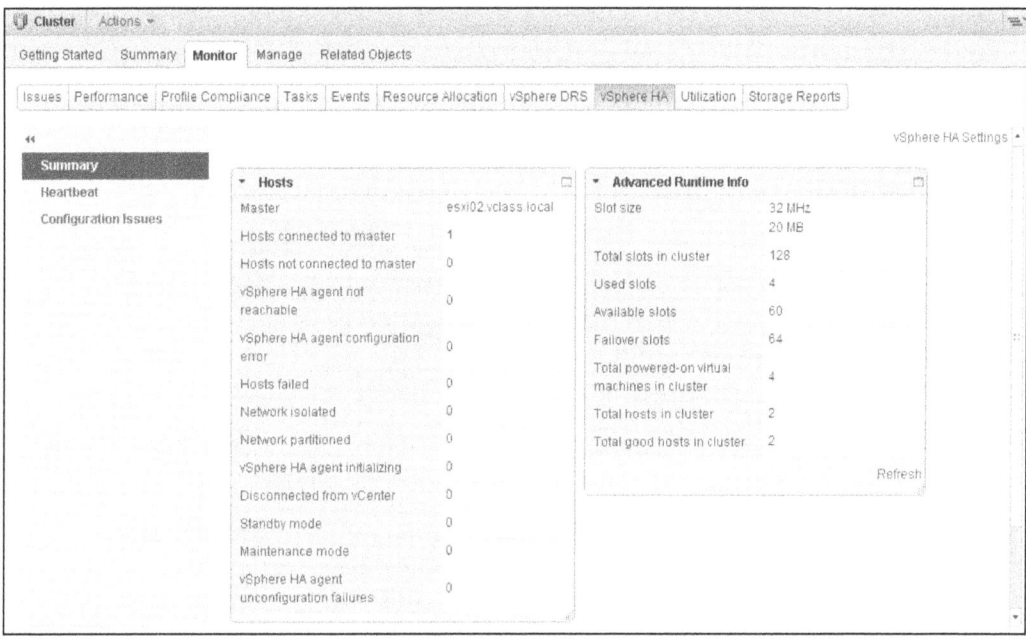

The **Hosts** pane specifies the **Master** host and the number of hosts that have failed, isolated, partitioned, and so on. This allows an administrator to quickly identify potential vSphere HA issues. The **Advanced Runtime Info** pane indicates the slot size and the number of slots, used slots, available and reserved for failover slots, and so on.

Storage Distributed Resource Scheduler (SDRS)

A datastore cluster is a collection of datastores that can be grouped together to work as a single unit or as separate entities. To gain full benefit of a datstore cluster, Storage DRS should be enabled. When a datastore cluster is enabled for **Storage Distributed Resource Scheduler** (**Storage DRS** or **SDRS**), this feature balances across the datastore cluster based on the datastore usage and the I/O latency. Datastore clusters are not necessarily connected or related to an ESXi host cluster.

Overview of SDRS

Storage DRS will manage the initial placement of virtual machines in a datastore cluster based on the space usage and I/O load balancing. The feature will attempt to keep the usage as evenly distributed as possible across the datastores in the datastore cluster. Storage DRS requires the vSphere Enterprise Plus license.

Storage DRS can also be configured to balance the I/O latency across the datastore members of the datastore cluster to help mitigate any kind of performance issues.

Depending on the automation level of the datastore cluster, Storage DRS will either automatically execute the placement recommendation or display it, allowing the user to decide whether to accept or reject the recommendation.

Storage DRS is called upon at a configured frequency, which is every eight hours by default, or when a datastore in a datastore cluster exceeds the space utilization thresholds. Storage DRS checks the datastore's I/O latency values and the space utilization against the configured threshold.

For Storage DRS to successfully function, there are a few requirements that should be adhered to. Follow these guidelines when creating a datastore cluster:

- Datastores clustered together should be similar. Ideally, the datastores will have similar sizes and I/O capacities; however, we can have a mixture, but keep in mind that this can potentially cause performance issues.
    - Replicated datastores should not be combined with nonreplicated datastores in the same datastore cluster enabled for Storage DRS. Automated movement of the virtual machines can cause a gap in protection. This can occur because a virtual machine that should be placed on a replicated datastore may be automatically migrated to a nonreplicated datastore.
    - The VMFS and NFS datastore cannot be combined in the same datastore cluster.
- All ESXi hosts attached to the datastores in the datastore cluster must run ESXi 5.0 and later.
- Datastores with hardware acceleration enabled shouldn't be placed in a datastore cluster with datastores that do not have the acceleration enabled.
- Datastores should not be shared across multiple datacenters if you desire to include it in a datastore cluster.

Ensure that these prerequisites are met before enabling Storage DRS on a datastore cluster.

Storage DRS is used so that datastore migrations are recommended or automatically applied, resulting in a load-balanced datastore cluster. If the datastore usage reaches 100 percent of its capacity, then the datastore disconnects from all ESXi hosts. This disconnection causes virtual machines residing on this datastore to be disconnected and no longer accessible to the end users. Storage DRS helps avoid situations like this.

Configuring SDRS

Before attempting to create and configure a datastore cluster, ensure that you are licensed for this feature.

To create a datastore cluster, perform the following steps:

1. Browse to the **Datastore and Datastore Cluster** inventory view using the vSphere Web Client.
2. Right-click on the datacenter object.
3. Choose **New Datastore Cluster...**.

    This is demonstrated in the following screenshot:

    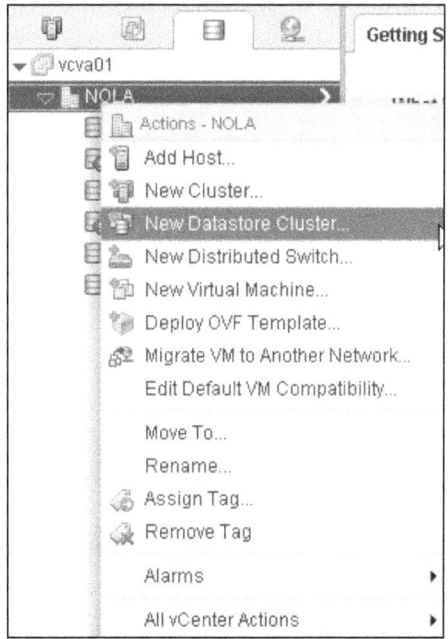

    Selecting this will launch the **New Datastore Cluster** wizard.

Balancing Resource Utilization and Availability

4. Enter a name in the **Datastore Cluster Name** field and select the checkbox next to **Turn ON Storage DRS** to enable this feature as shown in the following screenshot:

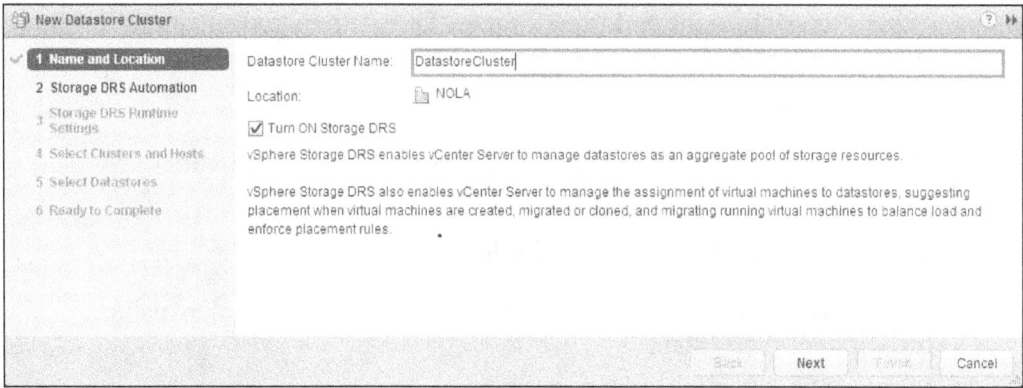

5. Click on **Next** after specifying this information.
6. For the **Automation level** section, choose either **No Automation (Manual Mode)** or **Fully Automated** as shown in the following screenshot:

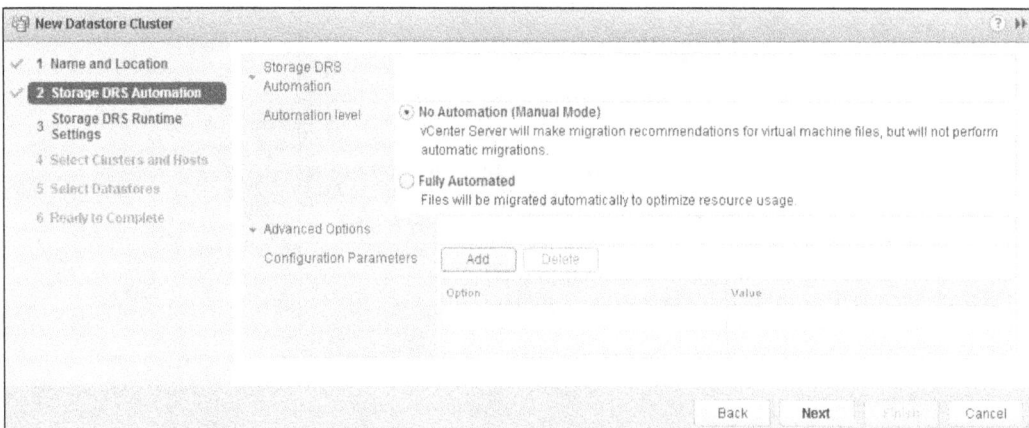

7. Click on **Next** after specifying the **Automation level** section.
8. If you wish to include the I/O metrics as part of the Storage DRS recommendations, select the checkbox next to **Enable I/O metric for SDRS recommendations**.

Chapter 9

There are two adjustable Storage DRS thresholds: **Utilized Space** and **I/O Latency**. The space utilization option for load-balancing generates a recommendation when the use of datastore space exceeds the threshold. An I/O latency threshold can be set to avoid bottlenecks. Whenever the I/O latency exceeds the configured threshold, migrations will occur to assist in alleviating the load. These I/O metrics are gathered using Storage I/O Control. The **Storage DRS Runtime Settings** pane is shown in the following screenshot:

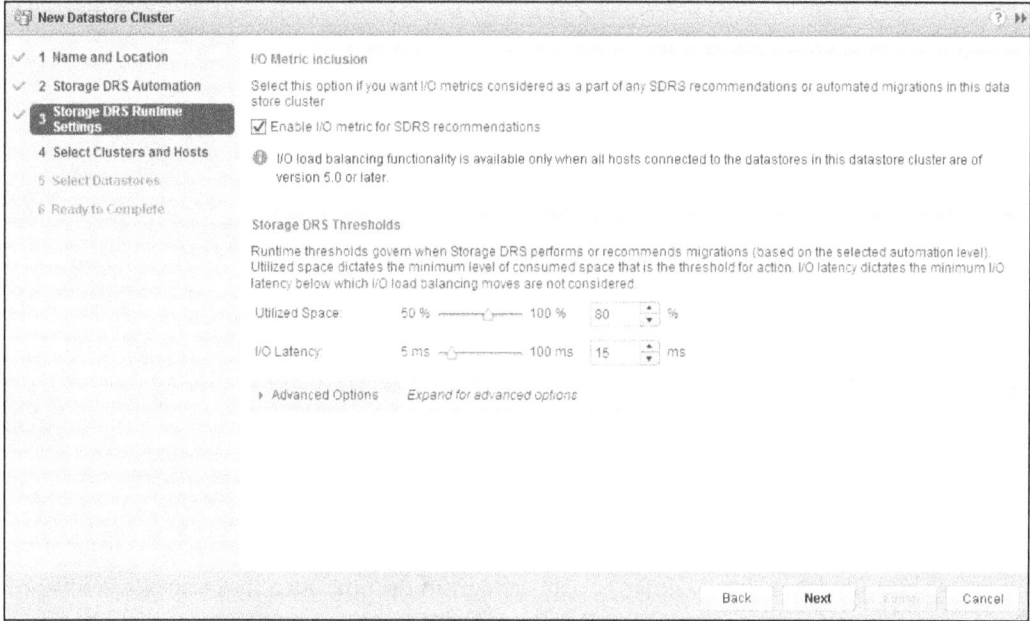

9. Click on **Next** after configuring the **Storage DRS Runtime Settings** pane.

[269]

Balancing Resource Utilization and Availability

10. On the **Select Clusters and Hosts** pane, select the objects that will have connectivity to the datastores in the newly created datastore cluster, as shown in the following screenshot:

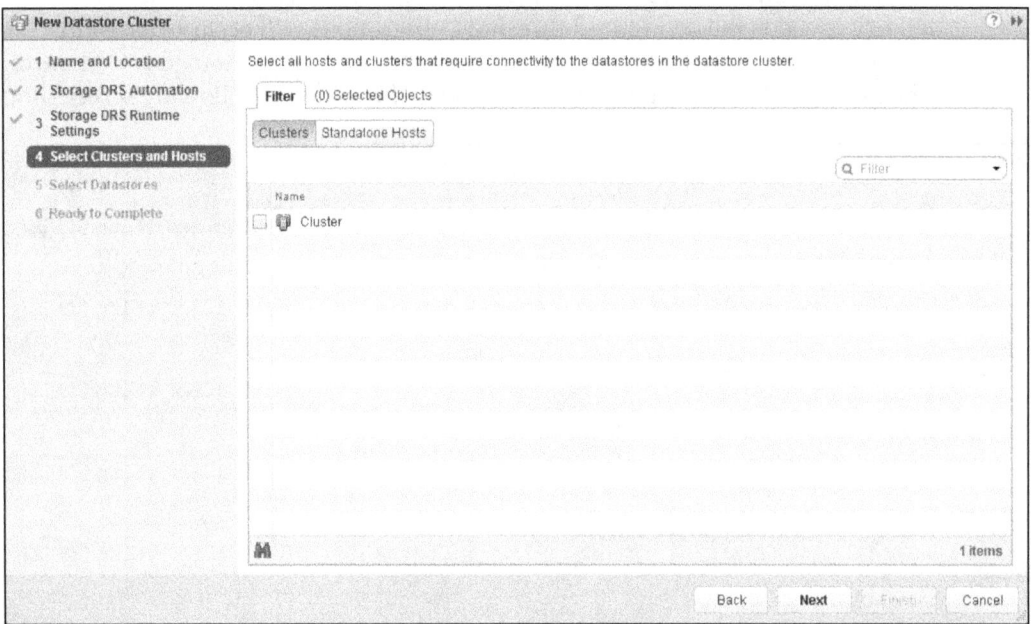

11. Click on **Next** after selecting the hosts and clusters.

    The following pane allows for the selection of datastore that should belong to this datstore cluster. By default, only datastores that are connected to all previously selected hosts will be displayed. This can be changed using the drop-down menu above the datastore pane.

12. Select the datastore that will be a part of this datastore cluster as shown in the following screenshot:

Chapter 9

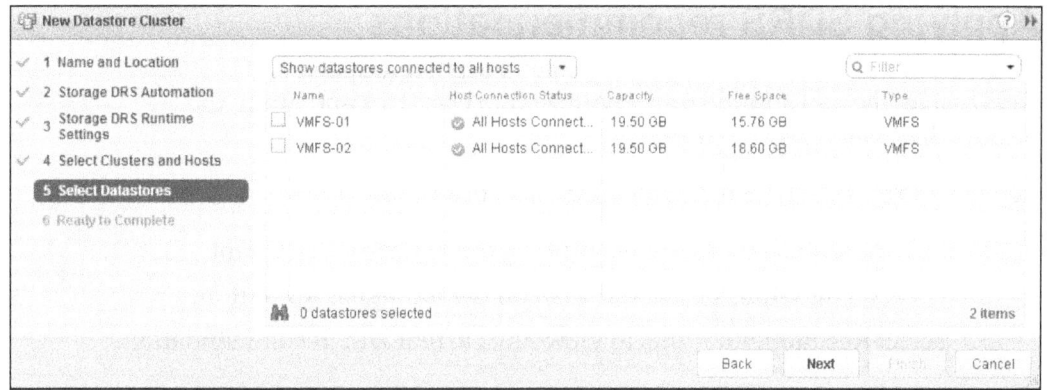

13. Click on **Next** after selecting the datastores.

    Review all the selections to verify the SDRS configuration as shown in the following screenshot:

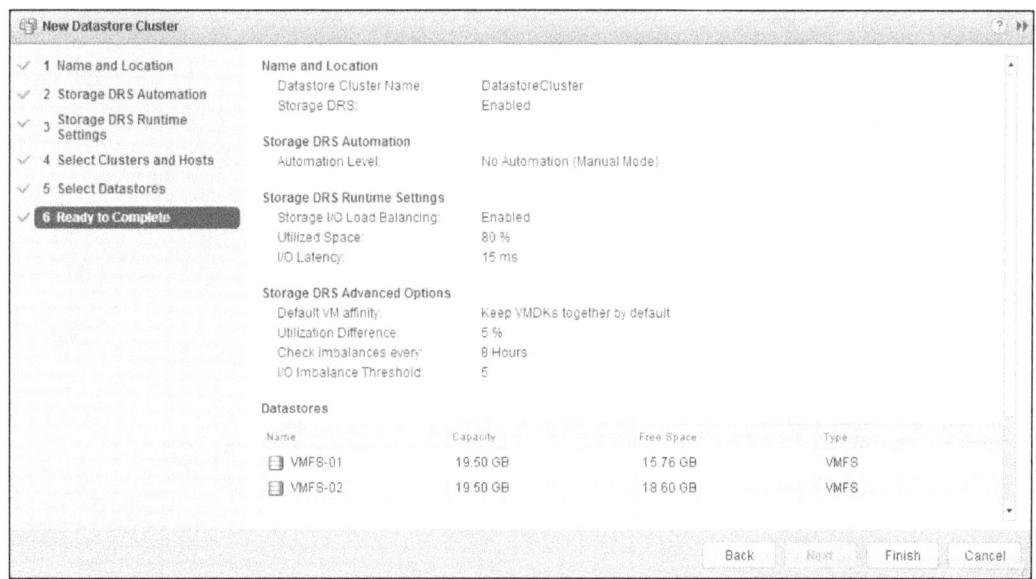

14. Click on **Finish** to complete the creation and configuration of the datastore cluster enabled with vSphere Storage DRS.

Applying SDRS recommendations

If SDRS is configured for anything less than **Fully Automated** and **Aggressive**, then an administrator will need to check for and apply the desired SDRS recommendations.

To view the Storage DRS recommendations, perform the following steps:

1. Browse to the datastore cluster using the vSphere Web Client.
2. Click on the **Monitor** tab and then on the **Storage DRS** button.
3. Select **Recommendations** to view any current DRS recommendation.

Click on the **Run Storage DRS Now** button to refresh the list of recommendations. If any recommendations are made, review them and click on the **Apply Recommendations** button. This is demonstrated in the following screenshot:

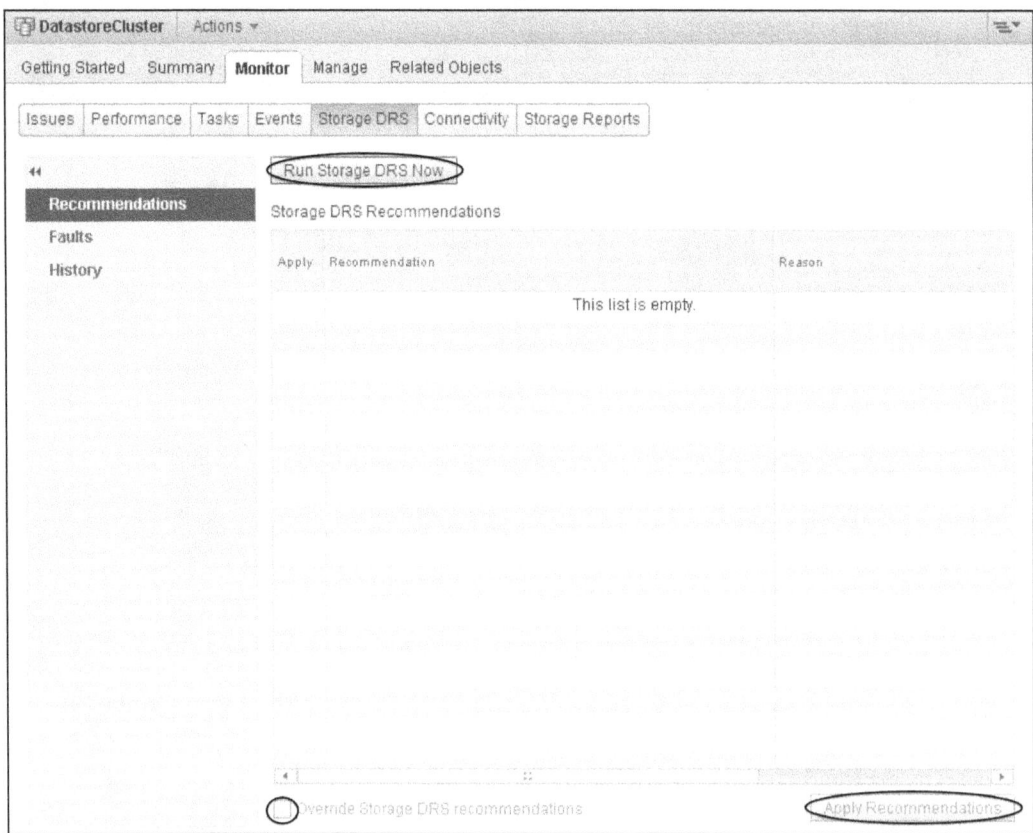

If multiple recommendations are made and you only desire to apply a subset of them, then select the checkbox next to **Override Storage DRS recommendations**. Deselect the recommendations that are not desired and click on the **Apply Recommendations** button.

Anti-affinity rules

Storage DRS anti-affinity rules can be created to control which virtual disk should not be placed on the same datastore within the datastore cluster. When an anti-affinity rule is created, it applies to the relevant virtual disks in the datastore cluster and these rules are enforced during initial placement and Storage DRS load-balancing recommendations. Keep in mind that the anti-affinity rules are not enforced when a user initiates a Storage vMotion.

> By default, a virtual machine's disks are placed together on the same datastore.

To configure the Storage DRS rules:

1. Go the **Manage** tab of the datastore cluster.
2. Under the **Settings** tab, select **Rules**.
3. To add a Storage DRS rule, click on the **Add** button.

Specify a name for the rule and the type of the DRS rule. Click on **Add** to choose which virtual machines this rule will apply to.

There are two types of rules that are available for Storage DRS:

- **VMDK anti-affinity**: This specifies which virtual disks from a particular virtual machine must be kept on separate datastores. For example, a database may be configured for its virtual disks to be stored on different datastores for performance reasons.
- **VM anti-affinity**: This type specifies which virtual machines should be kept on separate datastores.

Once you have specified a Storage DRS rule, click on **OK**. The **Add Storage DRS Rule** dialog box is shown in the following screenshot:

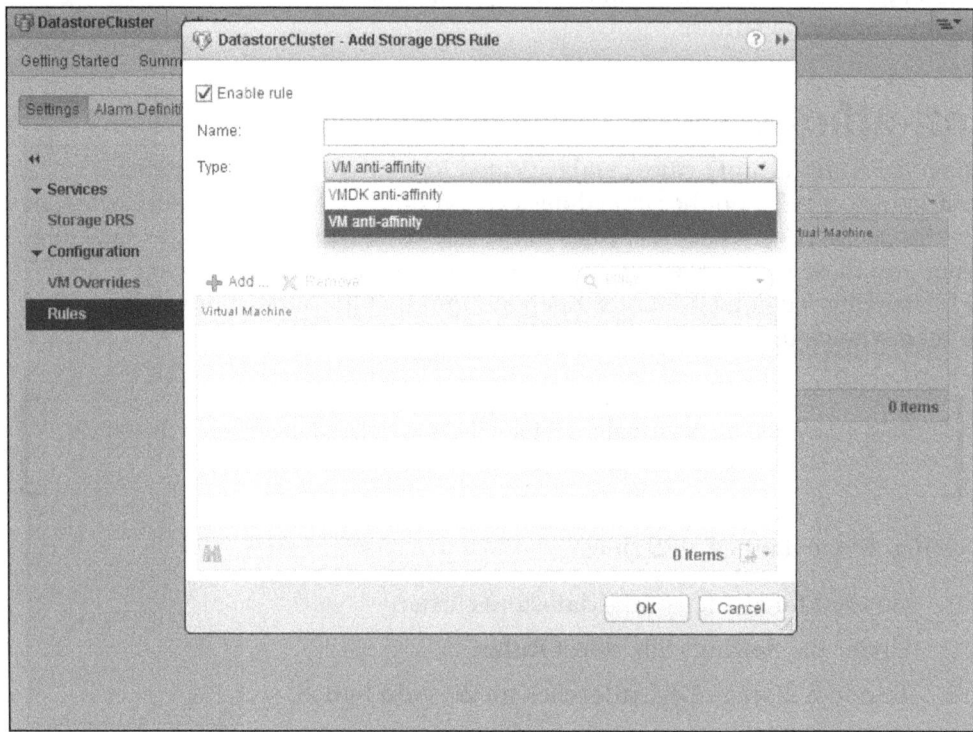

Summary

A cluster is a collection of ESXi hosts with shared CPU and memory resources. DRS provides the functionalities of initial placement and automated load balancing based on the CPU and memory usage. The DRS rules can be created to specify affinity or anti-affinity in order to keep virtual machines together or apart. vSphere HA is another cluster feature. vSphere HA continuously monitors the ESXi hosts in the cluster, and in the event of a failure, the virtual machines are restarted on an alternate ESXi host. Host network isolation occurs when an ESXi host is still up and running but no longer exchanges traffic from the HA agents on the management network.

A datastore cluster is a collection of datastores on which Storage DRS may be enabled. Storage DRS balances virtual machine files across the datastore cluster based on the datastore use and the I/O latency. The Storage DRS rules can be created to control the placement of virtual disks on a datastore within the datastore cluster.

The next chapter will discuss the virtual machine design.

10
Virtual Machine Design

This final chapter incorporates many of the topics discussed throughout the book. Now, it's time to focus on how the administrator should move forward in the creation and deployment of virtual machines. A review of our virtual machine resources as well as selecting a provisioning method is discussed here.

In this chapter, you will learn about the following topics:

- Which method should be used to provision the virtual machines
- Virtual hardware and resource configuration
- Other configuration considerations

Comparing provisioning methods

It is very possible that many of the virtual machines deployed in your environment will have similar requirements. If this is true for your environment, then it is advantageous and easy to create a standard build in the form of a template. This will allow for a more expeditious deployment of virtual machines. Standardization simplifies many configuration options; a well-designed, standardized build can be very beneficial with an optimized resource configuration. Templates are not the only method for standardizing, deployments; cloning, virtual appliances, and OVF templates may also be used. Don't forget that if these options do not suit your needs, a virtual machine can always be created from scratch! We'll be discussing a few provisioning methods that are native to vSphere, but keep in mind that there are many third-party automation tools that are available.

The provisioning method is not the only consideration for designing and deploying virtual machines. Don't forget to take performance and availability into consideration when deciding where to place the virtual machine.

Provisioning using templates

A **VM template** is a preconfigured virtual machine that is stored in a .vmtx format so that it cannot be powered on. This inability to power on the template protects it from being needlessly changed. You can create some kind of update and maintenance schedule in which the VM templates are brought into compliance for your corporate standards. Also, consider the use of the customization specifications for unique virtual machines deployed from the VM templates. Virtual machines can be created from VM templates and customized within minutes using these streamlined processes. We discussed how to deploy a VM from a VM template and its customization specifications in *Chapter 3, Other Ways to Provision a Virtual Machine*.

Consider how templates will fit into your environment's existing process for provisioning operating systems and applications. A template repository or library could be built for the different operating systems and application requirements, but don't plan to have a template for every single scenario. It's better to use the customization specifications to adjust to the newly deployed virtual machines to your needs. Create a reasonable number of templates that will fit the common needs of the environment; each template will take time to create and will require maintenance.

A template should be regularly updated. Administrators need to apply guest operating system and application patches as well as new antivirus definitions and other policies. A regular sequence of patching should occur. The process should include converting the template to a virtual machine, powering it on and making the necessary changes, and powering it off and converting it back to a template. This will ensure that all future virtual machines deployed from this template will remain updated.

Be careful not to over-provision resources for the standardized template. Provisioning virtual machines from templates that have too many unused resources could waste valuable resources. On the flip side, under-provisioning can also be harmful, requiring extra work to increase the resources after deployment. Different operating systems require different minimum resources; what works for a Windows Server 2000 virtual machine will not for a Windows Server 2012 virtual machine. Create a template for each of the common guest operating systems with the correct virtual hardware configuration. Remember to go through each template and disable or remove the virtual hardware that is not required.

Using clones for provisioning

Cloning a virtual machine will result in an exact copy of the source; the configurations as well as the disks are duplicated. Clone results have the same IP address, MAC address, and hostname as the source; remember to use guest customizations, as needed, to ensure uniqueness. Clones can be used to quickly replicate a production system so that it can be tested on an isolated network. We discussed this in *Chapter 3, Other Ways to Provision a Virtual Machine*.

Using virtual appliances

Virtual appliance is a generic term for a virtual machine that is built for a specific use case or purpose. The setup and configuration is simplified so that the administrators can quickly deploy it. Mostly, the operating system has a smaller footprint configured with only the necessary tools so that there are generally fewer updates required. Consider browsing the VMware Virtual Appliance Marketplace (`solutionexchange.vmware.com`) to see if there are any virtual appliances available that suit your environment's needs.

OVF templates

Standard virtual machine packages can be created and used for distribution. These packages are known as OVFs. The vSphere Web Client can be used to import and export OVF templates; this process was previously outlined in *Chapter 3, Other Ways to Provision a Virtual Machine*. The OVF is often used by software vendors because it is hypervisor agnostic. This can be used to export a virtual machine after a standardized build is created so that the VM may be distributed across different environments.

Virtual hardware and resource configuration

Appropriate virtual machine sizing as well as virtual hardware selection and configuration is an important part of the virtual machine design. Allocating too many resources can lead to waste and potentially even resource contention. Alternatively, if insufficient resources are provided to the virtual machines, it can cause resource issues as well as give users a poor impression of virtualization.

Generally speaking, it's easier to add more resources or virtual hardware to virtual machines than it is to take it away. Removing resources and virtual hardware can be difficult at times and almost always requires a reboot of the virtual machine. In some cases, a complete virtual machine rebuild is necessary. Often, resources or virtual hardware can be hot added to a virtual machine; the guest operating systems usually cope well with the addition too.

When sizing a virtual machine, begin with reasonable resource configurations. Benchmark the virtual machine to help identify any under- or over-provisioning of the virtual machine. Refer to *Chapter 6, Virtual Machine Performance and Resource Allocation* for more information. There are several tools available, such as VMware vCenter Operations Manager, that can assist in capacity management. Don't just give a virtual machine the same hardware present in equivalent physical servers; remember, virtualization is meant to be more efficient in its use of hardware as well as in saving money on server hardware. Allocating too many resources and wasting these resources will eventually hurt the virtual machines.

Virtual machine maximums

The virtual machine hardware version will ultimately dictate the features and the configurable maximums available. At the end of the day, you will not be able to give virtual machines any virtual hardware that is not available on the ESXi host. This means that if, for example, an ESXi host has 16 cores available, then the maximum vCPUs a virtual machine on this ESXi host can be configured with is 16, unless hyper-threading is enabled (even though virtual hardware Version 10 dictates up to 64 can be configured). The following table displays the available virtual hardware maximums associated with vSphere 5.5 and hardware Version 10:

Hardware component	Maximum
vCPU	64
RAM	1 TB
Virtual SCSI adapters per VM	4
Virtual SCSI targets per adapter	15
Virtual SCSI targets per VM	60
Virtual Disks per VM	60
Virtual Disk size	62 TB
IDE devices per VM	4
Floppy devices per VM	2
Virtual SATA adapters per VM	4
Virtual SATA devices per adapter	30
Virtual NICs per VM	10
USB devices per VM	20
Parallel ports per VM	3
Serial ports per VM	4
Video memory per VM	512 MB

Hardware maximums change with each vSphere version. Seek the *vSphere Configuration Maximums* guide for your specific vSphere version for more information.

Memory

The virtual machine is configured with a set of memory; this is the sum that is available to the guest OS. A virtual machine will not necessarily use the entire memory size; it only uses what is needed at the time for the guest OS and applications. However, a VM cannot access more memory than the configured memory size plus overhead. A default memory size is provided by vSphere when creating the virtual machine. It is important to know the memory needs of the application and the guest operating system being virtualized so that the virtual machine's memory can be sized accordingly. Shares, limits, and reservations can be used as needed; these topics were discussed in *Chapter 6, Virtual Machine Performance and Resource Allocation*.

CPU

VMware vSphere Virtual Symmetric Multiprocessing is what allows the virtual machines to be configured with up to 64 virtual CPUs, allowing a larger CPU workload to run on an ESXi host. The maximum number of vCPUs that can be allocated depends on the underlying logical cores that the physical hardware has. Another factor determining the maximum number of vCPUs is the tier of vSphere licensing; only Enterprise Plus licensing allows for 64 vCPUs. Check `www.vmware.com/files/pdf/vsphere_pricing.pdf` for more information on the licensing tiers.

Many guest operating systems and applications do not need and are not enhanced by having multiple CPUs; therefore, multiple CPUs should not be a standard configuration. Ideally, create virtual machines with one vCPU; configure multiple vCPUs only when the application or guest OS require them.

If multiple vCPUs are required, use as few vCPUs as possible in an attempt to lower the overhead and provide a potential performance improvement for the ESXi host and the virtual machine. Unused vCPUs can still consume timer interrupts, which may result in consuming resources that may otherwise be available for other uses.

The multicore virtual CPU was introduced in vSphere 4.1 so as to avoid socket restrictions used by the guest operating systems. In vSphere, a vCPU was presented to the guest OS as a single core within a single socket, which limits the number of vCPUs that can be presented to an operating system. Generally, the OS-vendor restricts only the physical CPUs (sockets) and not the logical CPUs (cores). To assist in solving this limitation, VMware introduced the vCPU configuration options of virtual sockets and cores per socket.

Eight single-core sockets equal eight vCPUs. Two quad-core sockets equal eight vCPUs. One eight-core socket equals eight vCPUs. The difference is how the CPU is presented to the guest operating system, not how the vCPUs will be scheduled on the underlying physical processors.

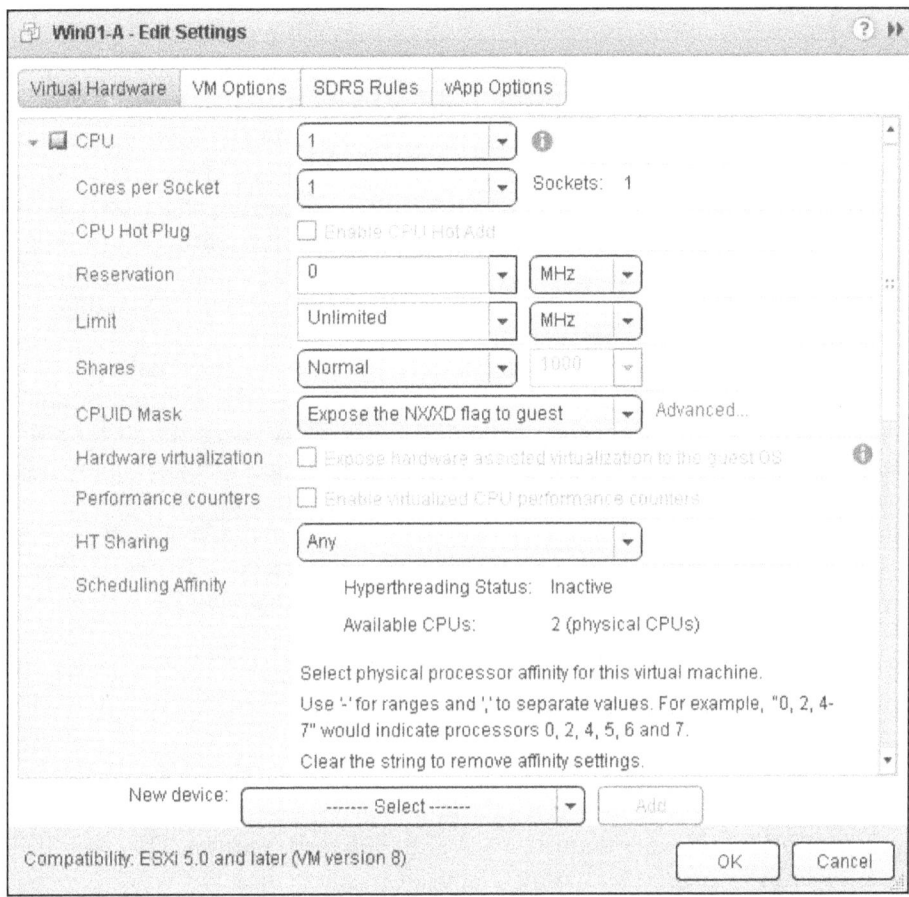

Will it impact performance if you use multiple sockets, and not one socket? No! There's no difference in performance; however, there's a change in the usable number of vCPUs. The vCPUs will be scheduled the same regardless of how they are presented to the guest operating system.

The operating system and application requirements will dictate how the vCPU(s) should be configured. As previously mentioned, some guest operating systems place a restriction on the amount of sockets that can be allocated, but usually the logical CPUs or cores do not. For example, Windows 7 allows only two CPU sockets but has no limitations on cores. Another consideration is how the application is licensed since CPUs can be used as a method to determine the amount of licenses needed. Shares, limits, and reservations can be used as needed; these topics were discussed in *Chapter 6, Virtual Machine Performance and Resource Allocation*.

Storage

Another virtual machine resource to consider and design for is storage. Accessing storage from the guest operating system of a virtual machine has been significantly simplified over the different vSphere versions. The virtual hardware presented to the guest operating system includes a set of familiar SCSI and IDE controllers as well as SATA, which was introduced in vSphere 5.5. Because of this, the guest OS sees a simple physical disk attached via a common controller. Presenting a virtualized storage view to the virtual machine's guest OS has many advantages such as expanded support and access, improved efficiency, and easier storage management.

When configuring the virtual disk, consider the number and size of disks presented to the virtual machine. It isn't uncommon to split up the disks of a virtual machine. For a Windows guest operating system, the C drive is often a separate disk from the program, files, user data, page file, and so on. This is not necessarily recommended; follow best practices set by the application vendor. Also, consider the **Disk Provisioning** type and **Disk Mode** when considering the virtual machine design. Shares and limits can be used as needed if licensed for Storage I/O Control; these topics were discussed in *Chapter 6, Virtual Machine Performance and Resource Allocation*.

The Disk Provisioning types

There are three different **Disk Provisioning** options:

- **Thin provision**: The disk is allocated and zeroed as needed as opposed to being fully provisioned and zeroed at the time of creation. This results in a thin-provisioned disk having a shorter creation time but with reduced performance for the first write to a block. Subsequent writes to the blocks will result in the same performance as that of the disks provisioned as eager-zeroed thick. This can be a more effective use of datastore space but can result in an over-provisioned datastore.

- **Thick provision eager zeroed**: The disk space is allocated and zeroed out during the disk creation. This increases the length of time that it takes to create the disk, but using this type of disk results in the best performance upon the first write to each block. This is required for using the Fault Tolerance feature with VMs.

- **Thick provision lazy zeroed**: The disk space is allocated during the disk creation, but each block is not zeroed until the first write. Comparatively, this results in a shorter creation time than eager-zeroed but reduces performance during the first write to a block. Subsequent writes to the blocks will result in the same performance as disks provisioned as eager-zeroed thick. This is the default option in the vSphere Client and is good for most cases.

The following screenshot demonstrates the options that are available when creating a new virtual disk. Click on **OK** after making selections.

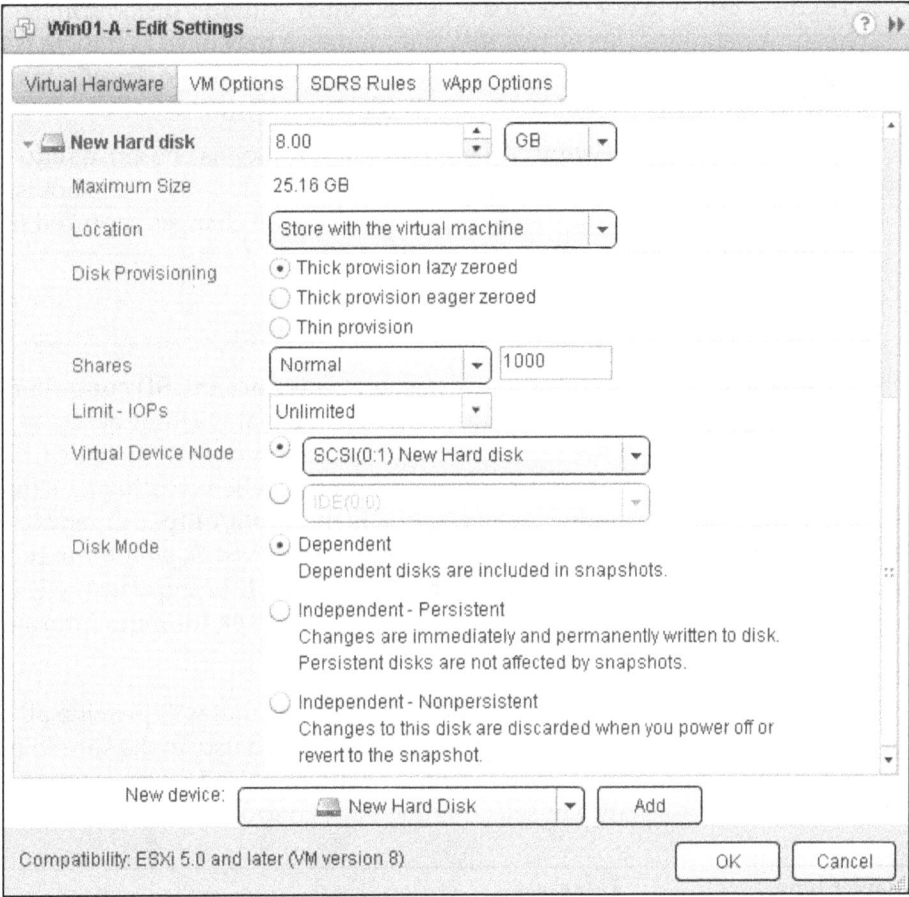

Disk Mode

Disk Mode describes how the virtual hard disk interacts with the virtual machine. By default, a disk is **Dependent**, meaning it is treated as part of the virtual machine for all operations. However, if a disk is **Independent**, then it can be omitted from a backup operation due to the fact that Independent disks do not support snapshot operations. Think of Independent disks as being "independent of snapshots." There are two types of **Independent** disks:

- **Independent-Persistent**: This commits changes immediately and permanently to the disk. You will not see a delta file associated with this disk during a snapshot operation. This virtual disk file continues to behave as if there is no snapshot being taken of the virtual machine and all writes go directly to the disk. All changes to the disk are preserved upon snapshot deletion.
- **Independent-Nonpersistent**: When this configuration is chosen, a redo log is created to capture all subsequent writes to this disk. If the snapshot is deleted, or if the virtual machine is powered off, the changes captured in that redo log are discarded.

The SCSI controller

The selection of the virtual **Small Computer System Interface** (**SCSI**) controller can also affect the virtual machine's performance. The virtual machine accesses each virtual disk using one of the virtual SCSI controllers. A default virtual SCSI controller is selected based on the guest operating system when creating a virtual machine using the wizard. Another consideration is the **Input/output Operations Per Second** (**IOPS**) required for this virtual machine. The PVSCSI adapter may be used for an increased throughput with lower CPU overhead for those heavy I/O virtual machines. Check http://kb.vmware.com/kb/1010398 for more information on the PVSCSI adapter.

If Storage Profiles are in use, ensure that you select the one that will provide all of the storage characteristics required. If Storage Profiles are not in use, make sure to place the virtual disk on a datastore that is best suited for the required performance. See the following chart for assistance in selecting the SCSI controller:

Adapter type	Use cases
Buslogic Parallel	• Default for Windows 2000
	• Considered a legacy adapter; no current updates or enhancements
LSI Logic Parallel	• Default for Windows 2003, Vista, Linux OSes
	• Most commonly used adapter, widely compatible

Adapter type	Use cases
LSI Logic SAS	• Default for Windows 2008, Windows 7
	• Newer LSI driver, used for MSCS support
VMware Paravirtualized	• Used for high I/O VMs (over 2000 IOPS)
	• Lower CPU utilization, check for OS support

Raw Device Mapping (RDM)

Raw Device Mappings are an alternative to the typical VMDK. These RDMs give a virtual machine direct access to a raw LUN as if it were a disk. It is recommended that RDMs be used only when necessary as there is no performance gain with this configuration. The RDM use case will dictate the compatibility mode. There are two compatibility modes for an RDM:

- **Physical compatibility mode**: Choosing this mode will result in minimal SCSI virtualization of the mapped device. This allows for greater flexibility for SAN management type software from various vendors. The VMkernel passes all SCSI commands, with the exception of the REPORT LUNs command, to the device. Other than that, all characteristics of the underlying hardware are exposed. The maximum size is 64 TB.

- **Virtual compatibility mode**: This option will result in full virtualization of the mapped device, sending only READ and WRITE commands. The characteristics of the real underlying hardware are hidden and the mapped device appears the same as a virtual disk file in a VMFS volume to the guest operating system. Due to this, the virtual mode is more portable across storage hardware because it presents behavior the same as the virtual disk file. The maximum size, as of vSphere 5.5, is 62 TB.

There are a few use cases associated with the configuration of RDMs:

- **SAN-Aware Technologies**: Some SAN management and storage resource management applications that are virtualized may need direct access to the lower-level storage.

- **N-Port ID Virtualization (NPIV)**: With this feature, one Fibre Channel HBA port is able to register to a fabric while using multiple **World Wide Port Names (WWPNs)**. This effectively means that there are more than one Virtual HBAs per physical HBA. NPIV allows for a **World Wide Name (WWN)** to be assigned at the virtual machine level instead of the more common ESXi host level. This can allow for fine-tuning of per port zoning and QoS.

- **Data migration to virtual**: RDMs can provide a transitional stage for a large LUN that is attached to a physical server being converted to a virtual machine.
- **Application clustering**: Certain applications, such as Microsoft cluster, require the ability to make direct calls to the block table of a LUN.

An RDM should not be the first choice for configuration. However, this option has proved invaluable in certain situations and is useful in certain virtual machine designs. For more information on RDMs, check http://kb.vmware.com/kb/2009226.

The virtual network adapters

vNICs are the virtual network adapters presented to the virtual machines. Do not confuse these with the vmnics, which are the names given to the ESXi host physical network adapters, or vmknics, which are VMkernel interfaces. A virtual machine can be configured with up to 10 virtual Ethernet adapters. Normally, a virtual machine is configured with just a single vNIC because there is no increased bandwidth by adding a second vNIC.

A vNIC driver should be chosen based on the features and the performance that the virtual machine requires. The following table describes the available virtual network adapter options:

Network adapter	Description
vlance	Emulated version of the AMD 79C970 PCnet32. Older 10 Mbps NIC with drivers available in most 32-bit guest OSes, except Windows Vista and newer.
VMXNET	Paravirtualized adapter, optimized for performance in virtual machines. VMware Tools is required for VMXNET drivers.
e1000	Emulated version of the Intel 82545EM 1Gbps NIC. Available in Linux Versions 2.4.19 and later, Windows XP Professional x64 Edition and later, and Windows Server 2003 (32-bit) and later. No jumbo frames support prior to ESX/ESXi 4.1.
e1000e	Emulated version of the Intel 82574 1Gbps NIC. Only available on hardware Version 8 or newer VMs in vSphere 5.x. This is the default vNIC for Windows 8 and newer Windows guest OSes. Not available for Linux from the UI.
VMXNET2	Paravirtualized adapter, providing more features than VMXNET, such as hardware offloads and jumbo frames. Limited guest OS support for VMs on ESX/ESXi 3.5 and later.
VMXNET3	Paravirtualized adapter unrelated to previous VMXNET adapters. Offers all VMXNET2 features as well as multiqueue support, MSI/MSI-X interrupt delivery, and IPv6 offloads. Supported only for hardware Version 7 or later with limited guest OS support.

The paravirtualized drivers (VMXNET family) improve performance since they share a ring buffer between the virtual machine and the VMkernel. This uses zero-copy, reducing internal copy operations between buffers, thus saving CPU cycles. Shares and limits can be used as needed if licensed for Network I/O Control. These topics are discussed in *Chapter 6*, *Virtual Machine Performance and Resource Allocation*.

Other considerations

In addition to the configurable virtual hardware options, there are other considerations for the implementation of virtual machines. This section will only cover a few of the considerations that are incorporated into a design that has vSphere virtual machines. These topics will cover the available vSphere options. With this in mind, remember that there are many things that you can do within the guest operating system to optimize it for virtualization. For example, stop any unused service in an attempt to lower CPU consumption by this virtual machine. Seek out VMware and other vendor documentation for further guidance.

Renaming virtual machines

A virtual machine's files reflect the name given to the virtual machine during creation. If a virtual machine's inventory name is changed later, the filenames do not automatically reflect the name change; the original virtual machine name is retained. A virtual machine's files are renamed during a disk migration operation, such as a Storage vMotion or cold storage migration, by manually renaming the files or by cloning to a new virtual machine (see *Chapter 3*, *Other Ways to Provision a Virtual Machine* and *Chapter 8*, *Migrating Virtual Machines*). Since a Storage vMotion allows the virtual machine to remain on and simply migrate the files to a new datastore, this is the preferred method. To manually rename the virtual machine files, check http://vmware.com/kb/1029513.

Upgrading virtual hardware version

If a virtual machine was created on an older version of vSphere, then the hardware version may be out of date. Upgrading the virtual machine hardware version to the newest version can provide more functionality and hardware choices. Before upgrading the virtual machine's hardware version, VMware Tools should be updated. Check http://kb.vmware.com/kb/1010675 for more information. To upgrade the virtual hardware version, we need to execute the following steps:

1. Browse to the virtual machine in the vSphere Web Client inventory.
2. Power off the virtual machine.

Virtual Machine Design

3. Right-click on **All vCenter Actions**.
4. Navigate to **Compatibility | Upgrade VM Compatibility**. The entire process is demonstrated in the following screenshot:

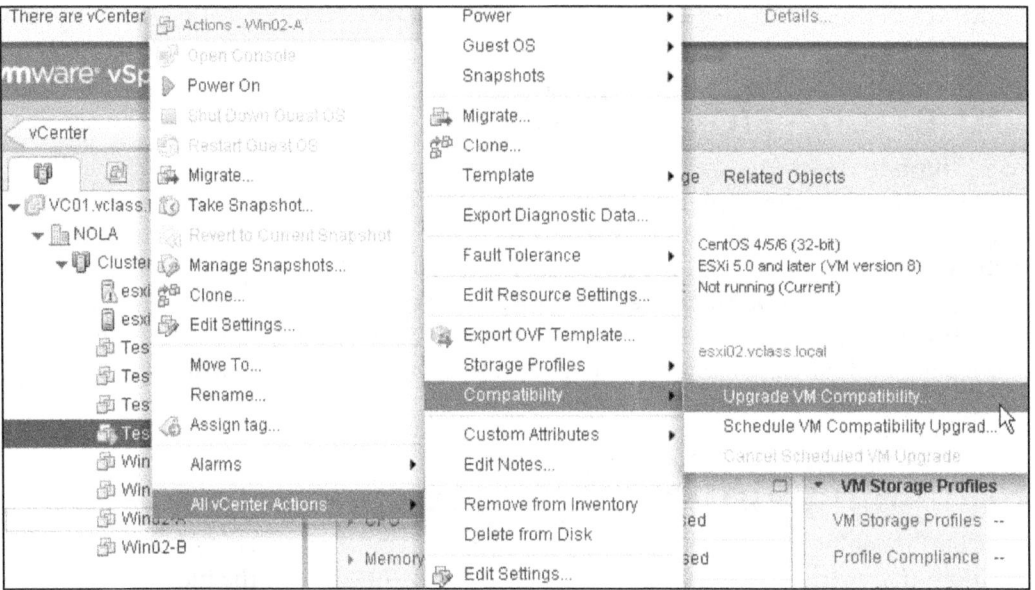

5. This will bring up a warning message that specifies that this is irreversible and makes the virtual machine incompatible with older versions of vSphere.

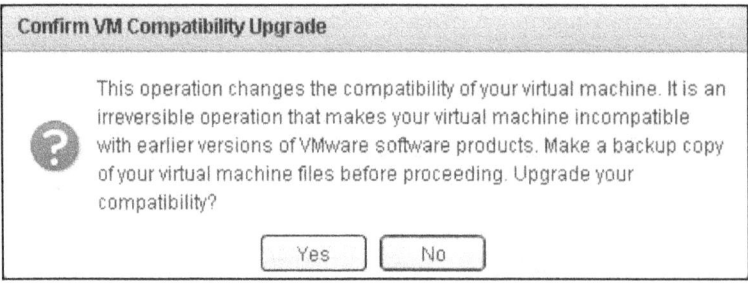

6. Click on **Yes**. Select the compatibility level for this virtual machine. For example, ESX 5.1 and later is selected, which specifies Version 9. This virtual machine can now run on vSphere 5.1 and 5.5 ESXi hosts. For assistance in this selection, see the following chart:

Version	Product version	Max memory size	Max vCPUs	Additional features
10	ESXi 5.5	1 TB	64	Extended vGPU support, SATA controller enhancements (up to 4 controllers and 30 devices per controller)
9	ESXi 5.1	1 TB	64	Improved 3D graphics
8	ESXi 5.0	1 TB	32	USB 3.0 device support
7	ESX/ESXi 4.x	255 GB	8	Hot Plug support for CPU and memory, VMXNET3
4	ESX 3.x	64 GB	4	

7. Select the compatibility level for the virtual machine.

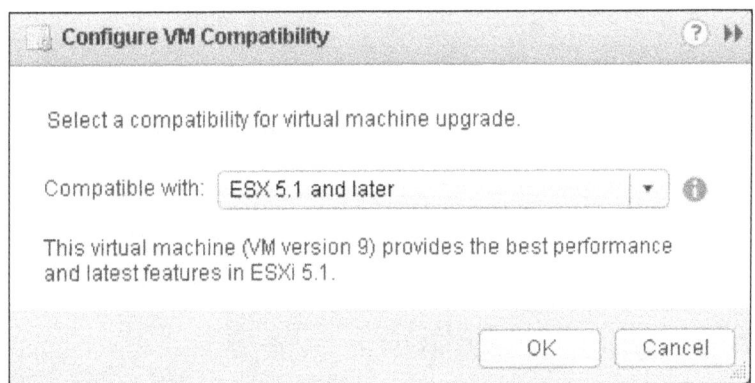

8. Click on **OK**.

Alternatively, this could be done using VMware vSphere Update Manager.

Using tags

A feature that was introduced in the vSphere 5.1 Web Client to further enhance search capabilities is called a **tag**. Tags give the administrators the ability to create custom labels that can be applied to any object within the vCenter inventory. These can be used for organization, grouping, or even for configuration management databases to specify ownership. Any object can have more than one tag so that you are not limited with objects that can only exist within a single folder. My favorite feature of tags is that they are fully searchable. This means that I can execute a search for the criteria set in the tags rather than a potentially long inventory name.

For example, many organizations have somewhat complex naming standards for their server inventory, so looking at the name BLG-BG-0106 would not be helpful unless you knew what the different values meant. This may be the sixth domain controller in the Bruges, Belgium site, but unless you knew the naming convention, you would have no idea. An administrator can now set tags that could specify criteria such as Belgium, Bruges, domain controller, and so on, so that the virtual machine was more easily searchable. To configure tags for an inventory object, we need to execute the following steps:

1. Browse to that object using the vSphere Web Client.
2. Click on the **Manage** tab.
3. Click on the **Tags** button.
4. Click on the **Add Tag** button. From here you can assign or create tags. This is shown in the following screenshot:

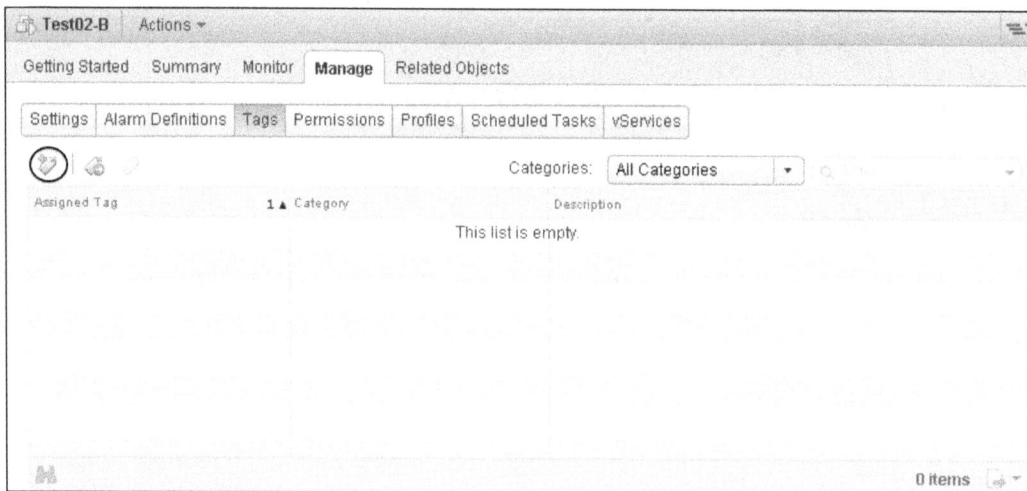

Chapter 10

5. This will bring up a dialogue that will allow an administrator to specify a tag's **Name** and **Description** as well as create or specify **Category**, which allows for multiple tags or a single tag, and **Object Type**.

6. Click on **OK** after configuring the tag.

NTP configuration

Time synchronization is an important consideration for virtual machines as it can affect application replication, authentication, and so on. This is also an important consideration for the ESXi hosts. The ESXi hosts should be syncing time with an NTP source so that the timestamps for logging, debugging, and performance monitoring are accurate. To configure NTP for an ESXi host, we need to execute the following steps:

1. First browse to the ESXi host in the vSphere Web Client inventory.
2. Select the **Manage** tab.
3. Navigate to **Settings | Time Configuration**.

Virtual Machine Design

4. If an external time source has not been configured, click on the **Edit** button. This is shown in the following screenshot:

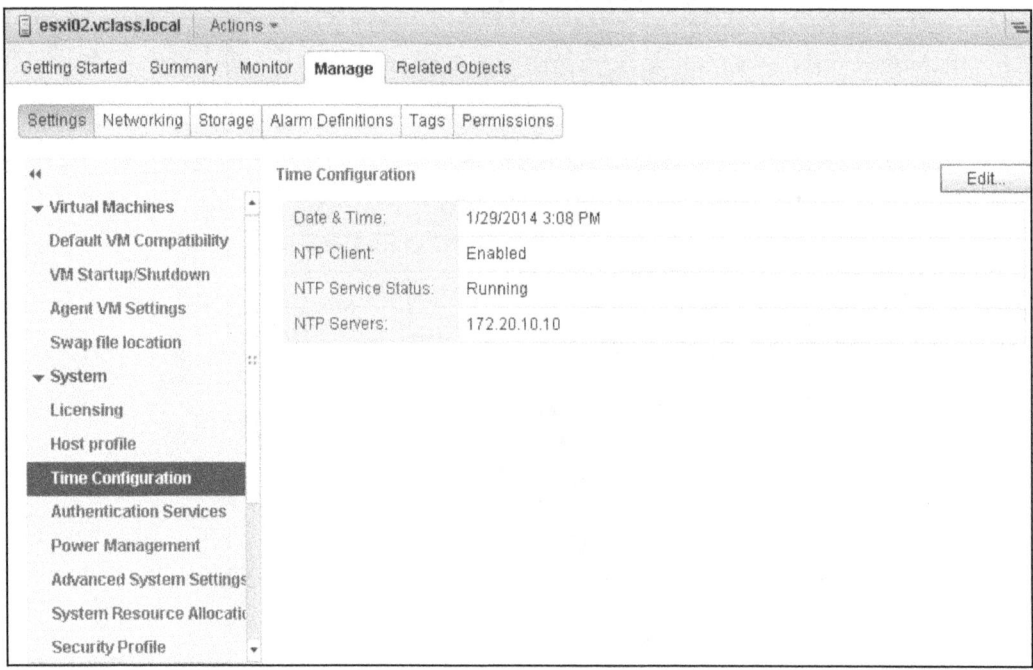

5. This will open a dialogue, which will allow for the specification of an **NTP Server** and selection of the **NTP Service Startup Policy**. After entering a time source, click on the **Start** button, as shown in the following screenshot, to begin running the service:

Chapter 10

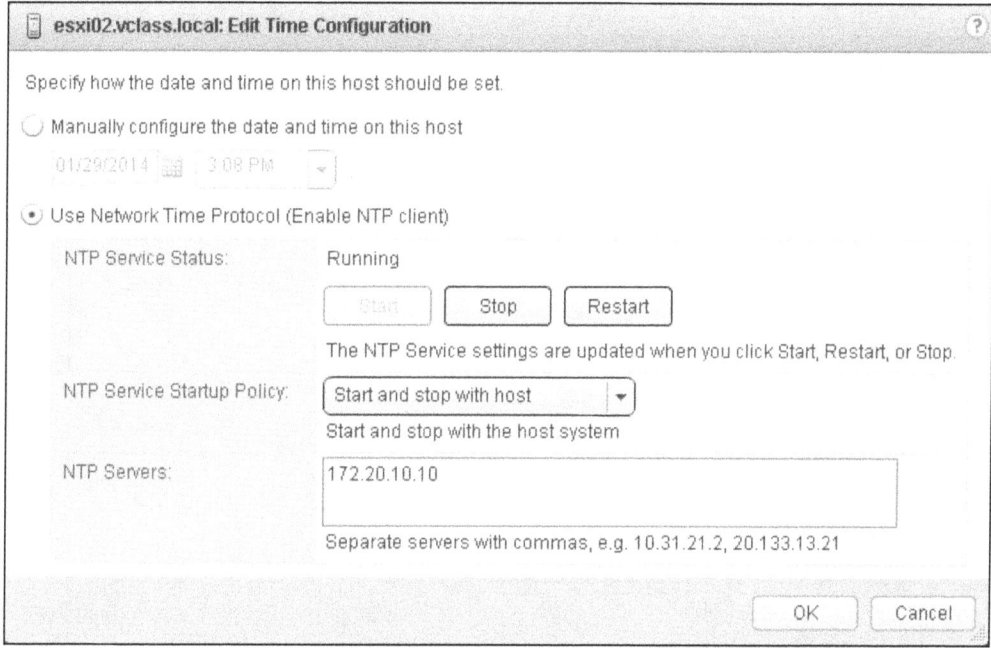

6. Click on **OK** after configuring NTP.

It is not necessarily recommended for your virtual machines to use VMware Tools for time synchronization. Using **Network Time Protocol (NTP)** or **Win32Time** is generally more accurate and preferred overall. For more information regarding guest operating system timekeeping, check http://vmware.com/kb/1318 for Windows guest operating systems or http://vmware.com/kb/1006427 for Linux guest operating systems.

Disabling unused virtual hardware

A virtual machine should only be presented with the hardware that it requires. Configure what is needed and remove, disable, or disconnect the rest to prevent waste of ESXi host resources. Hardware that isn't needed can sometimes be disabled in the virtual machine BIOS and/or in the guest operating system. For example, floppy drives are rarely used these days, and are therefore good candidates for removal. To remove and disable a floppy drive, we need to execute the following steps:

1. Browse to the virtual machine in the vSphere Web Client inventory.
2. Right-click on the virtual machine and click on **Edit Settings**.

Virtual Machine Design

3. Hover the cursor near **Floppy drive 1** and an **X** should appear on the right-hand side.
4. Click on **X** to remove the device:

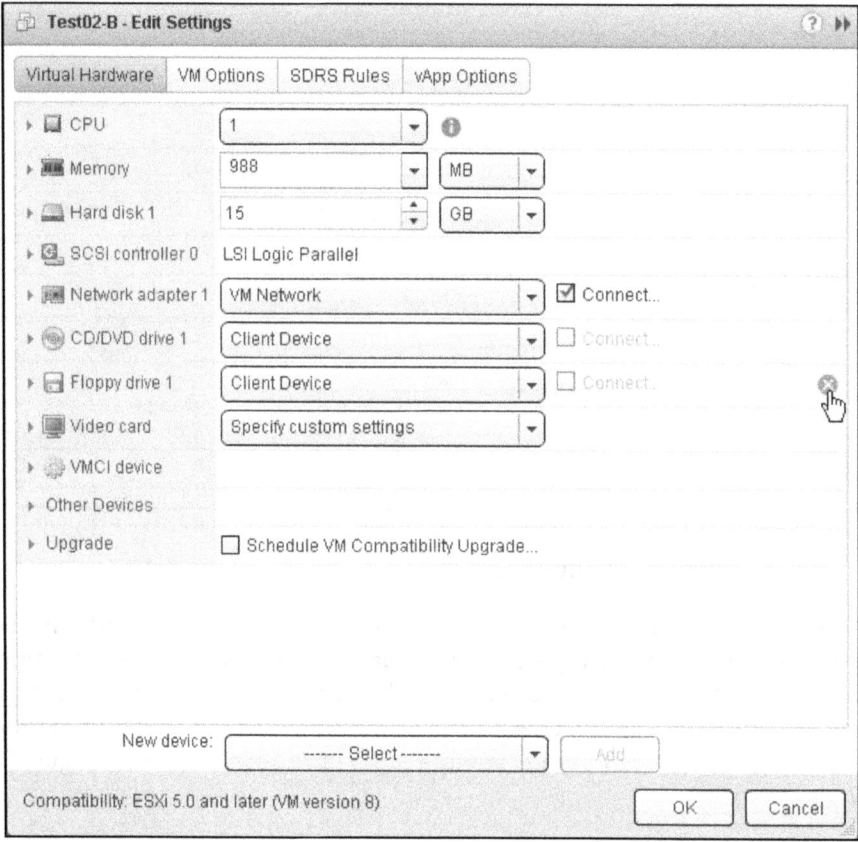

To also disable the floppy disk controller in the BIOS, we need to execute the following steps:

1. Go to the **VM Options** tab while the settings dialogue is still open.
2. Expand ***Boot Options** and click on the **Force BIOS setup (*)** checkbox. This will force the virtual machine to enter the BIOS setup and process the net power cycle.

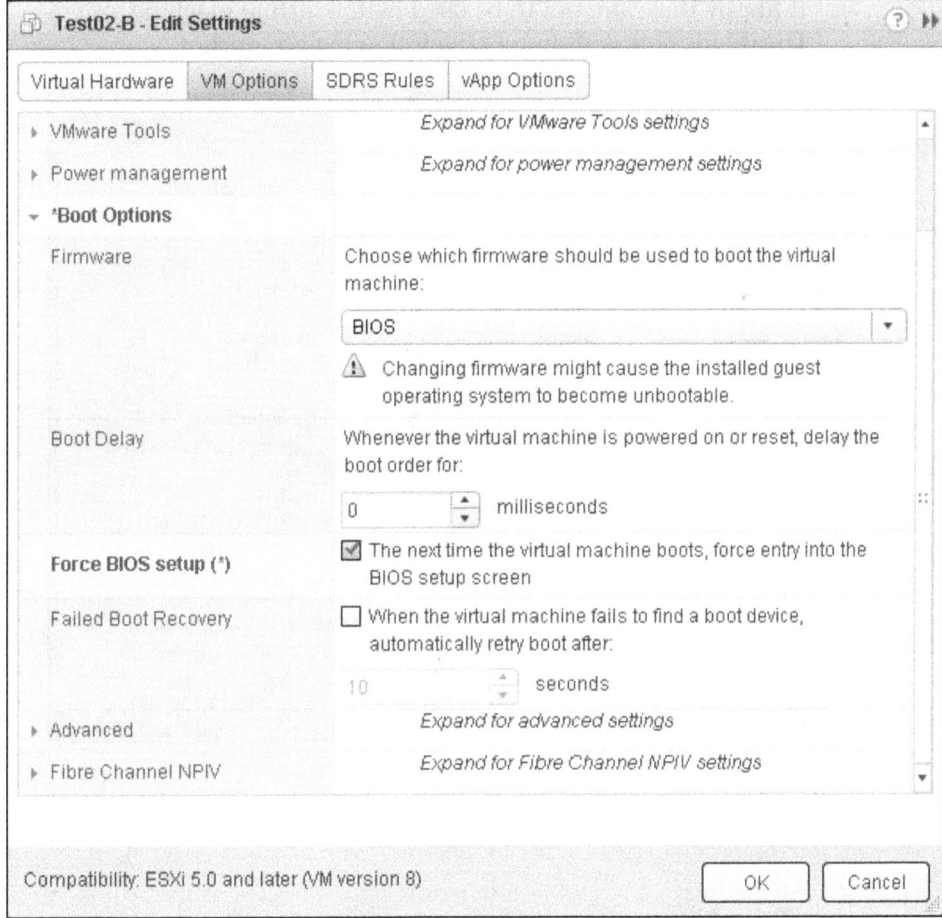

3. Click on **OK** after making these configuration changes.
4. At the next power cycle, the virtual machine will enter the BIOS setup screen, which is shown in the following screenshot. For a Phoenix Technologies 6.00 BIOS (standard for vSphere virtual machines), we need to execute the following steps:

    1. Go to the **Advanced** tab
    2. Select **I/O Device Configuration** by pressing the *Enter* key.
    3. Choose the **Floppy disk controller** by pressing *Enter*.

Virtual Machine Design

4. If floppy disks are not to be used by the virtual machine, select **Disabled**. This is shown in the following screenshot:

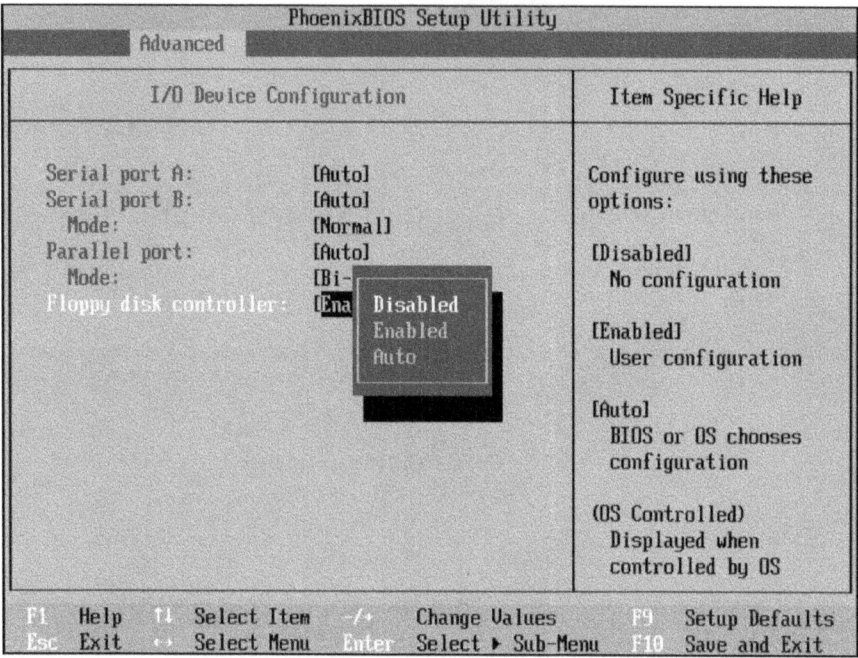

Disable any other devices in the BIOS that are not planned to use by the virtual machine.

VMware Tools

VMware Tools is a utility suite that enhances the performance of a virtual machine's guest OS. If VMware Tools is not installed in the guest operating system, the guest will be lacking some important functionality. VMware Tools utility improves virtual machine management by replacing the generic OS drivers with VMware drivers optimized for virtual hardware. Make sure that VMware Tools is always installed in the virtual machines and that it is kept updated. For more information on VMware Tools, see *Chapter 3, Other Ways to Provision a Virtual Machine*.

Summary

Standardization simplifies many configuration options; a well-designed standardized build can be very beneficial with an optimized resource configuration. A template is a preconfigured virtual machine that is in a `.vmtx` format so that it cannot be powered on. Cloning a virtual machine will result in an exact copy of the source. Use customization specifications to prevent IP address and MAC address conflicts. Virtual appliance is a generic term for a virtual machine that is built for a specific use case or purpose. Appropriate virtual machine sizing as well as virtual hardware selection and configuration is an important part of the virtual machine design. Benchmark the virtual machine to help identify any under- or over-provisioning of the virtual machine. A virtual machine's files are based on the name given to it during creation; if later changed, the filenames do not automatically reflect the name change. Upgrading the virtual machine hardware version to the newest version can provide more functionality and hardware choices.

Throughout this book, we discussed how to create virtual machines using different methods, including using the wizard from scratch, deploying from a template, cloning, and using VMware vCenter Converter. Use the method that best suits your needs for the virtual machine being created. Monitor ESXi hosts for over-commitment and your virtual machines and ESXi hosts for contention. Virtual machines may be migrated using vMotion and Storage vMotion. Cluster features such as DRS and Storage DRS leverage these technologies to ensure the environment is well balanced. Shares, limits, and reservations may be used to control how virtual machines access and compete for resources. Check `https://www.vmware.com/pdf/Perf_Best_Practices_vSphere5.5.pdf` for more best practices on performance.

Index

Symbols

-delta.vmdk file 18, 24
-flat.vmdk file 18, 23
.log file 18, 25
.nvram file 18, 22
-rdm.vmdk file 18, 23
.vmdk file 18, 22
.vmfx file 18
.vmsd file 18, 24
.vmsn file 18, 24
.vmss file 18, 24
.vmtx file 18, 22
.vmx file 18, 19, 22
.vswp file 18, 22
.vswp file location
  setting 124-126

A

Accept EULAs pane 102
advanced options, vSphere virtual machine
  Boot Options 130
  General Options 127
  VMware Remote Console Options 128
  VMware Tools 128, 129
advanced performance chart
  about 199-202
  viewing 200
  vs, overview performance chart 202
affinity/anti-affinity rules, DRS
  configuring 255
alarms
  condition-based alarms 210
  event-based alarms 210
  using 210

AMD No eXecute (NX) 122, 223
AMD Rapid Virtual Indexing (RVI) 117
anti-affinity rules, SDRS
  about 273
  VM anti-affinity 273
  VMDK anti-affinity 273
application clustering 286
Array Integration (VAAI) 232
Audio driver 29

B

balloon driver 30
ballooning 163
BIOS 9
Boot Options 130
BT 116

C

clones
  used, for provisioning vSphere virtual machine 277
cloning
  vSphere virtual machine, creating by 99
cloning, vApp 152-157
cluster
  about 245
  creating 246, 247
  features 245
command line
  used, for viewing vSphere virtual machine files 28
components, vSphere virtual machine
  BIOS 9
  DVD/CD-ROM 9

floppy drive 9
hard disk 9
IDE controller 10
keyboard 10
memory 10
Motherboard/Chipset 10
network adapter 10
parallel port 10
PCI controller 10
PCI device 10
pointing device 10
processor 11
SCSI controller 11
SCSI device 11
serial port 11
SIO controller 11
USB controller 11
USB device 11
Video controller 11
VMCI 11
compute resource
  selecting 95
condition-based alarms
  about 210
  creating 210-213
configuration, DRS 248, 250
configuration file 19, 21
configuration, HA 259-265
configuration, NTP 291-293
configuration, SDRS 267-271
configuration, vMotion
  prerequisites 222, 223
Configure Network pane 88-90
considerations, vSphere virtual machine
  NTP configuration 291-293
  tags, using 290, 291
  unused virtual hardware, disabling 293-296
  virtual hardware version,
    upgrading 287-289
  virtual machine, renaming 287
  VMware Tools 296
core 4 8
CPU
  about 14, 280, 281
  monitoring, esxtop used 205
CPU affinity
  setting 123, 124

CPU hot plug
  enabling 120, 121
CPU identification (CPUID) mask 122
CPU virtualization 160, 161
cross-host Storage vMotion
  about 237
  used, for migrating virtual
    machine 237-243
custom configuration wizard
  CPUs pane 52
  Guest Operating System pane 50, 51
  Memory pane 53
  Name and Location pane 47
  Network pane 54
  Ready to Complete pane 68
  SCSI controllers 55, 56
  Storage pane 48
  Virtual Machine Version pane 49, 50
  vSphere virtual machine, creating with 46
customization, vSphere virtual machine
  Configure Network pane 88-90
  configuring 79
  creating 82
  Enter Windows License 86
  Ready to complete pane 92
  Run Once pane 88
  Set Administrator Password pane 86, 87
  Set Computer Name pane 84, 85
  Set Operating System Options 91
  Set Registration Information pane 84
  Set Workgroup or Domain pane 90
  Specify Properties pane 83
  Sysprep files, copying to vCenter directory 80, 81
Customize template pane 104, 105

D

data link 16
data migration 286
datastore heartbeating 258
Dependent disk 284
Deploy OVF Template
  Accept EULAs pane 102
  Customize template pane 104, 105
  Ready to complete pane 105, 106
  Review details pane 101

[300]

Select name and location pane 102
Select source 101
Select storage pane 103
Setup networks pane 104
Deploy VM from this Template option 94
Destination Location pane 111
Destination System pane 109, 110
Destination Virtual Machine pane 110
device drivers, VMware Tools
Audio driver 29
Memory control driver 30
Mouse driver 29
Paravirtual SCSI driver 29
SCSI driver 29
SVGA driver 29
ThinPrint driver 30
VMCI Sockets drivers 30
VMXNET NIC drivers 29
vShield Endpoint 29
disk 17
disk alignment 192
Disk Mode
Dependent disk 284
Independent disk 284
Disk Provisioning
Thick provision eager zeroed 282
Thick provision lazy zeroed 283
Thin provision 282
Distributed Power Management. *See* **DPM**
Distributed Resource Scheduler. *See* **DRS**
DPM 246
DRS
about 96, 177, 221, 245
affinity/anti-affinity rules 255
configuring 248, 250
enabling 248
initial placement 248
load balancing 248
monitoring 251-254
overview 248
recommendations, viewing 251-254
requirements 248
DVD/CD-ROM 9

E

e1000 286

e1000e 286
e1000e network adapter 40
e1000 network adapter 40
Edit settings, vApp
IP allocation policy 146-148
virtual machine shutdown action 149, 150
virtual machine startup action 149, 150
election 257
End User License Agreement (EULA) 102
Enhanced vMotion Compatibility. *See* **EVC**
Enter Windows License pane 86
ESXi host 8
esxtop
batch mode 203
help option 209, 210
interactive mode 203
Replay mode 203
used, for monitoring CPU 205
used, for monitoring memory 205, 206
used, for monitoring network 207
used, for monitoring storage 208
using 203
EVC 246
event-based alarms
about 210
creating 214, 215
expandable reservation 181
Extensible Firmware Interface (EFI) 130

F

Fault Domain Manager (FDM) 257
floppy drive 9

G

General Options 127
group ID (GID) 205

H

HA
about 245, 256
configuring 259-265
overview 257, 258
responsibilities 257
hard disk 9

[301]

help option, esxtop 209, 210
High Availability. *See* HA
host network isolation 258
HV 117
HWMMU 117
hypervisor 8
hypervisor swapping 168, 169

I

IDE controller 10
Independent disk
  Independent-Nonpersistent 284
  Independent-Persistent 284
initial placement 248
Input/Output Operations Per Second
    (IOPS) 170, 284
installation, VMware Tools
  in Linux virtual machine 135-137
  in Windows virtual machine 131-134
Integrated Drive Electronics (IDE) 10
Intel eXecute Disable (XD) 122, 223
Intel Extended Page Tables (EPT) 117
IP allocation policy
  about 146-148
  DHCP option 147
  Static - IP Pool option 147
  Static - Manual option 147
  Transient option 147

K

keyboard 10

L

limits 173, 174
Linux virtual machine
  VMware Tools, installing 135-137
load balancing 248

M

Managed Object ID (MOID) 257
megabytes (MB) 205
memory
  about 10, 15, 279
  monitoring, esxtop used 205, 206

memory compression 164, 165
Memory control driver 30
memory hot add
  enabling 120, 121
memory management unit (MMU) 116
memory overcommitment (memory
    reclamation)
  about 161
  ballooning 163
  compression 164, 165
  hypervisor swapping 168, 169
  swapping, to host cache 165-167
  transparent page sharing (TPS) 162
monitor mode
  about 116-119
  BT 116
  HV 117
  HWMMU 117
Motherboard/Chipset 10
Mouse driver 29

N

network
  about 16
  monitoring, esxtop used 207
  virtual Ethernet adapters 16
  virtual switch 16
network adapter 10
Network Attached Storage (NAS) 17
network constraint, resource contention 170
network interface card (NIC) 16
Network I/O Control
  about 182
  set up 182
network partition 258
network resource pool
  assigning, to distributed port group 185,
      186
  configuring 183, 184
Network Time Protocol. *See* NTP
N-Port ID Virtualization (NPIV) 285
NTP
  about 291
  configuration 291-293

O

Open Virtualization Appliance (OVA) 100
Open Virtualization Format. *See* OVF
operating system (OS) 7
Options pane 112, 113
overview performance chart
  about 198
  viewing 198
  vs, advanced performance chart 202
OVF 100, 140
OVF file
  Deploy OVF Template 100
  vSphere virtual machine, creating from 100
OVF template
  used, for provisioning vSphere virtual machine 277

P

parallel port 10
Paravirtual SCSI driver 29
PCI controller 10
PCI device 10
Perfmon 215-218
performance charts
  about 197
  advanced performance chart 199-202
  overview performance chart 198
performance tuning, vSphere virtual machine 192
performance, vSphere virtual machine
  problem, determining 193
  traditional practices 193
  troubleshooting 194
Physical compatibility mode, RDM 285
pointing device 10
primary resources, vSphere virtual machine
  CPU 14
  disk 17
  memory 15
  network 16
processor 11
provisioning, vSphere virtual machine
  clones, used 277
  OVF templates, used 277
  virtual appliance, used 277
  VM template, used 276

R

Raw Device Mapping (RDM)
  about 23, 58, 285
  configuration issues 285
  Physical compatibility mode 65, 285
  Virtual compatibility mode 65, 66, 285
Ready to complete pane 92, 105, 106
recommendations, DRS
  viewing 251-254
recommendations, SDRS
  applying 272, 273
reservations 175, 176
Resource allocation, vApp
  Limit option 144
  Reservation option 143
  Reservation type option 143
  Shares option 143
resource contention
  about 159
  CPU virtualization 160, 161
  memory reclamation 161
  network constraint 170
  storage constraint 170
resource controls
  about 170
  limits 173, 174, 180
  reservations 175-179
  reservation type 180
  shares 171, 172, 179
resource pool
  about 177
  creating 178-180
  usage 177
  with expandable reservation 181
resxtop
  Batch mode 203
  Interactive mode 203
  Replay mode 203
  using 203
Reverse Address Resolution Protocol (RARP) 222
Review details pane 101
Run Once pane 88

S

SAN-Aware Technologies 285
SCSI controller
  about 11, 284
  adapter type 56
  Do not create disk pane 67
  existing virtual disk, using 59-61
  new virtual disk, creating 57-59
  RDM 62-64
SCSI device 11
SCSI driver 29
SDRS
  about 221, 265
  anti-affinity rules 273
  configuring 267-271
  overview 266
  recommendations, applying 272, 273
  requirements 266
Security ID (SID) 91
Select a name and folder option 94
Select clone options 97, 98
Select name and location pane 102
Select source pane 101
Select storage pane 96, 103
serial port 11
service level agreement (SLA) 193
Set Administrator Password pane 86, 87
Set Computer Name pane 84, 85
Set Operating System Options pane 91
Set Registration Information pane 84
Setup networks pane 104
Set Workgroup or Domain pane 90
shares 171, 172
SIO controller 11
Small Computer System Interface controller. See SCSI controller
snapshot file 24
socket 160 14
solid-state drives (SSD) 165
Source Machine pane 108, 109
Source System pane 108
Specify Properties pane 83
storage
  about 282
  Disk Mode 284
  Disk Provisioning 282, 283
  monitoring, esxtop used 208
  RDM 285, 286
  SCSI controller 284
Storage Area Networks (SAN) 17
storage constraint, resource contention 170
Storage Distributed Resource Scheduler. See SDRS
Storage I/O Control
  about 187
  configuring 188
  enabling 187
  setting 189, 190
  vStorage API 191
Storage vMotion
  about 37, 231
  used, for migrating vSphere virtual machine 231-236
Summary pane 114
SVGA driver 29
Swap file 22
symmetric multiprocessing (SMP) 160
Sysprep files
  copying, to vCenter directory 80, 81

T

tags
  about 290, 291
  using 290, 291
template
  about 93
  compute resource, selecting 95
  creating 93
  Deploy VM from this Template option 94
  Select a name and folder option 94
  Select storage pane 96
  vSphere virtual machine, creating from 92
Thick provision eager zeroed 282
Thick Provision Eager Zeroed virtual disk 41
Thick provision lazy zeroed 283
Thick Provision Lazy Zeroed virtual disk 41
ThinPrint driver 30
Thin provision 282
Thin Provision virtual disk 41
Translation Lookaside Buffer (TLB) 117

transparent page sharing (TPS) 162
troubleshooting, vSphere virtual machine
      performance 194
typical configuration wizard
   Create a Disk pane 40, 41
   Guest Operating System pane 38
   Name and Location pane 36
   Network pane 39, 40
   Ready to Complete pane 42
   Storage pane 37
   virtual machine settings, editing 43-45
   vSphere virtual machine, creating
         with 34, 35

U

unused virtual hardware
   disabling 293-296
USB controller 11
USB device 11

V

vApp
   about 140
   benefits 140
   cloning 152-157
   creating 141-144
   Edit settings 145
   exporting 150, 151
   Resource allocation 143
vCenter directory
   Sysprep files, copying to 80, 81
Video controller 11
virtual appliance
   used, for provisioning vSphere virtual
         machine 277
Virtual compatibility mode, RDM 285
virtual CPUs (vCPUs) 160
virtual disk
   Thick Provision Eager Zeroed 41
   Thick Provision Lazy Zeroed 41
   Thin Provision 41
virtual disk descriptor 22
virtual disk file 22, 23
virtual Ethernet adapter 16

virtual hardware configuration
   about 278
   CPU 280, 281
   memory 279
   storage 282
   virtual hardware maximums 278, 279
   virtual network adapters 286
virtual hardware maximums 278, 279
virtual hardware version
   upgrading 287-289
Virtual Machine Communication Interface.
      See VMCI
Virtual Machine Executable (VMX) 116
virtual machine files
   renaming 287
Virtual Machine File System (VMFS) 17
virtual machine hardware version
   features 50
virtual machine monitor. See VMM
virtual machine settings
   editing 43-45
virtual machine shutdown action 149, 150
virtual machine startup action 149, 150
virtual machine (VM) 7
virtual network adapters
   about 286
   e1000 286
   e1000e 286
   vlance 286
   VMXNET 286
   VMXNET2 286
   VMXNET3 286
virtual resource configuration. See virtual
      hardware configuration
Virtual SAN. See VSAN
virtual switch 16
vlance 286
vlance network adapter 40
VM anti-affinity 273
VMCI 11
VMCI Sockets drivers 30
VMDK anti-affinity 273
VMkernel port
   creating 223-227
VMM
   about 116
   monitor mode 116-119

vmnics 16
vMotion
  about 221, 222
  configuring 222, 223
  used, for migrating virtual
    machine 228-231
VM template
  used, for provisioning vSphere virtual
    machine 276
VMware Hardware Compatibility List
  (HCL) 12
VMware Remote Console Options 128
VMware Tools
  about 28, 30, 128, 129, 296
  device drivers 29, 30
  installing 131
  installing, in Linux virtual machine 135,
    136, 137
  installing, in Windows virtual
    machine 131-134
VMware Tools service 28
VMware user process 30
VMware vCenter Converter
  about 106
  Destination Location pane 111
  Destination System pane 109, 110
  Destination Virtual Machine pane 110
  Options pane 112, 113
  Source Machine pane 108, 109
  Source System pane 108
  Summary pane 114
  used, for creating vSphere virtual
    machine 106
VMware vSphere Virtual Symmetric
  Multiprocessing (SMP) 14
VMXNET 286
VMXNET2 286
VMXNET2 network adapter 40
VMXNET3 286
VMXNET3 network adapter 40
VMXNETnetwork adapter 40
VMXNET NIC driver 29
vNIC 286
vNICs 16
Volume Shadow Copy Services (VSS) 30
VSAN 246
vShield Endpoint 29

vSphere Client
  used, for viewing vSphere virtual machine
    files 25, 26
  vs, vSphere Web Client 33, 34
vSphere Management Assistant (vMA) 203
vSphere virtual machine
  about 8
  components 9
  creating, by cloning 99
  creating, from OVF file 100
  creating, from template 92
  creating, VMware vCenter Converter used
    106
  creating, vSphere Web Client used 69, 70
  creating, with custom configuration wizard
    46
  creating, with typical configuration wizard
    34, 35
  migrating, cross-host Storage vMotion used
    237-243
  migrating, Storage vMotion used 231-236
  migrating, vMotion used 228-231
  other considerations 287
  performance tuning 192
  primary resources 13
  provisioning 275
  usage 12
vSphere virtual machine clone
  creating 99
  Select clone options 97, 98
vSphere virtual machine files
  about 18
  configuration file 19, 21
  other files 24, 25
  snapshot file 24
  Swap file 22
  viewing, command line used 28
  viewing, vSphere Client used 25, 26
  viewing, vSphere Web Client used 27
  virtual disk file 22, 23
vSphere Web Client
  Customize hardware pane 75
  Ready to complete pane 76
  Select a compute resource pane 71
  Select a guest OS pane 74
  Select a name and folder pane 70, 71
  Select compatibility pane 73

Select storage pane 72
used, for creating vSphere virtual machine 69, 70
used, for viewing vSphere virtual machine files 27
vs, vSphere Client 33, 34

vStorage API for Array Integration (VAAI) 191

vStorage API for Data Protection (VADP) 191

vStorage API for for Storage Awareness (VASA) 191

vStorage API for Multipathing Pluggable Storage Architecture 191

W

Win32Time 293

Windows virtual machine
 VMware Tools, installing 131-134

World Wide Name (WWN) 285

World Wide Port Names (WWPNs) 285

Thank you for buying
vSphere Virtual Machine Management

About Packt Publishing

Packt, pronounced 'packed', published its first book "Mastering phpMyAdmin for Effective MySQL Management" in April 2004 and subsequently continued to specialize in publishing highly focused books on specific technologies and solutions.

Our books and publications share the experiences of your fellow IT professionals in adapting and customizing today's systems, applications, and frameworks. Our solution based books give you the knowledge and power to customize the software and technologies you're using to get the job done. Packt books are more specific and less general than the IT books you have seen in the past. Our unique business model allows us to bring you more focused information, giving you more of what you need to know, and less of what you don't.

Packt is a modern, yet unique publishing company, which focuses on producing quality, cutting-edge books for communities of developers, administrators, and newbies alike. For more information, please visit our website: www.packtpub.com.

About Packt Enterprise

In 2010, Packt launched two new brands, Packt Enterprise and Packt Open Source, in order to continue its focus on specialization. This book is part of the Packt Enterprise brand, home to books published on enterprise software – software created by major vendors, including (but not limited to) IBM, Microsoft and Oracle, often for use in other corporations. Its titles will offer information relevant to a range of users of this software, including administrators, developers, architects, and end users.

Writing for Packt

We welcome all inquiries from people who are interested in authoring. Book proposals should be sent to author@packtpub.com. If your book idea is still at an early stage and you would like to discuss it first before writing a formal book proposal, contact us; one of our commissioning editors will get in touch with you.

We're not just looking for published authors; if you have strong technical skills but no writing experience, our experienced editors can help you develop a writing career, or simply get some additional reward for your expertise.

VMware vSphere 5.1 Cookbook

ISBN: 978-1-84968-402-6   Paperback: 466 pages

Over 130 task-oriented recipes to install, configure, and manage various vSphere 5.1 components

1. Install and configure vSphere 5.1 core components.
2. Learn important aspects of vSphere such as administration, security, and performance.
3. Configure vSphere Management Assistant(VMA) to run commands/scripts without the need to authenticate every attempt.

vSphere High Performance Cookbook

ISBN: 978-1-78217-000-6   Paperback: 240 pages

Over 60 recipes to help you improve vSphere performance and solve problems before they arise

1. Troubleshoot real-world vSphere performance issues and identify their root causes.
2. Design and configure CPU, memory, networking, and storage for better and more reliable performance.
3. Comprehensive coverage of performance issues and solutions including vCenter Server design and virtual machine and application tuning.

Please check **www.PacktPub.com** for information on our titles

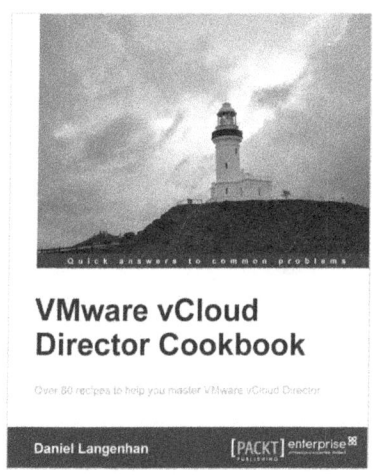

VMware vCloud Director Cookbook

ISBN: 978-1-78217-766-1   Paperback: 364 pages

Over 80 recipes to help you master VMware vCloud Director

1. Learn how to work with the vCloud API.
2. Covers the recently launched VMware vCloud Suite 5.5.
3. Step-by-step instructions to simplify infrastructure provisioning.
4. Real-life implementation of tested recipes, packed with illustrations and programming examples.

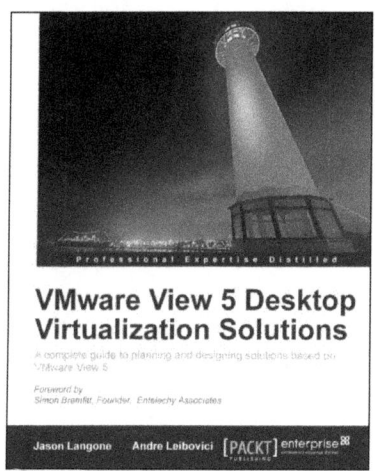

VMware View 5 Desktop Virtualization Solutions

ISBN: 978-1-84968-112-4   Paperback: 288 pages

A complete guide to planning and designing solutions based on VMware View 5

1. Written by VMware experts Jason Langone and Andre Leibovici, this book is a complete guide to planning and designing a solution based on VMware View 5.
2. Secure your Visual Desktop Infrastructure (VDI) by having firewalls, antivirus, virtual enclaves, USB redirection and filtering and smart card authentication.

Please check **www.PacktPub.com** for information on our titles

www.ingramcontent.com/pod-product-compliance
Lightning Source LLC
Chambersburg PA
CBHW080926220326
41598CB00034B/5699